AFGHANISTAN BETWEEN HOPE AND FEAR

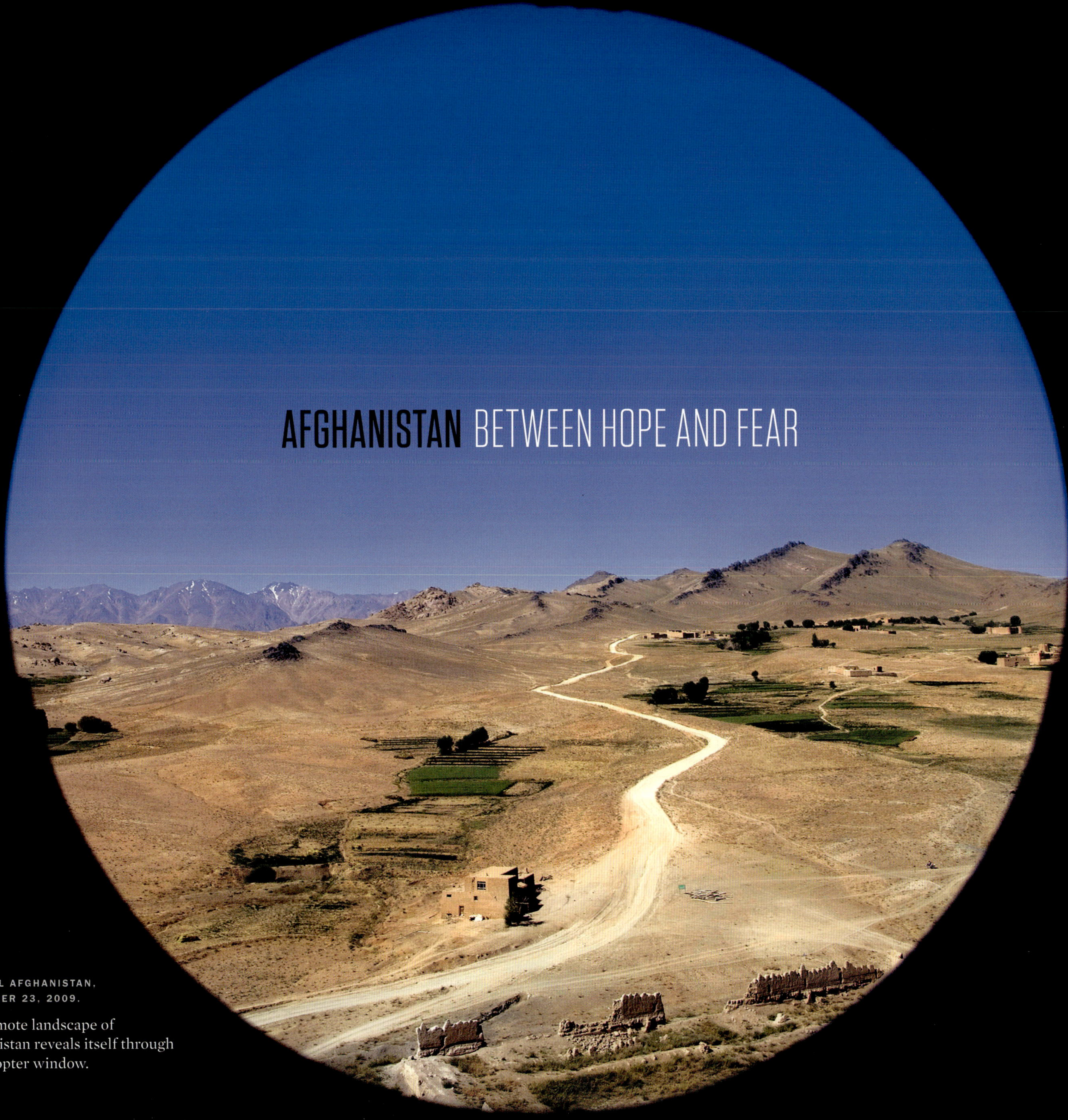

CENTRAL AFGHANISTAN,
NOVEMBER 23, 2009.

The remote landscape of Afghanistan reveals itself through a helicopter window.

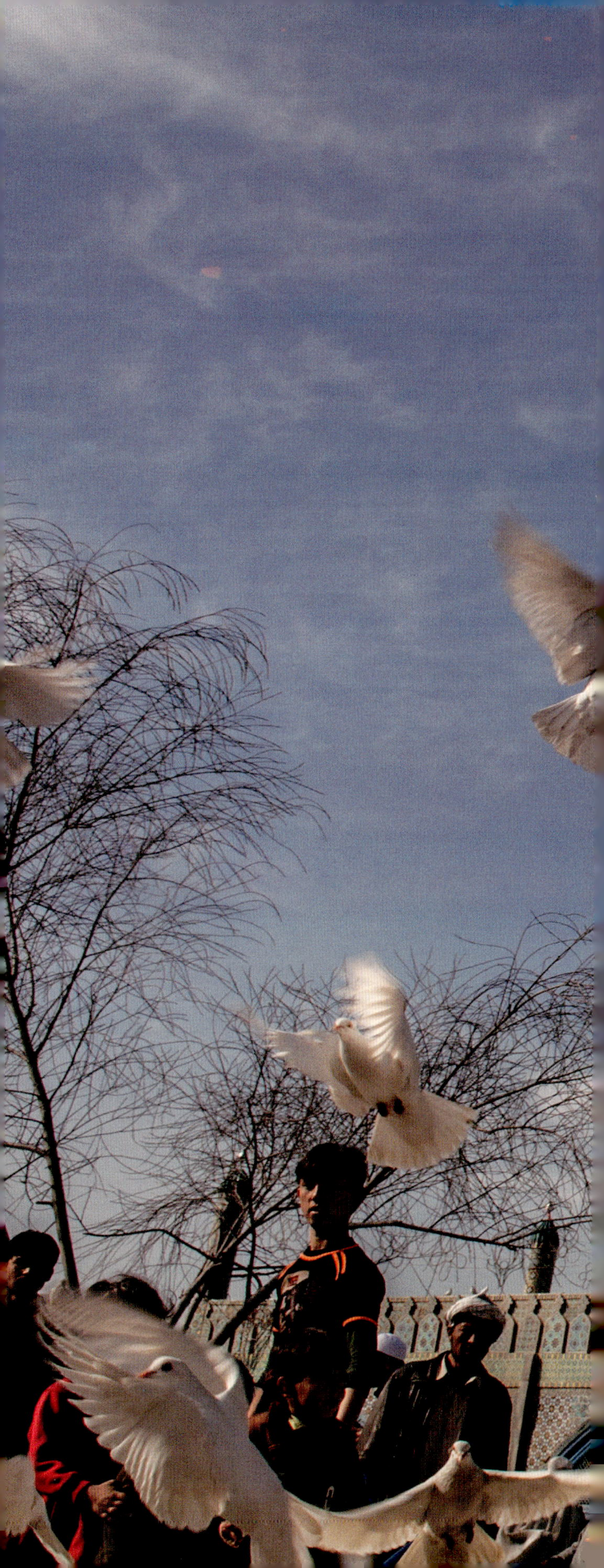

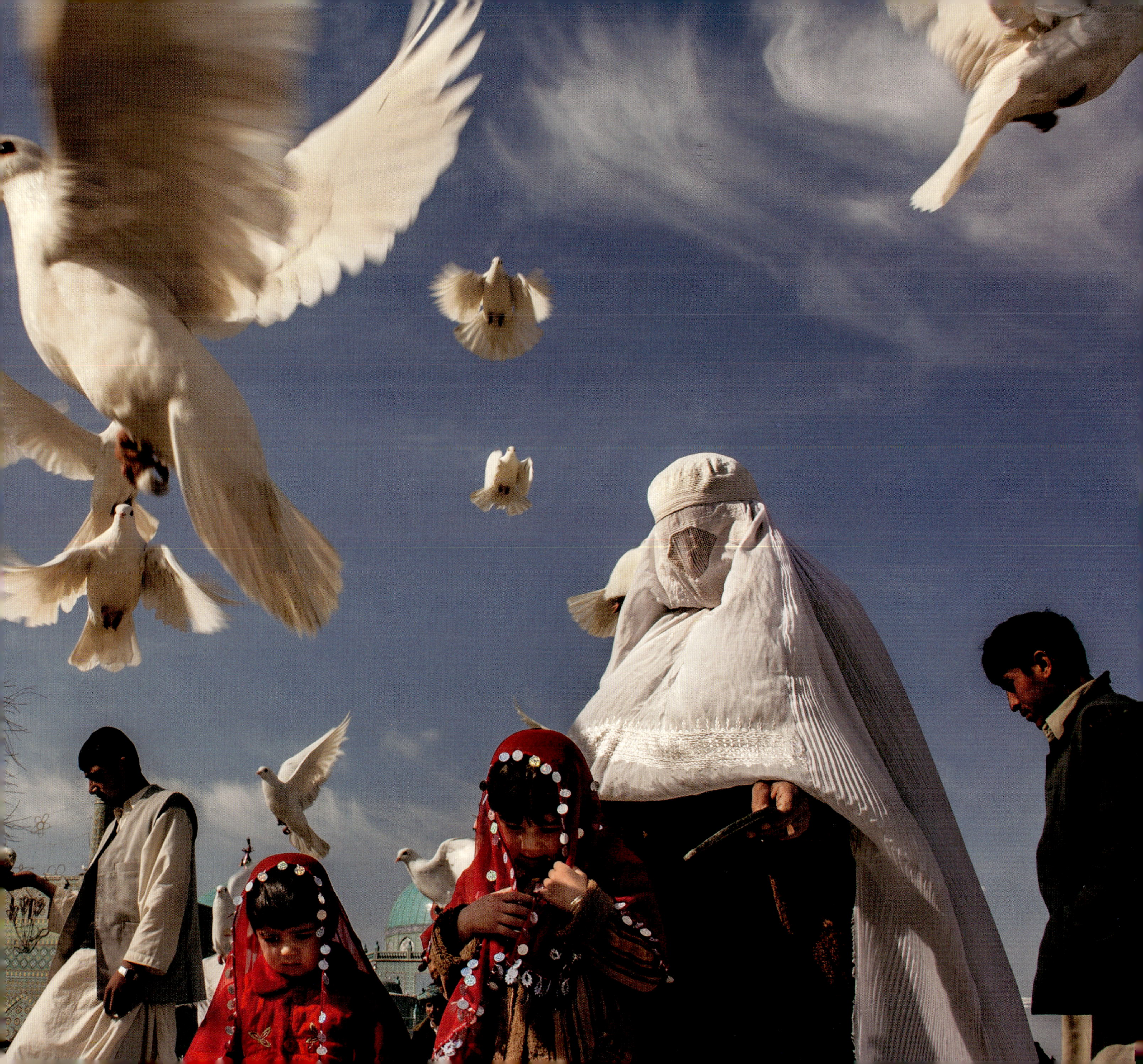

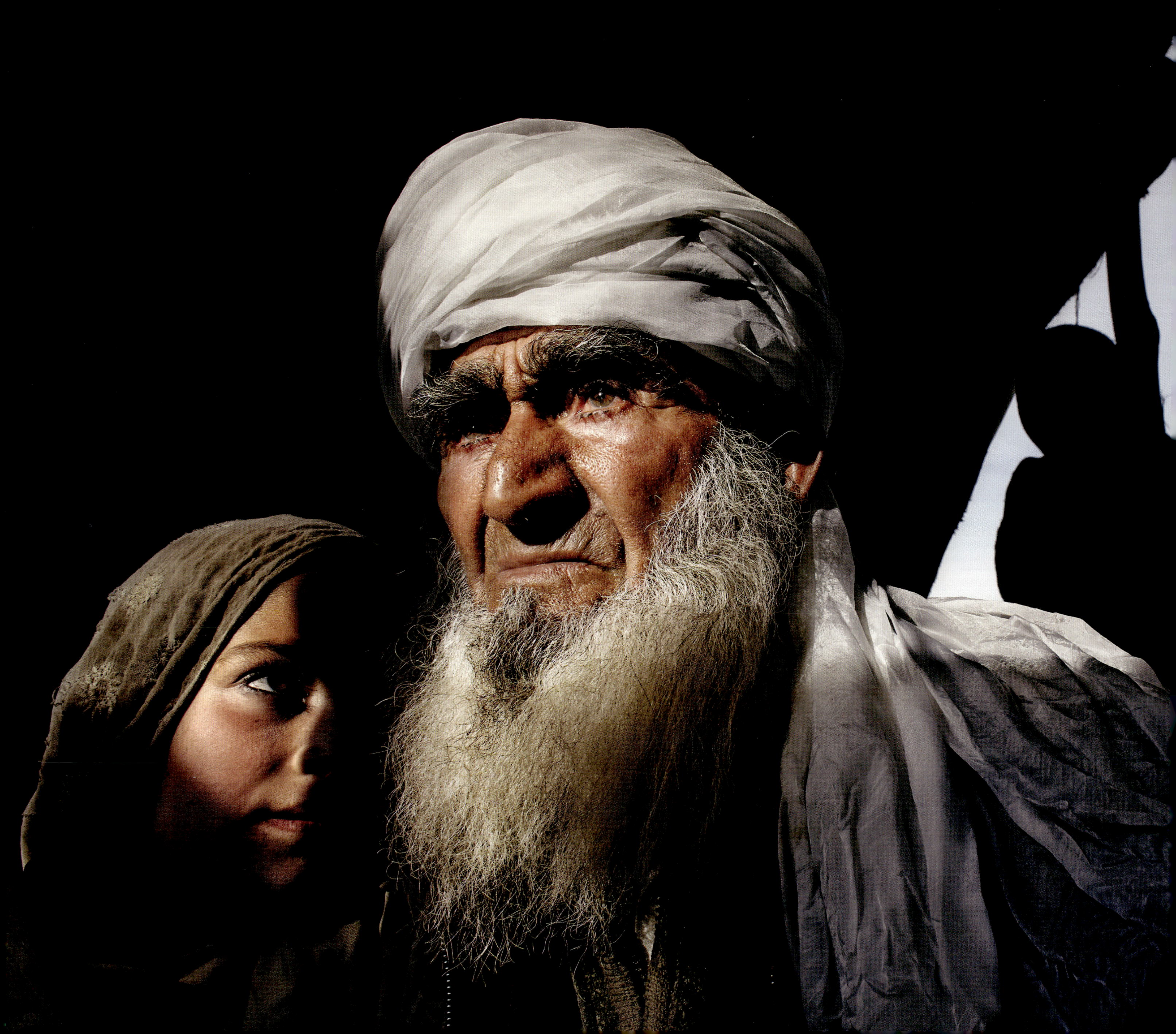

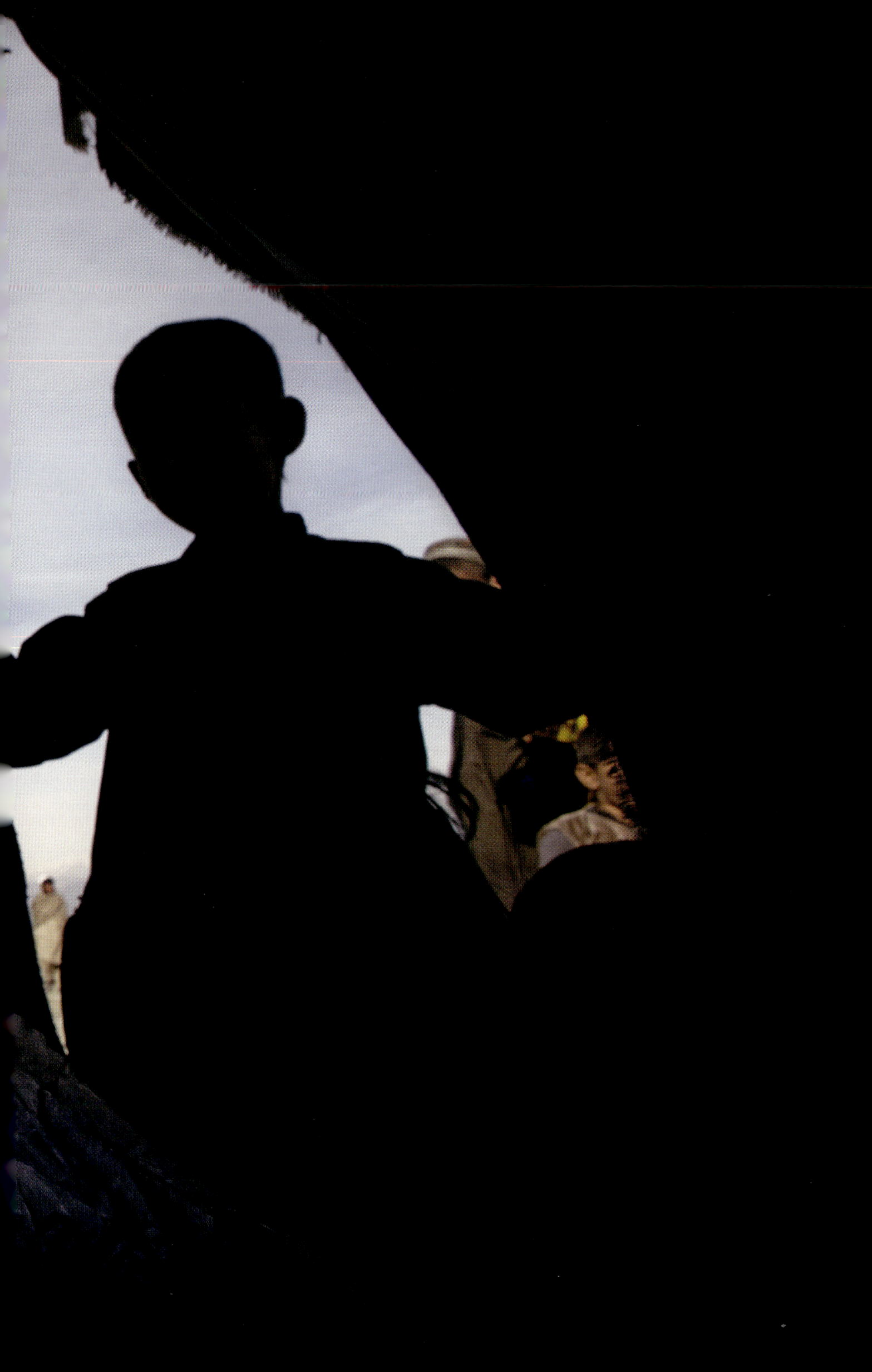

SURUBI, NANGARHAR PROVINCE, FEBRUARY 7, 2009.

An elderly man holds his granddaughter in their tent at a refugee camp after they were forced to flee their village, which US and NATO forces had bombed because, they claimed, it was a Taliban hideout.

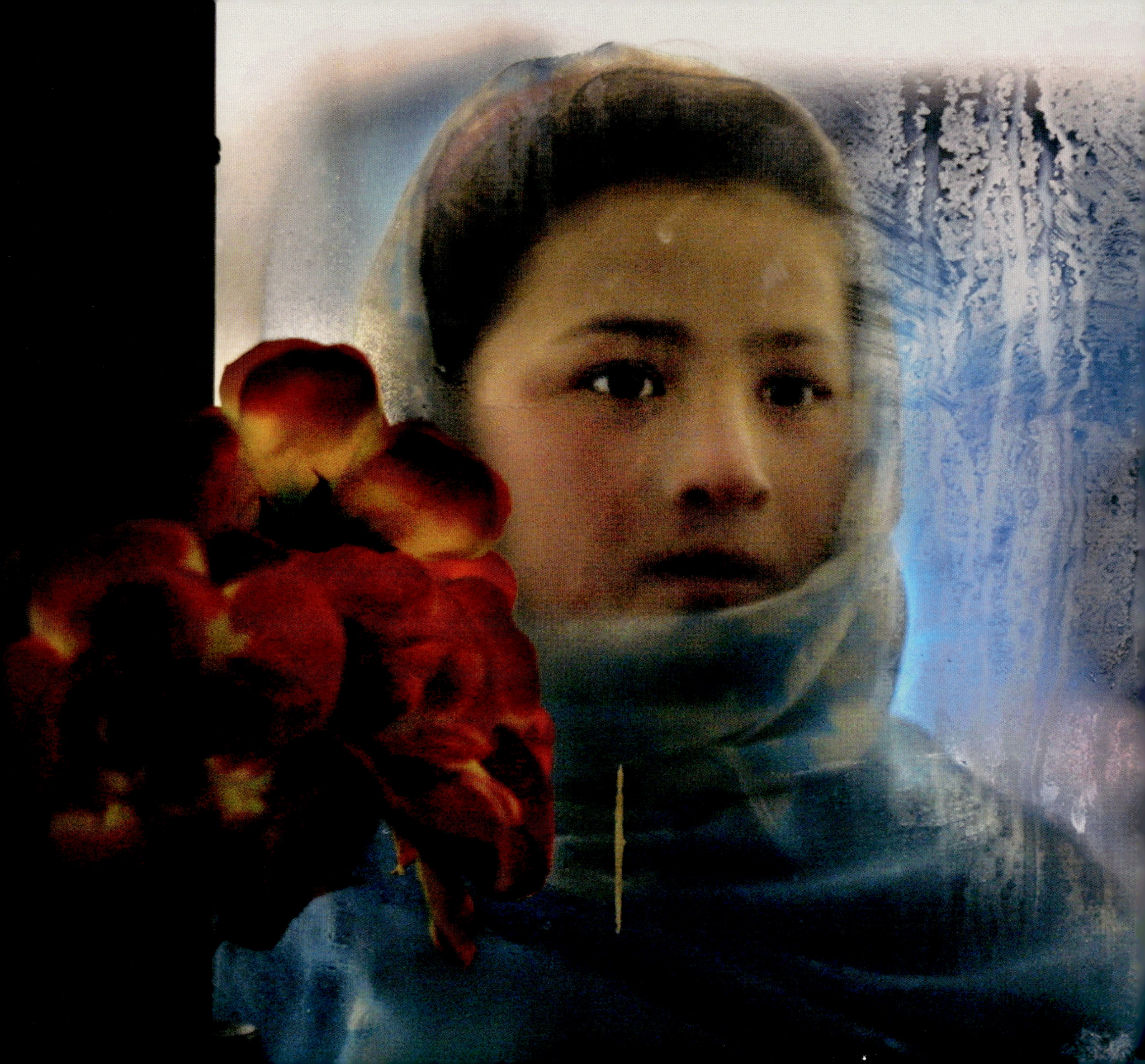

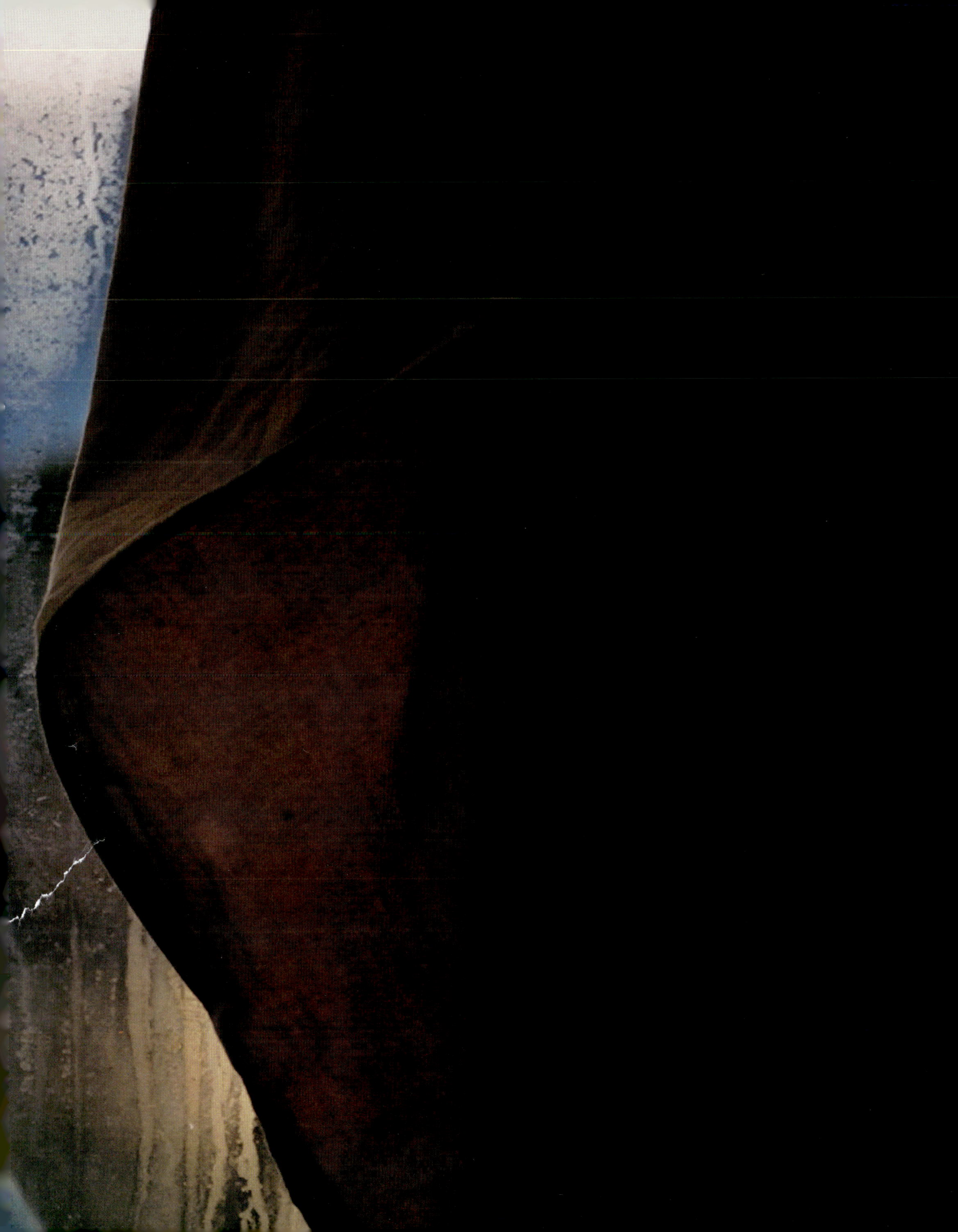

KABUL, JANUARY 13, 2002.

A girl looks through the frosted window of a restaurant, hoping to get leftovers. She begs after school to help out her family.

AFGHA

NISTAN

BETWEE

N HOPE

AND FE

AR

PAULA BRONSTEIN

FOREWORD BY KIM BARKER

INTRODUCTION BY CHRISTINA LAMB

UNIVERSITY OF TEXAS PRESS
AUSTIN

LASHKAR GAH, HELMAND PROVINCE.
JUNE 23, 2014.

Razima holds her two-year-old son, Malik, while waiting for medical attention at the Boost Hospital emergency room.

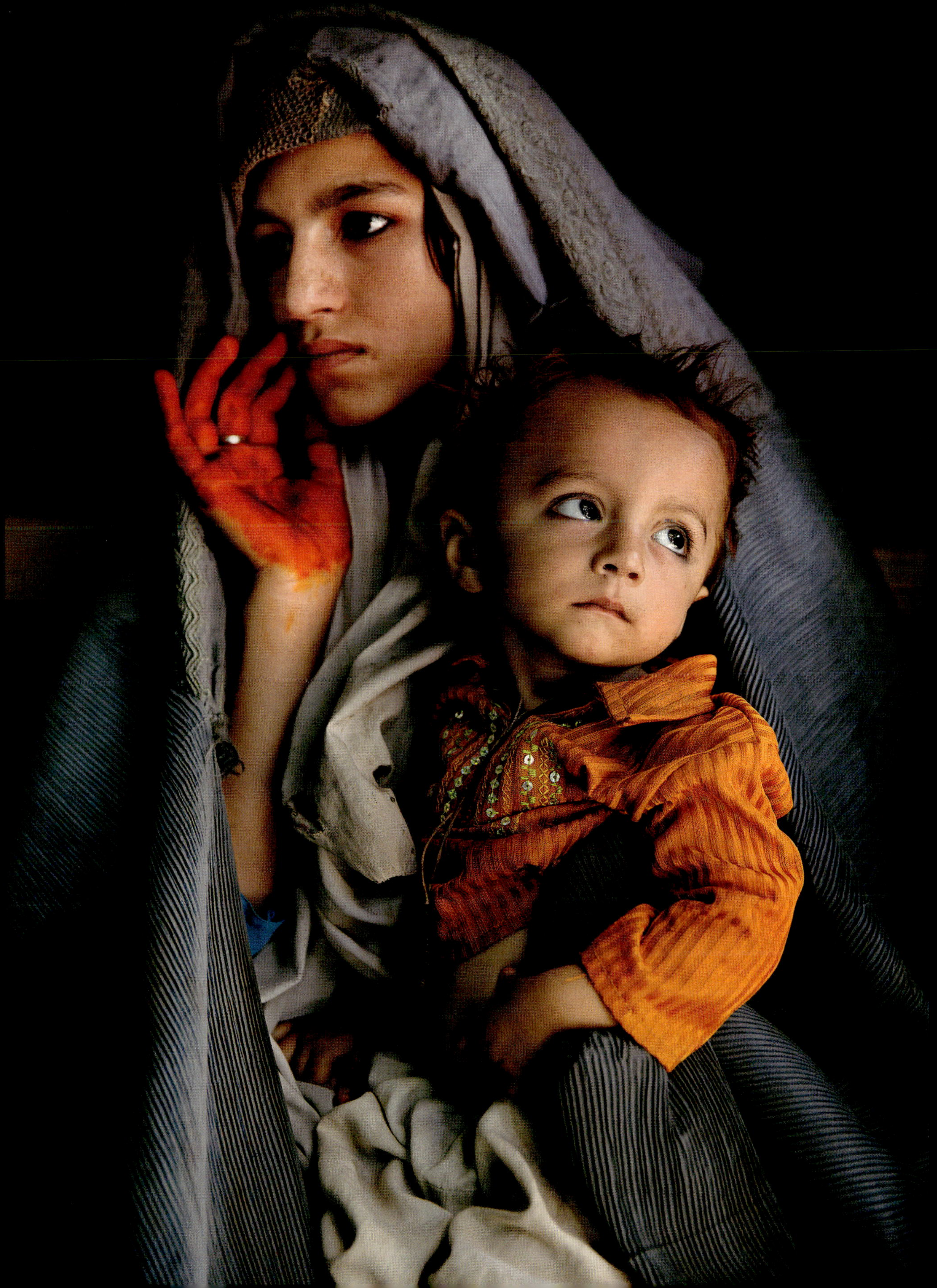

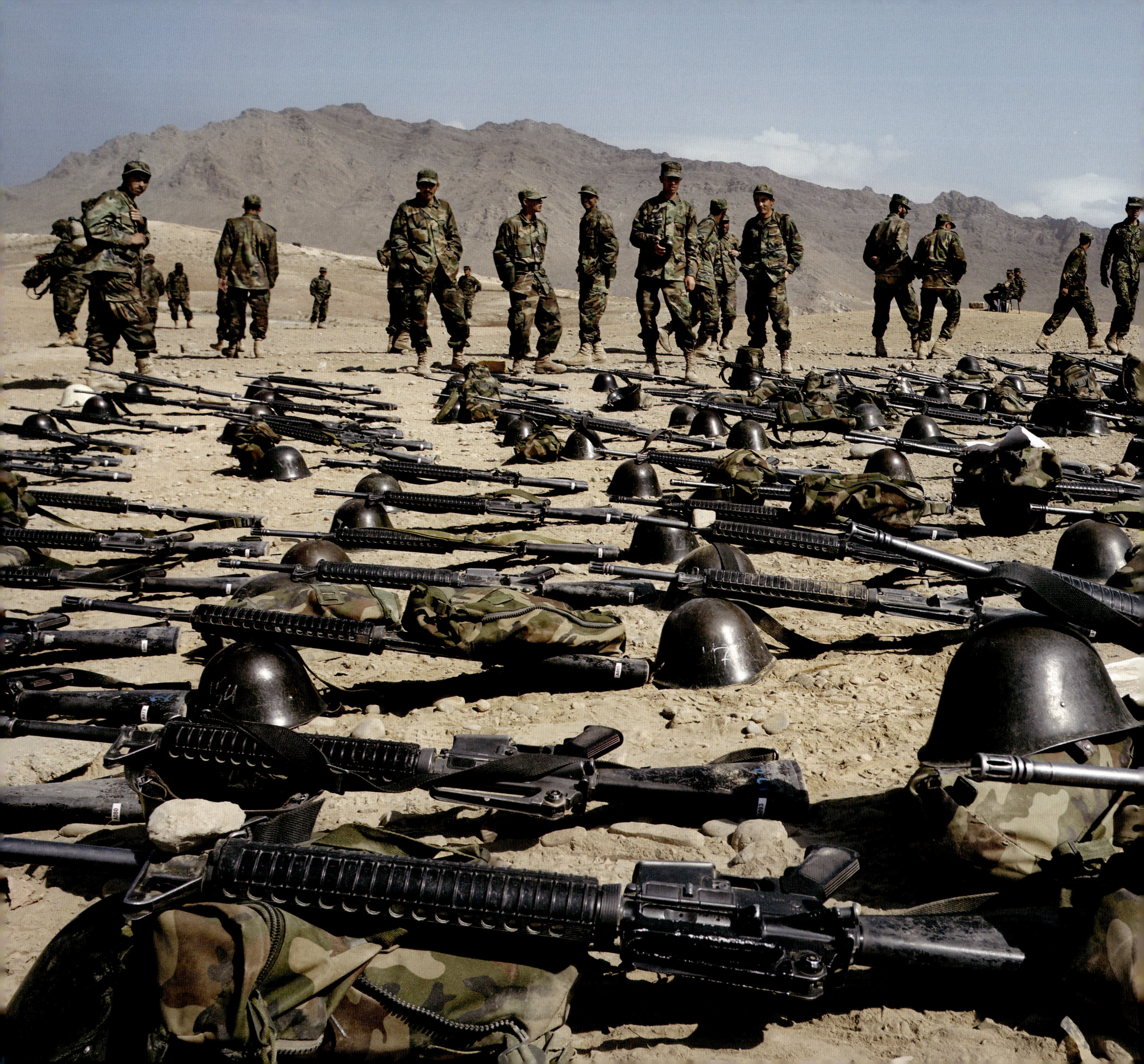

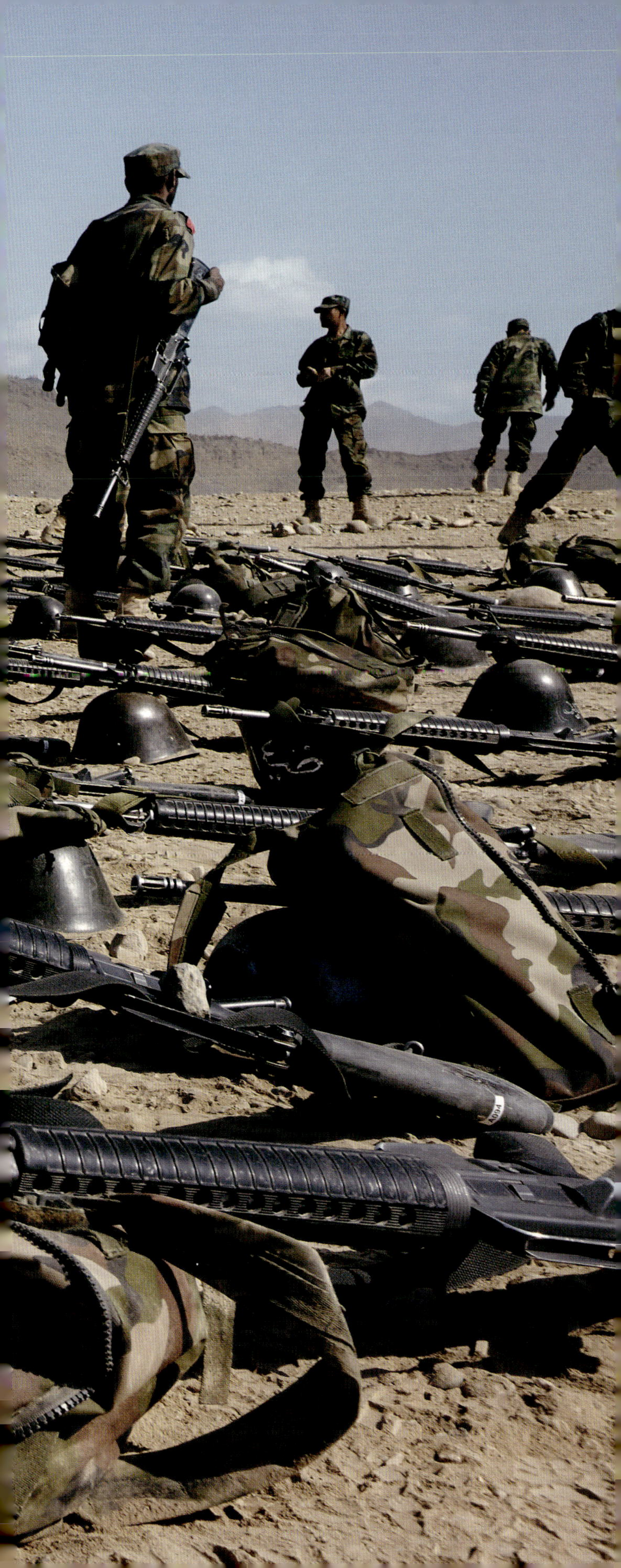

BAMIYAN, NOVEMBER 19, 2003.

A mother and her two children look out from their cave dwelling. Many families who, fleeing the Taliban, took refuge inside caves adjacent to Bamiyan's destroyed ancient Buddha statues now have nowhere else to live.

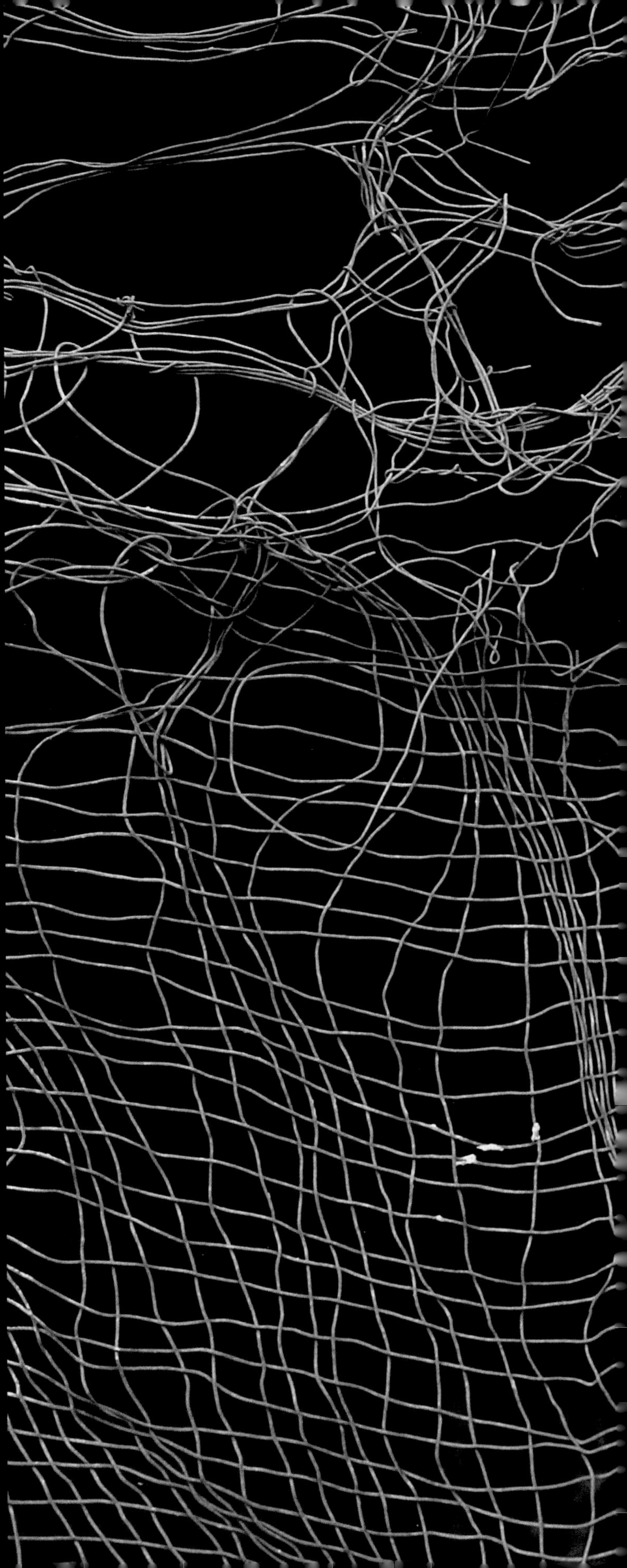

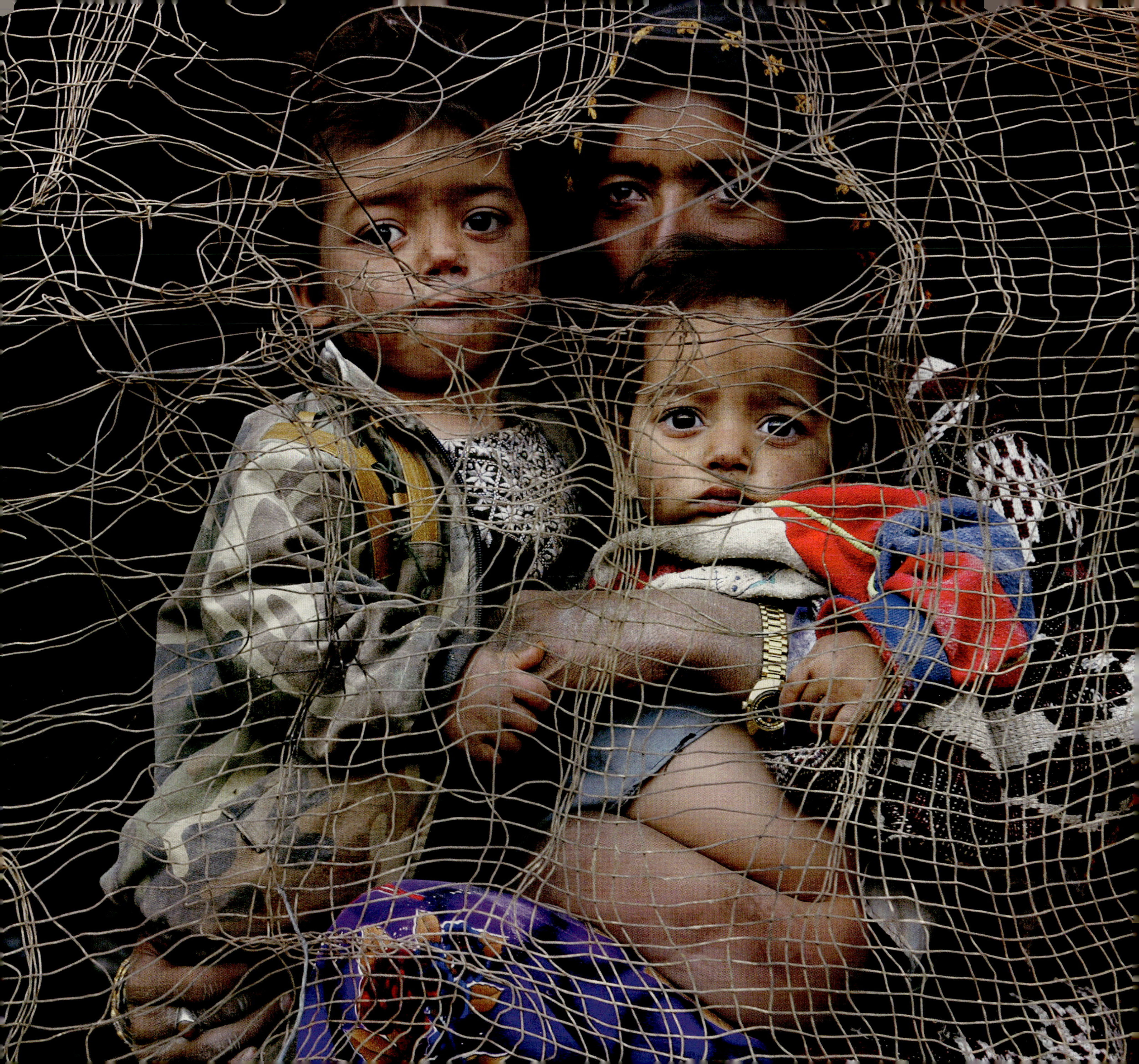

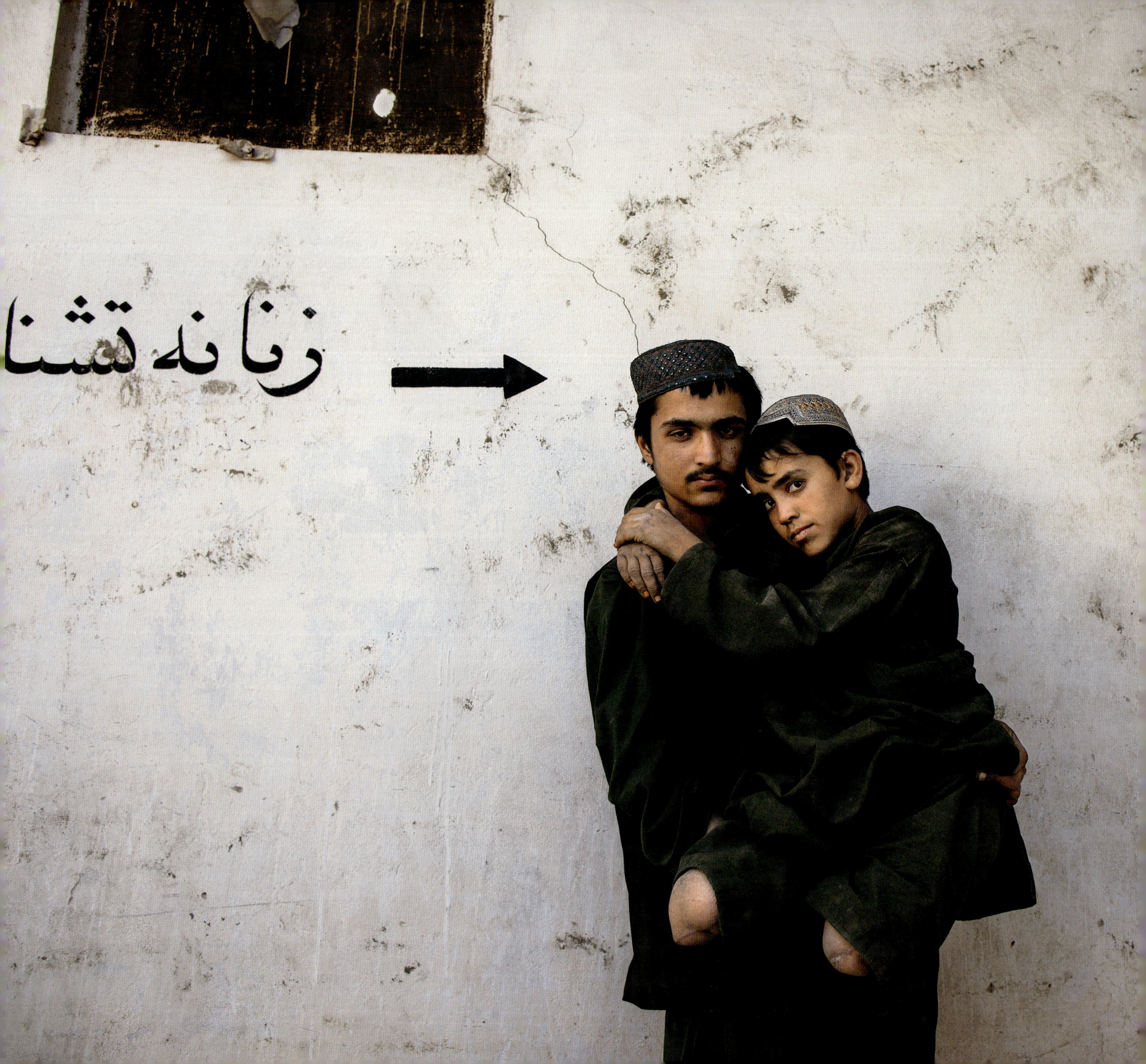
زنانه تشنا

KANDAHAR, OCTOBER 11, 2009

Twelve-year-old Rozi Muhammad is held by his brother, Yar Muhammad, at Handicap International's clinic inside the Mirwais Hospital compound. Rozi lost both his legs in a bomb attack on a military convoy that passed him while he was working at his drink cart.

Printed in China
First edition, 2016

The Louann Atkins Temple Women & Culture Series is supported by Allison, Doug, Taylor, and Andy Bacon; Margaret, Lawrence, Will, John, and Annie Temple; Larry Temple; the Temple-Inland Foundation; and the National Endowment for the Humanities.

∞ The paper used in this book meets the minimum requirements of ANSI/NISO Z39.48-1992 (R1997) (Permanence of Paper).

Library of Congress Cataloging-in-Publication Data

Names: Bronstein, Paula, author, photographer. | Barker, Kim, 1970– writer of supplementary textual content. | Lamb, Christina, writer of supplementary textual content.
Title: Afghanistan : between hope and fear / Paula Bronstein ; foreword by Kim Barker ; introduction by Christina Lamb.
Other titles: Louann Atkins Temple women & culture series ; bk. 42.
Description: First edition. | Austin : University of Texas Press, 2016. | Series: Louann atkins temple women & culture series ; book forty-two
Identifiers: LCCN 2015039025 | ISBN 9781477309391 (cloth : alk. paper)
Subjects: LCSH: Afghanistan—History—2001—-Pictorial works. | Women—Afghanistan—Pictorial works. | Families—Afghanistan—Pictorial works. | Afghanistan—Social conditions—21st century—Pictorial works. | Women and war—Afghanistan—Pictorial works. | Photojournalism—Afghanistan—Pictorial works.
Classification: LCC DS371.4.B76 2016 | DDC 958.104/7—dc23
LC record available at http://lccn.loc.gov/2015039025

doi:10.7560/309391

I dedicate this book to my father,
who is a pillar of strength and has always been
a guiding light throughout my career.

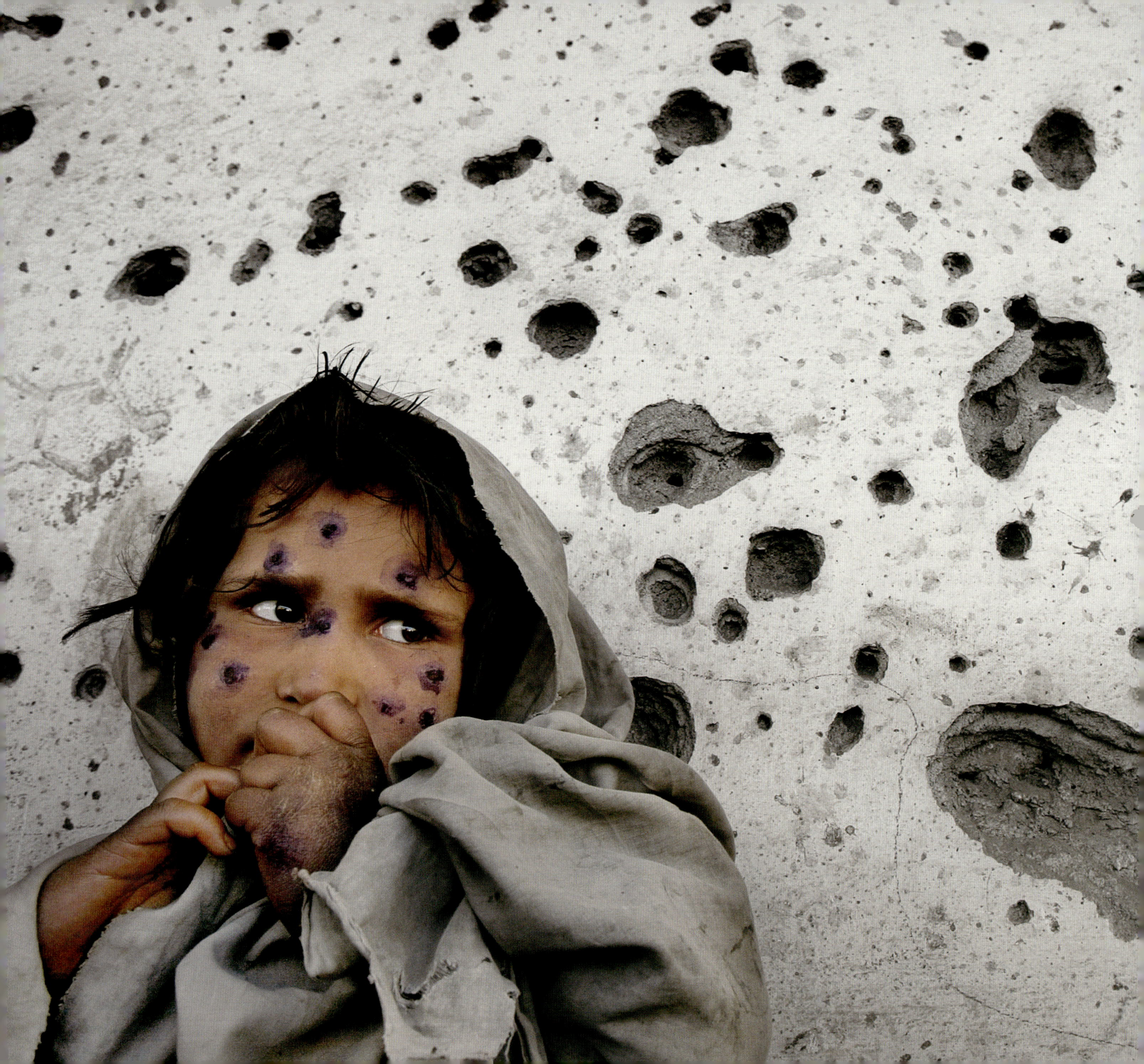

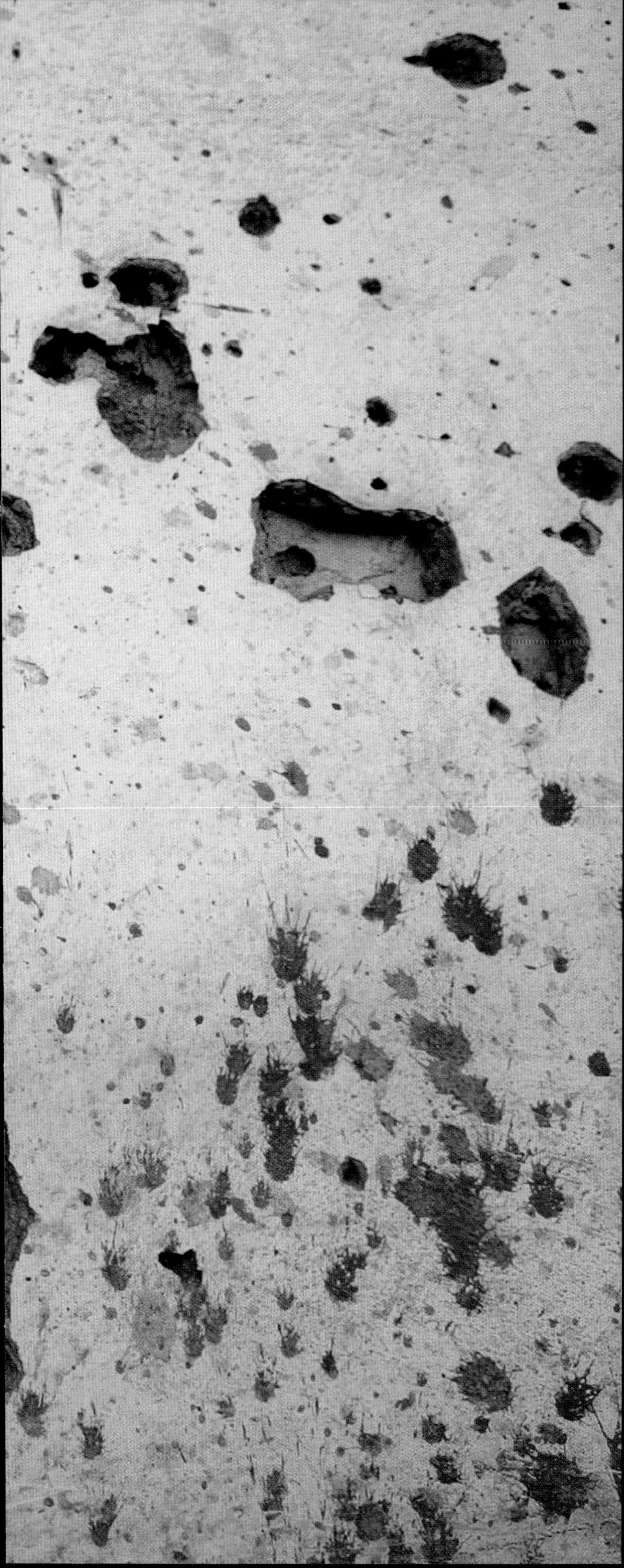

CONTENTS

KABUL, MARCH 1, 2002.

Mahbooba stands against a bullet-ridden wall, waiting to be seen at a medical clinic. The seven-year-old girl suffers from leishmaniasis, a parasitical infection.

FOREWORD

KIM BARKER

Afghanistan is home to our longest war. Making sense of it will take a generation or two, but the numbers provide one way to tell the story up to this point. More than 3,400 members of the armed forces from thirty countries, mostly Americans, have been killed in the conflict. More than 20,000 Afghan soldiers and police officers have died from the violence, as have more than 18,000 Afghan civilians—mainly victims of the Taliban. So far, the United States has spent more than $790 billion on this war. That's enough dollar bills to stretch around the world more than 3,000 times, or enough money to buy twenty-three Big Macs for every human on earth. America will spend trillions more rebuilding and caring for a military exhausted by more than ten years of fighting.

Yet despite this, despite the tremendous cost, despite the dead and the wounded, many Americans are tired of hearing about Afghanistan, tired of this war. Perhaps that's understandable. The numbers—thousands killed, more than $790 billion spent—are so large that they start to lose any meaning. Statistics are bloodless. They tend to sanitize how war can crush a family. As a result, many people have stopped paying attention to what happens in an unforgiving nation 7,000 miles away, and that includes the media, which have dramatically reduced their coverage of Afghanistan.

But Paula Bronstein forces them to pay attention. Her pictures bring the cold numbers to life. She first visited Afghanistan in late 2001, right as the Taliban was being driven from power after the September 11 attacks. Afghanistan worked its magic on her, just as it does on many journalists. The country got under her skin. Harsh mountains, a wide sky, craggy faces, turbans and burqas—the country is so different from what we know, so foreign, that words can do it little justice. Photographs are almost the only way to prove the reality of life there.

As a reporter for the *Chicago Tribune* who covered Afghanistan for five years, I know the pull of both Afghanistan and Bronstein's photography. I worked with Paula as she painstakingly followed the story of Afghans becoming hooked on their own chief export: heroin. We even sat in the same dark room with a mother and her two children as they smoked the drug. Showing how heroin was infecting the country was not easy, but it was important. Yet Bronstein is not some impassive journalist—after finding the family, she helped get them into rehab. Bronstein was continually adopting Afghans she met while on the job, always trying to help in some small way.

That's not the only thing that makes Bronstein different from many other journalists who have spent time in Afghanistan. She made the country a mission, returning frequently over the years and choosing to spend most of her time with Afghans rather than on embeds with international troops. And while she has certainly documented how people die, she also shows how they live. Some of these pictures are difficult to view—a mother next to her starving son with rib bones as visible as those of a skeleton, a five-year-old girl with vacant eyes lying on the cold concrete floor of a mental institution, or the aftermath of different bomb blasts. Bronstein's photographs of Afghan women who set themselves on fire to both protest and escape their treatment—because they would rather die an agonizing death than stay in their agonizing lives—are particularly tough to look at.

But Bronstein also catches the small moments that show how Afghans live, how they vote, how they laugh. She captures the straight lines of new soldiers in the Afghan army, the nervous moments before a wedding, a father and a son in a burqa shop, and a woman in a tattered burqa begging on a snowy, muddy street. She tells a story with every picture—just the eyes of an older woman carrying a pail of water on her head seem to ask, "Is this all there is?"

Some of Bronstein's images are arresting: a NATO soldier in camouflage against a beige background, wearing oddly purple gloves as he looks at the scene of a suicide bombing; a woman draped in a pink scarf and covered in white bandages; or an Afghan girl showing her face in a sea of women in all-encompassing blue burqas. Others are inspiring: Afghan girls all raising their hands to answer a question in an English class or a particularly defiant Afghan girl on a skateboard, her hands shoved in her pockets.

And other photographs highlight the stark beauty of this hardscrabble land: a view through a helicopter window of blue sky and a beige landscape stretching into the mountains; one of the deep blue lakes at the country's first national park; or yellow flowers in front of the cliffs in Bamiyan, where the Taliban destroyed giant Buddhas, leaving behind cavities resembling giant coffins.

More than numbers can, Bronstein's photographs and their individual stories illustrate the larger narrative of Afghanistan since the attacks of September 11, 2001, and the war that followed. Bronstein has put together one of the richest portraits there is of modern Afghanistan—complicated, conflicted, and contradictory, but always compelling. Just try to put down this book without looking at every image, without feeling each person in your gut, in your heart. It's impossible.

This commitment to showing how people live through war is admirable also because Bronstein has continued to travel to Afghanistan even as the situation (for some reason, people always describe life in Afghanistan as "the situation") has worsened, even as friends and colleagues have been injured or killed covering the wars there and in Syria, Libya, and other sites of chaos. As the threat to journalists has grown, Bronstein has stayed committed to Afghans.

In writing this, I looked through Bronstein's pictures, some for the first time, many for the umpteenth time. They brought me back to a country that I also fell in love with and to the various stages in this phase of Afghanistan's long war—when there was hope, so much hope; when Afghan women first emerged from their burqas; when civilian casualties first became a wedge issue between the United States and Afghanistan; and when the United States decided that enough was enough. This book is a marker in time, for there are still more photographs to come and more of a story yet to tell.

I'm writing this in March 2015, shortly after the White House announced, with much fanfare, the end of the US combat phase in Afghanistan, more than thirteen years after it began. The remaining 13,500 individuals in the international military units could be gone by the end of 2016—or not, if the threat from Islamic militants in the region grows. When the Western troops leave, the Afghan democracy, as gawky and awkward as a newborn foal, will be largely left to secure itself against insurgents. What will happen is anybody's guess, but I know that Bronstein will be there to capture it and that her photographs will document what we leave behind.

KIM BARKER is the author of *The Taliban Shuffle: Strange Days in Afghanistan and Pakistan* and the former South Asia bureau chief for the *Chicago Tribune*.

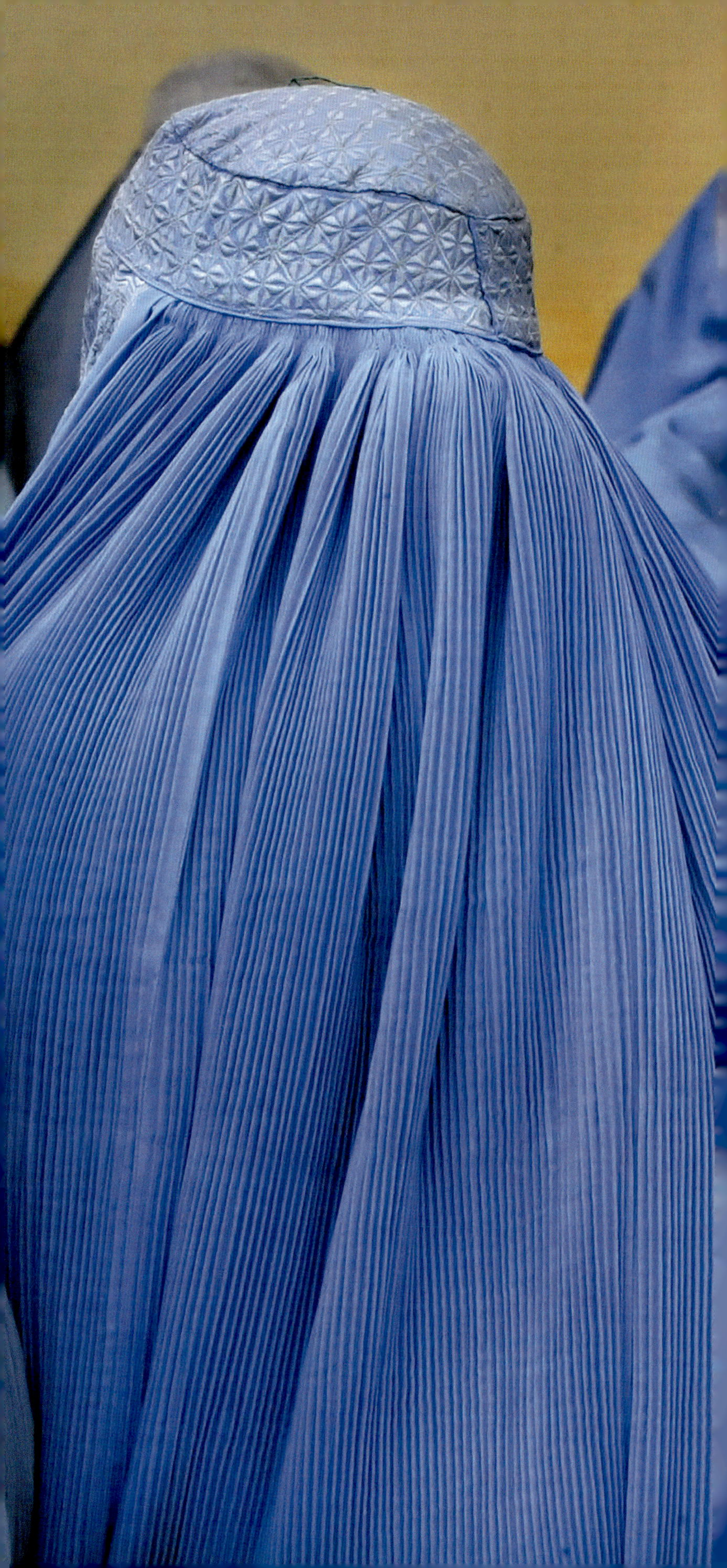

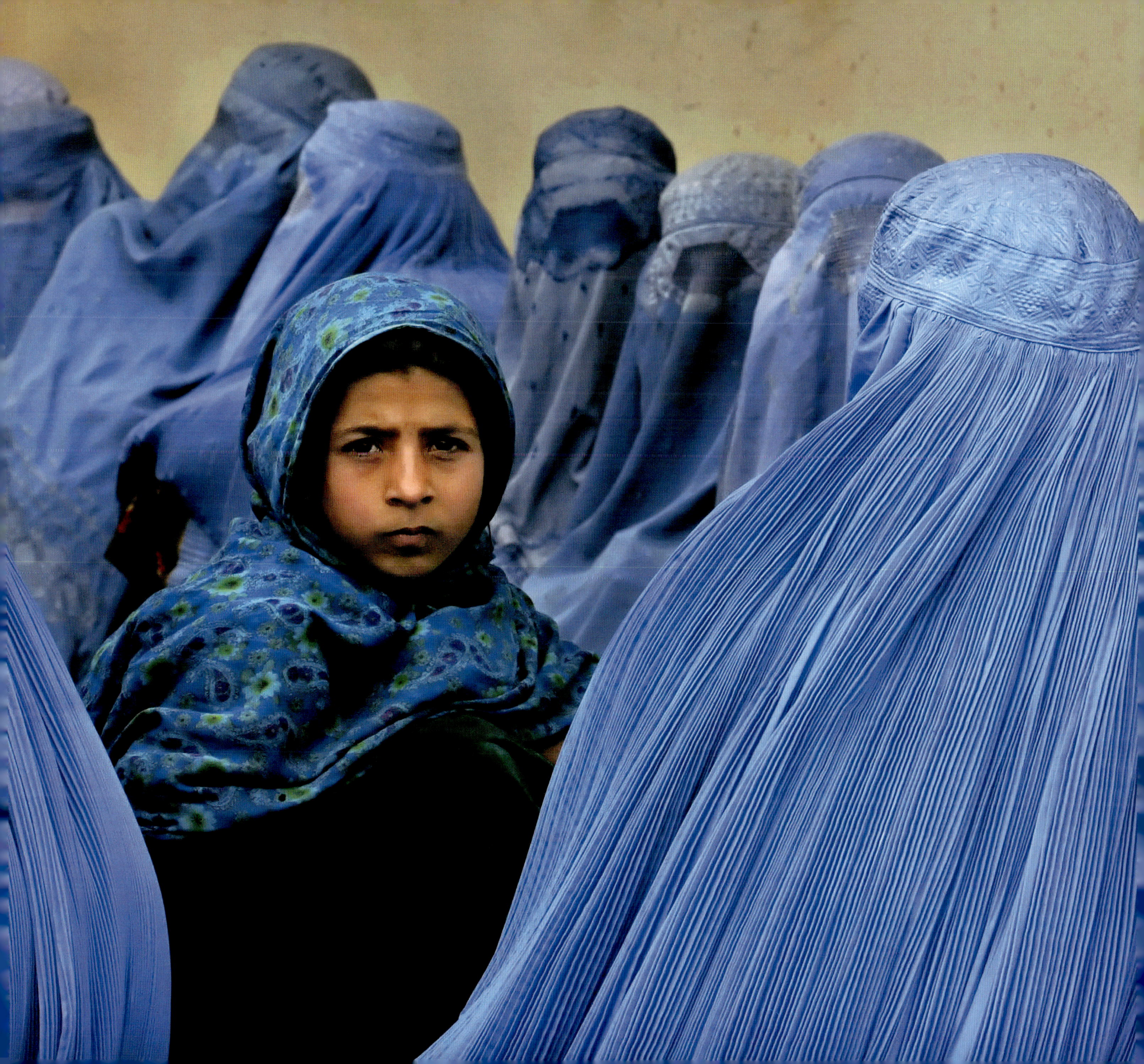

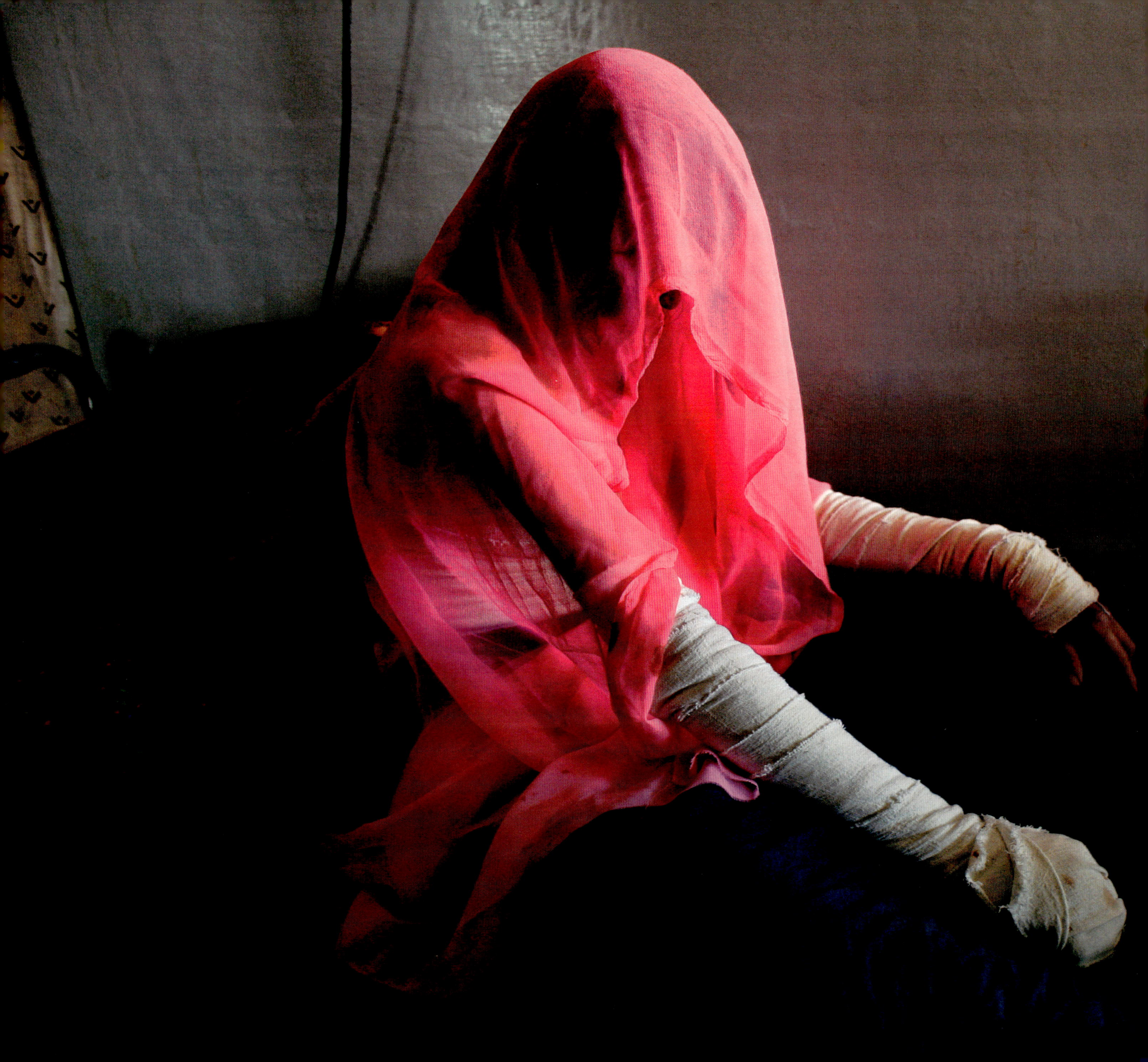

HERAT, FEBRUARY 3, 2006.

Nazgul, age thirty-five, a self-immolation victim, is shrouded by her headscarf at the Herat Regional Hospital. Every home has cooking oil, and so immolation is available for any woman or girl who seeks to end her suffering by killing herself.

GHARMBOLOQ, JUNE 12, 2011.

Hava Gul, seventy, waits to see a doctor at a makeshift local mobile health clinic. Mobile health units provide care to communities that are inaccessible, underprivileged, and underserved.

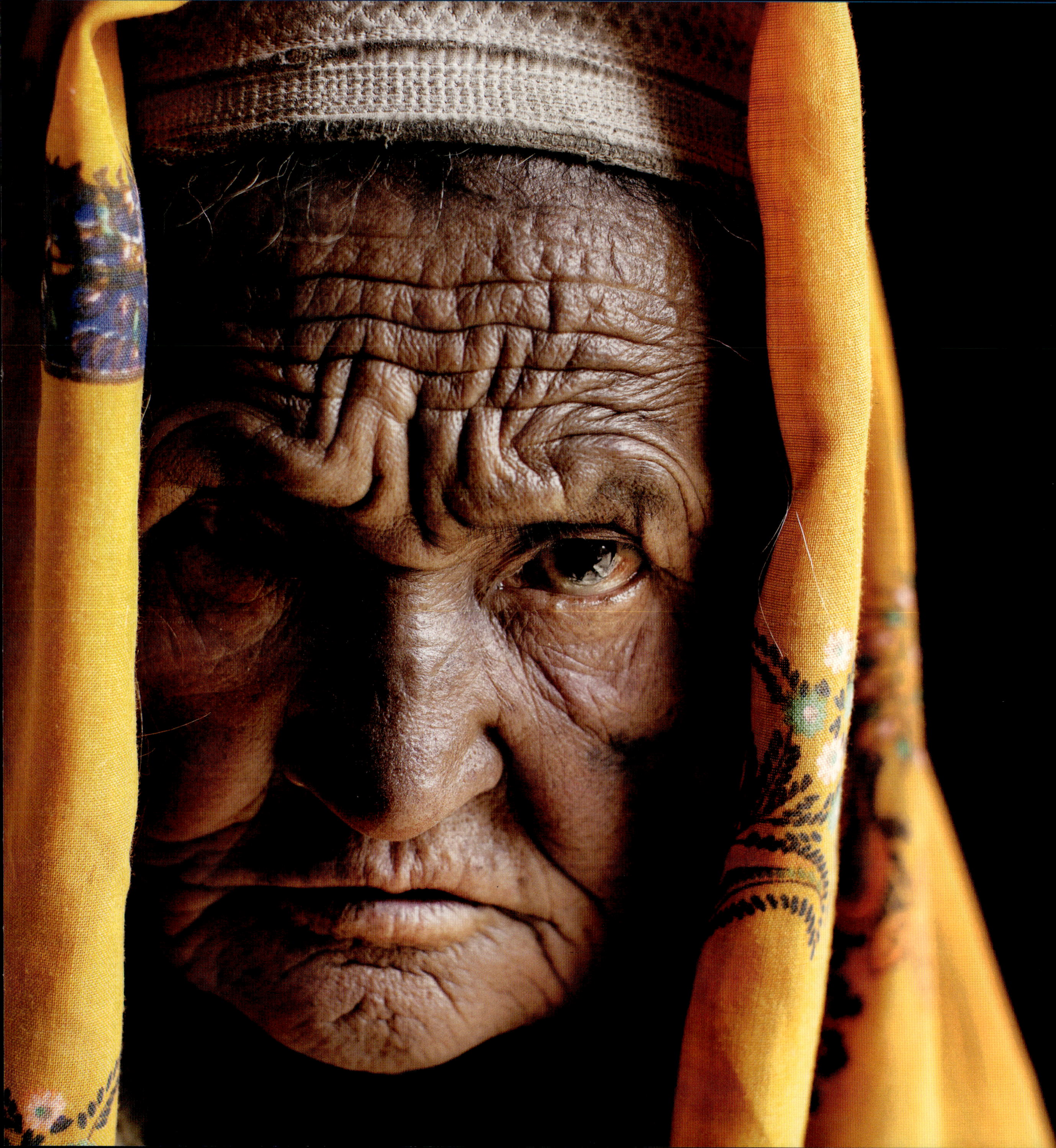

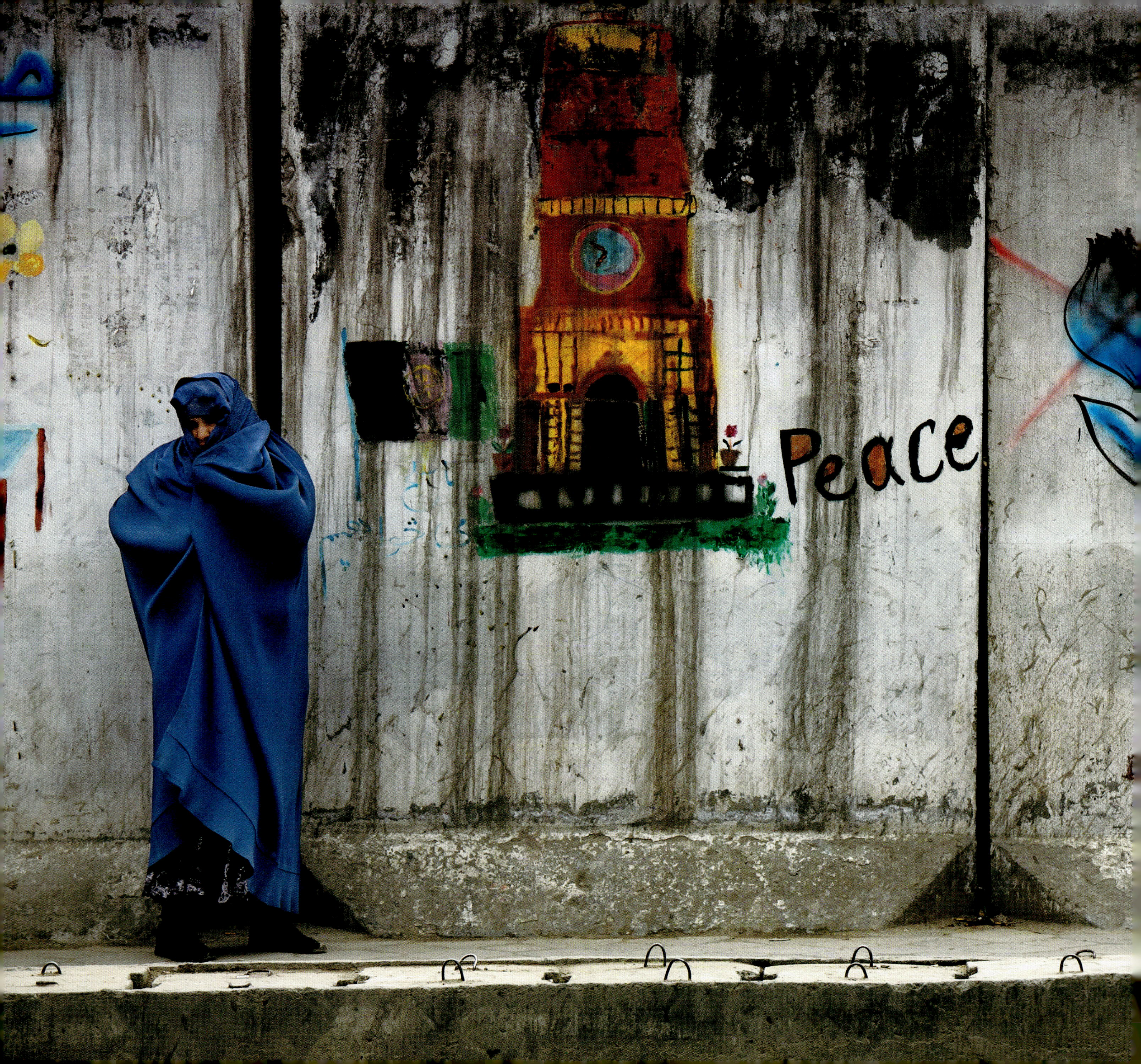
Peace

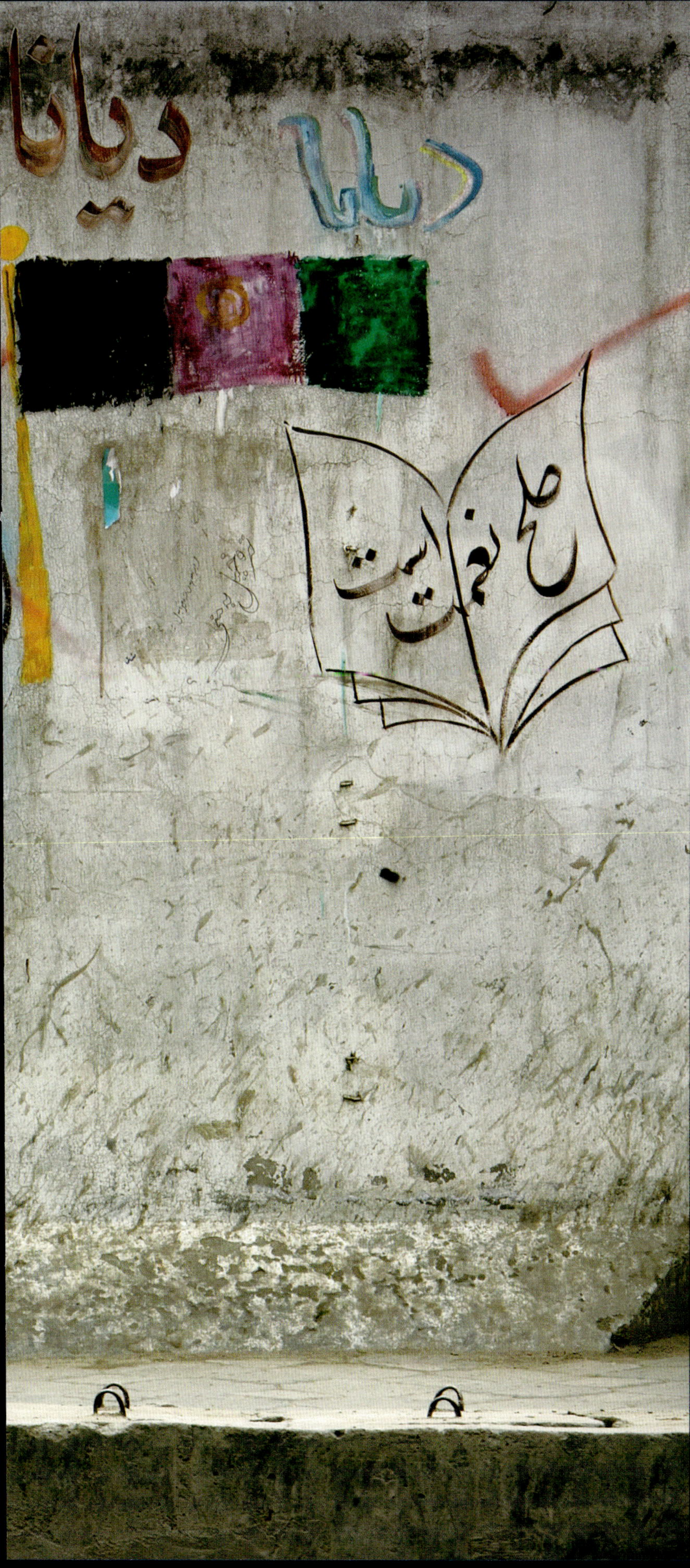
دیانا
دیانا
صلح نعمت است

KABUL, JUNE 19, 2014.

Farzana begs for alms outside a bread shop; she says that her husband died while serving with the Afghan National Army. Farzana is just one of the women, numbering in the hundreds of thousands or perhaps millions, who have been widowed by the war and now live in extreme poverty, often begging in Kabul's traffic-choked streets.

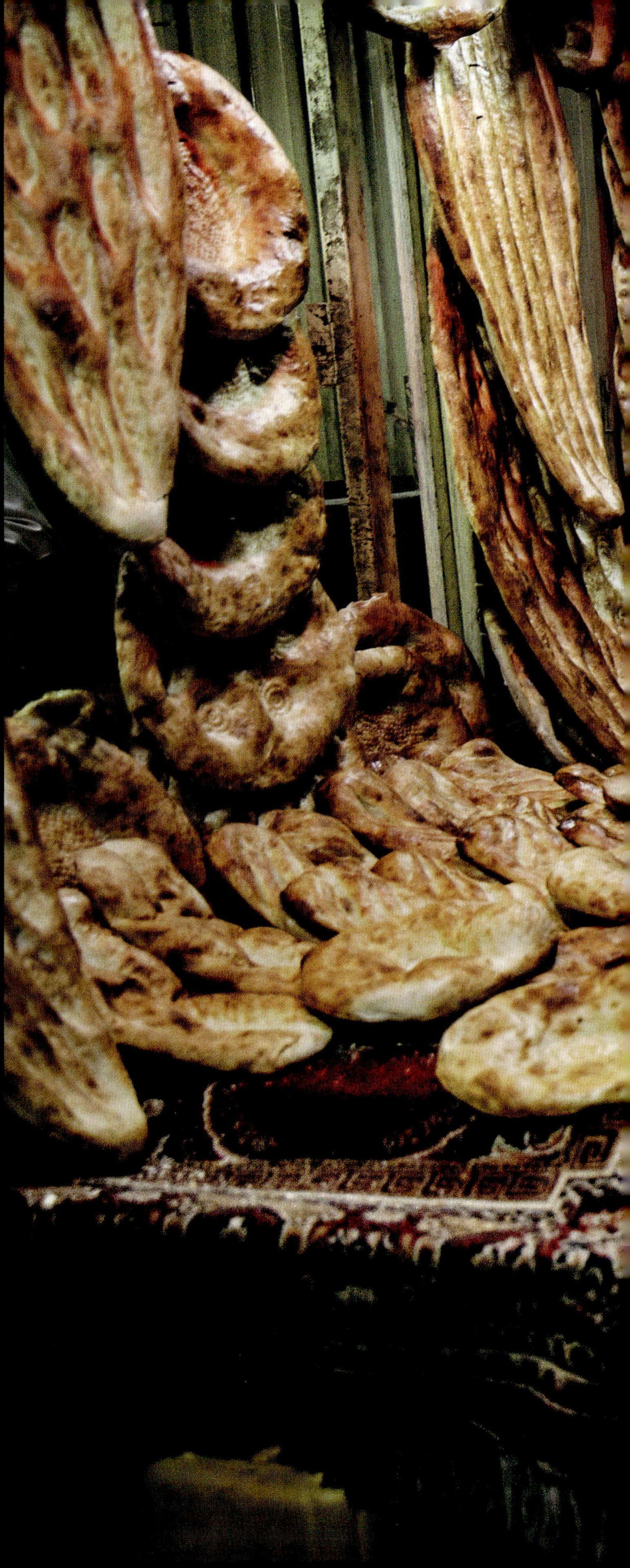

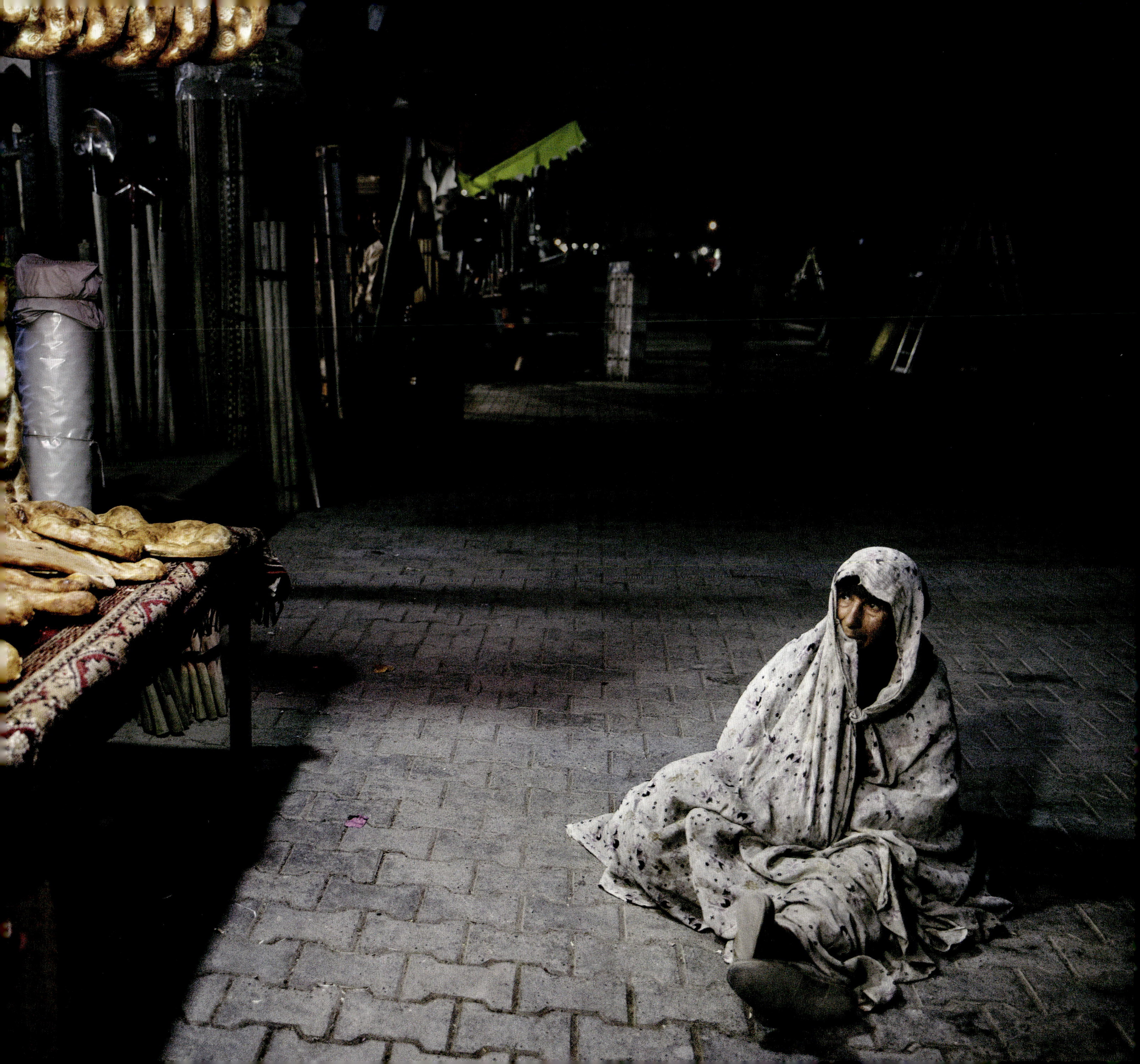

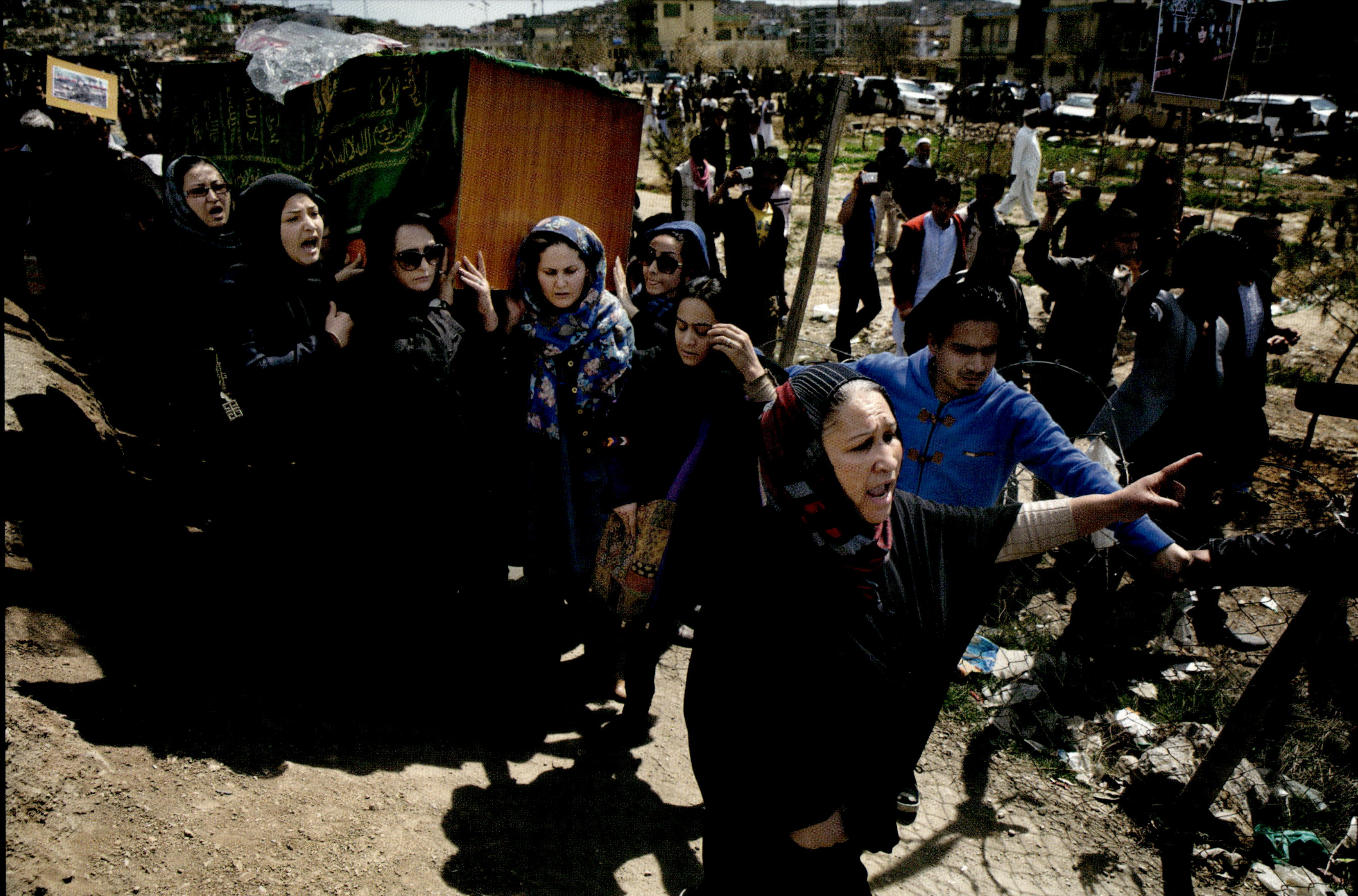

KABUL, MARCH 22, 2015.

Relatives, friends, and women's rights activists carry the casket of Farkhunda Malikzada during her funeral

AFGHAN WOMEN

CHRISTINA LAMB

The image of Afghan women breaking a traditional taboo and bravely holding aloft the coffin of twenty-seven-year-old Farkhunda Malikzada, burned to death by a mob in central Kabul in March 2015, was Shakespearean in its power. Robed in black, their faces riven with pain as they stood in a circle and refused to let a raging mullah pass through them, these women inspired support across Afghanistan and around the world. Yet the fact that a woman could be lynched in the center of the capital in broad daylight by a mob of mostly young men who beat her, set her on fire, ran her over with a Toyota pickup, and then threw her in the Kabul River showed how little things have changed since the Taliban era. Not only did others stand by and watch—including police—but some even posted footage of the assault on their Facebook pages. These show Farkhunda, face smeared with blood, repeatedly trying to get up.

As Paula Bronstein's photographs in this book vividly illustrate, there are two very different sides to the lives of women in Afghanistan. In the following pages, we see women eagerly queuing up to vote in elections and girls intent on their lessons at school and happily skateboarding, doing this in a country where girls form cycling teams and women work as entrepreneurs, rappers, and, in one case, a police chief. But we also see the almost unbearable anguish of girls in shelters fleeing forced marriages and the horribly burned figures of women so desperate to escape their lives that they have set themselves alight. International rights groups continue to cite Afghanistan as one of the world's worst places to be a woman.

"What we're seeing in Afghanistan today is two opposite faces," says Hassina Safi, executive director of the Afghan Women's Network. "On one side we're seeing promotion of women to key positions as a result of our advocacy over the last years, but at the same time there is no security for women, and we're seeing the systematic killing of women working outside."

It's easy to forget this now, but Western leaders often cited the repression of Afghan women as a key reason for toppling the Taliban regime after 9/11. In his State of the Union speech in January 2002, after the fall of the Taliban, President George W. Bush declared:

"The last time we met in this chamber, the mothers and daughters of Afghanistan were captives in their own homes, forbidden from working or going to school. Today women are free."

As someone who has visited and reported on Afghanistan throughout the fourteen years since the Taliban regime was ousted, I have seen the situation of women visibly improve. Under the harsh Islamic rule of the Taliban, women could not work, go to the bazaar without a male relative, wear white shoes, or laugh out loud. The shapeless blue burqas they were forced to wear became synonymous with women's repression, and they could be beaten or jailed for wearing nail varnish or lipstick. Girls were not allowed to go to school. Today, however, the bazaars are full of women, and lines of girls head to school with book bags proudly held on their backs, a sight that still makes me smile. Of the estimated 8 million Afghan children at school, 2.4 million are girls. The numbers of students going into higher education increased from just 4,000 in 2004 to over 120,000 in 2012, and about a quarter of these are young women.

Even in the remotest villages, life has changed for women. Microfinance loans for projects such as dressmaking or beekeeping have turned illiterate women who had never worked into entrepreneurs supporting their families.

Samangan is one of Afghanistan's poorest provinces, its land so arid that the mud-walled villages meld into the mountains like ancient ruins. Many are ghost villages completely abandoned as people fled war and poverty. In a village called Asiabad I was surprised to see a cow and two white-and-yellow taxis parked outside one house. I was even more surprised when their owner turned out to be a woman. Like most Afghan village women, Kubra looked much older than the fifty years she claimed, but while her skin might have been leathery and wrinkled, she was a human dynamo, her hands waving round and round like windmills and her black-button eyes flashing as she led the way into a pink-painted room decorated like a treasure palace with ribbons and sequins. In the center, taking pride of place, was a line of hand-operated Chinese sewing machines.

Samangan is one of Afghanistan's poorest provinces, its land so arid that the mud-walled villages meld into the mountains like ancient ruins. Many are ghost villages completely abandoned as people fled war and poverty. In a village called Asiabad I was surprised to see a cow and two white-and-yellow taxis parked outside one house. I was even more surprised when their owner turned out to be a woman.

Kubra's backstory was typical. Married off at thirteen because her parents could not afford to feed her, she had eleven children. Many days they survived on just one meal or sometimes only tea, for her husband was a subsistence farmer growing wheat, and with no rain the crops often failed. A few years after the Taliban fell, though, the village was visited by workers from Afghanaid, a British charity that had been working in the region for some thirty years. They offered the women training in tailoring and lent Kubra AFN 80,000 ($1,300) to buy a sewing machine and material.

"I worked day and night so I could buy another," she said. She shared her new skills with others and eventually had sixteen village women sewing. They were soon getting orders for weddings and selling in nearby villages. "Now my income is more than my husband's!" she said, revealing a mouthful of gold teeth as she laughed.

The women then formed a savings group and used the money they pooled to rent a shop, dividing the profits. Kubra saved her share to buy the cow, which provides curd, and she used the money from that to buy the sewing group a car, which doubles as a taxi driven by her son. Recently she added another taxi. "I am slowly moving up the ladder," she said, laughing and wiggling her fingers to mimic climbing the rungs.

The economic empowerment has had other effects. "Before, I couldn't even go to the bazaar on my own," she said. "No female was allowed to sit with men. Now our men have accepted that women can go outside. My daughters go to school, and one even got a job registering the voters for [the] election."

Kubra also administers TB and polio vaccines to people in her community; she says she learned to do this by watching a video. "I'm illiterate but am good at working things out in my head," she said.

Having tasted independence, she says, the women of her village will never relinquish it. "If the Taliban tried to come back now, although we don't have weapons, we have power and we would resist," she vowed.

THE CHANGE GOES TO THE HIGHEST LEVEL. AT THE START OF 2014 HISTORY WAS MADE when Afghanistan's first female police chief was appointed. Colonel Jamila Bayaz heads the station in the Mandayi bazaar, a market set in the teeming Old City district of Kabul and full of wooden stalls where vendors sell combs, old clothes, and Justin Bieber posters. She commands around 400 police officers serving a local population of around 1.5 million.

"This is a chance not just for me but for all women of Afghanistan," she said, sitting in her upstairs office surrounded by plastic flowers and glass dishes of almonds and pistachios. The fifty-year-old mother of five said she always dreamed of following in her father's footsteps and becoming a police officer. "I saw it as a way to help people, and I loved the uniform!" she said, laughing. Indeed, she looks resplendent in her gray uniform with silver-and-red epaulets and black headscarf. When she carries out her weekly inspection of Kabul's District 1 police force, she presents a stark contrast to her male officers, who offer a shambolic sight in a mishmash of uniforms, leather jackets, torn parkas, and assorted headgear.

Bayaz first trained as a policewoman in the 1980s, during the Soviet occupation, and worked in that capacity until Taliban fighters invaded the capital on September 26, 1996, a day she says she will never forget. "The Taliban stopped everything," she said. "It was as if they had stopped life itself." Twice she was beaten—once for showing an ankle and another time for taking off her burqa before she entered her house, unaware anyone was watching.

After the Taliban fell, she went back to the police and received new training from US, British, and Norwegian instructors. They sent her on trips to Colorado, Miami, and New York, as well as Dubai, Cairo, and—strangely—Siberia. "It was all very different to policing here," she said.

Bayaz described her promotion as a "victory for all women of Afghanistan." She would not comment on the assassination of a number of fellow female police officers in Helmand and Kandahar—or on the increase in attacks on women, which rose 28 percent in 2014, with little rise in prosecutions, according to a United Nations report.

Although on paper the new Afghan constitution guarantees women equal rights and protection from violence, in practice these guarantees are rarely enforced. Women are generally treated as inferior, and almost nine women in ten experience some kind of abuse. A UN report from April 2015 said that Afghanistan's judicial system is still failing women and that only 5 percent of cases involving violence against women result in punishment for the criminals.

The problems remain because men are still running things, and male attitudes have not changed. Though the Afghan Parliament reserves a fifth of its seats for women, meaning it has a higher percentage of female delegates than does the US Congress, which claims only 18.5 percent female membership, female MPs say they have little power.

In 2013 Afghan women made up just 8 percent of the nation's judges, 6 percent of its prosecutors, and less than 20 percent of its lawyers. Most of the female judges work in Kabul. In the provinces, not even one in thirty prosecutors is a woman. And though women went to election rallies and voted in force in the 2014 presidential elections, none of the nine candidates were women. Indeed, the slates included six warlords known for trampling on women's rights.

Happily, the eventual winner, Ashraf Ghani, put women's rights and equality at the heart of his presidential campaign. He appointed four women to his cabinet and has given his wife, Rula, a highly public profile. A Christian of Lebanese descent, she regularly speaks up for women's rights in Afghanistan and has set up a First Lady's office. President Ghani even recently joked that Afghanistan might have a woman president before the United States does.

President Ghani's fine words aside, it's easy to get despondent about Afghanistan. Kabul, Herat, and other such cities are full of shelters crammed with girls who have fled forced marriages. Some 60 percent of marriages are forced, with girls as young as nine handed over as bargaining chips to resolve feuds between tribes or as opium brides to repay loans.

One bitter January morning I met a girl who had been compelled to relinquish her five-month-old baby to get a divorce from the man who had beaten her with cables and a belt day after day.

One of the most horrific stories in recent years was that of twenty-one-year-old Lal Bibi, a shepherd's daughter from Kunduz. She was repeatedly raped for five days in May 2012 by four local policemen as revenge after a dispute between one of them and her cousin. Such stories are sadly common in Afghanistan and usually end there, with the girl shamed, unmarriageable, and perhaps living as an outcast in a shelter while the perpetrators go free, for this is a society where men with guns have virtually all the power.

One of the most horrific stories in recent years was that of twenty-one-year-old Lal Bibi, a shepherd's daughter from Kunduz. She was repeatedly raped for five days in May 2012 by four local policemen as revenge after a dispute between one of them and her cousin. Such stories are sadly common in Afghanistan and usually end there, with the girl shamed, unmarriageable, and perhaps living as an outcast in a shelter while the perpetrators go free, for this is a society where men with guns have virtually all the power.

Predictably, Lal Bibi ended up in a shelter, broken and unable to speak. But unusually, her family stood up for her, particularly her grandfather, and in the shelter she met Mary Akrami, an activist who runs the Afghan Women's Skills Development Center and was one of the first women in Afghanistan to set up shelters. Backed by her tribe and helped by Akrami, Lal Bibi and her family bravely went to court in Kabul. In November 2012 they made history when they succeeded in getting the rapists convicted—a decision hailed by human rights groups worldwide.

For most people the story stopped there. As the judge announced the sixteen-year sentence, however, the police commander pointed at the family and shouted, "I'll be free one day, and I'll deal with you people!" The family members were scared and remained in Kabul, sheltered by Akrami. Then, in 2014, Lal Bibi's grandfather died, and so they went back to their village. Within hours her father was arrested by the commander's men and falsely accused of killing someone. He remains in jail, and the family was forced to go back in hiding.

Mary Akrami will be among the first to say things have improved enormously for women compared to life under the Taliban. "Then women couldn't go out of house. Now they're going to court," says Akrami. "But as Lal Bibi's case shows, society is not ready." Indeed, Akrami herself gets threats every day. The stress has damaged her health, and her husband has pleaded with her to stay at home, but she refuses to give up. "We are the only ones to stand up to these powerful people," she said. "We can't give in."

Akrami and other activists fear that the Western powers have forgotten their commitment to freedom for Afghan women in the rush to get out. They are terrified of what will happen to women after NATO troops have left this region. "People need to realise the gains we have made are fragile and we still need help," said Hassina Safi of the Afghan Women's Network.

A few miles away from Jamila's police station is the Kabul stadium where women once were publicly lashed by the Taliban. A cavernous room inside offers an unexpected scene: a dozen female boxers sparring and aiming punches, laughing and teasing, as their trainer barks instructions. They are hoping to qualify for the 2016 Olympics. Once there were twenty-five of them, each receiving $100 per month, as well as transport provided by international aid. But the aid money has dried up. Now all they have is the room for training and the boxing gloves. More than half have dropped out.

Akrami says that all the women's groups once feted by Western donors are now seeing funding collapse as the outside world loses interest in Afghanistan. "I believed women's rights were a global issue and thought we had women from all the world behind us, but now I see we're alone," she said.

Some hope that the tragic story of Farkhunda Malikzada will reawaken that interest. A memorial has been built on the bank of the Kabul River to mark the spot where she was thrown in that Thursday in March 2015, ending her young life and all the dreams therein, including that of becoming a teacher. It has become a shrine to local women as well as a reminder to the outside world of promises once made.

CHRISTINA LAMB is an award-winning British journalist and best-selling author who has been traveling to Afghanistan since 1987. Her most recent book is *Farewell Kabul: From Afghanistan to a More Dangerous World* (HarperCollins 2015).

The Situation

KANDAHAR, DECEMBER 15, 2001.

A man walks along the rubble of a Taliban munitions bunker that was destroyed during extensive US bombing.

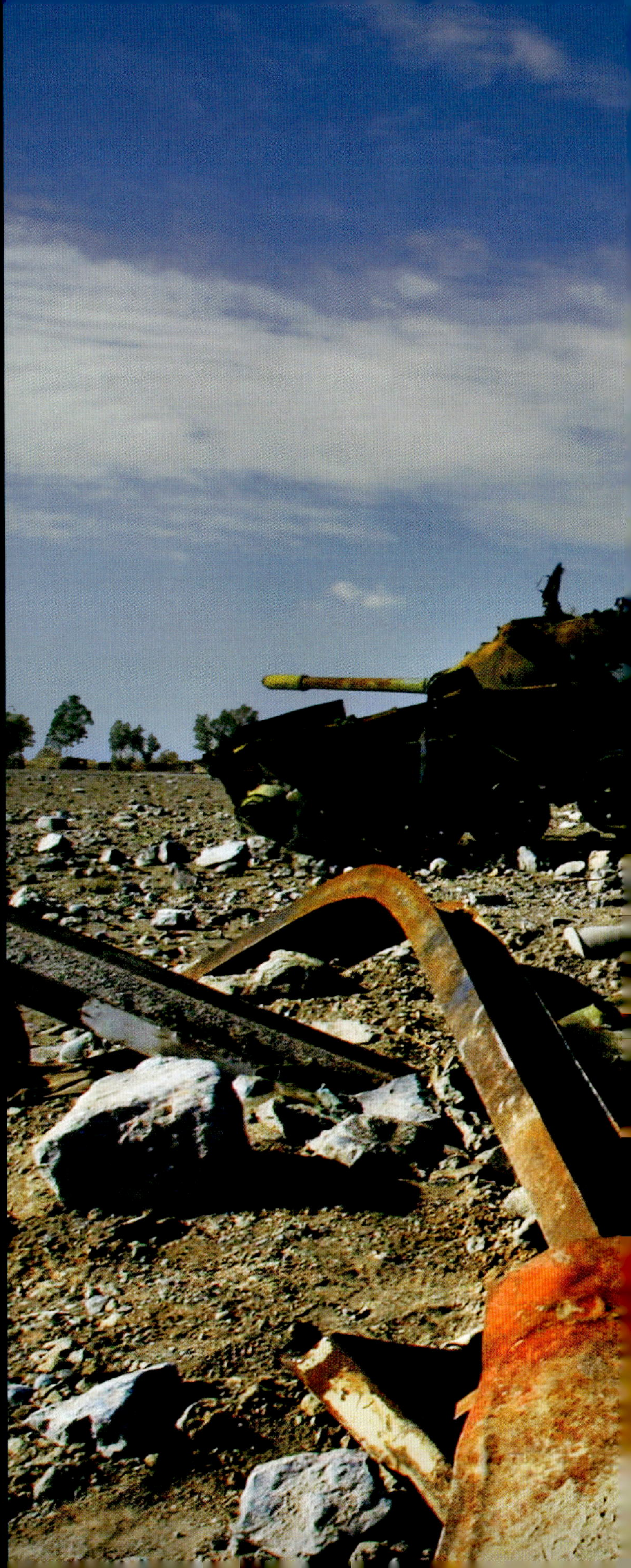

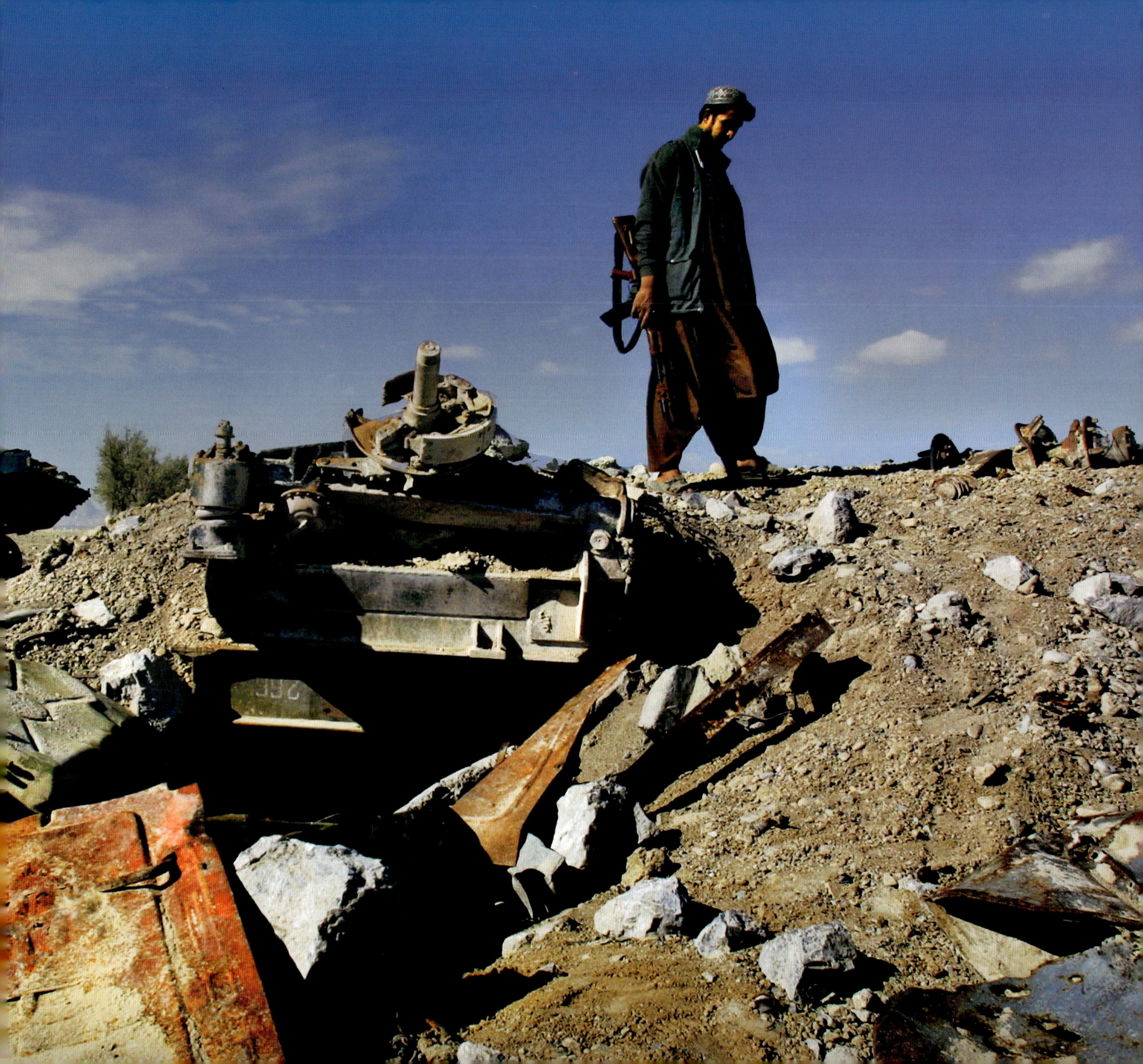

KABUL, JANUARY 11, 2002.

Bullets cover a checkpoint manned by a Northern Alliance soldier at the entrance to the city of Kabul.

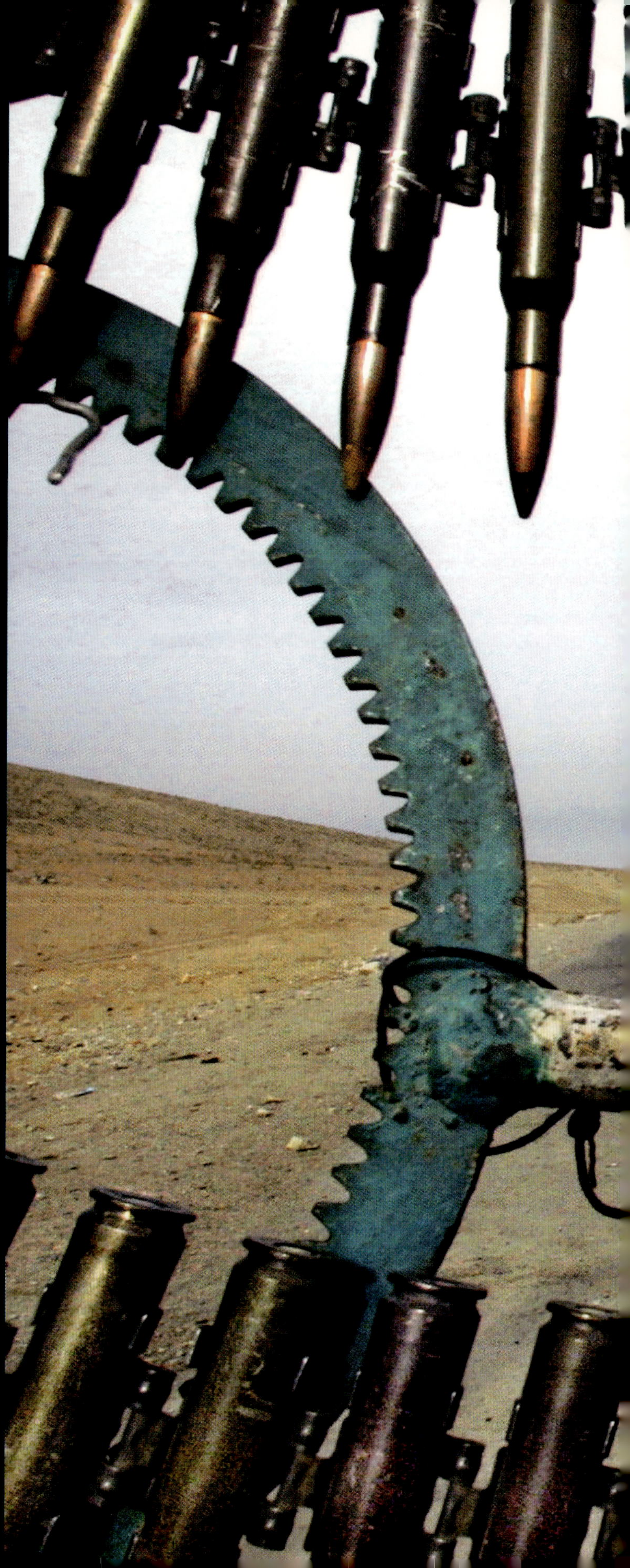

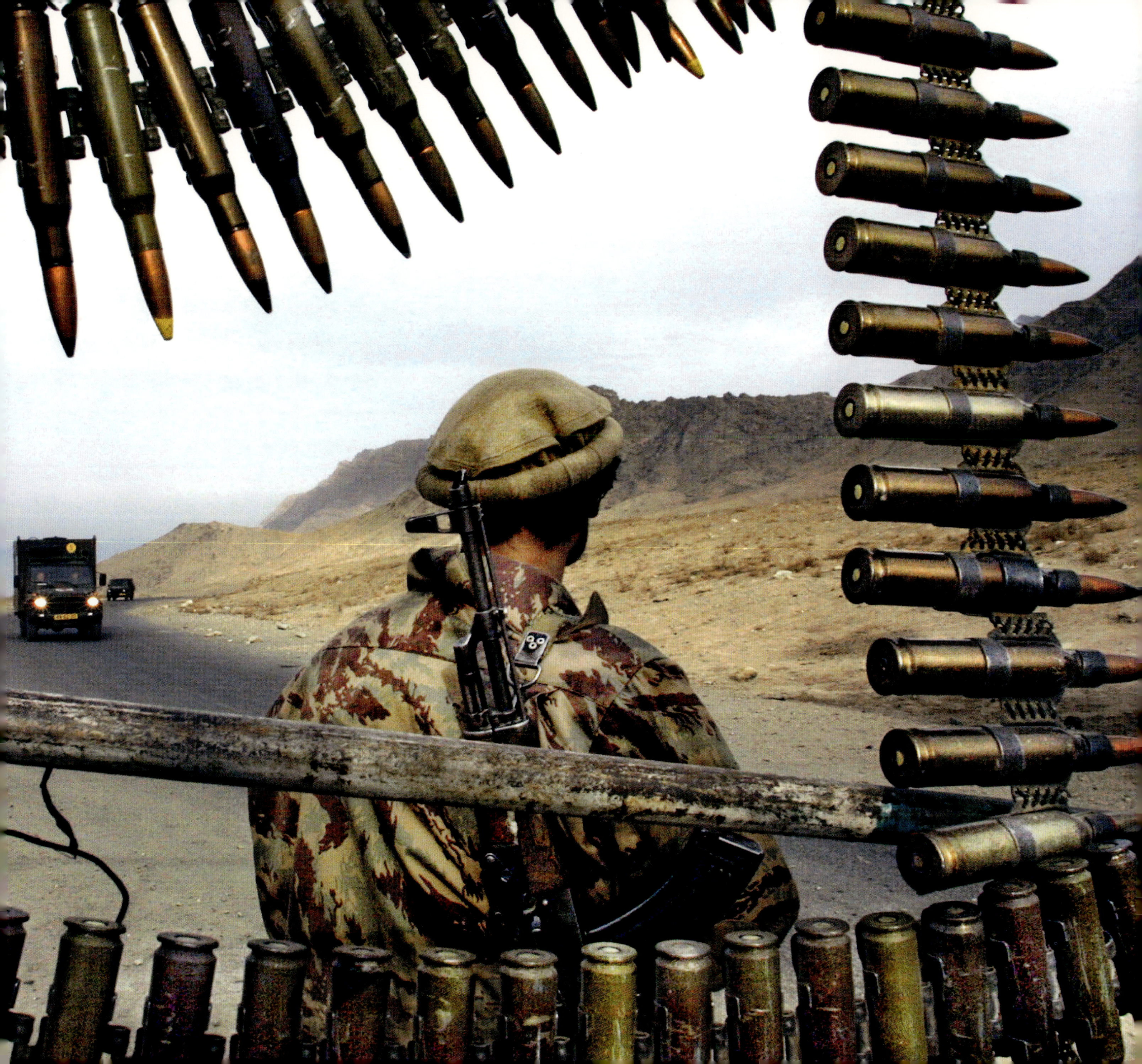

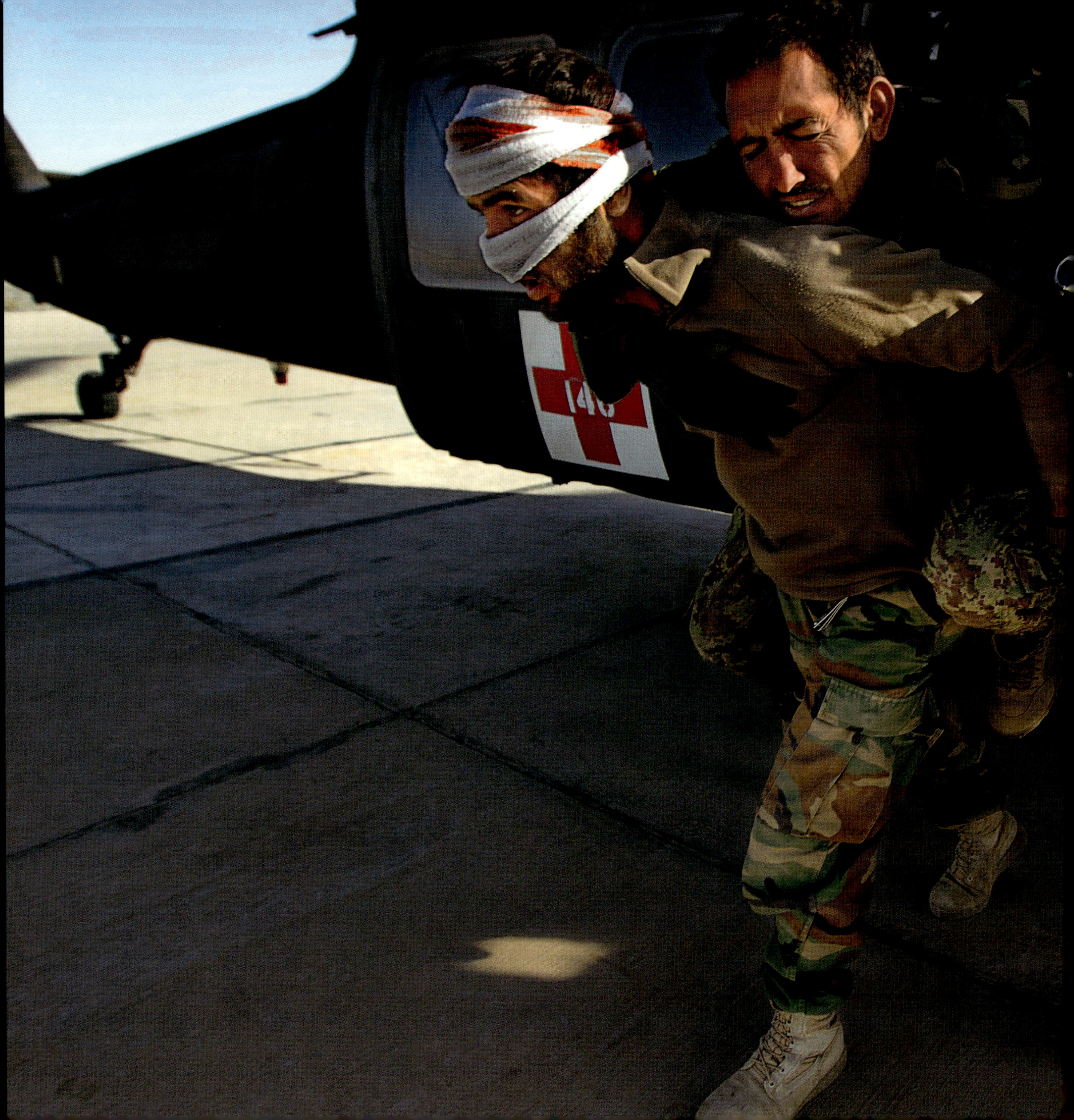

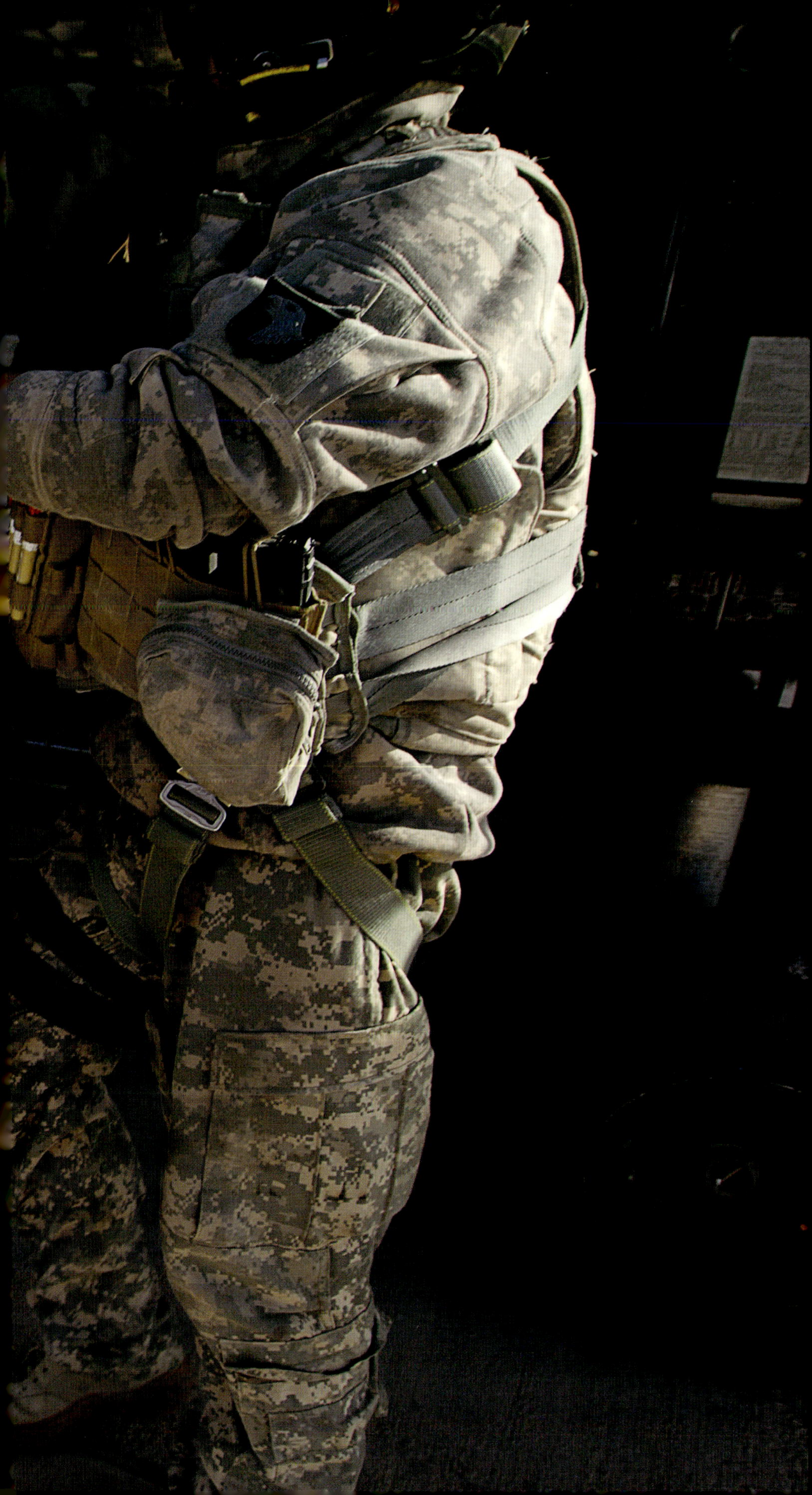

KANDAHAR, DECEMBER 12, 2010.

US Army Sergeant Jay Kenney (right), with Task Force Destiny, helps wounded Afghan National Army soldiers exit a Blackhawk helicopter after they have been rescued in an air mission.

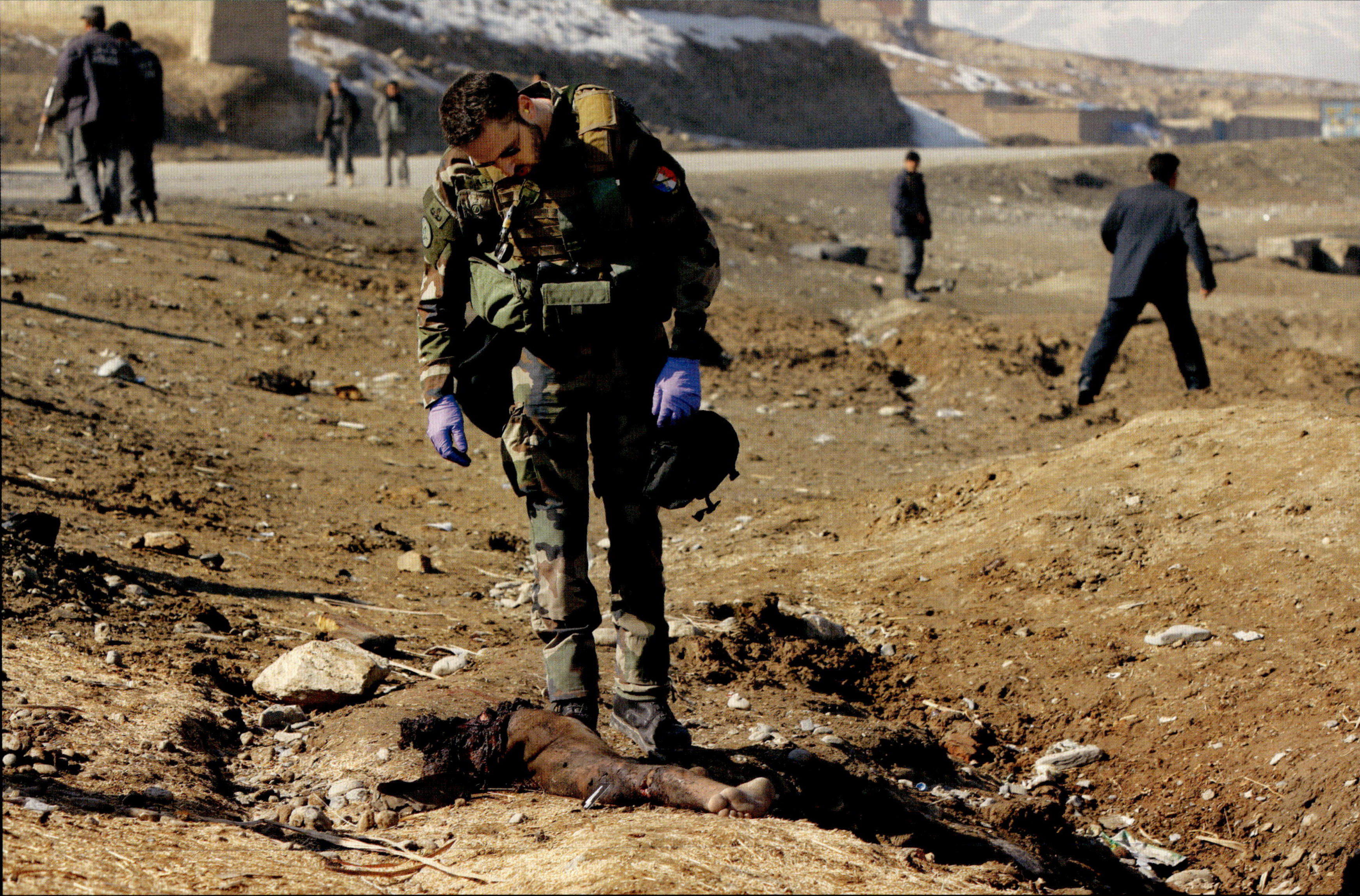

KABUL, FEBRUARY 1, 2009.

A NATO medic looks at the severed leg of a suicide bomber after an attack on a convoy of foreign troops.

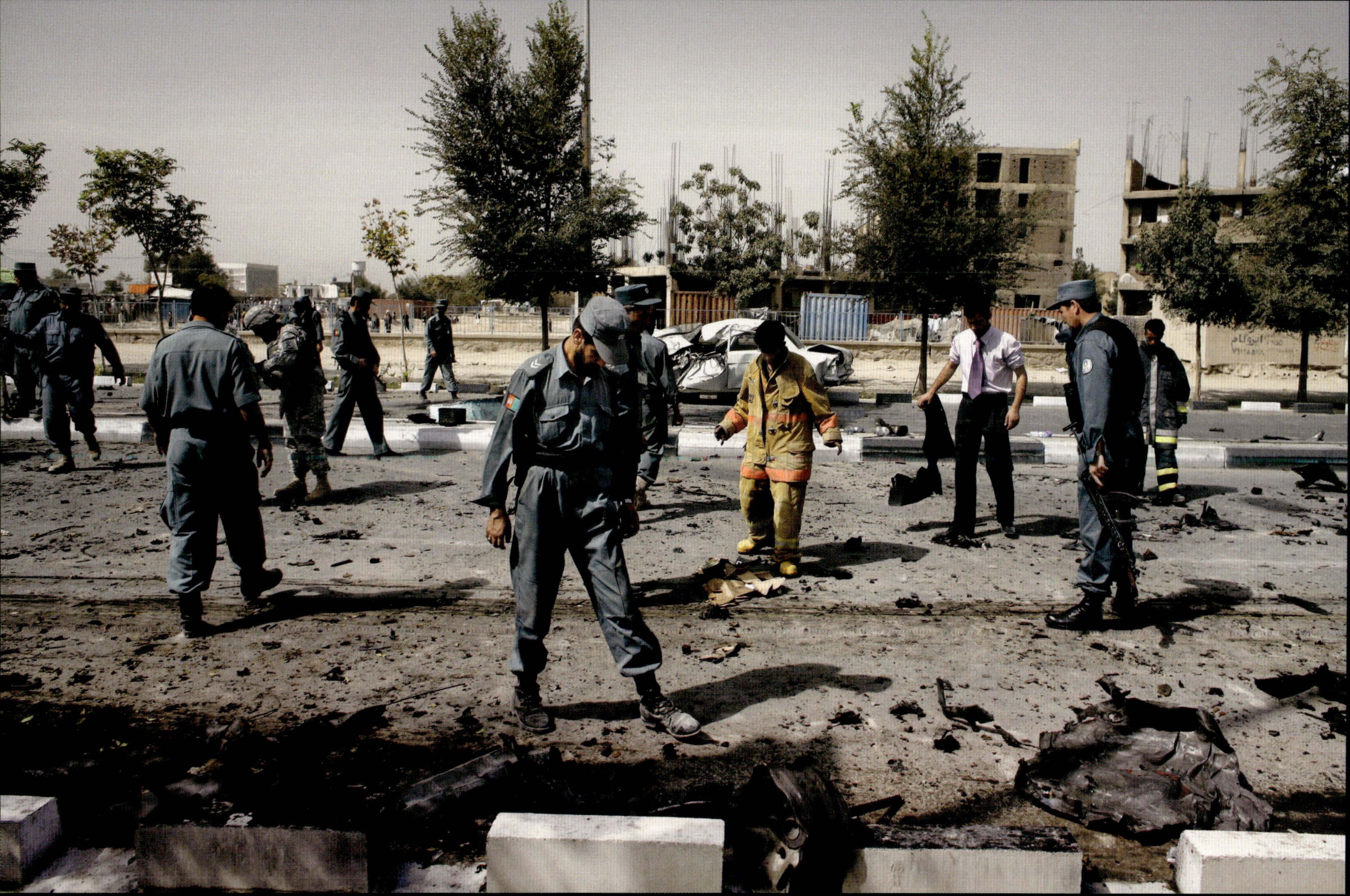

KABUL, OCTOBER 6, 2007.

Afghan police and US military personnel comb the scene for evidence following a suicide car bomber's attack on a US-led coalition convoy near Kabul International Airport. The attack killed one US soldier and five Afghans.

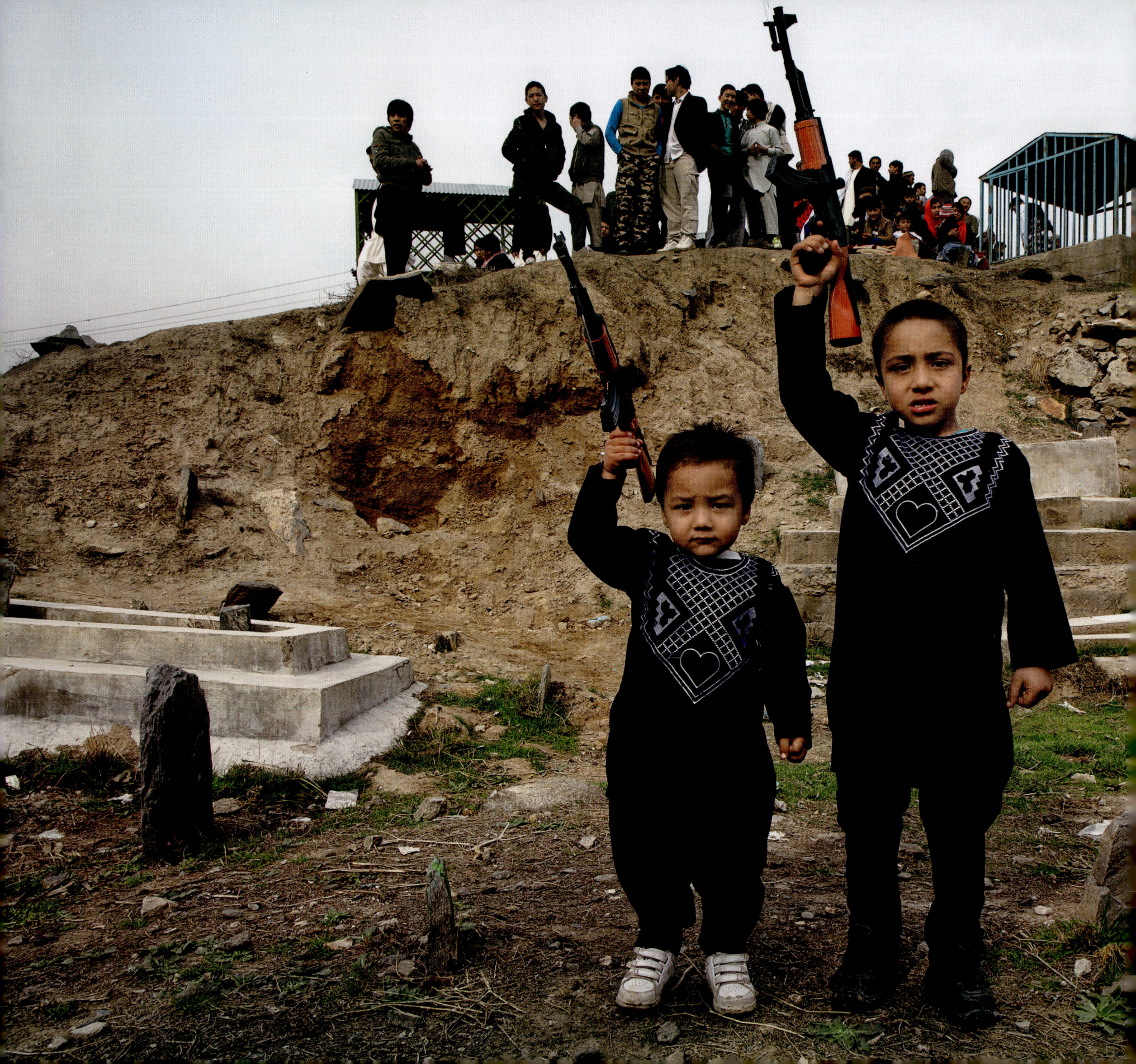

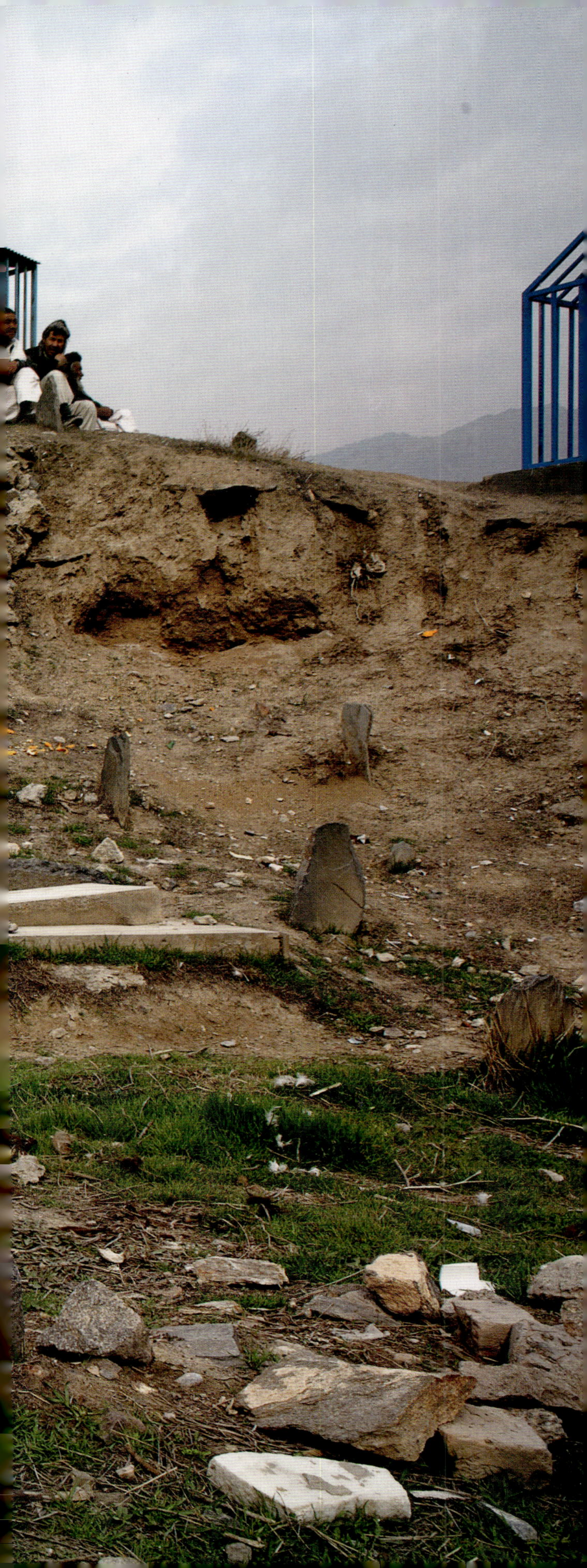

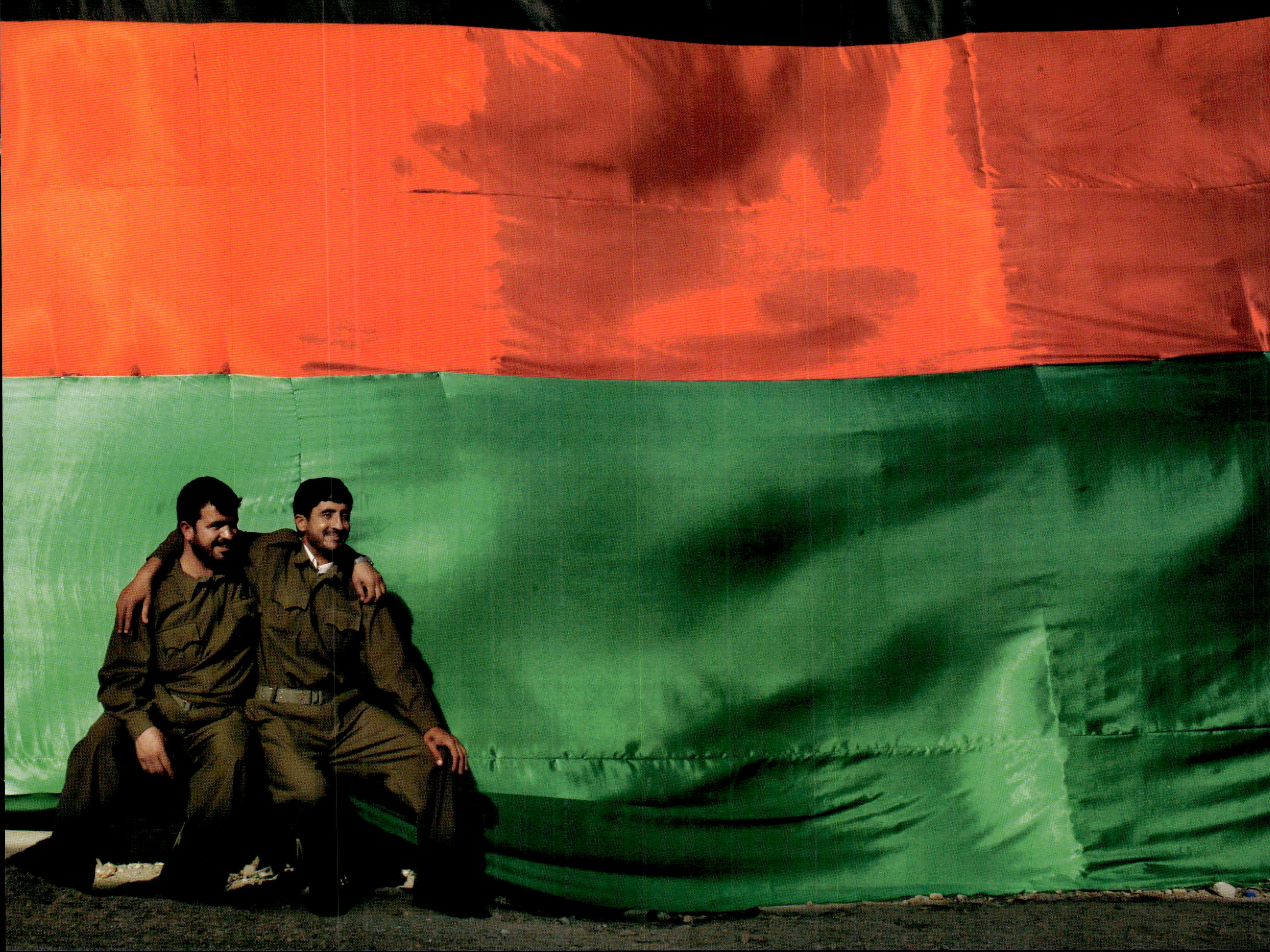

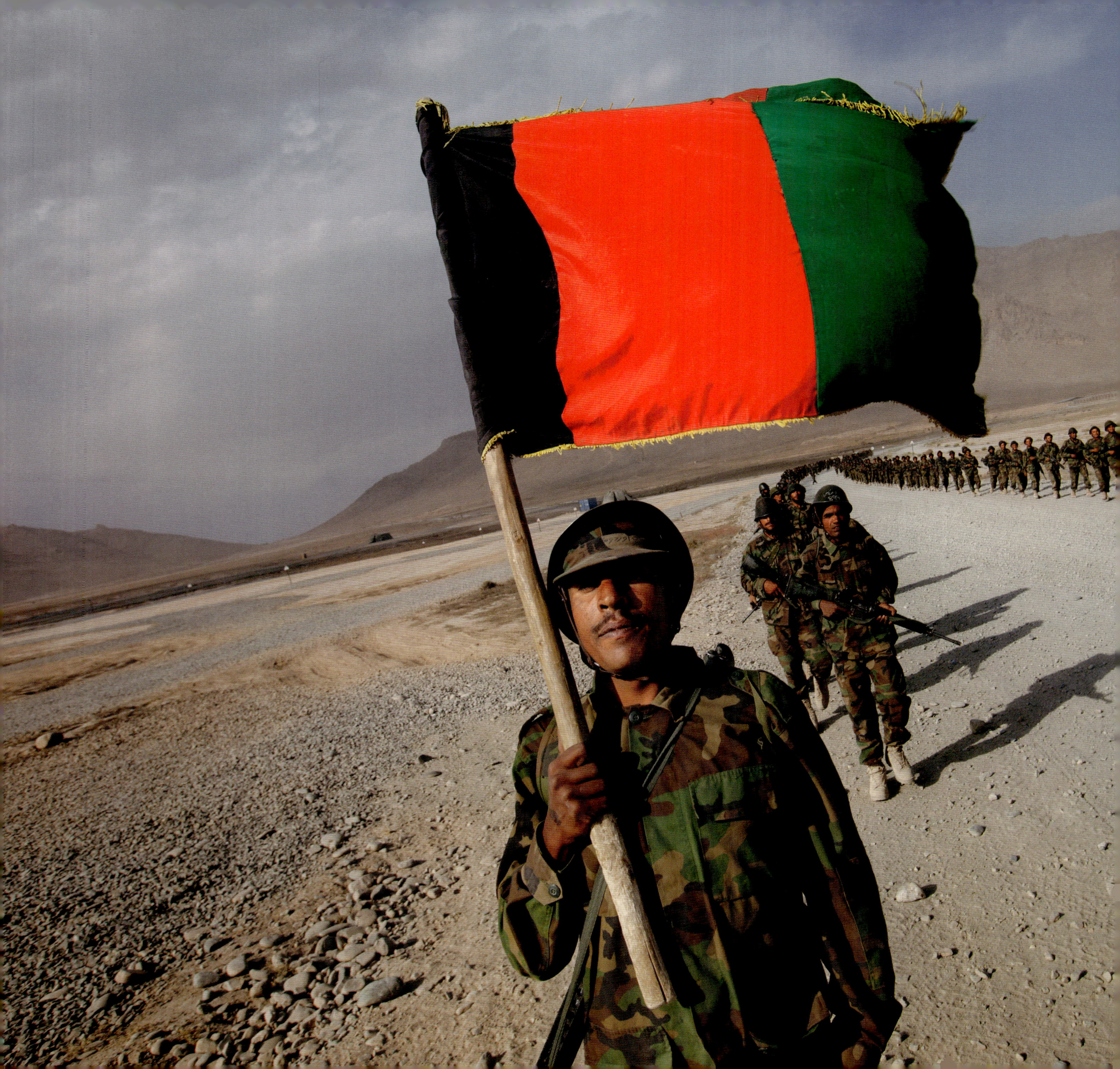

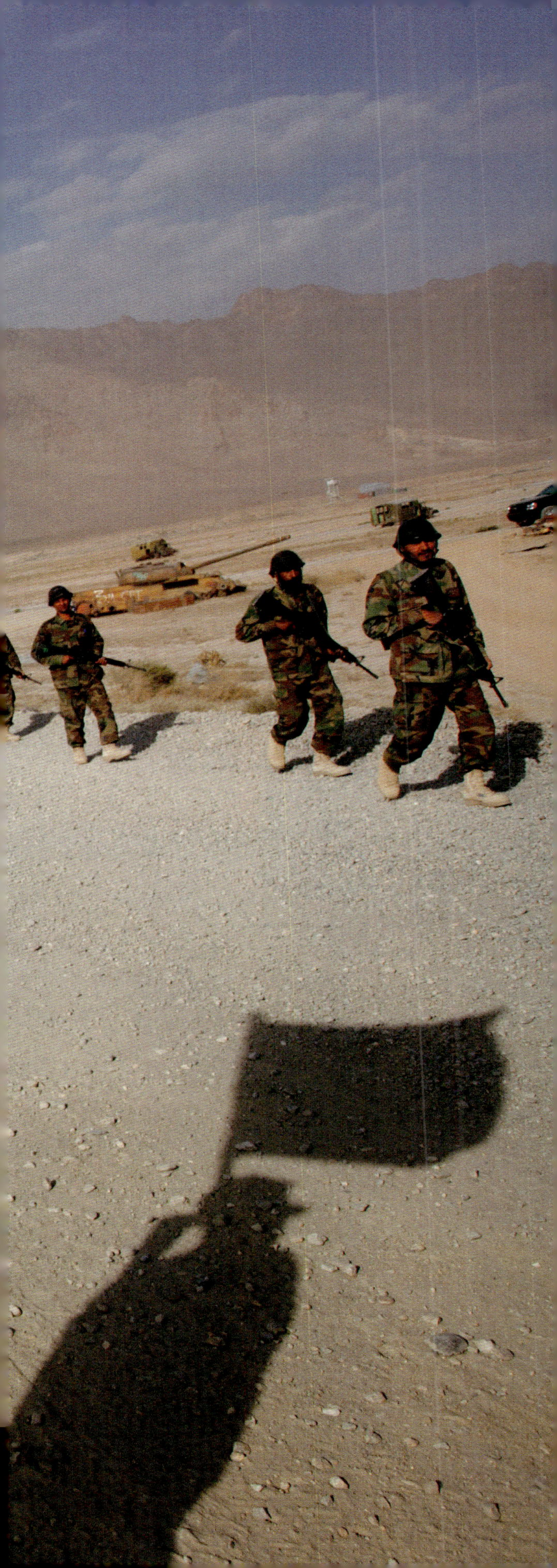

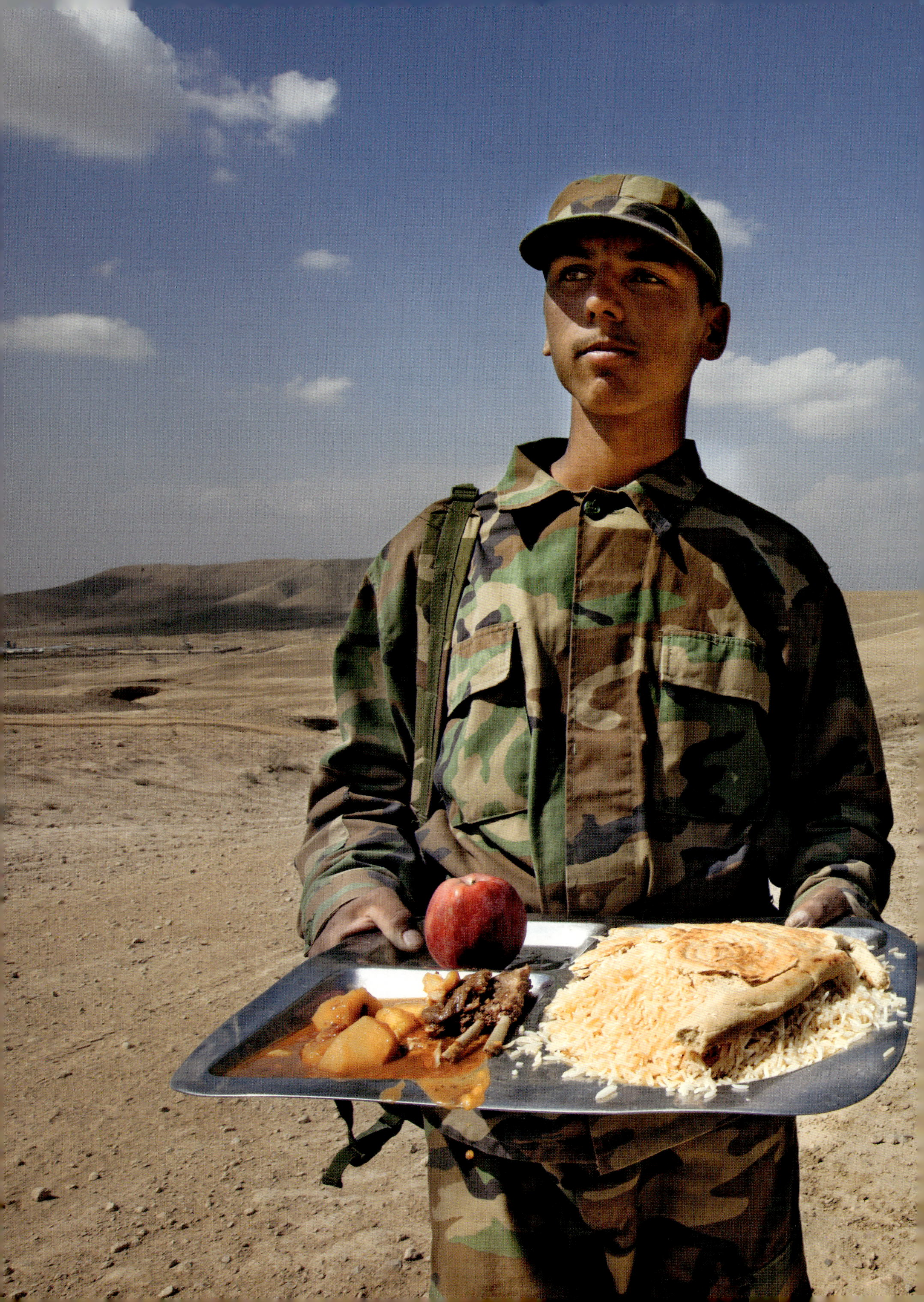

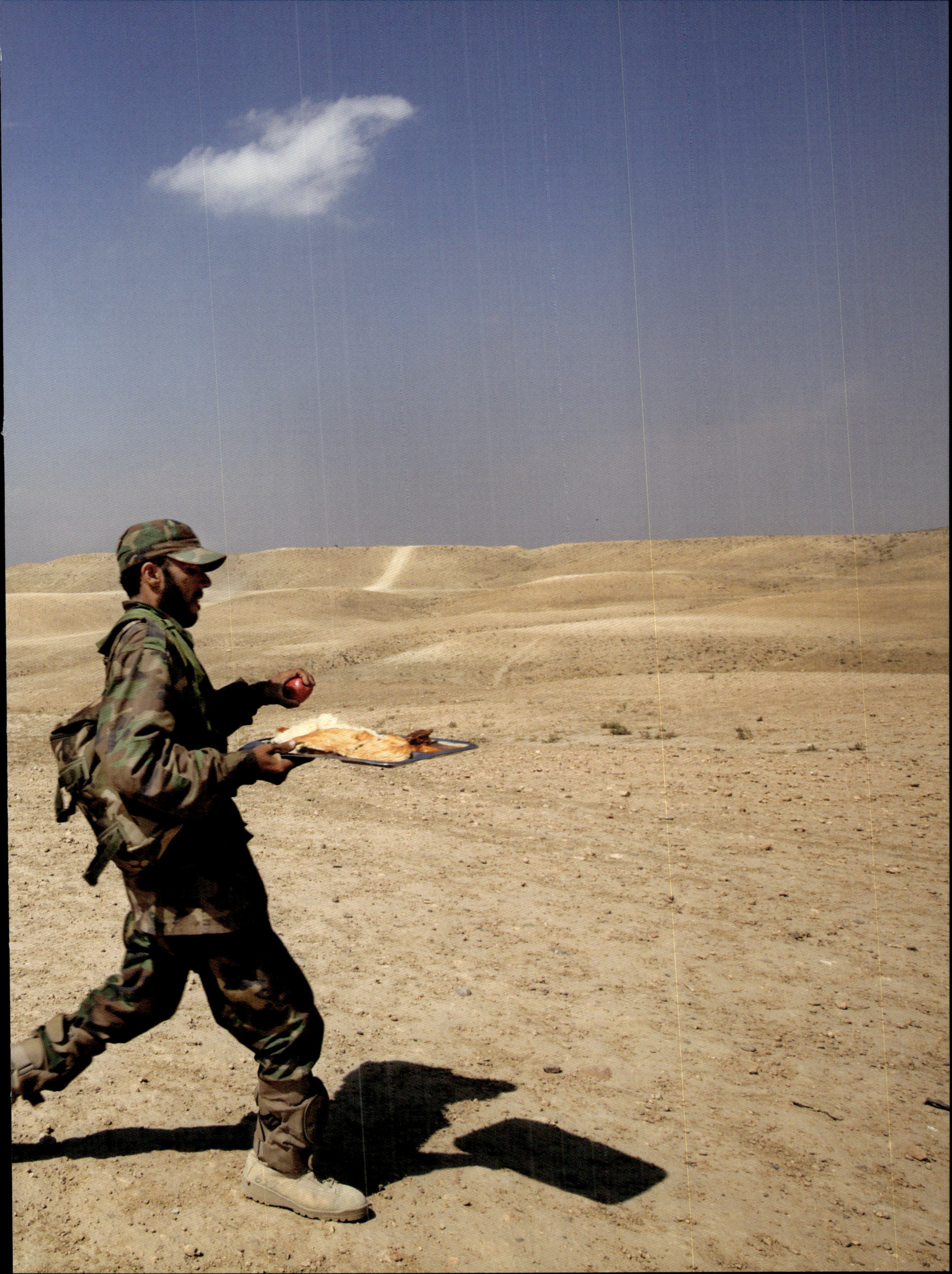

KABUL, OCTOBER 1, 2010.

A member of the Afghan National Army holds his lunch as others in the battalion eat at the training grounds of the Kabul Militar Training Center.

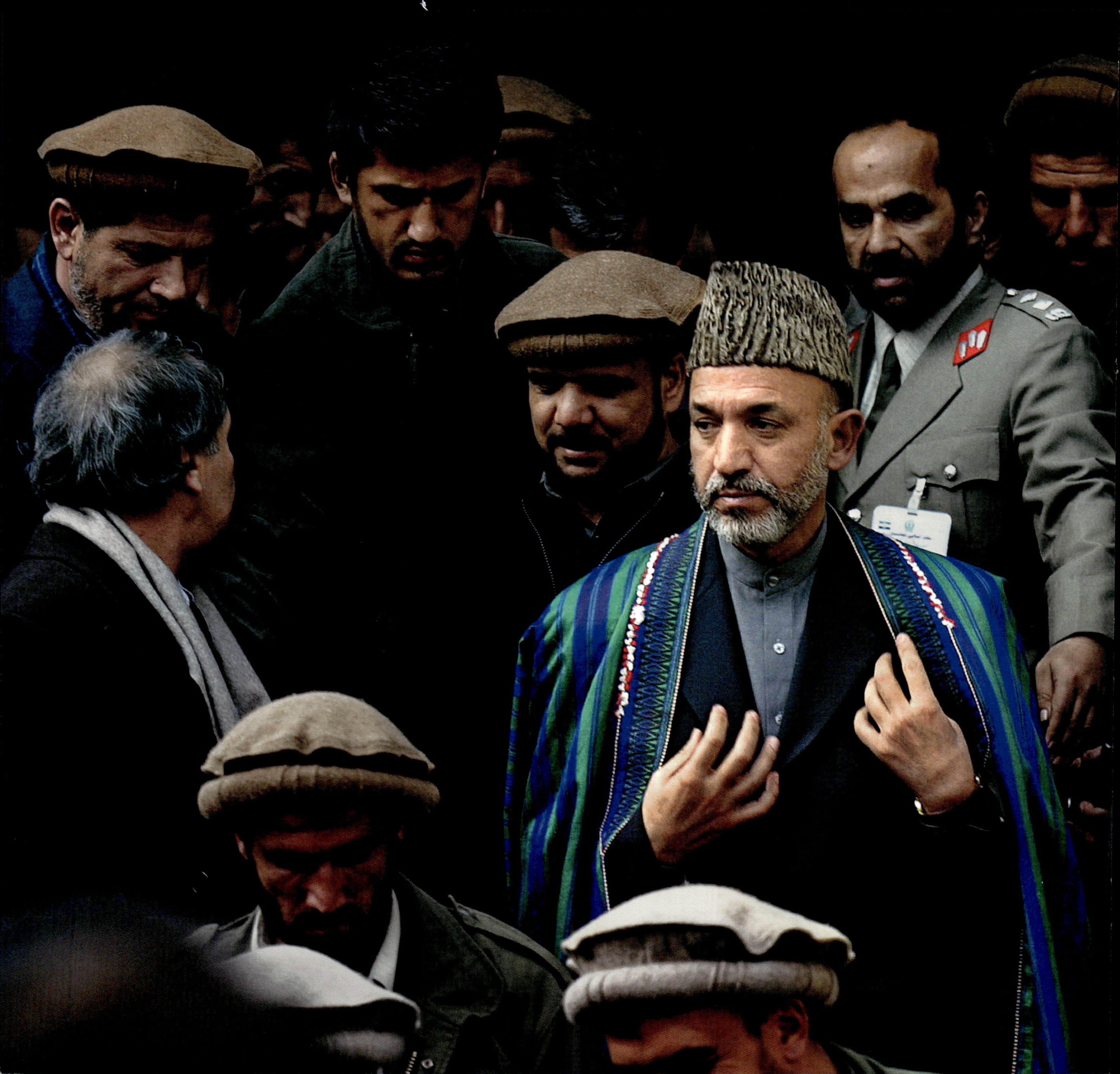

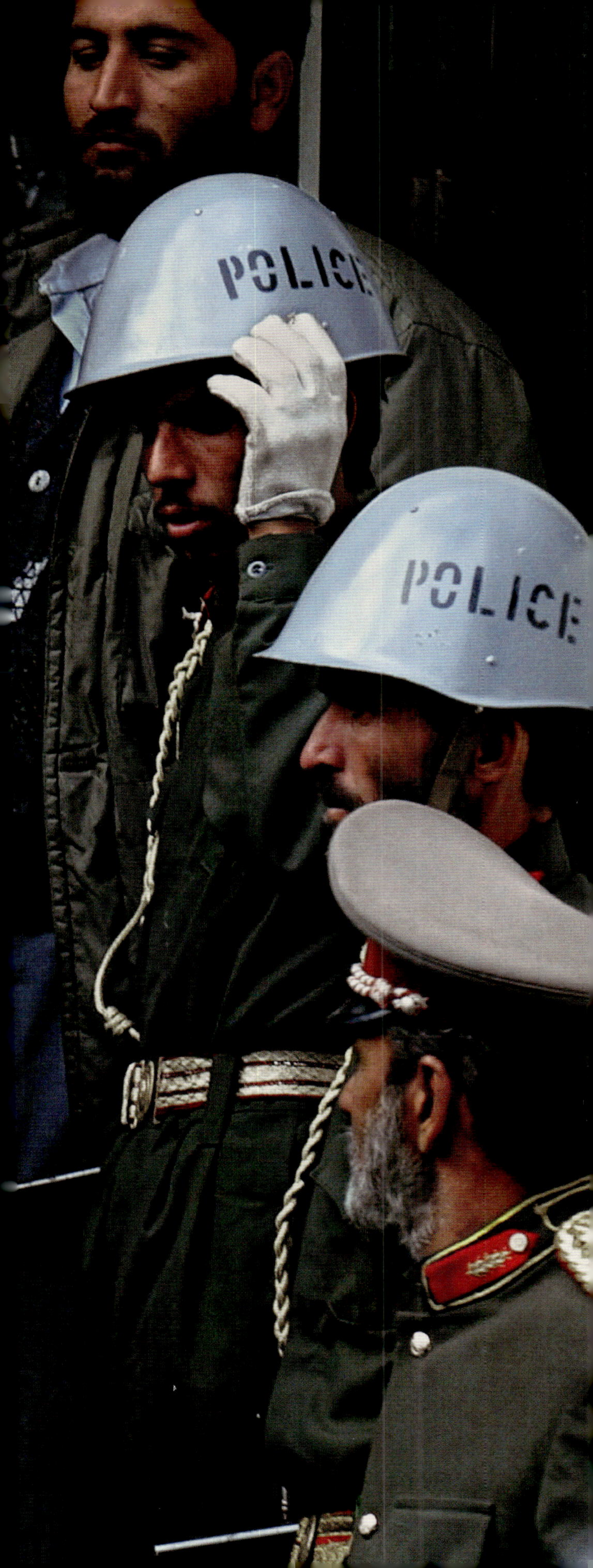
POLICE
POLICE

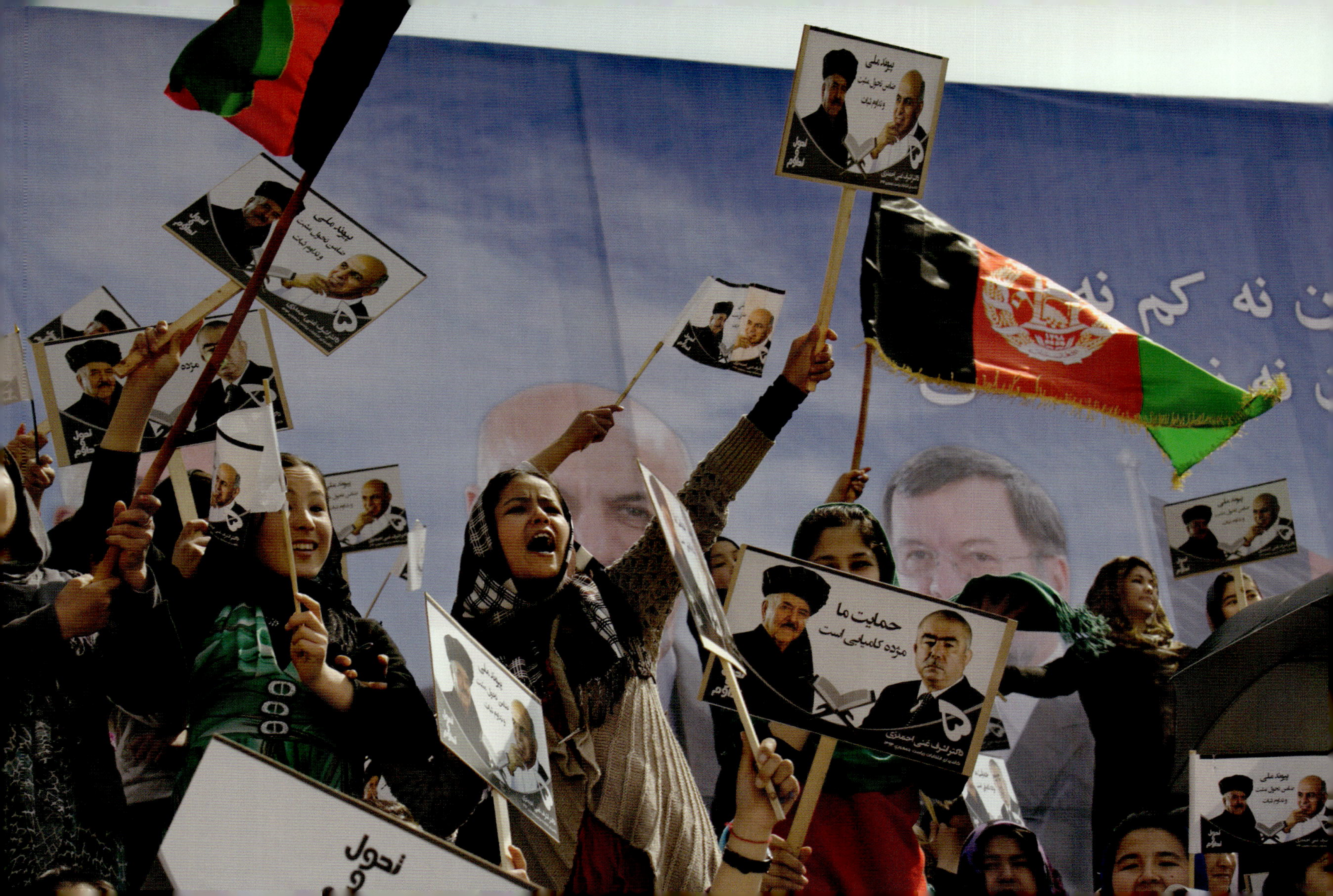

حمایت ما
مژده کامیابی است
تحول

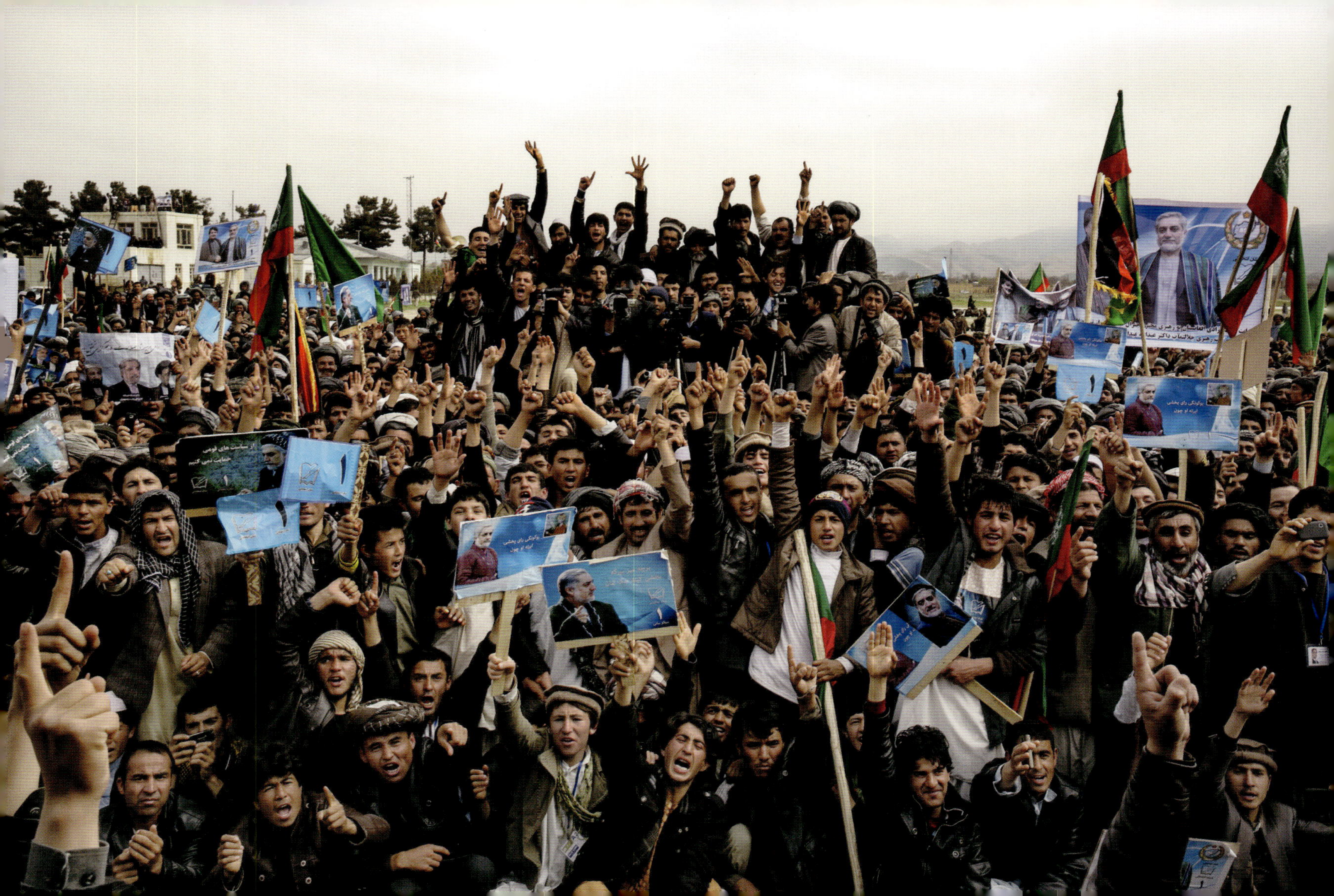

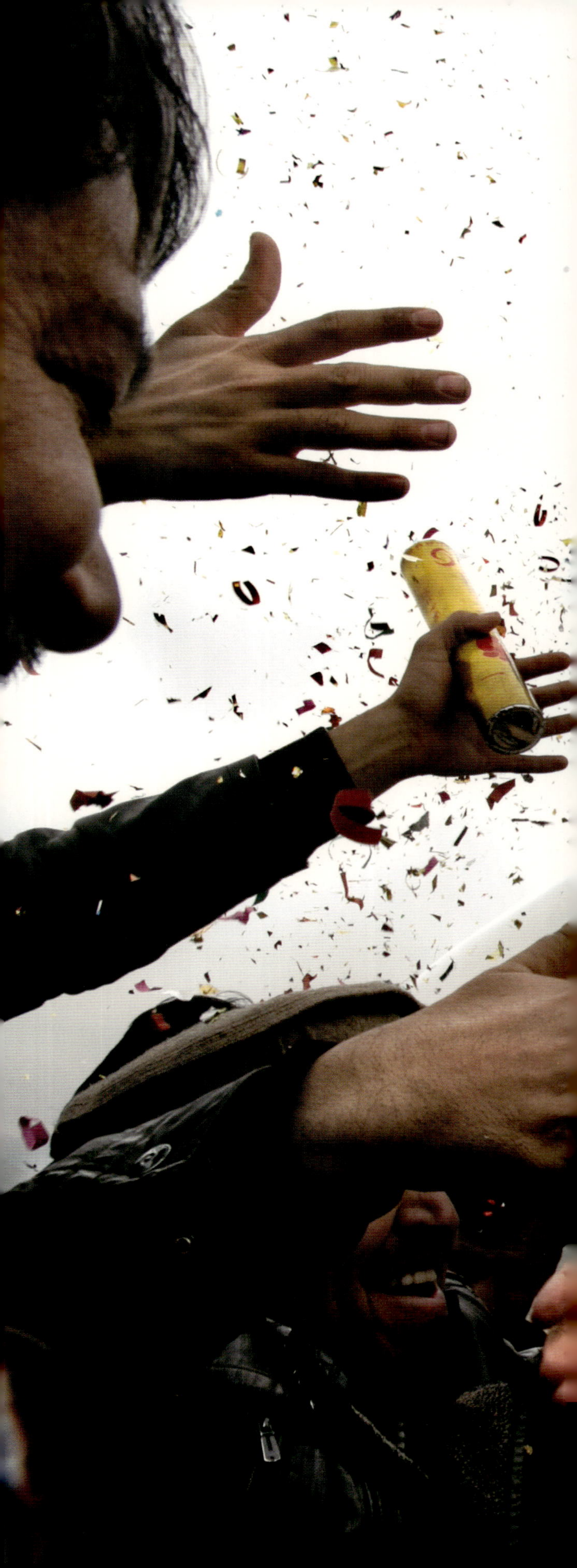

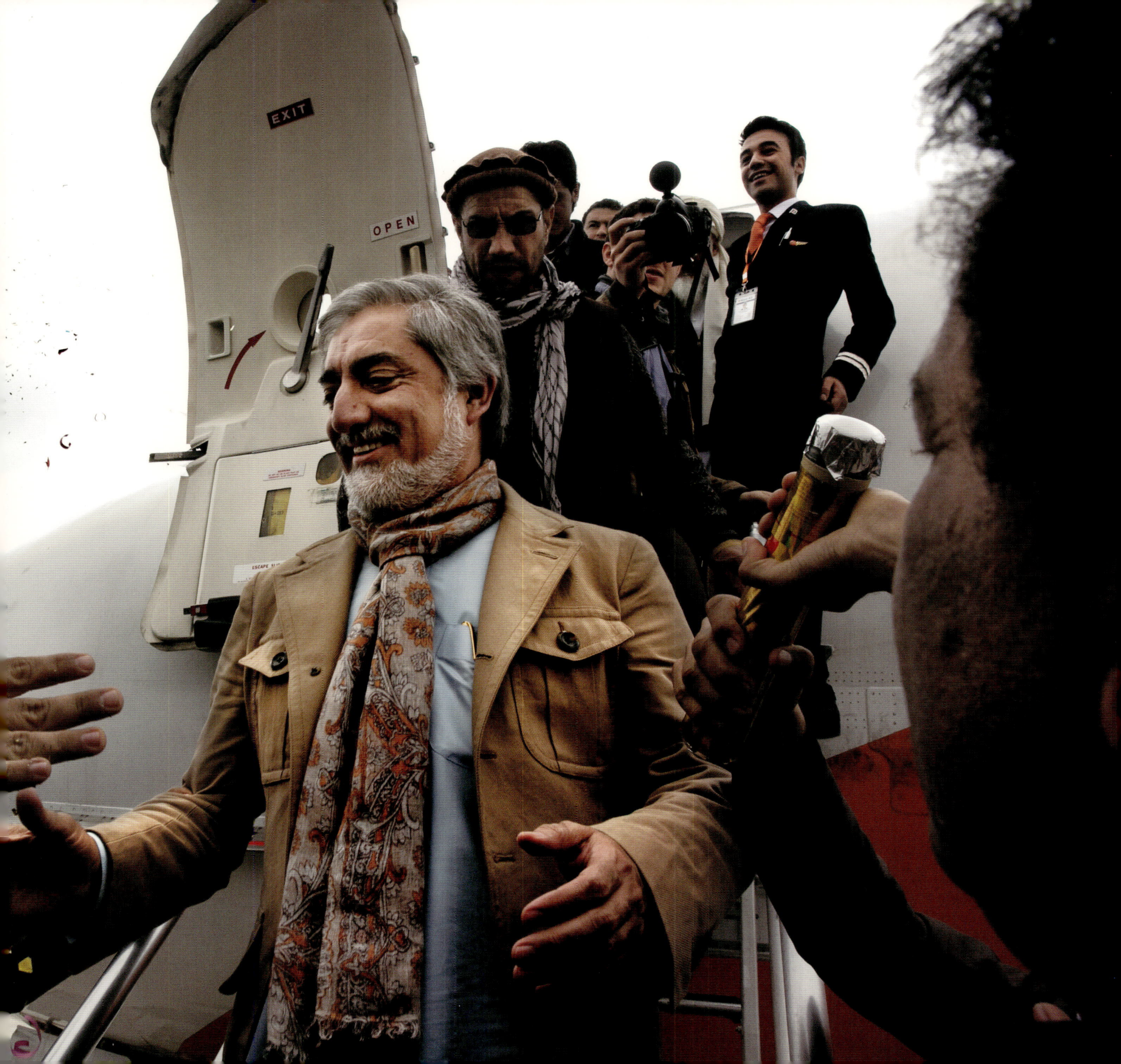
EXIT
OPEN

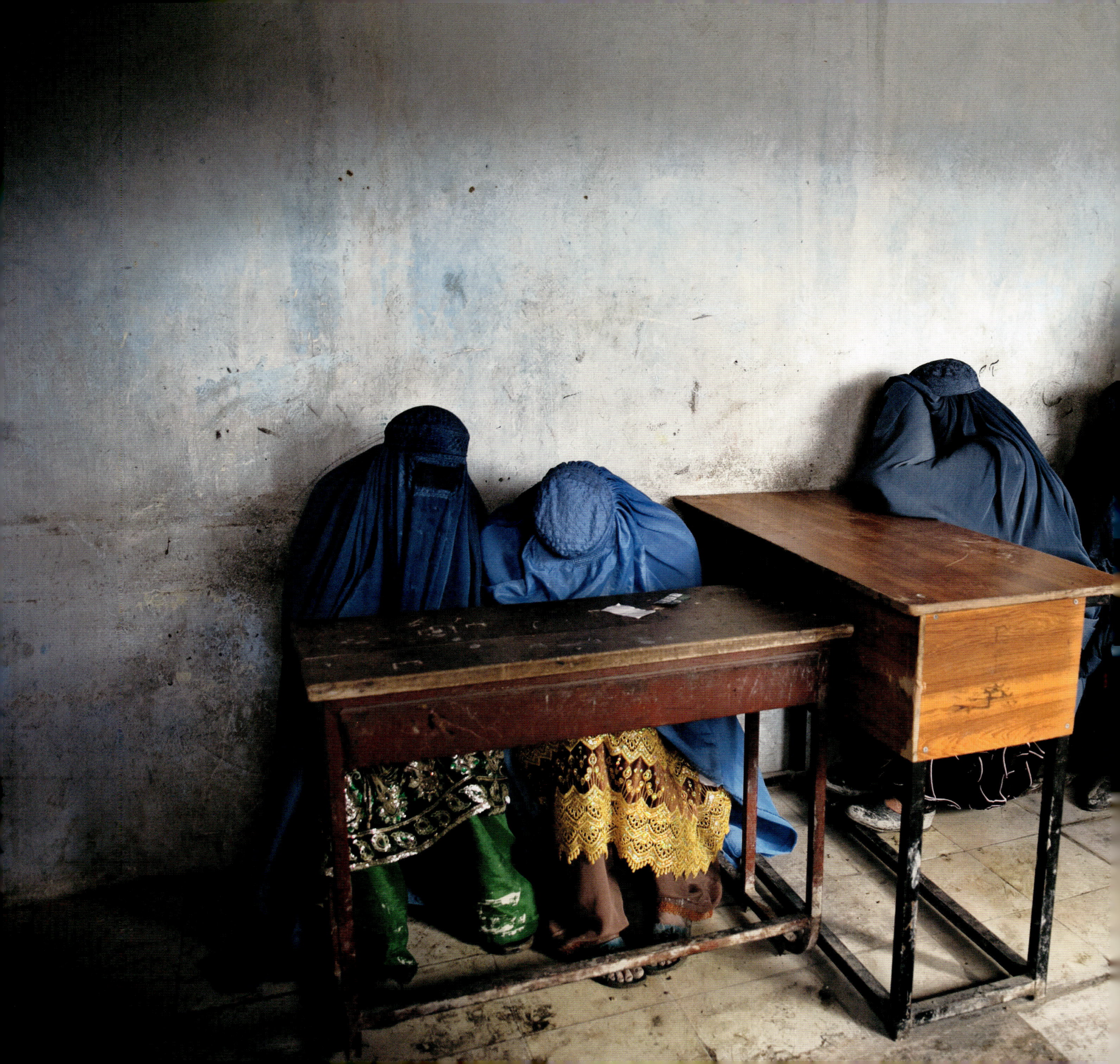

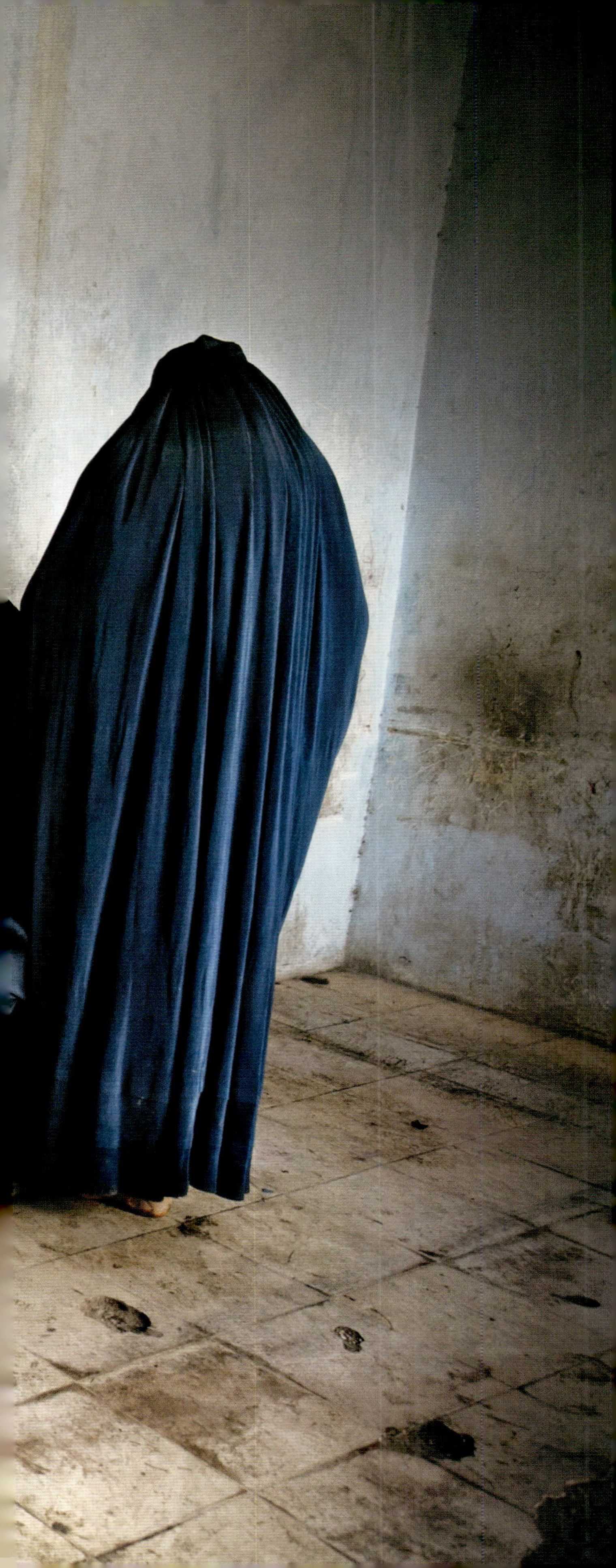

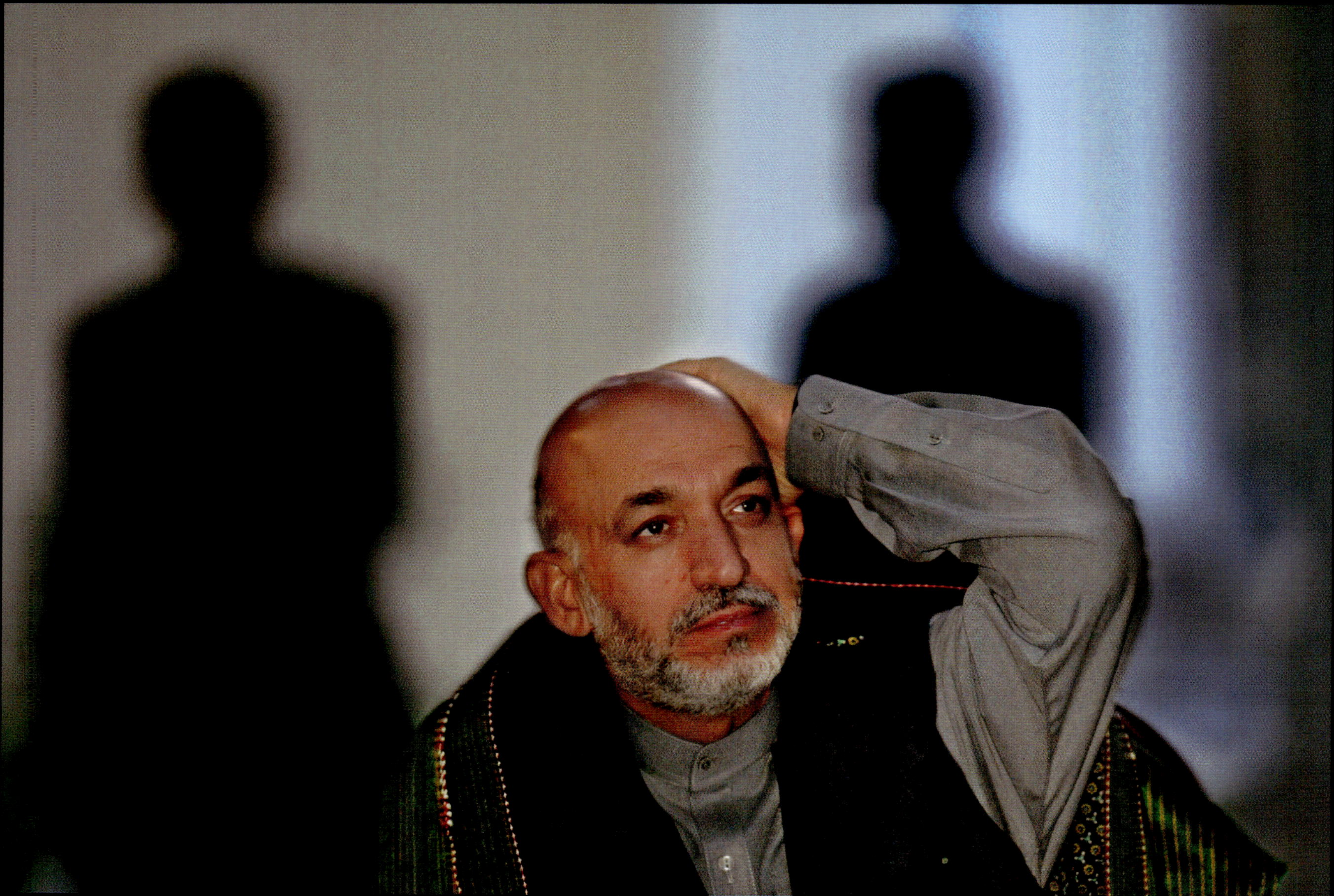

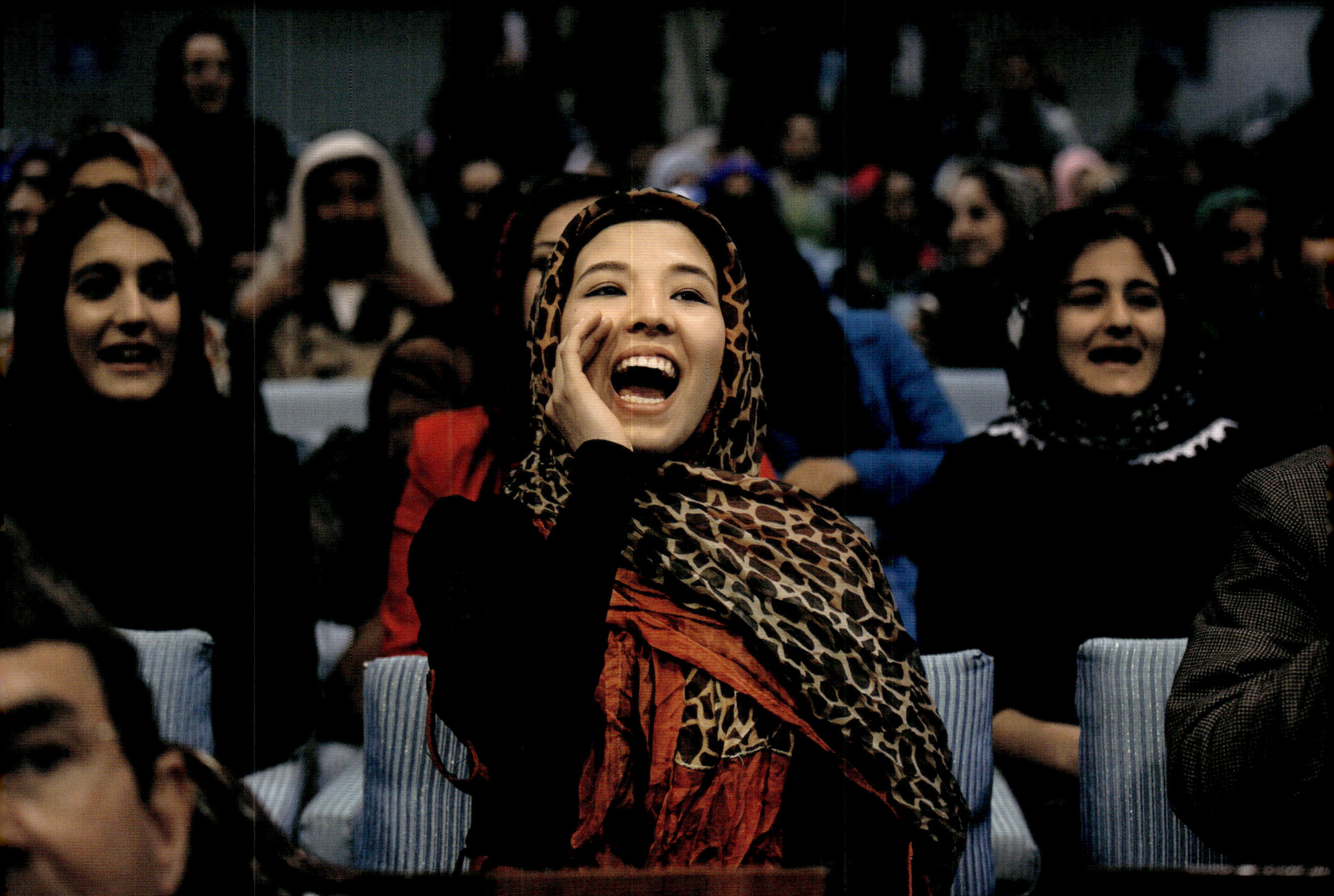

KABUL, MARCH 31, 2014.

Women cheer while attending an election rally for the Afghan vice-presidential candidate Habiba Sarabi.

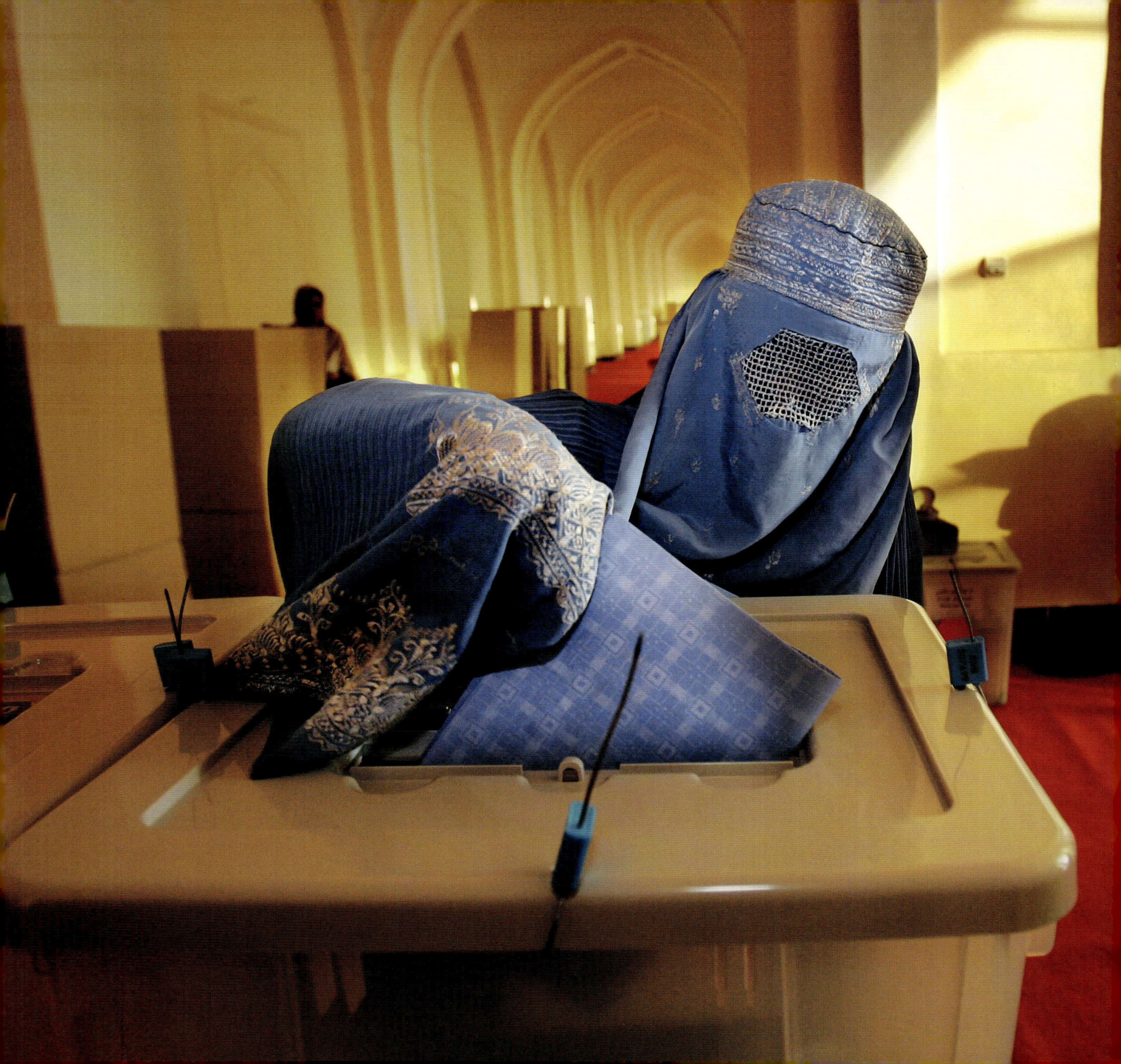

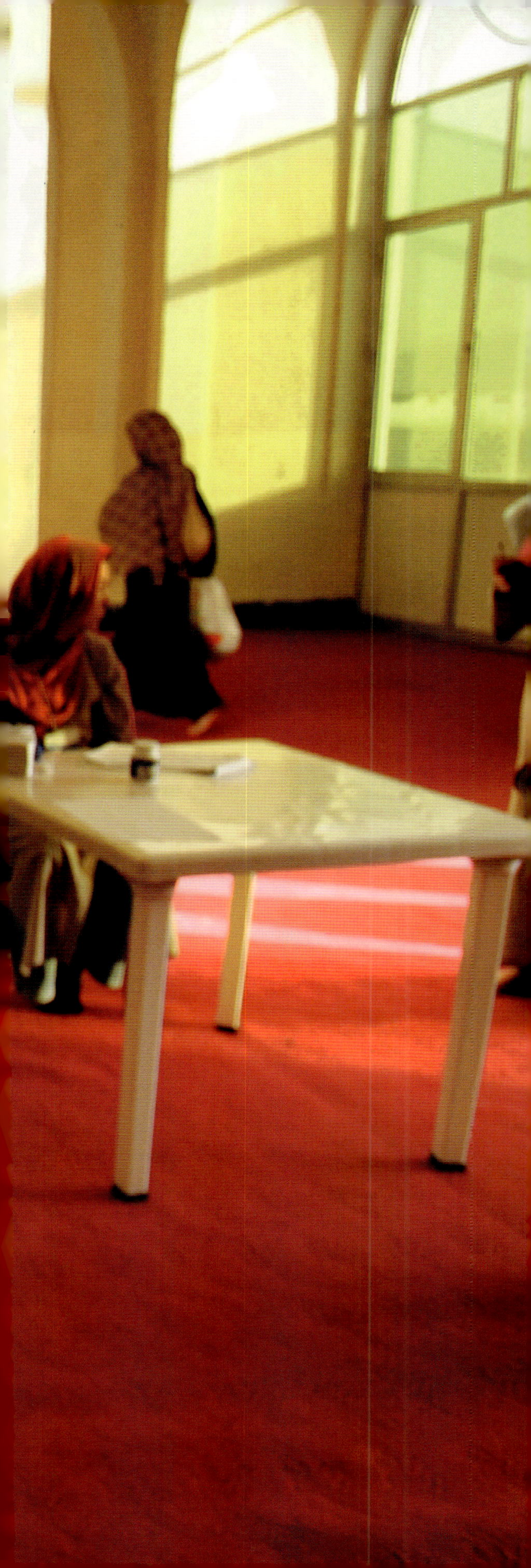

The Casualties

KANDAHAR, OCTOBER 13, 2009.

Seven-year-old Attiullah, a patient at Mirwais Hospital, stands alongside an X ray showing the bullet that entered his back, nearly killing him. Attiullah was shot by US forces when he was caught in crossfire as he was herding sheep.

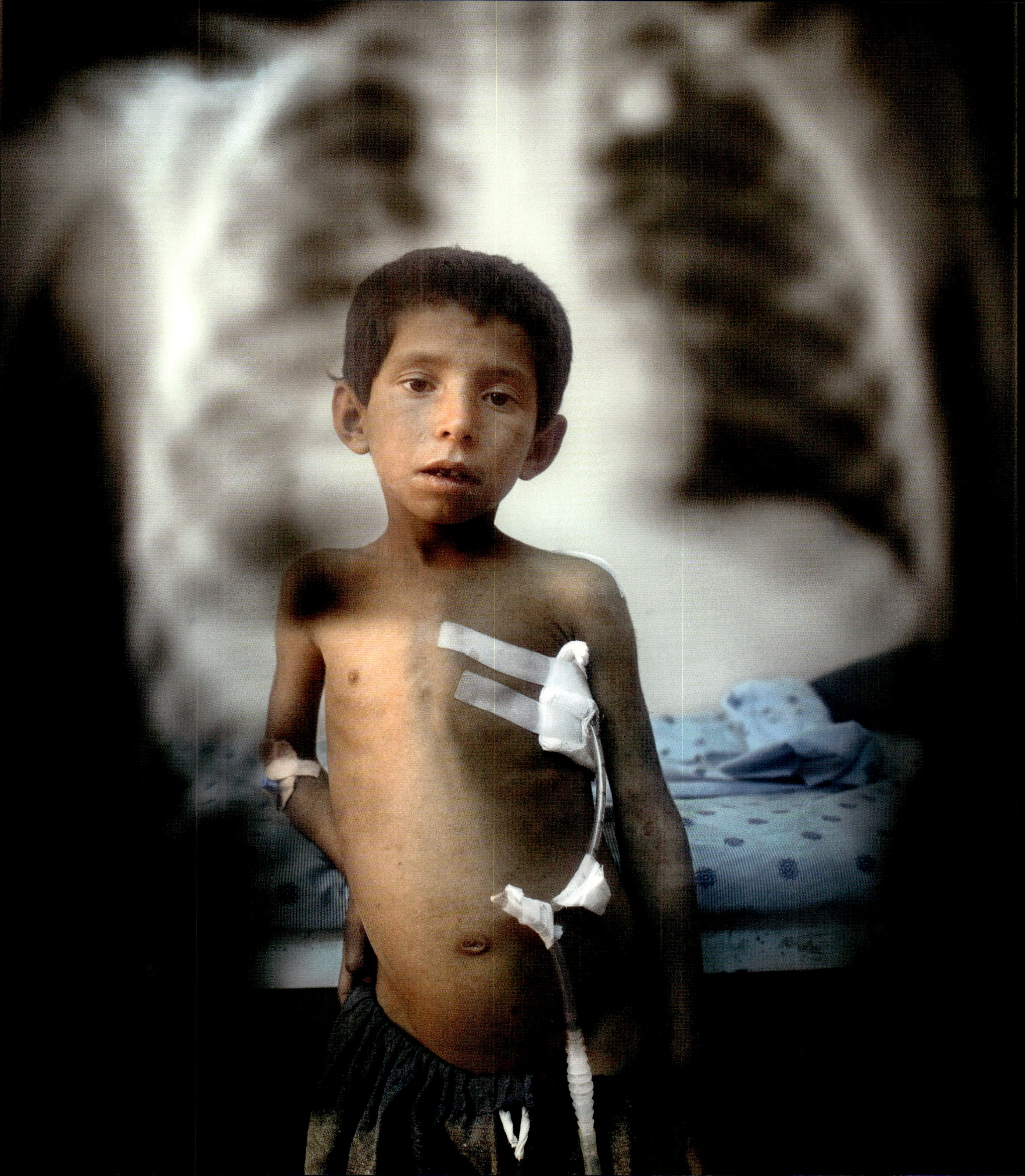

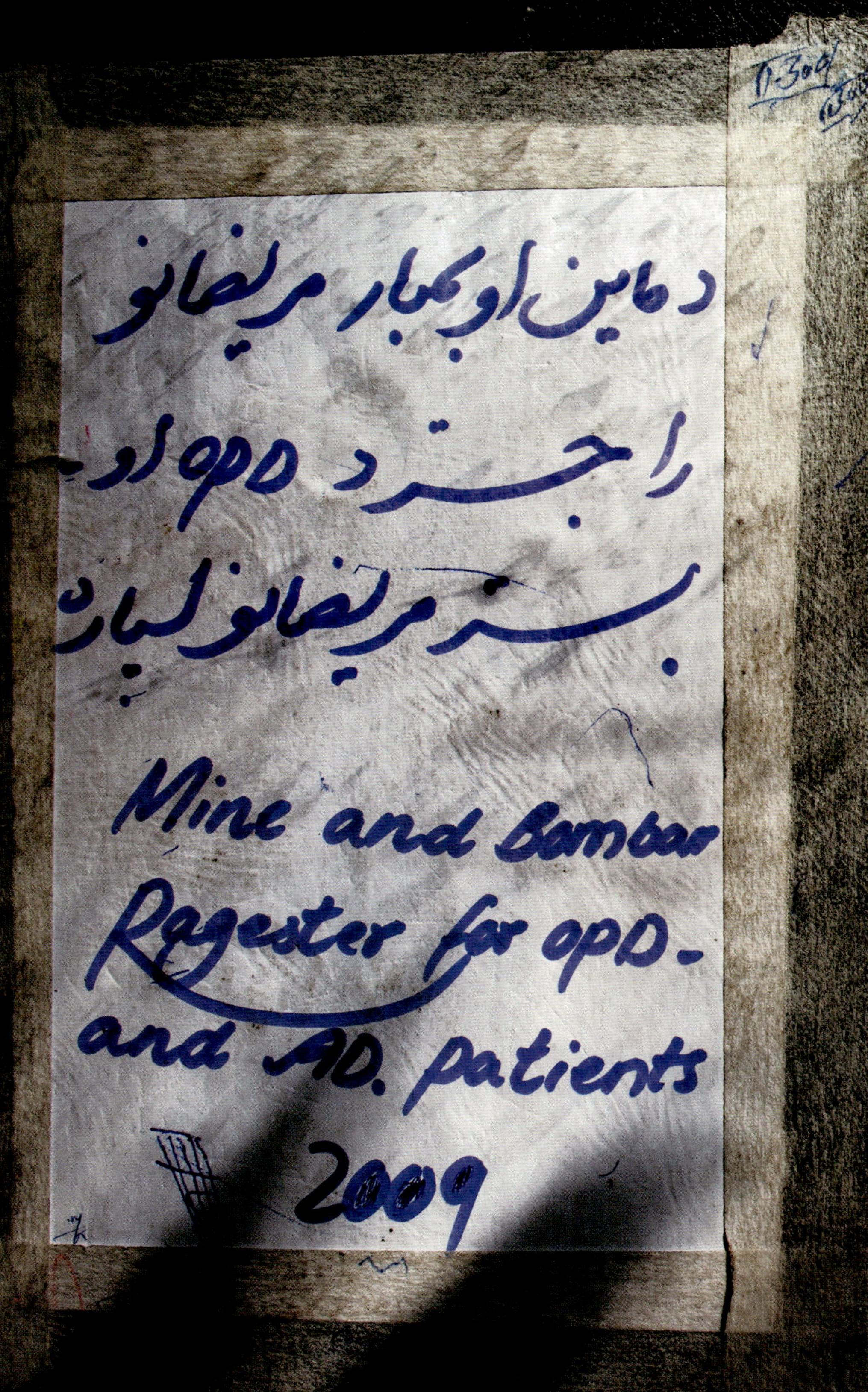
دماین او بمبار مریضانو
راجستر د opd او
بستر مریضانو لپاره
Mine and Bambar
Ragester for OPD-
and AD. patients
2009

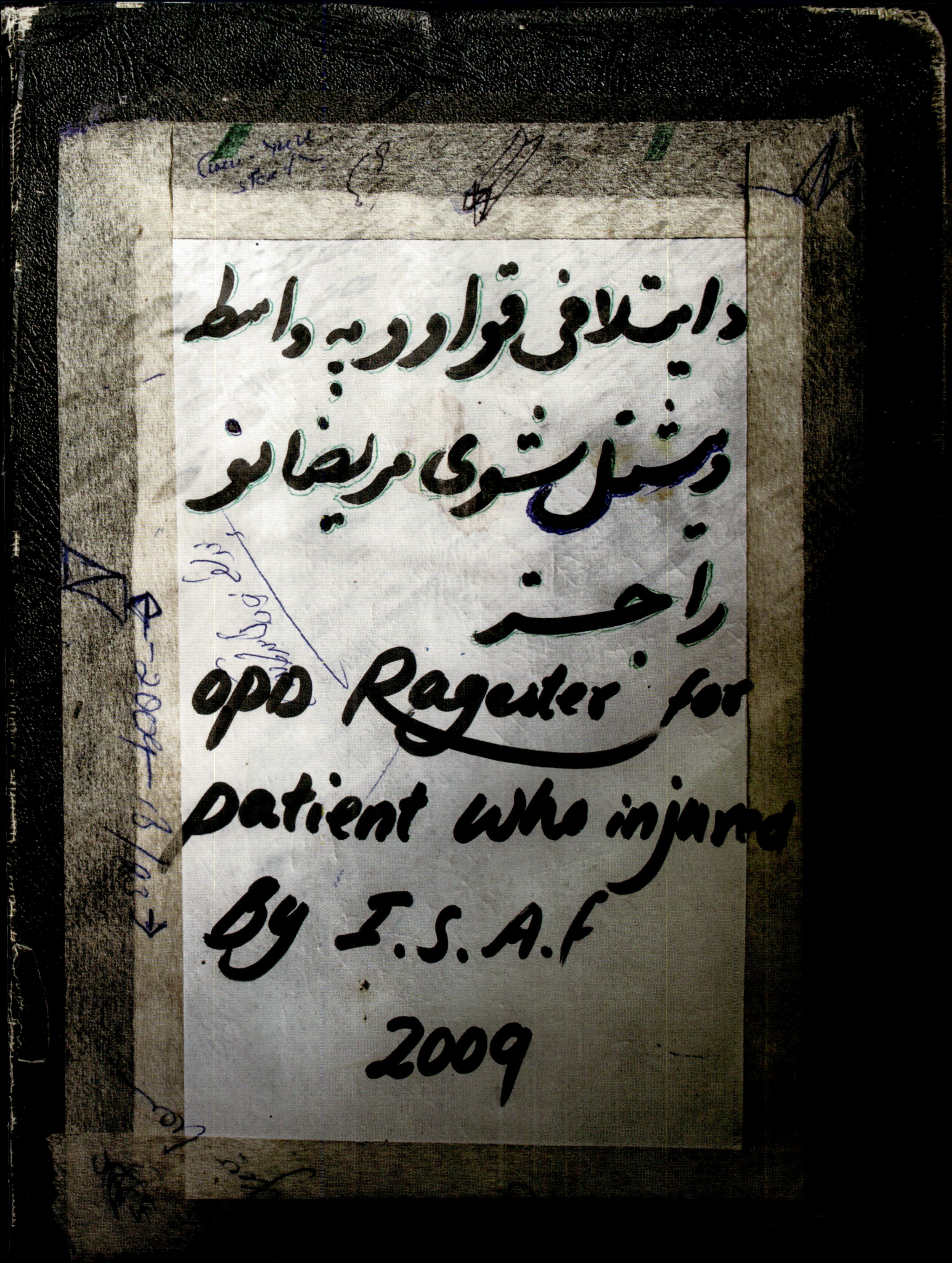

KANDAHAR, OCTOBER 15, 2009.

A handwritten book at the emergency room of Kandahar's Mirwais Hospital lists the injured, distinguishing those who were wounded by the military from those injured by an improvised bomb.

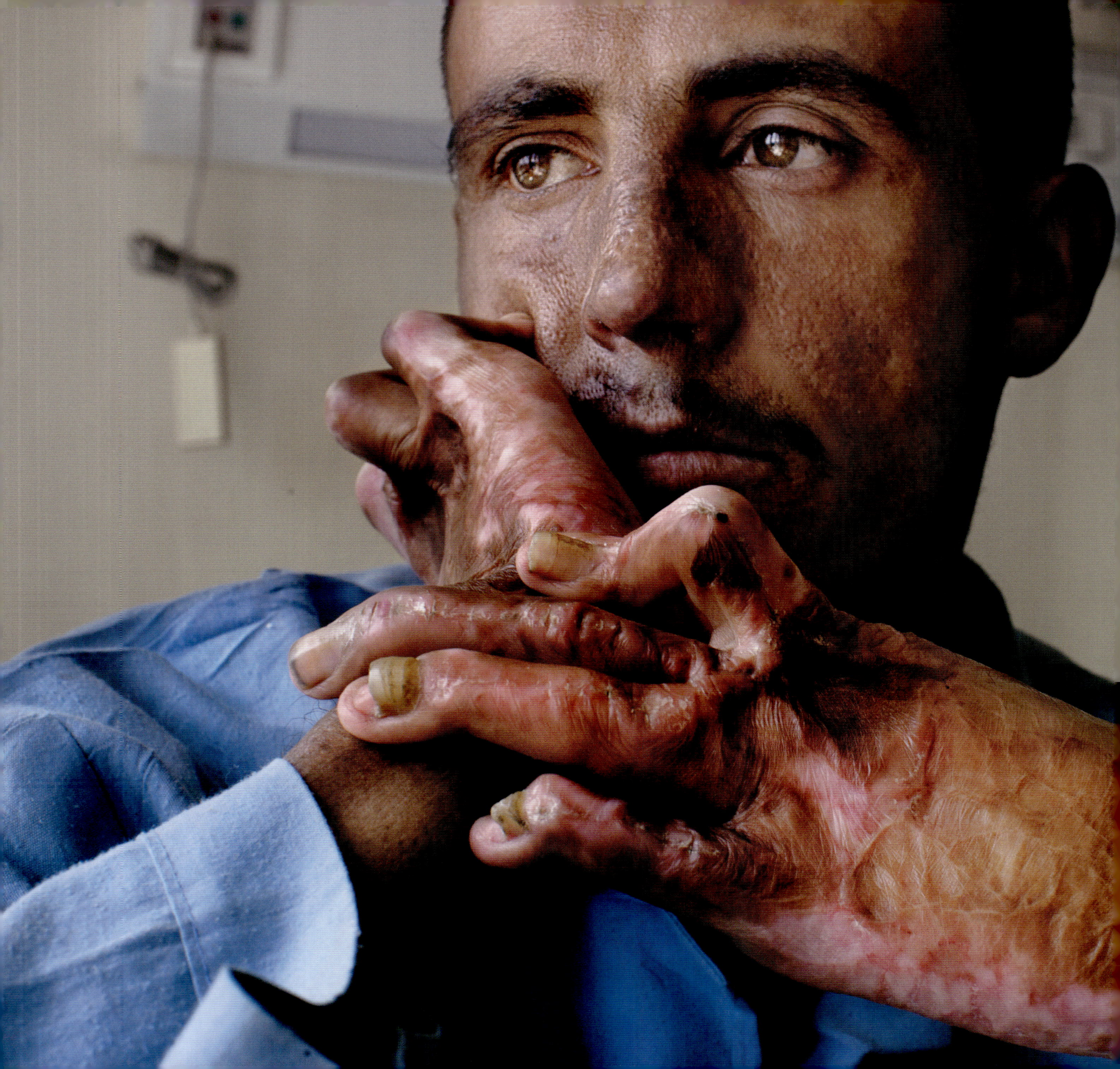

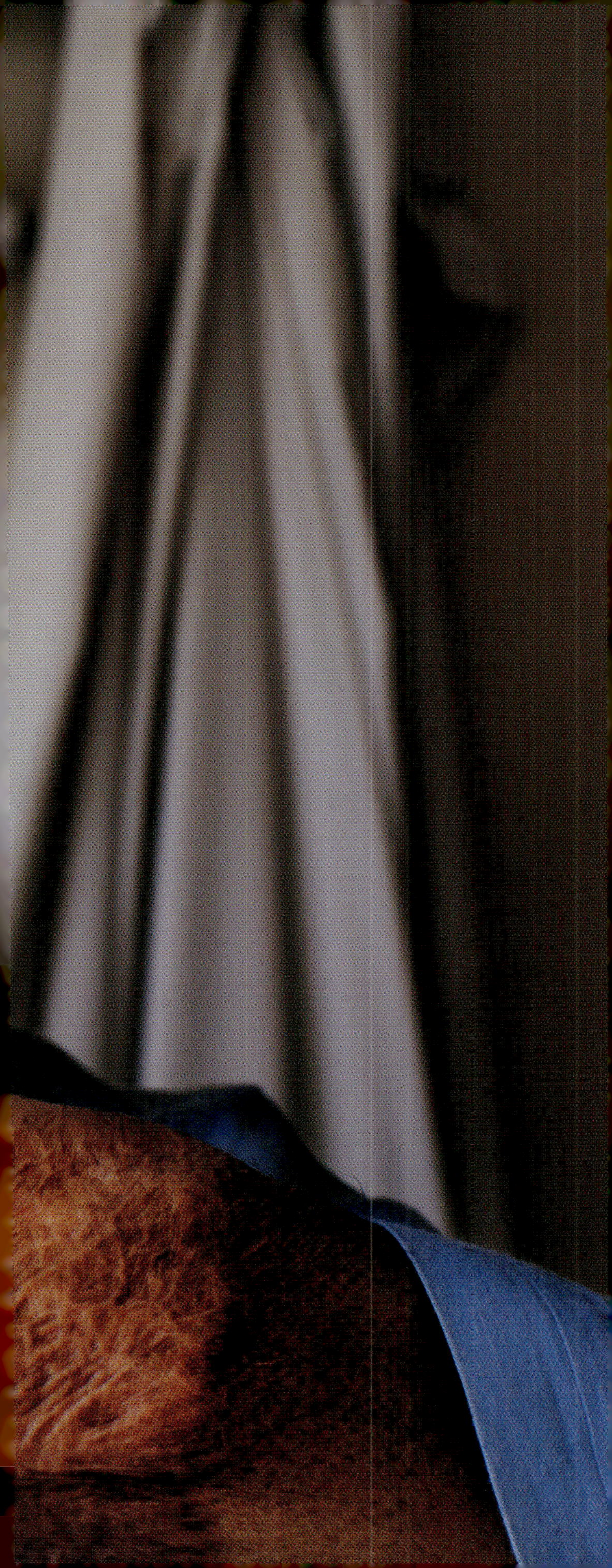

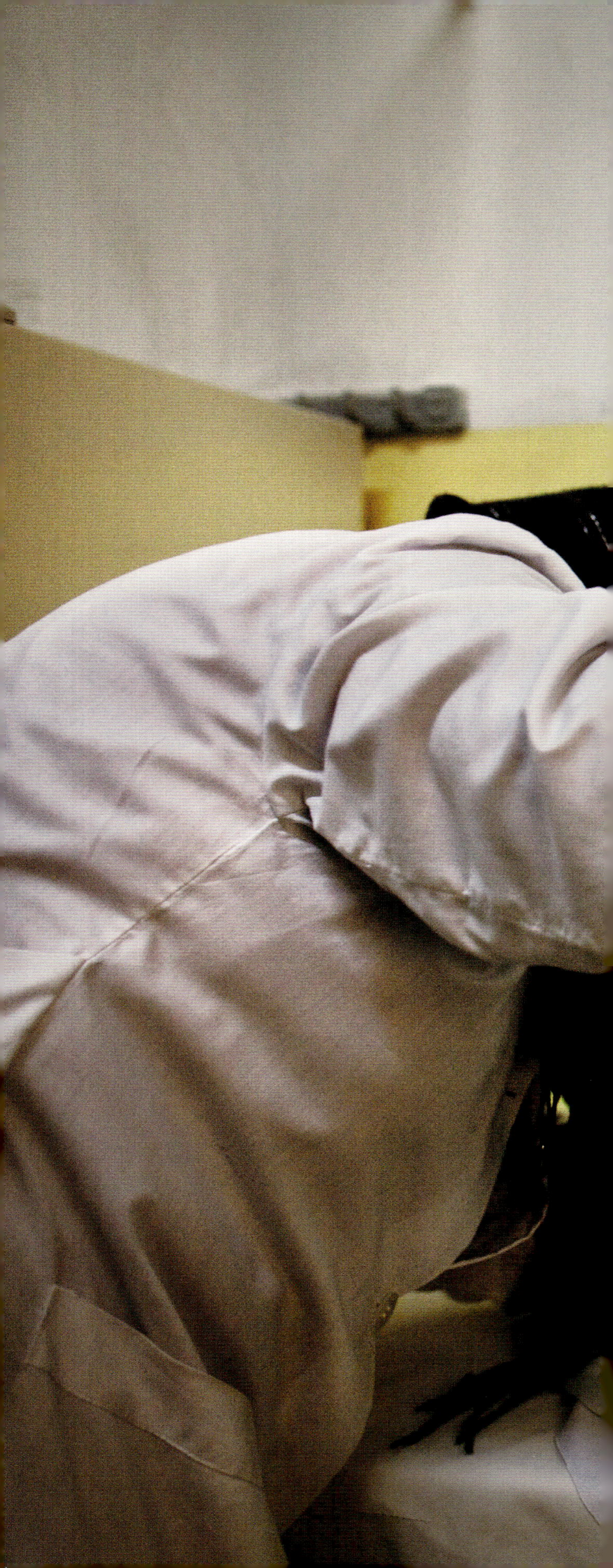

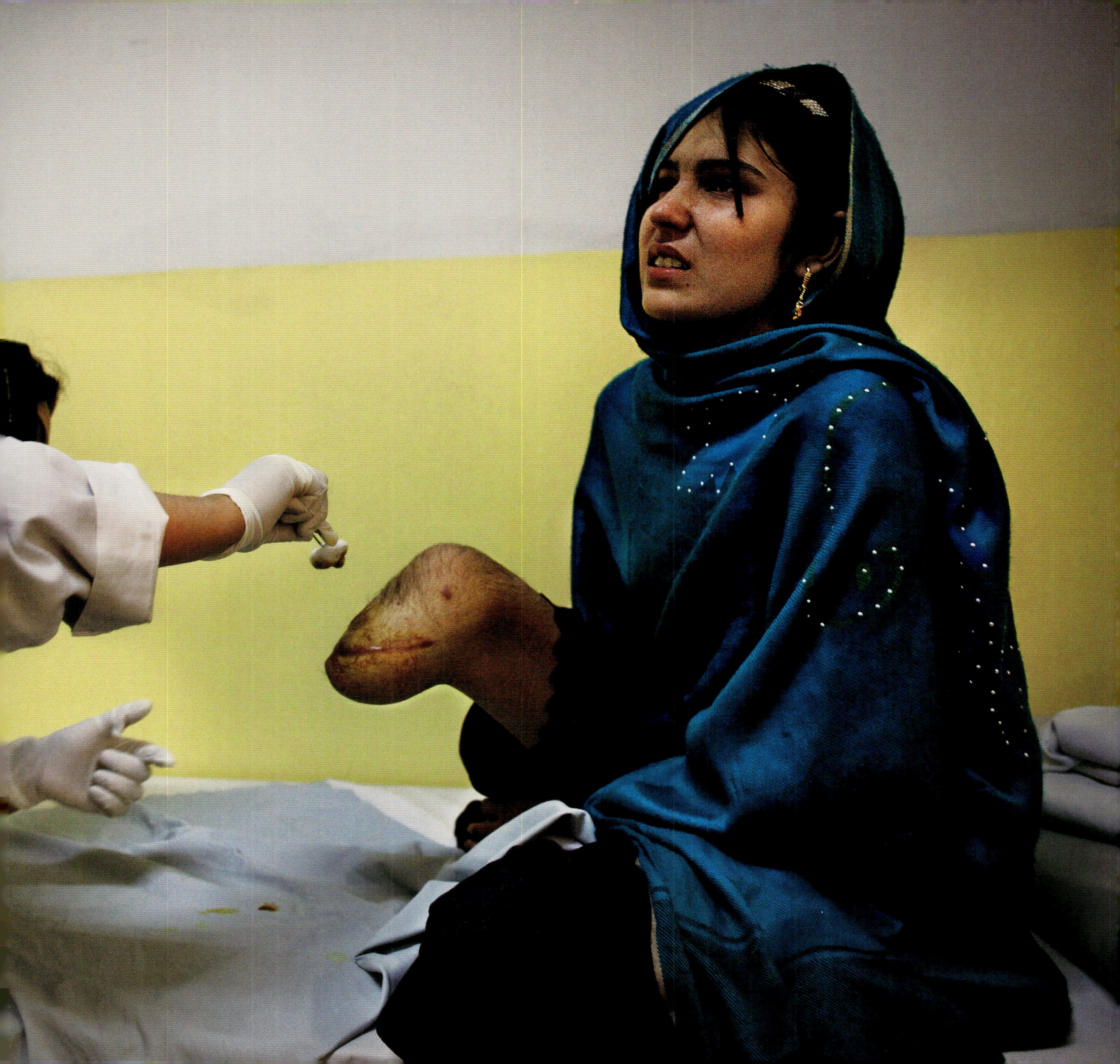

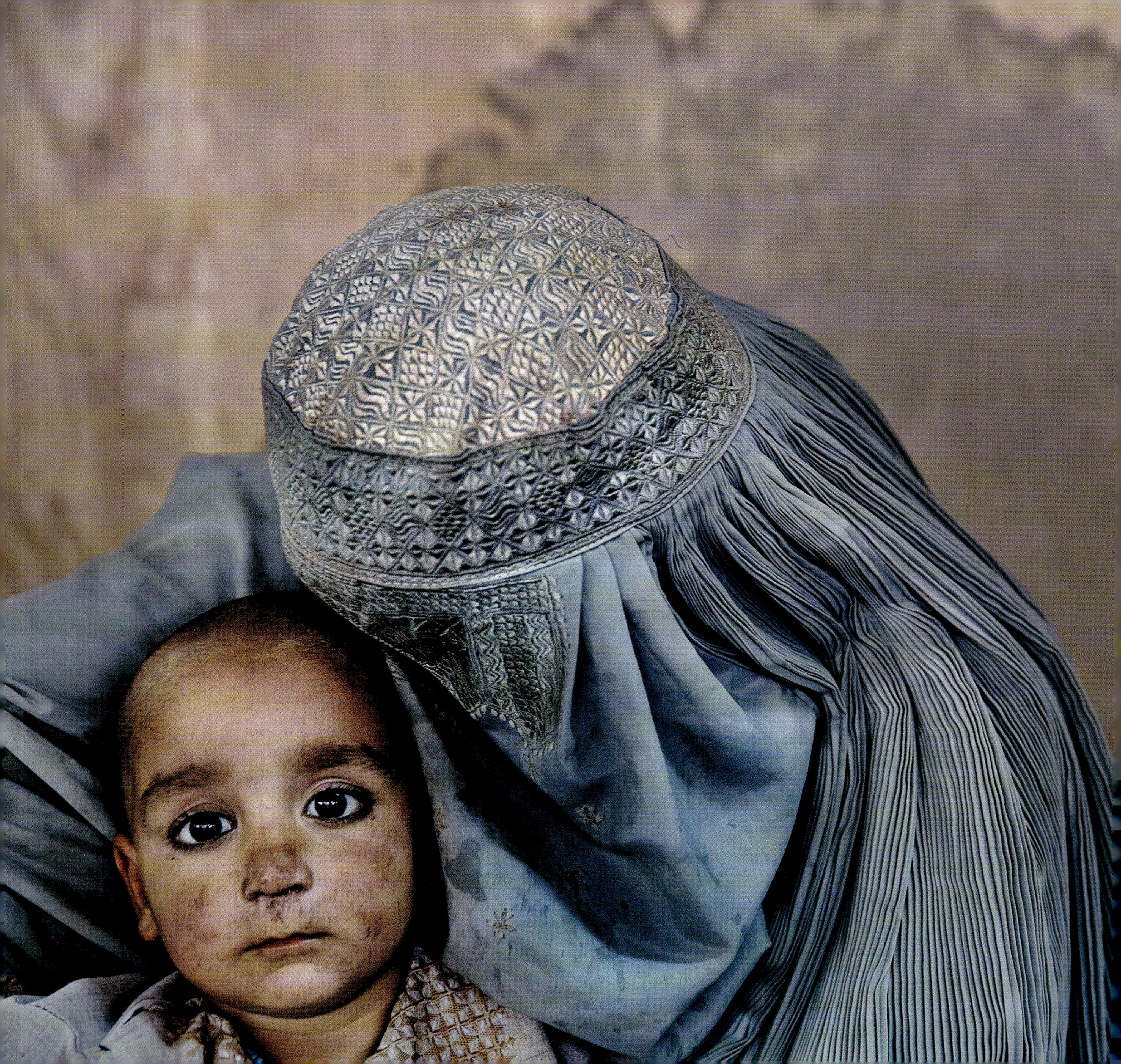

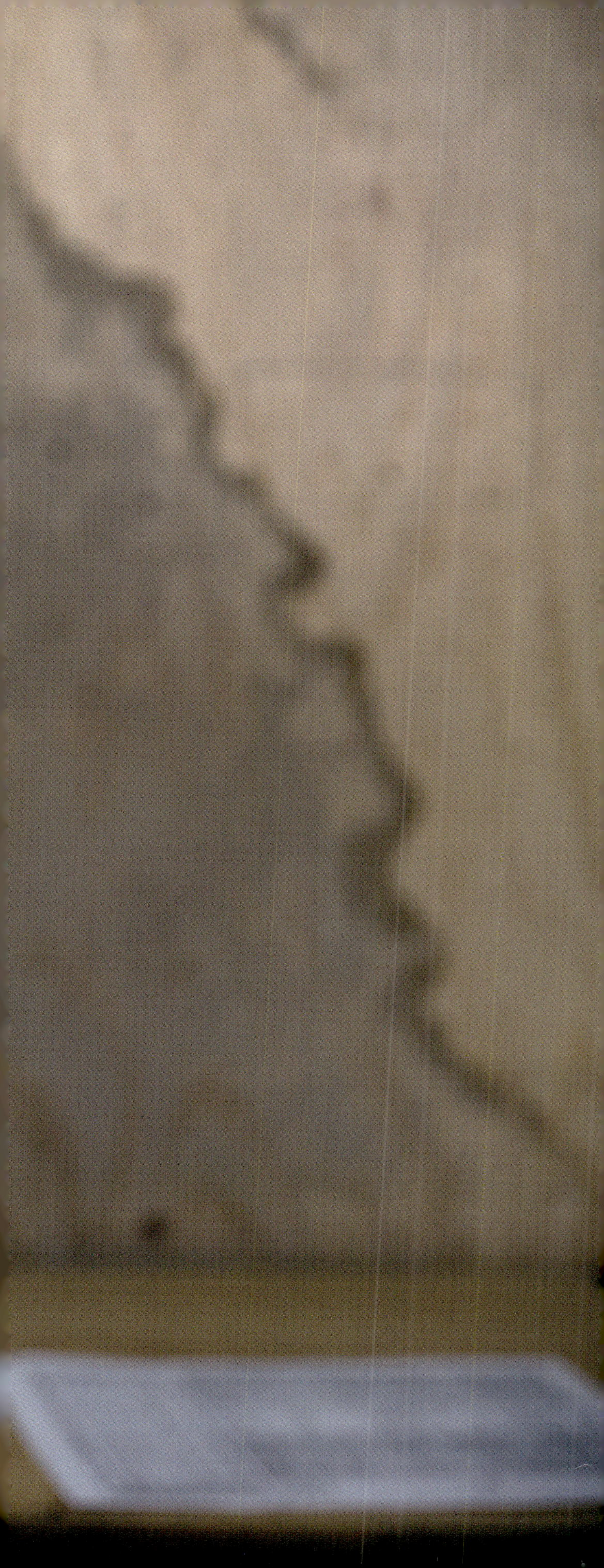

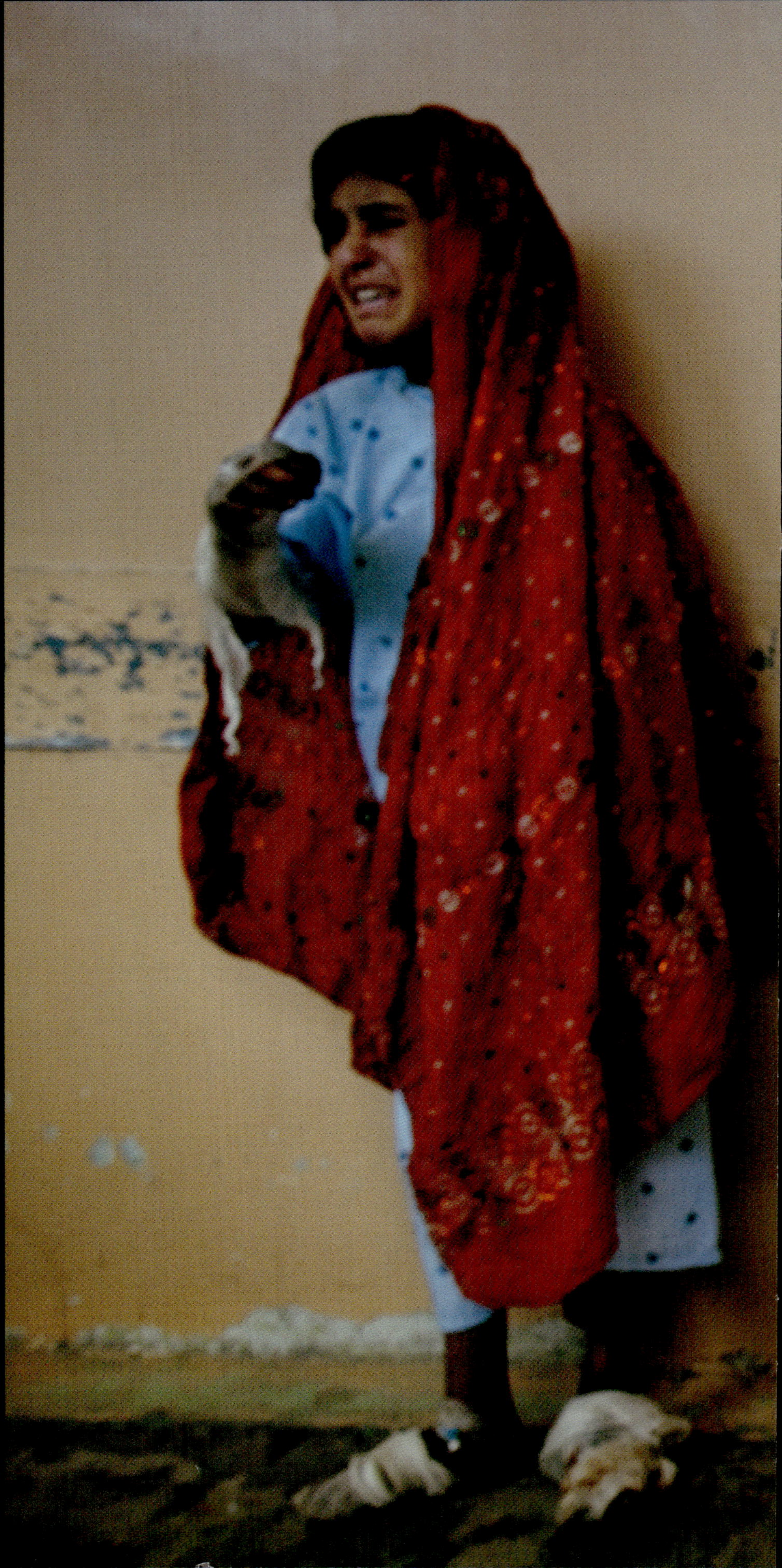

KANDAHAR, OCTOBER 13, 2009.

Asan, age nine (right), and her sister Saleema, age thirteen (left), stand in the hallway of the Mirwais Hospital. The two girls, members of the nomadic and vulnerable Kuchi tribe, were severely burned when a US military helicopter accidentally bombed their tent, killing three members of the family.

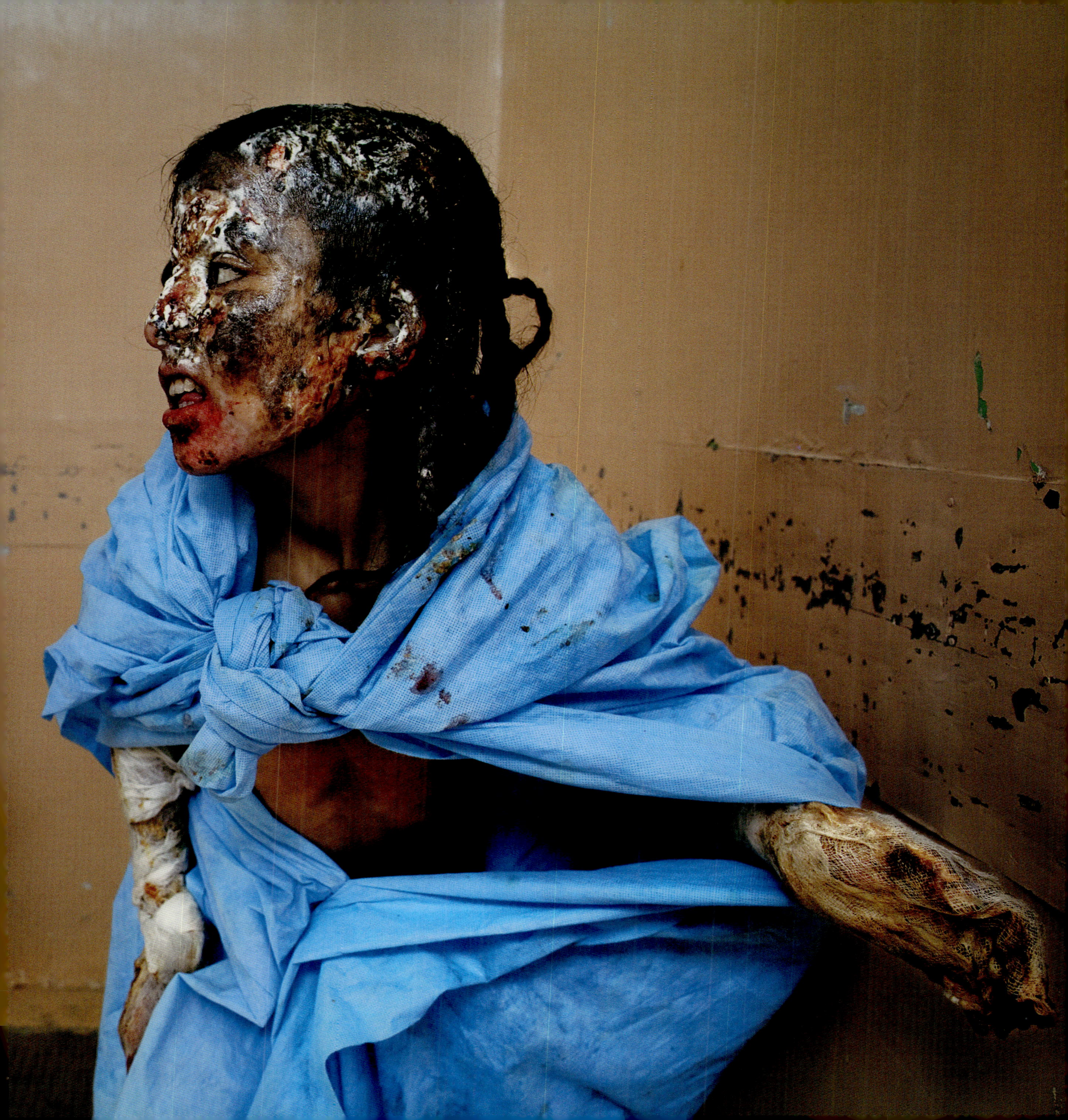

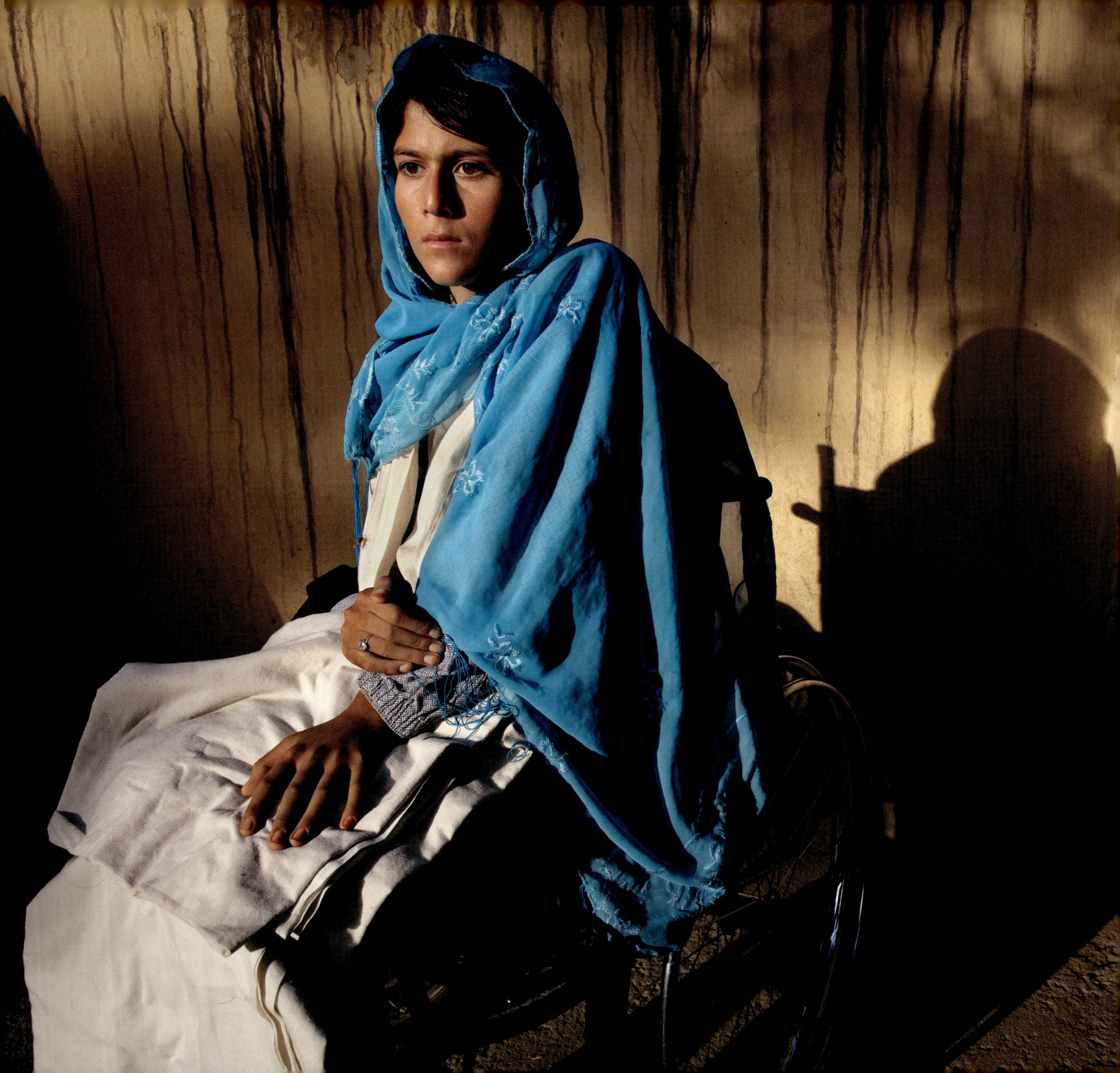

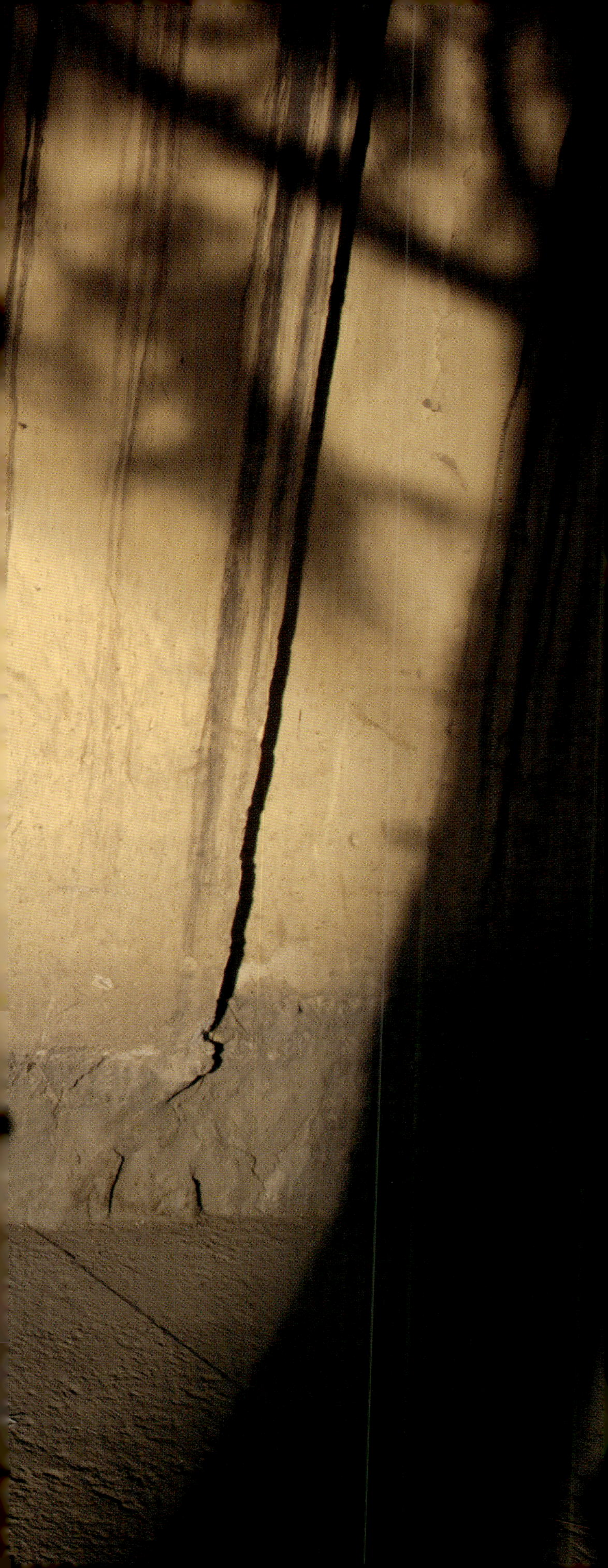

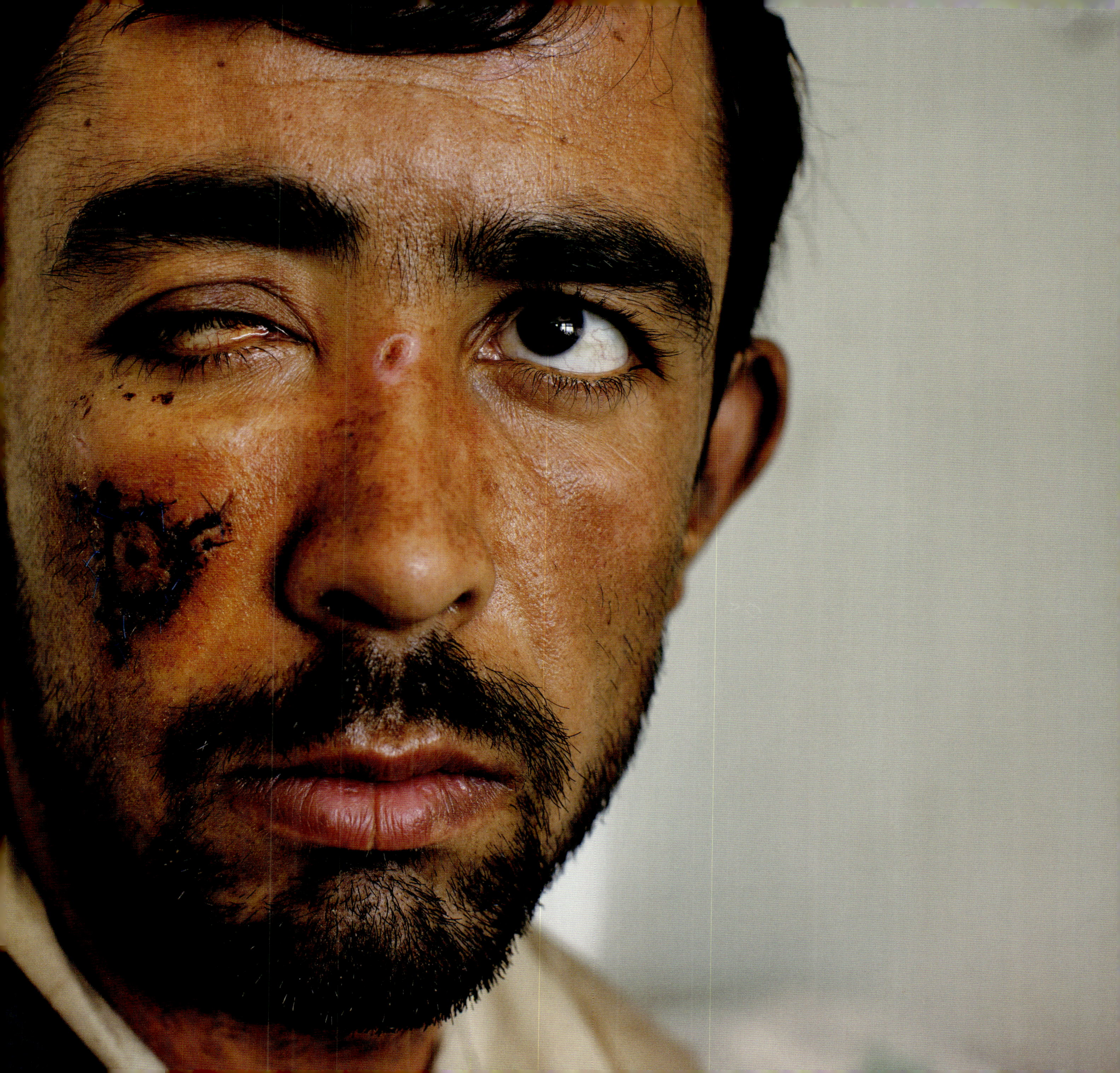

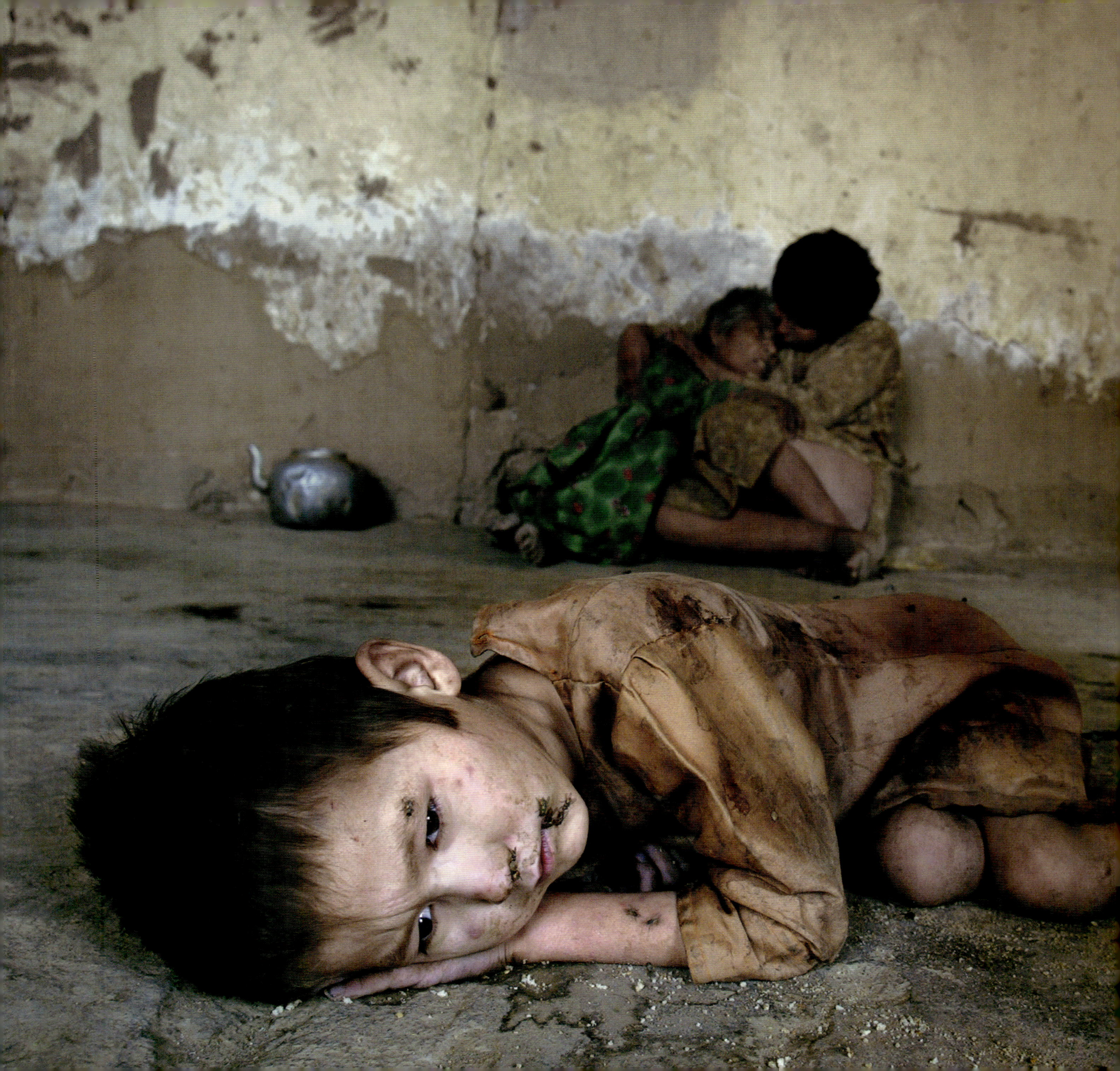

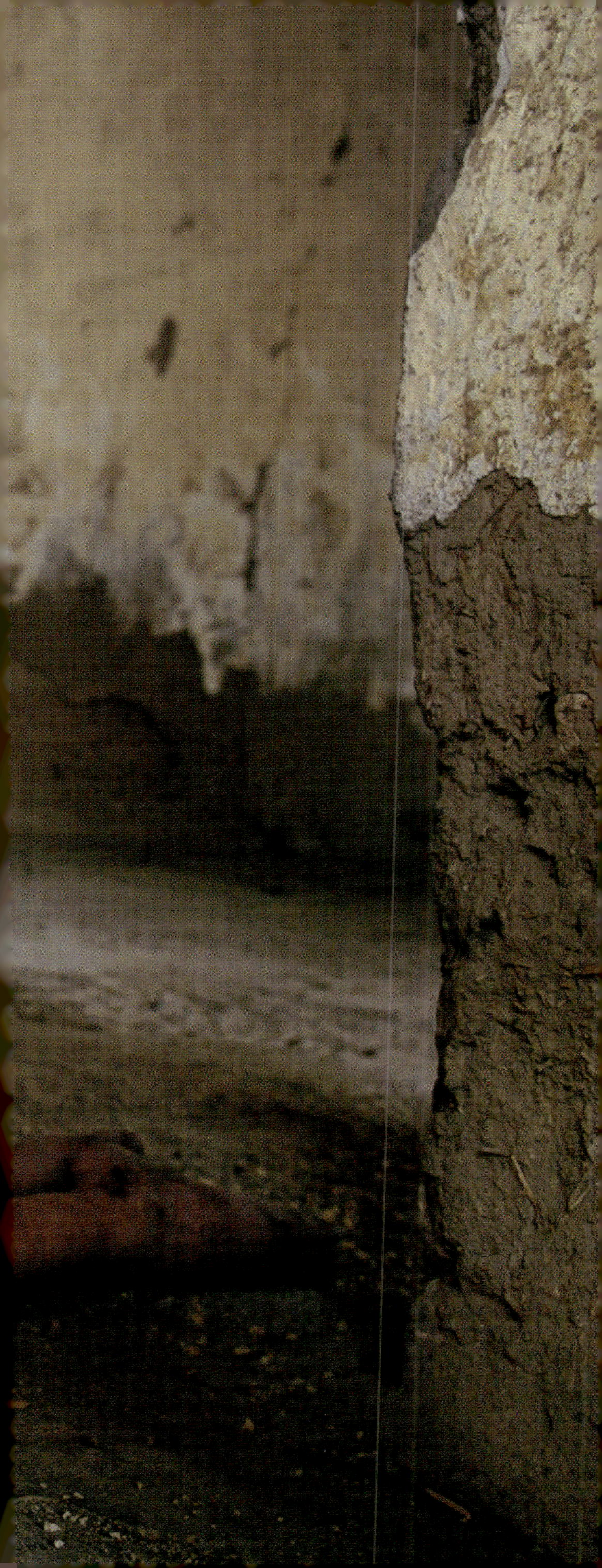

HERAT, OCTOBER 21, 2004.

Having attempted suicide by setting herself on fire, eighteen-year-old Masooma now has severe burns on 70 percent of her body. Forced marriages, domestic violence, poverty, and lack of access to education are the main reasons Afghan women try to kill themselves.

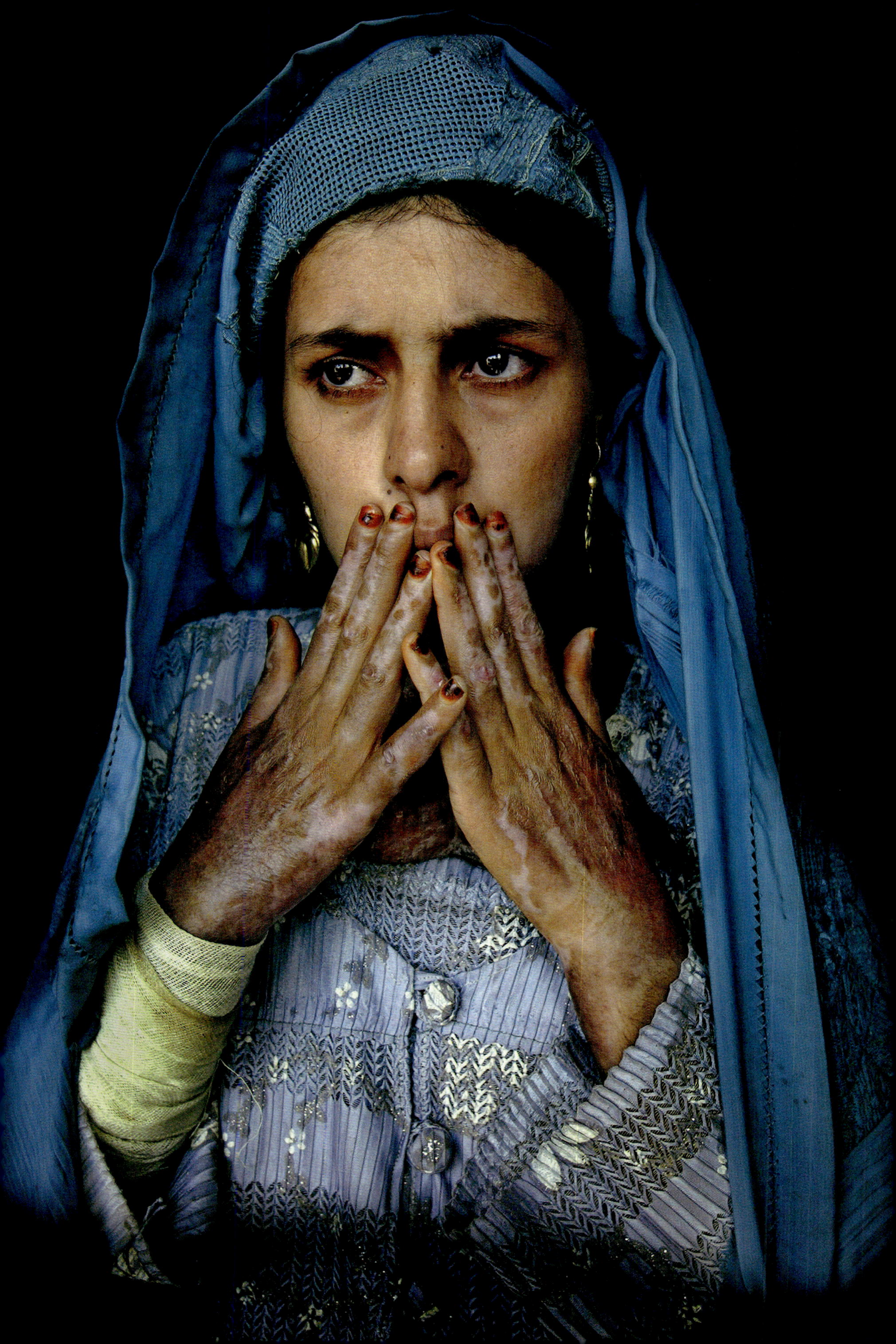

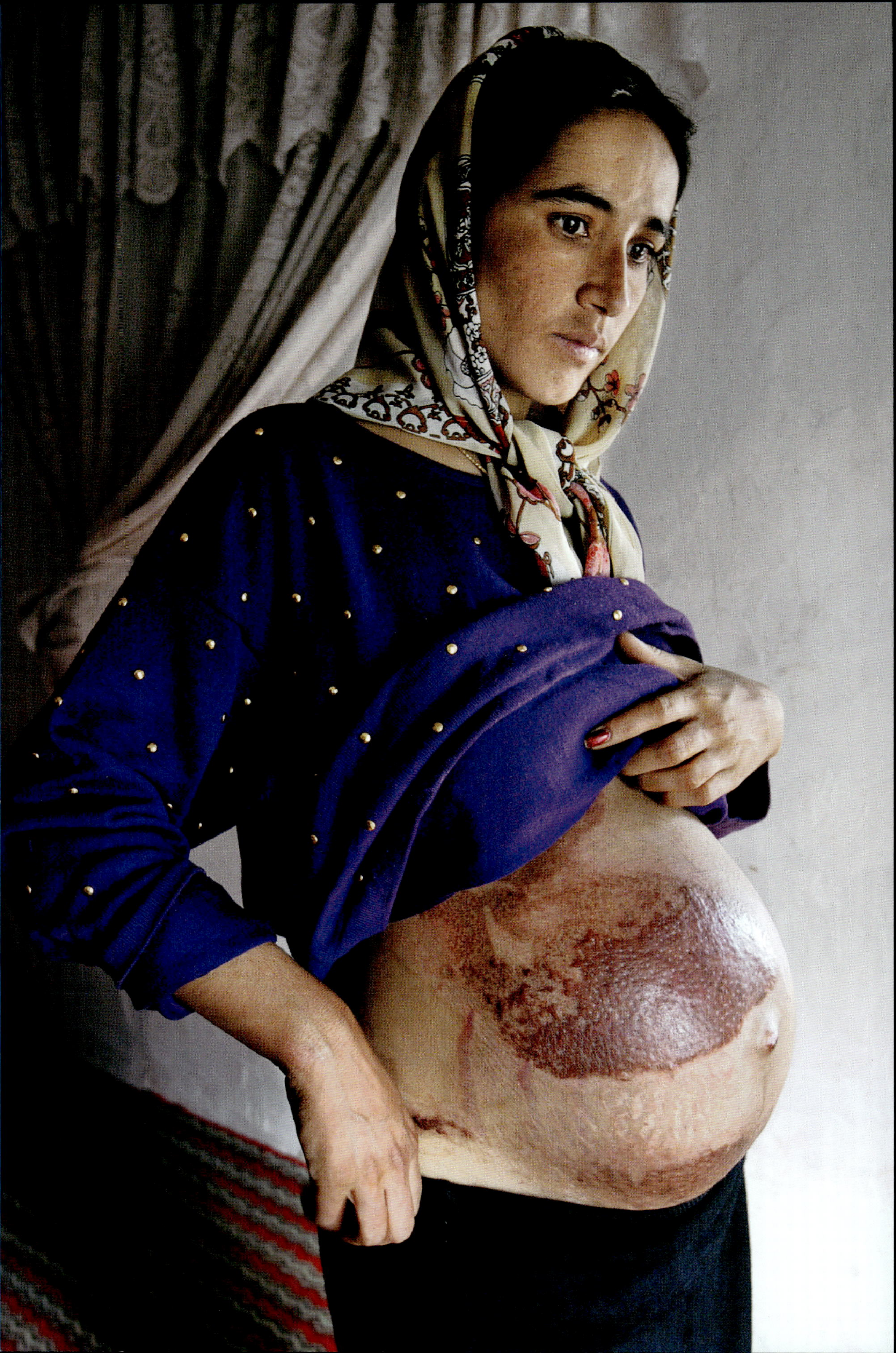

HERAT, OCTOBER 21, 2004.

Twenty-year-old Mariam, who is nine months pregnant here, shows the scars that resulted from her suicide attempt three months earlier. Devastated by an abusive, violent marriage, she doused herself with household fuel and set it alight, subsequently spending twenty-eight days in the hospital. She now lives with her mother, and her husband is moving back in with her and her two-year-old daughter.

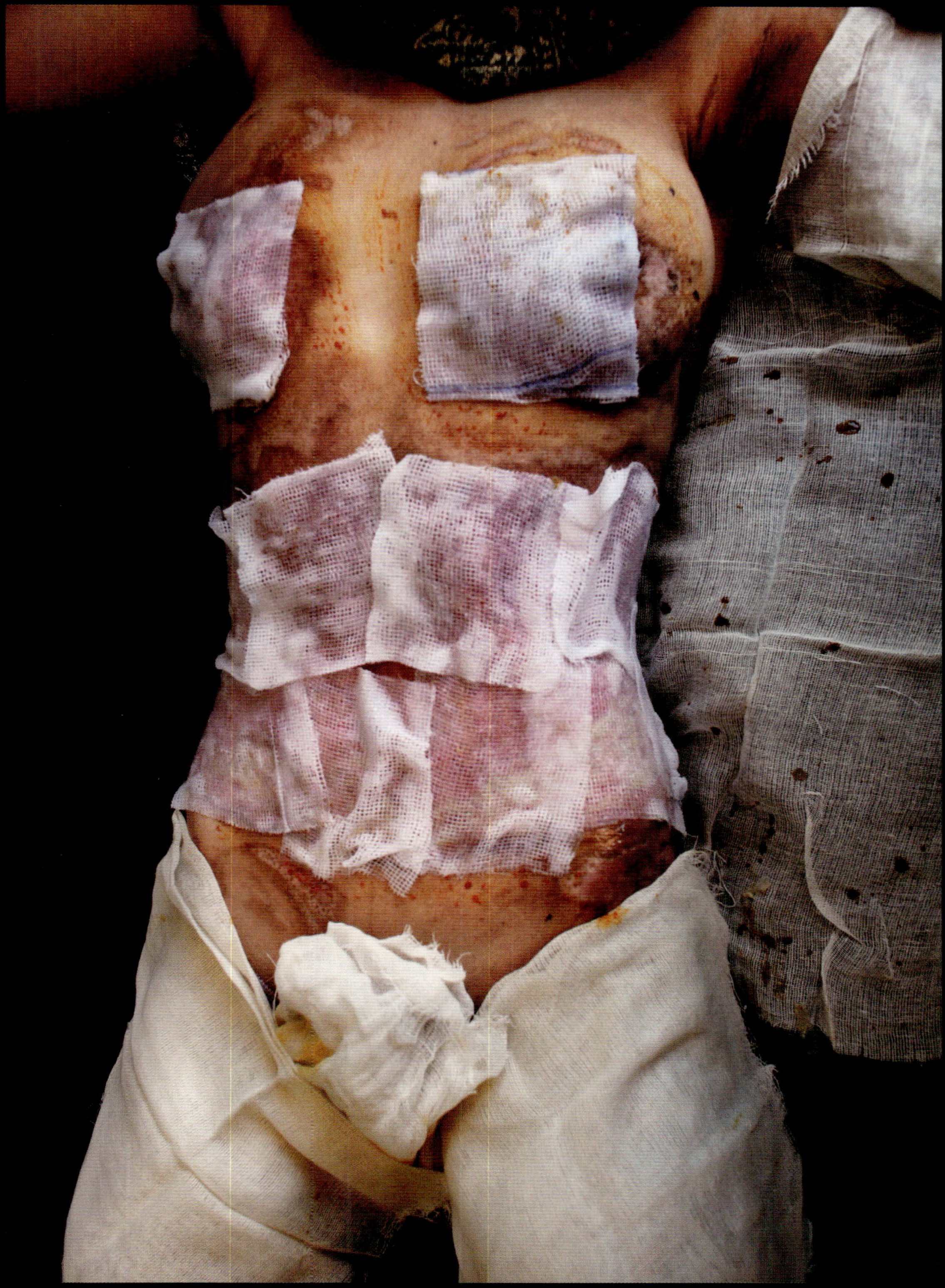

HERAT, NOVEMBER 16, 2006.

The burned body of twenty-two-year-old Sima Gul, who set herself on fire, lies on a bed at the Herat hospital. She had complained that she was too lonely because her husband was forced to work in Iran to make money for her family.

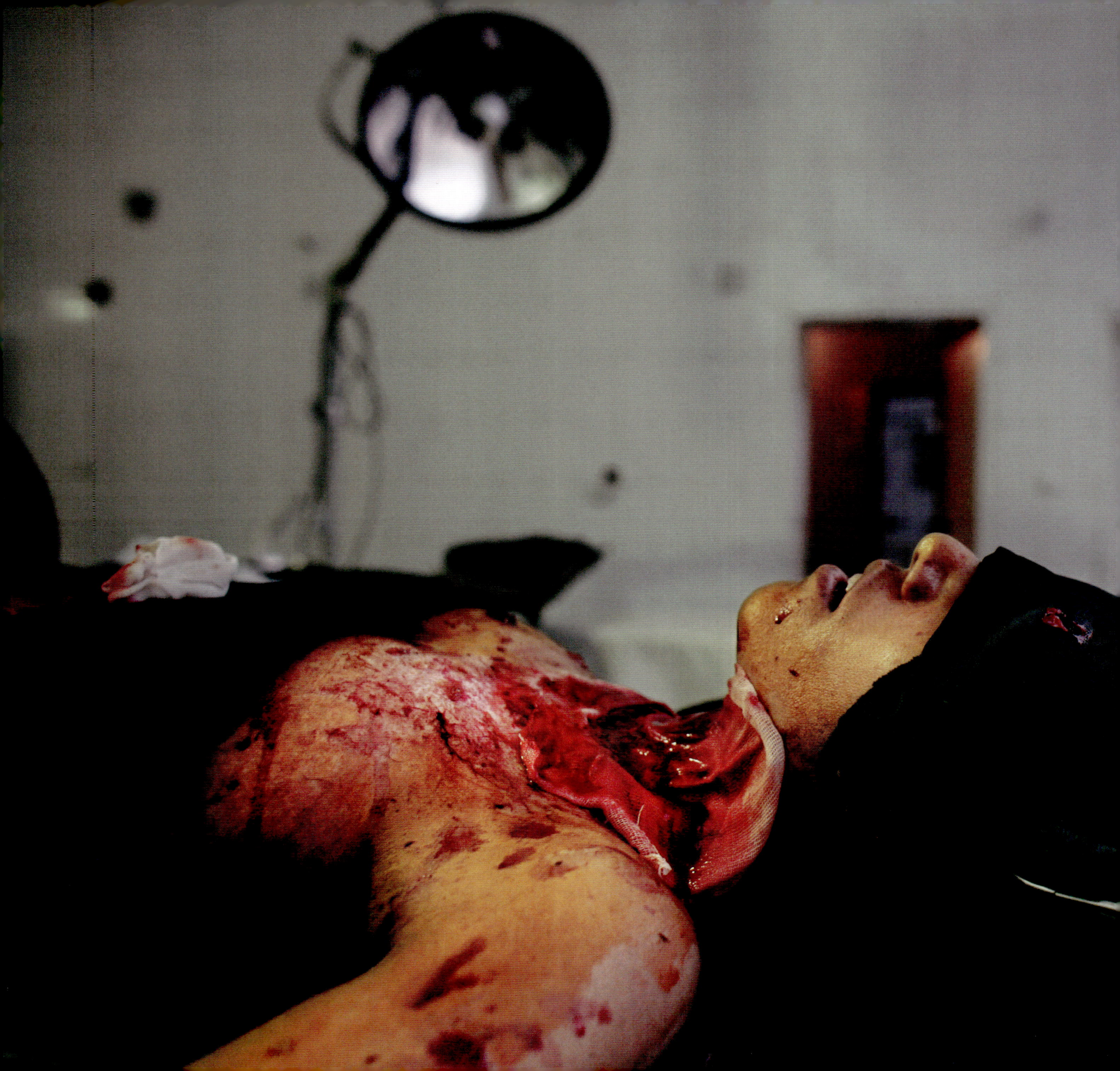

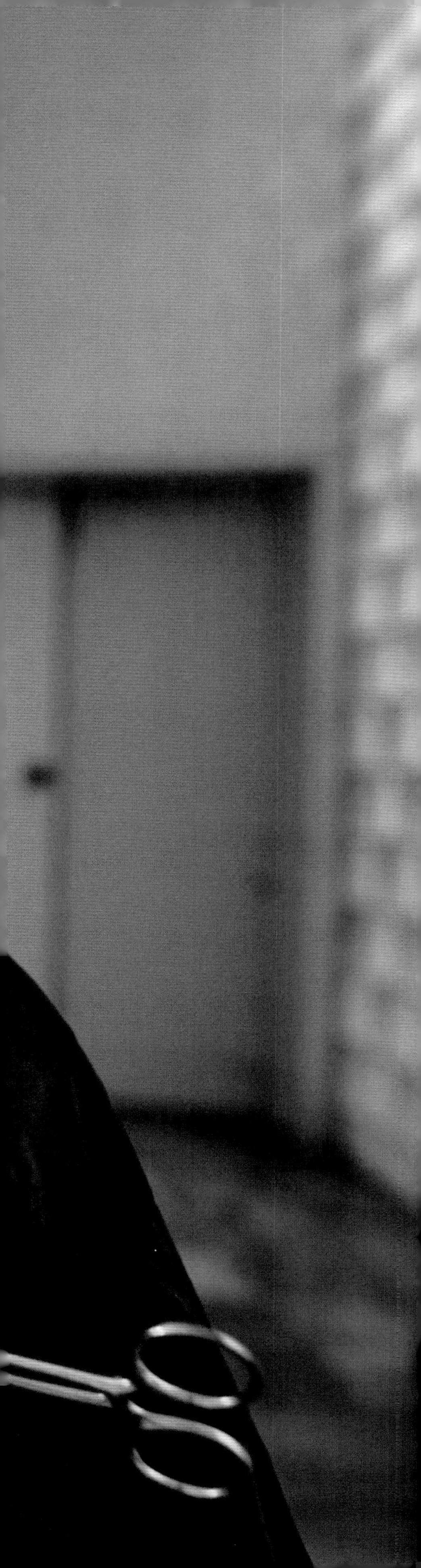

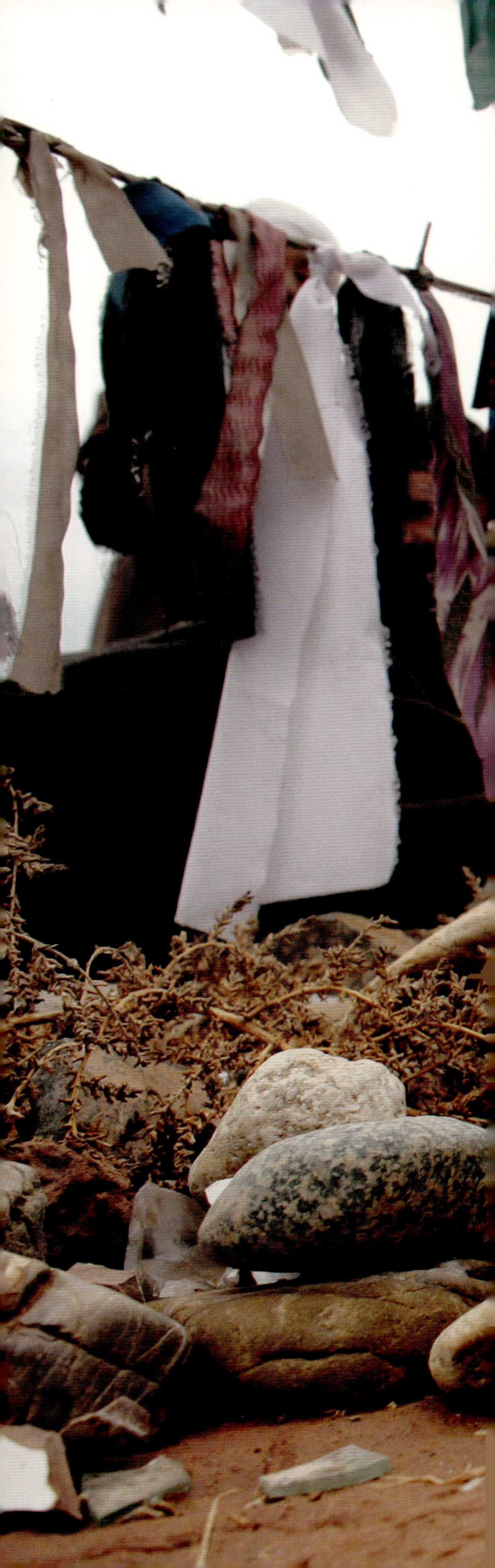

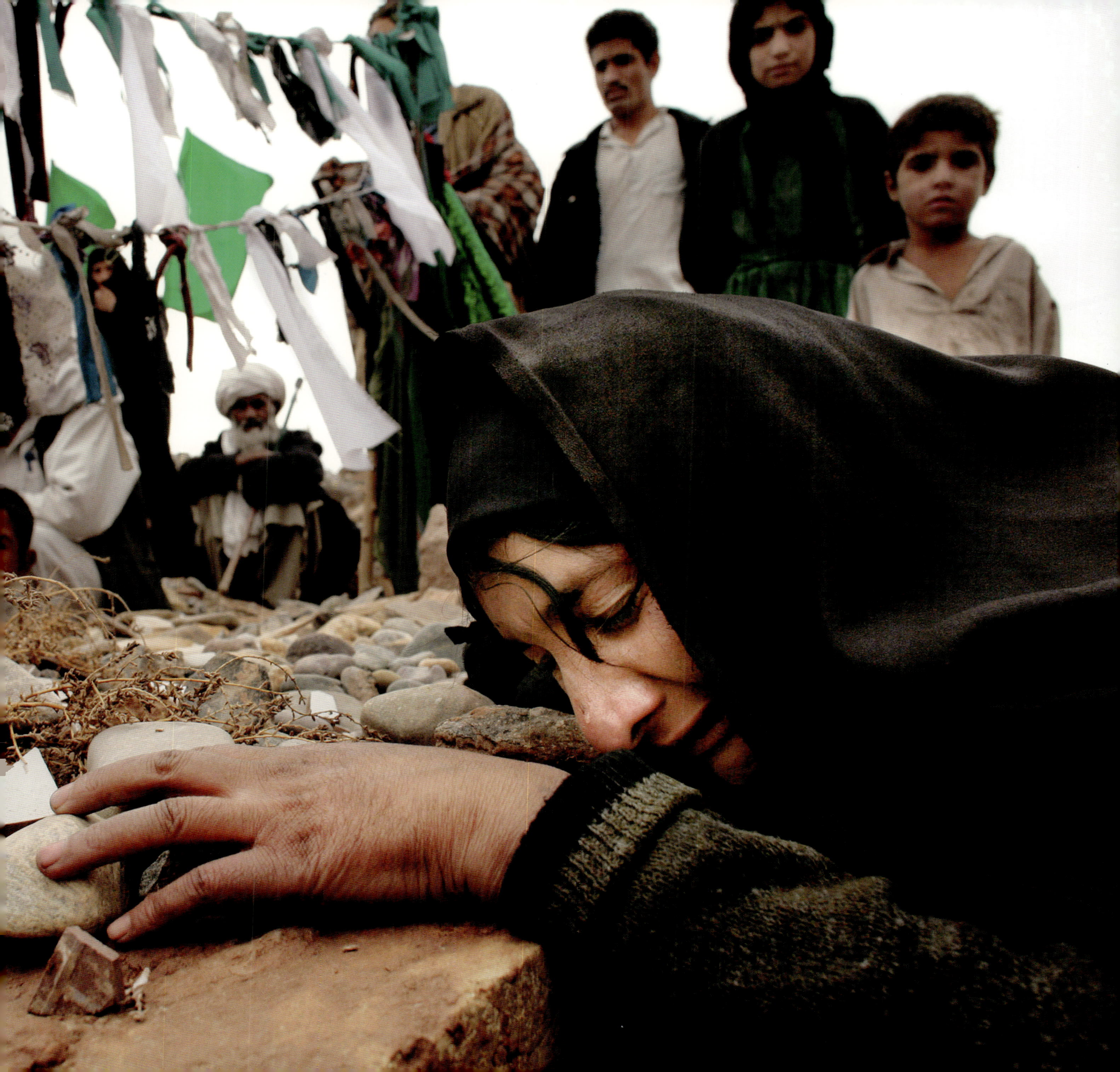

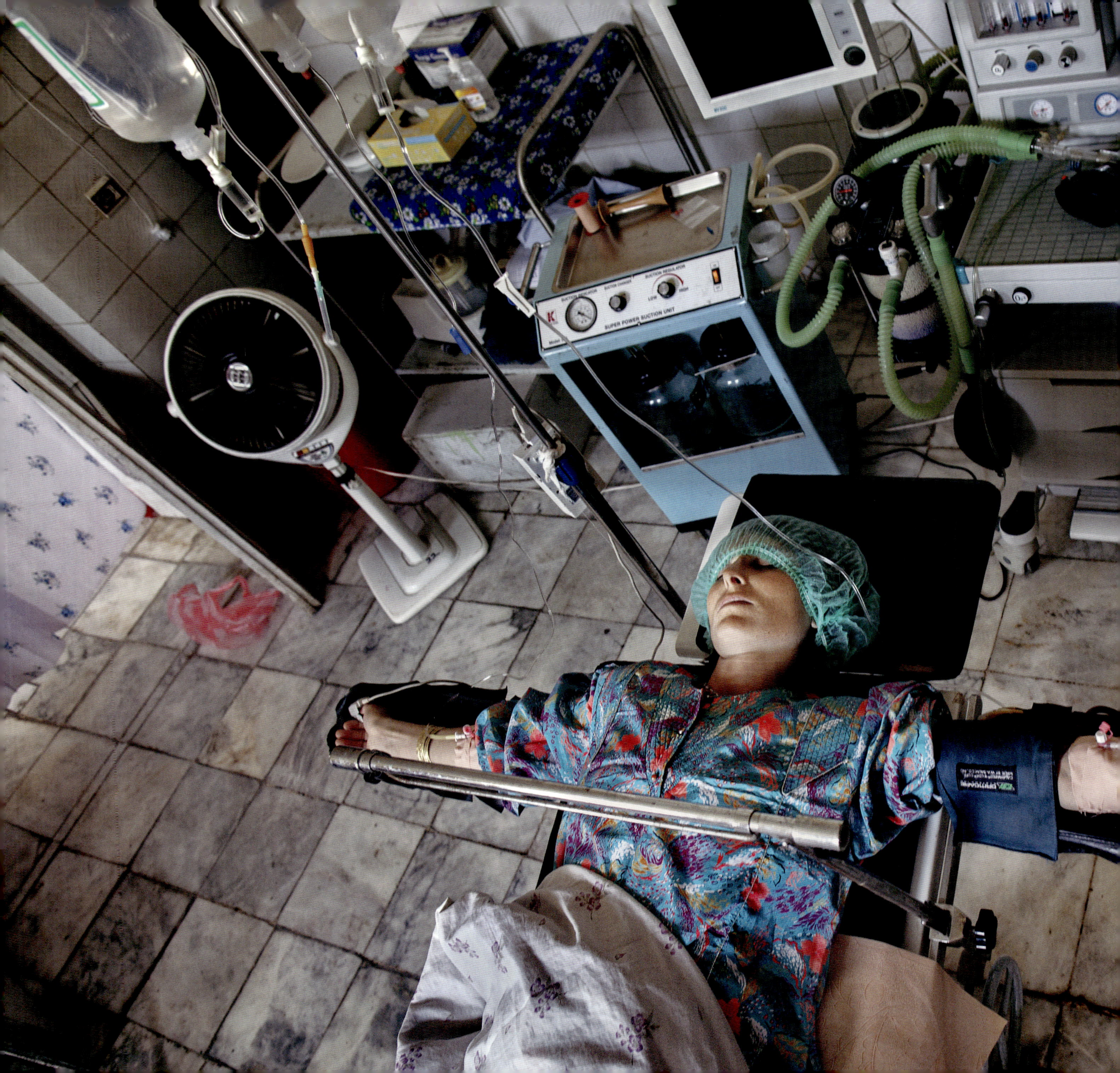
SUPER POWER SUCTION UNIT

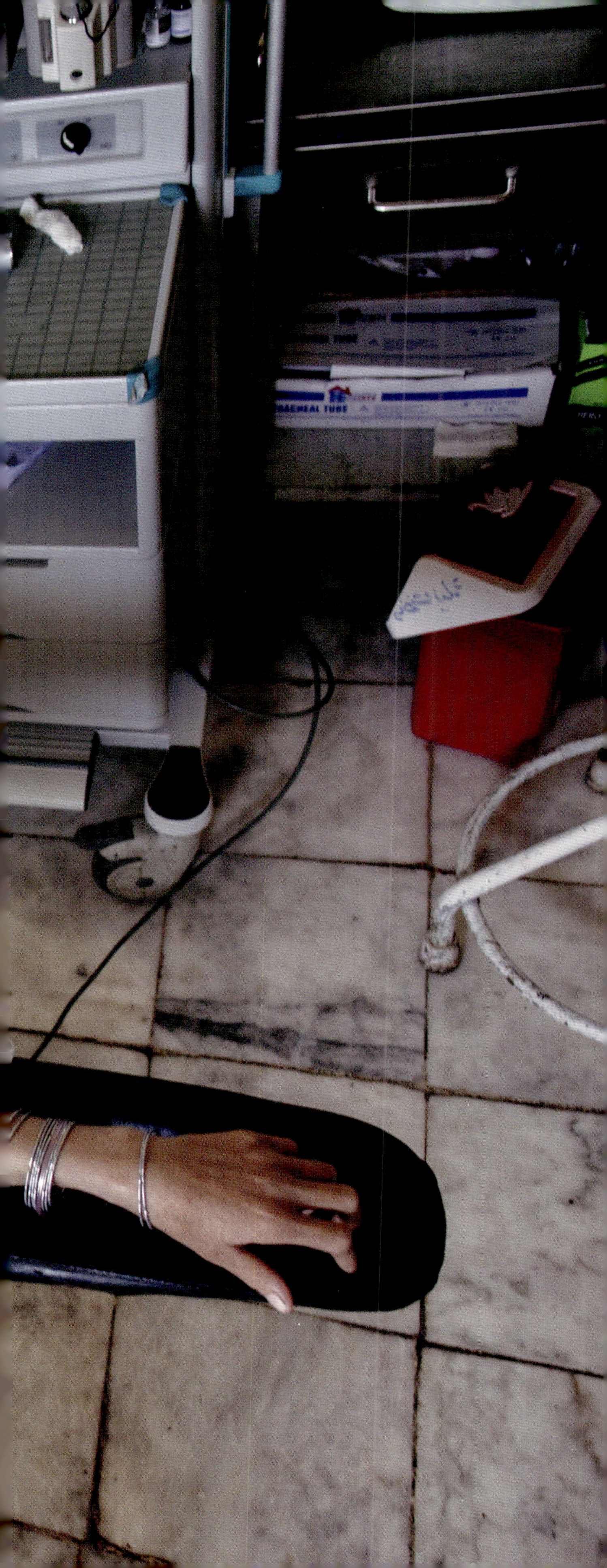

KABUL, APRIL 10, 2015.

Naiz Bibi, who was blinded in one eye, claims she is sixty-eight but really can't remember clearly. After a NATO air strike killed seven members of her family, including her husband, a daughter, and two sons, she and eight remaining family members fled north, ending up in the squalid Nasaji Bagrami camp along with thousands of other war refugees.

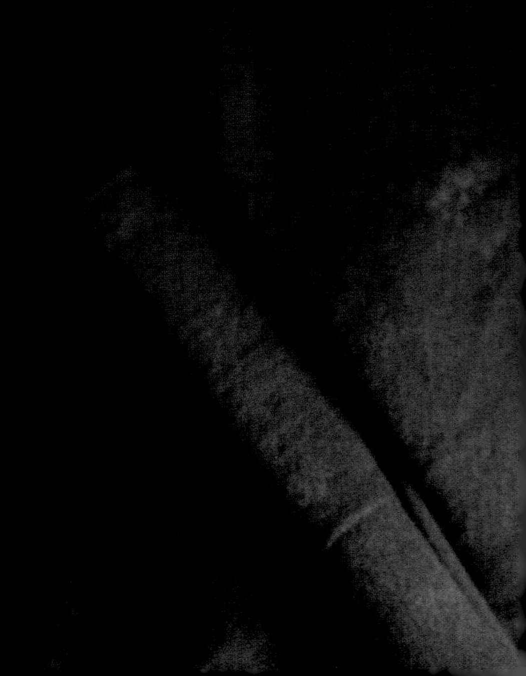

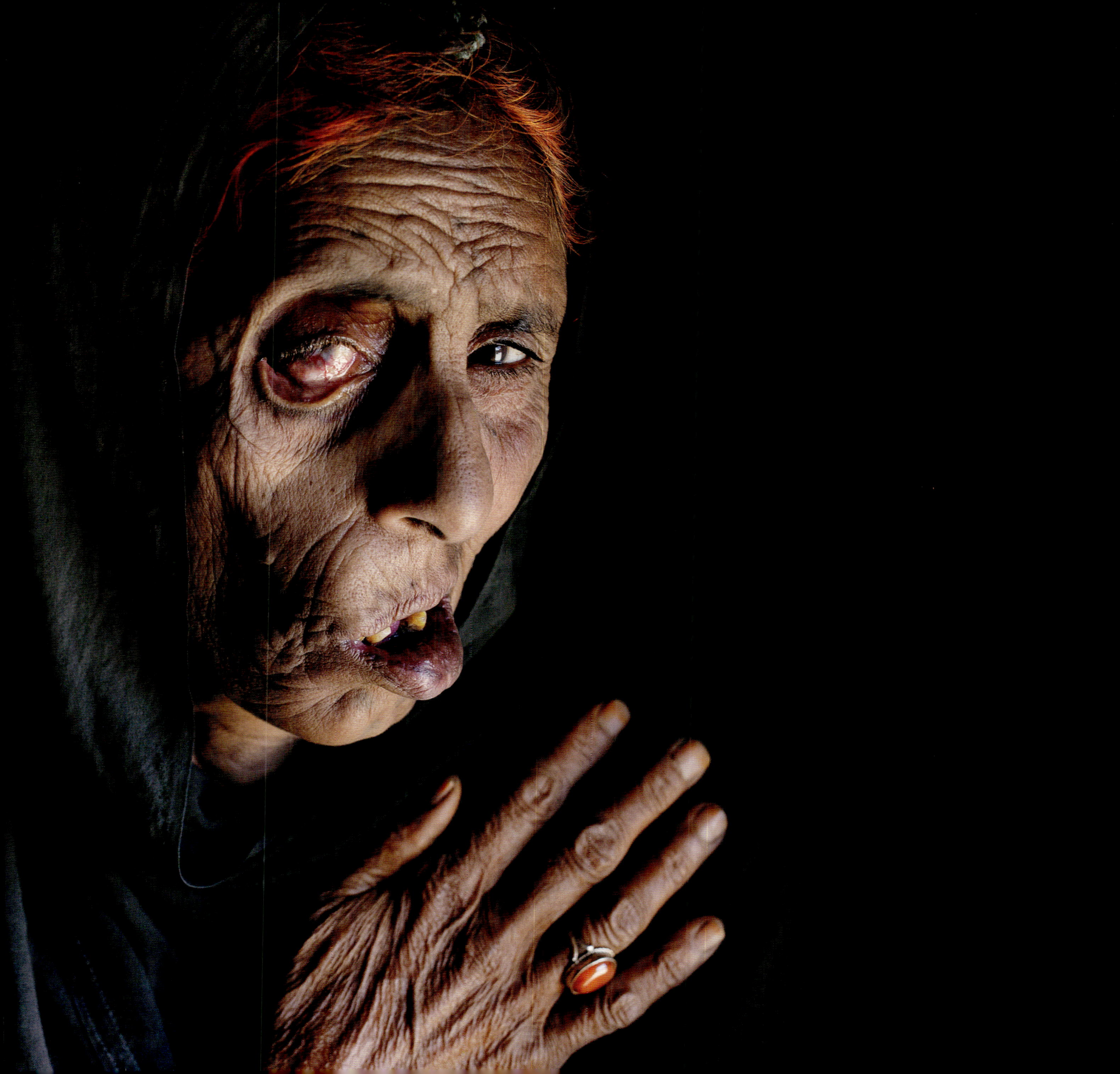

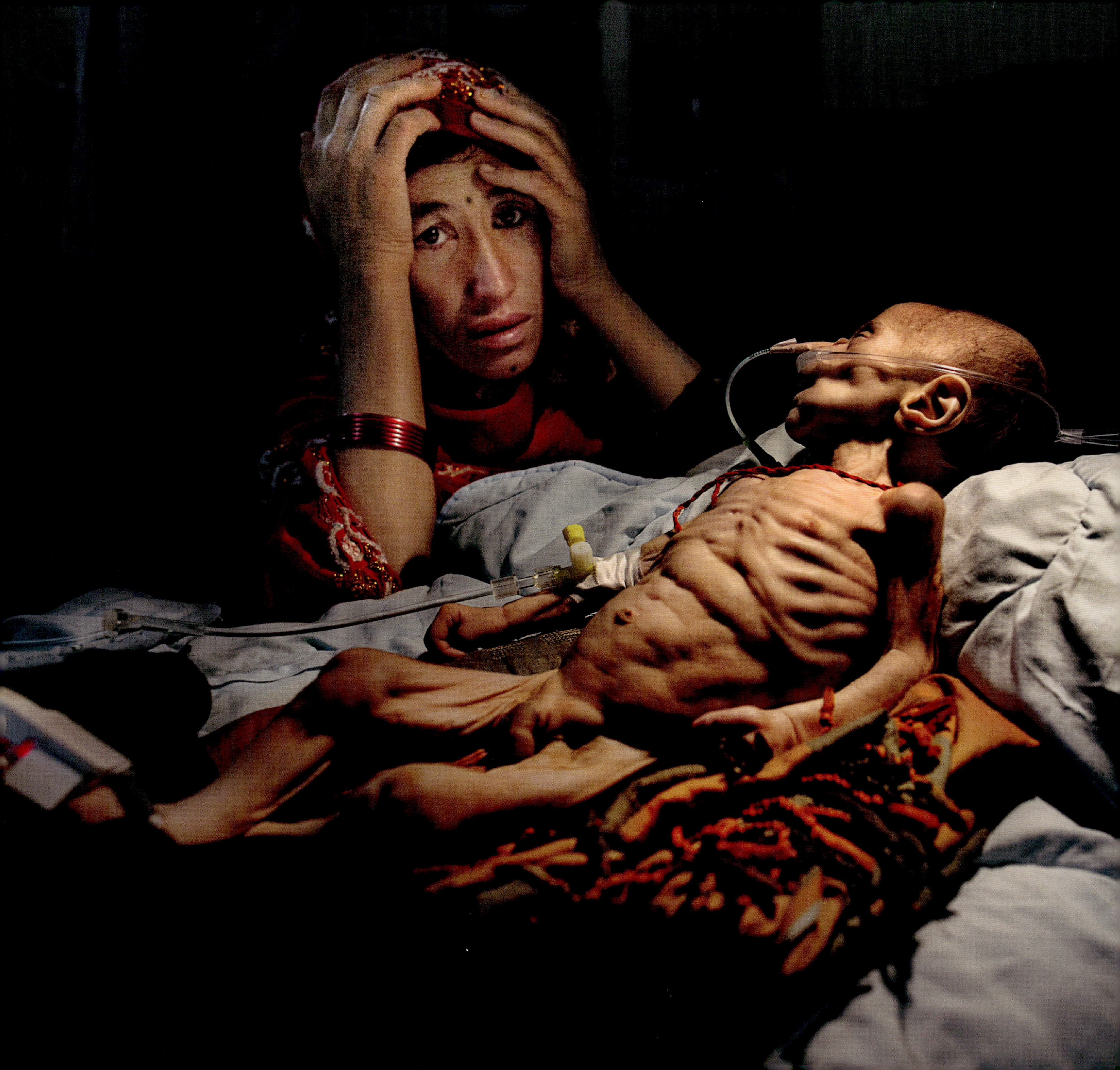

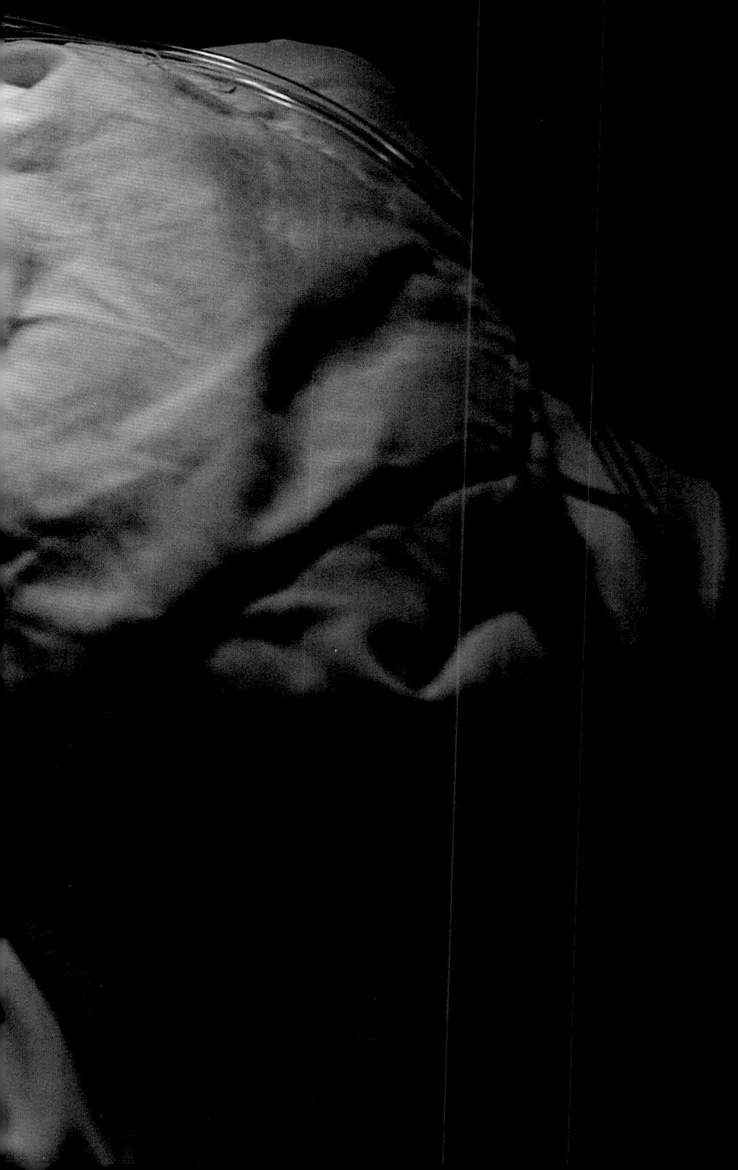

LASHKAR GAH, HELMAND PROVINCE, JUNE 22, 2014.

Noor Bibi stays at the bedside of her dying son, Ghulam Hazrat. The ten-month-old infant weighs 2.3 kg (5 lb.) and is being treated for severe malnutrition at the Pediatric Intensive Care Unit at Boost Hospital. When the mother could no longer breast-feed, she fed her child cow's milk, which caused severe diarrhea.

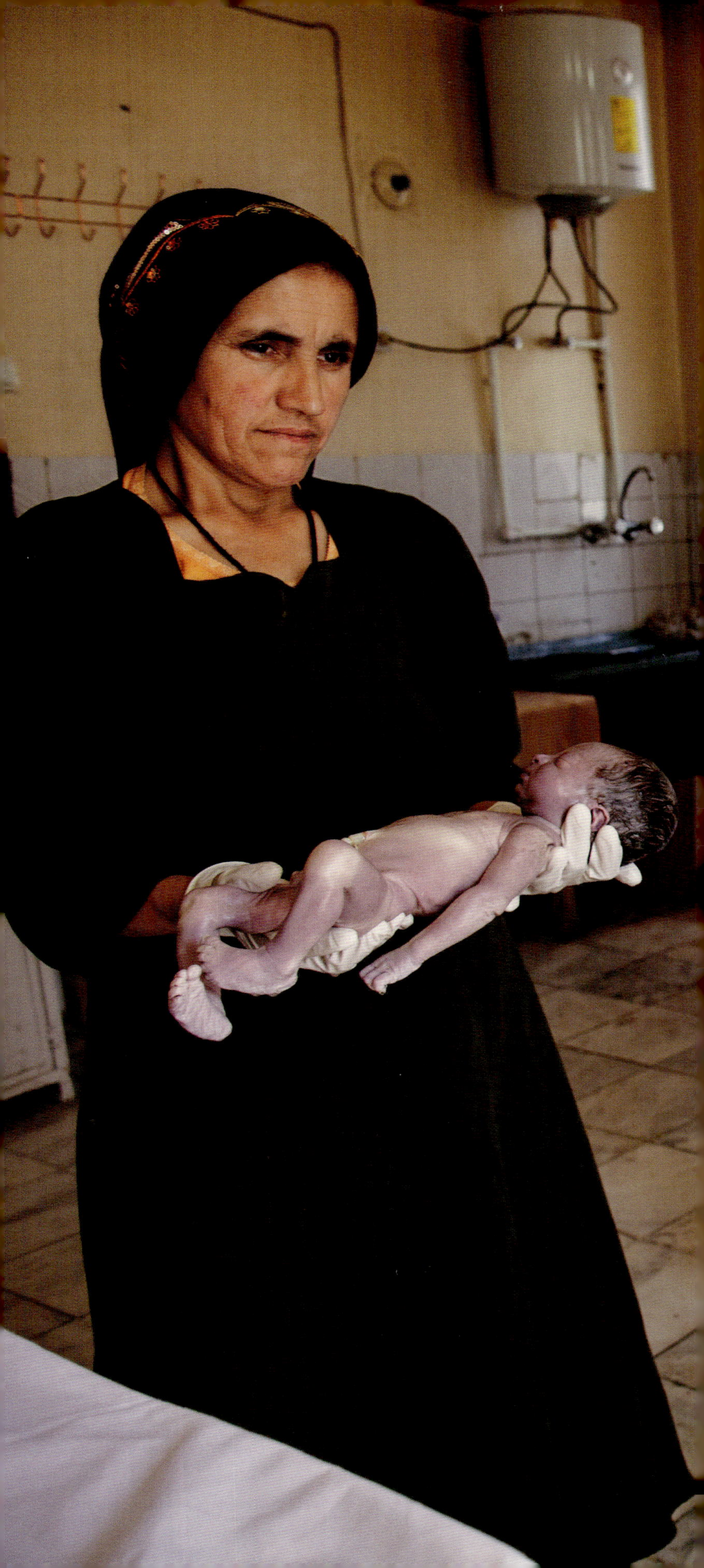

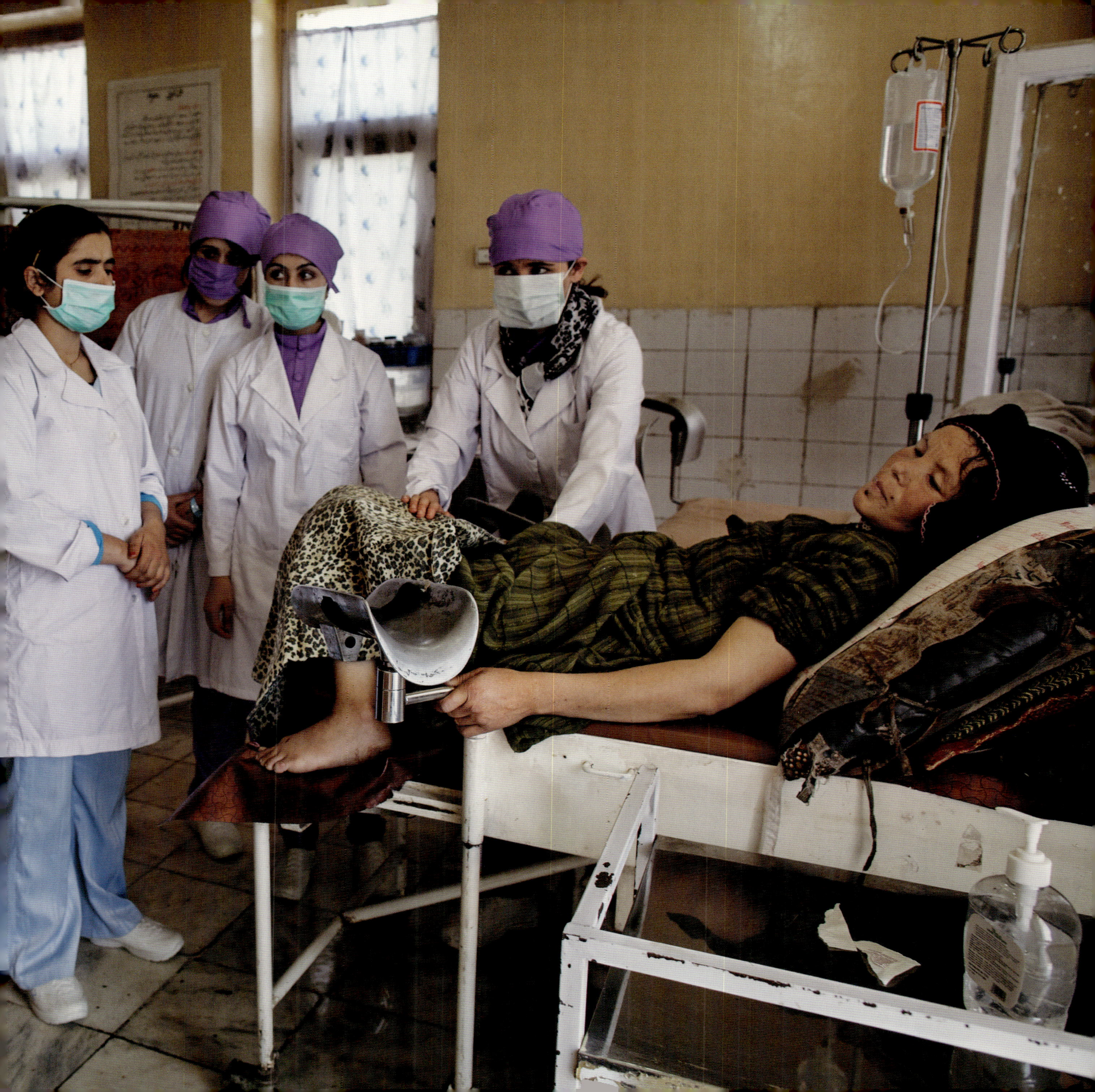

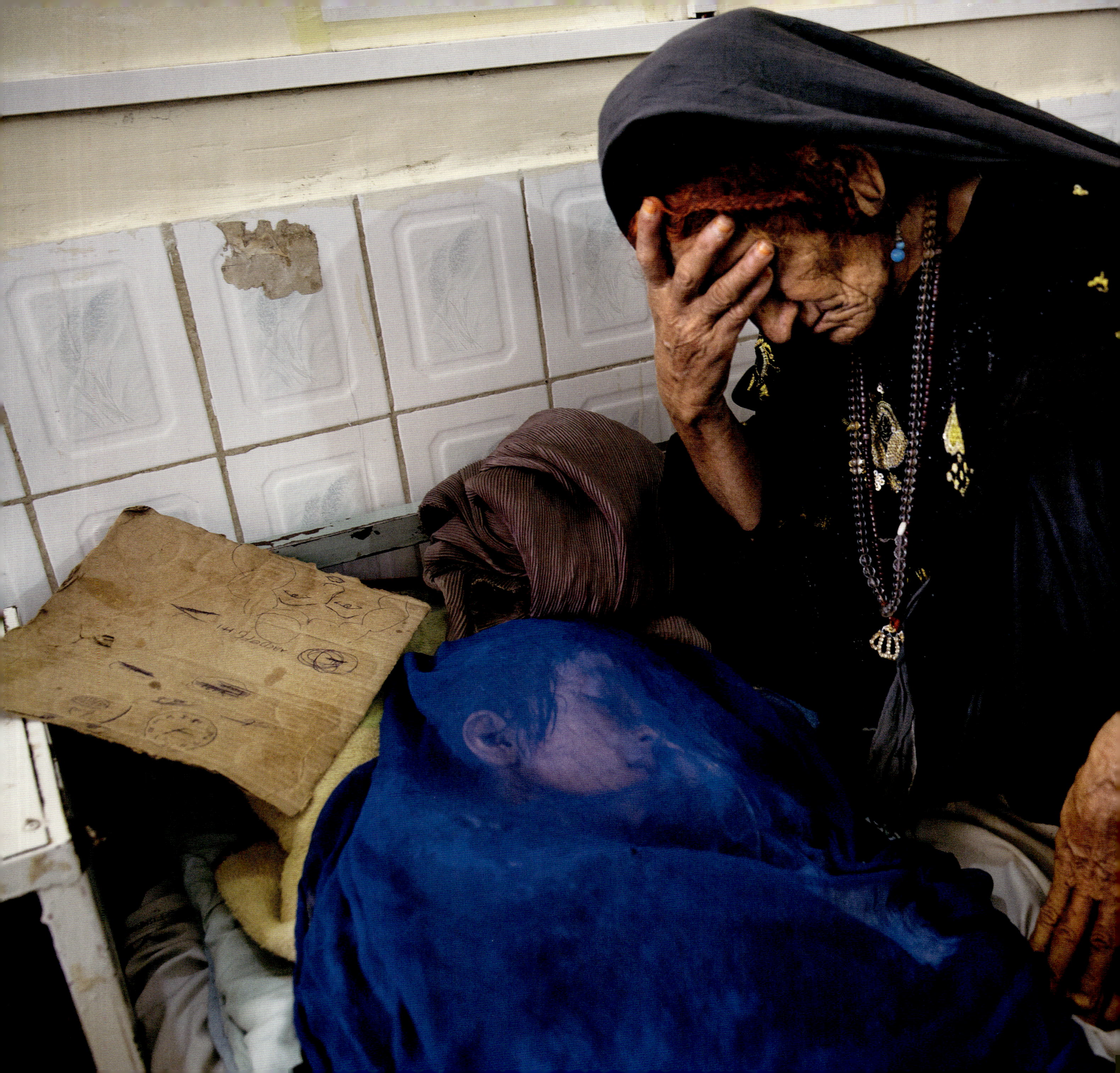

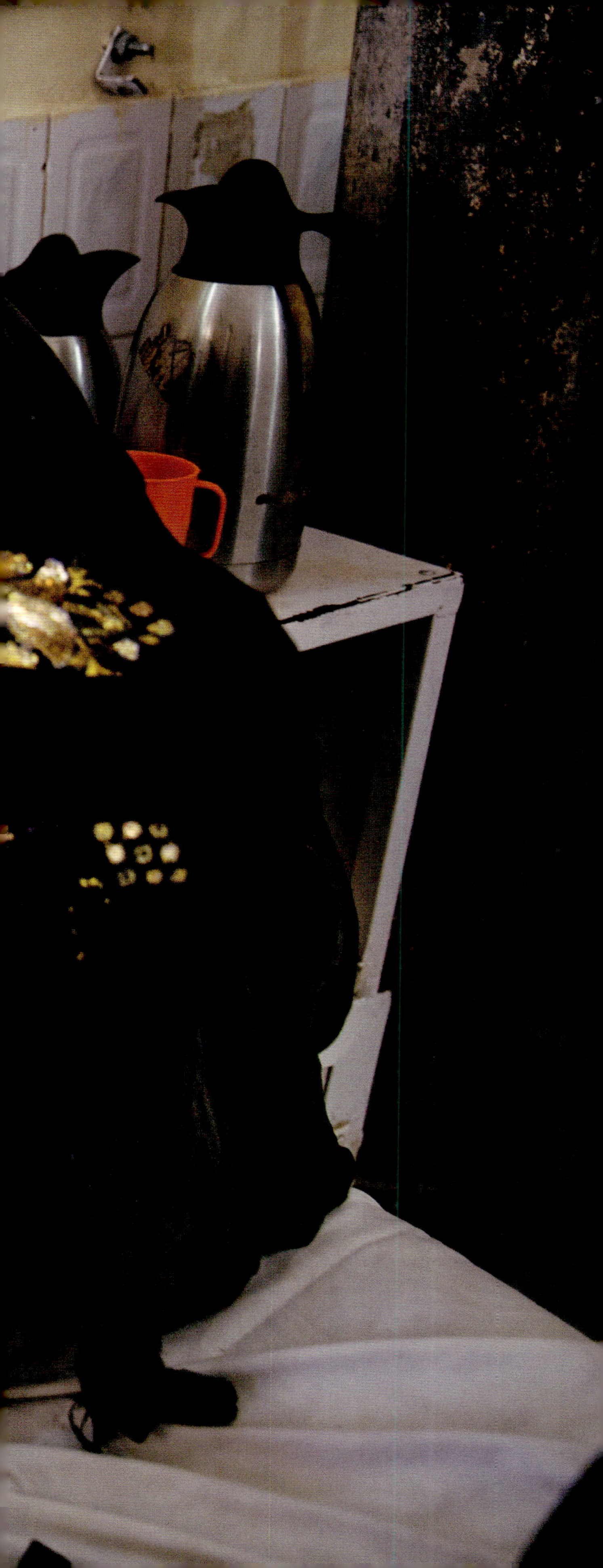

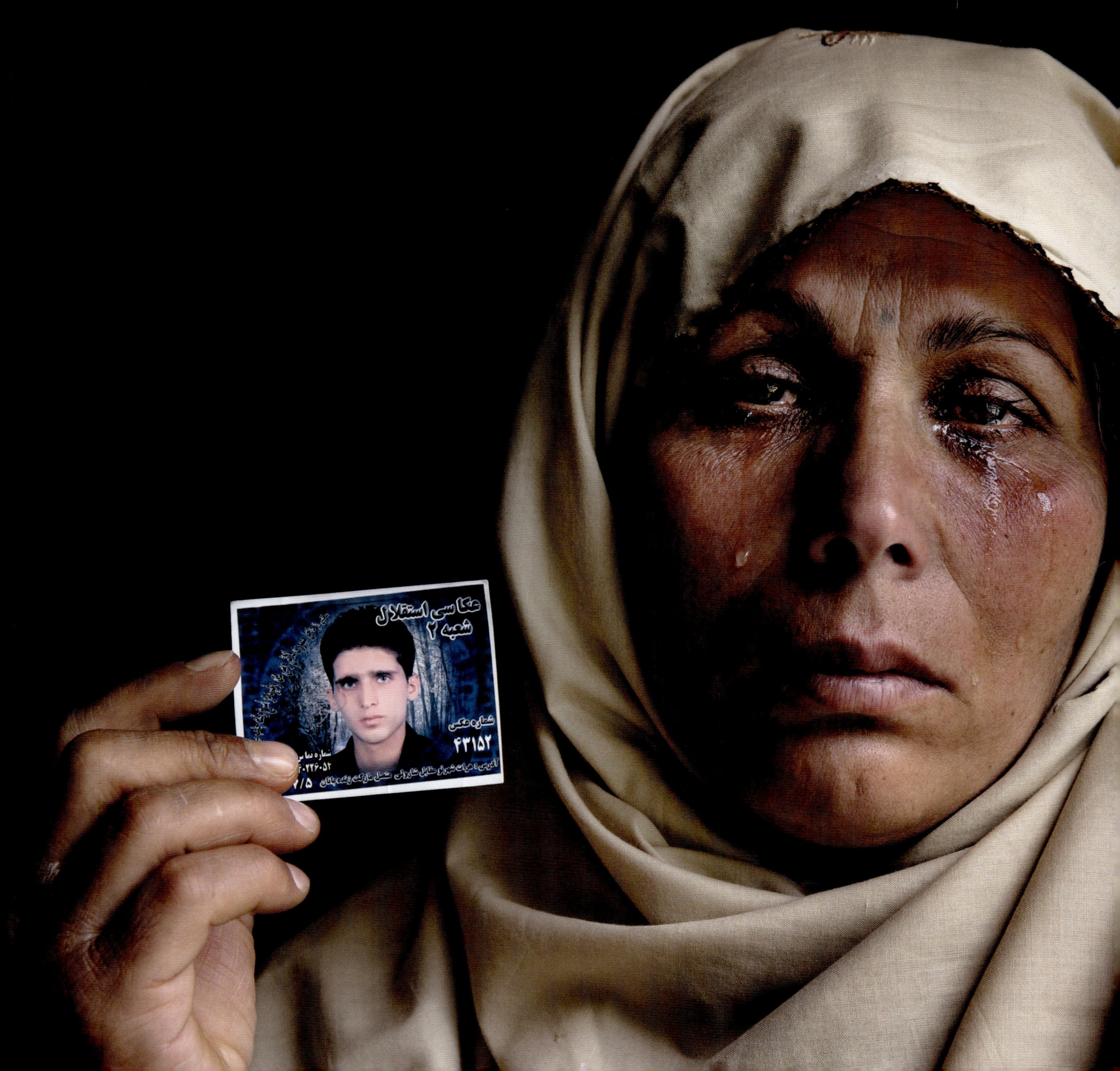

عکاسی استقلال
شعبه ۲
شماره عکس
۴۳۱۵۲
آدرس : هرات شهرنو مقابل شاروالی متصل مارکت زنده بانان

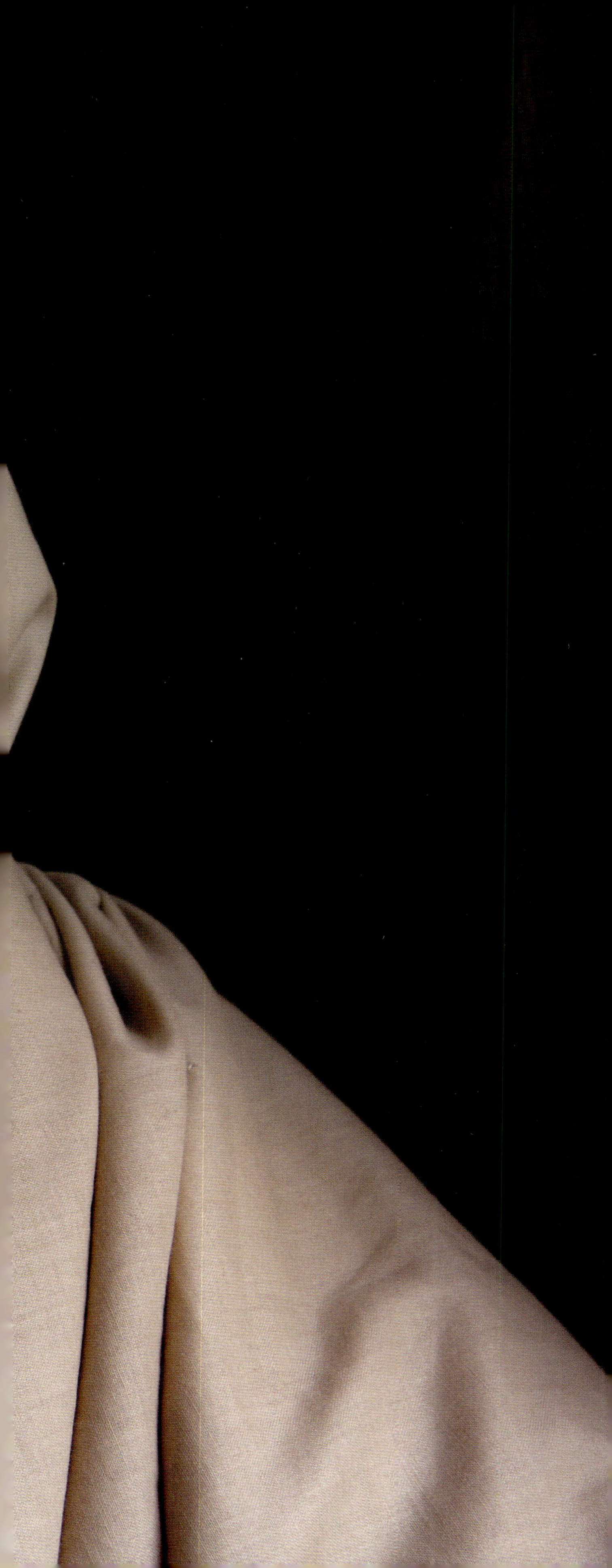

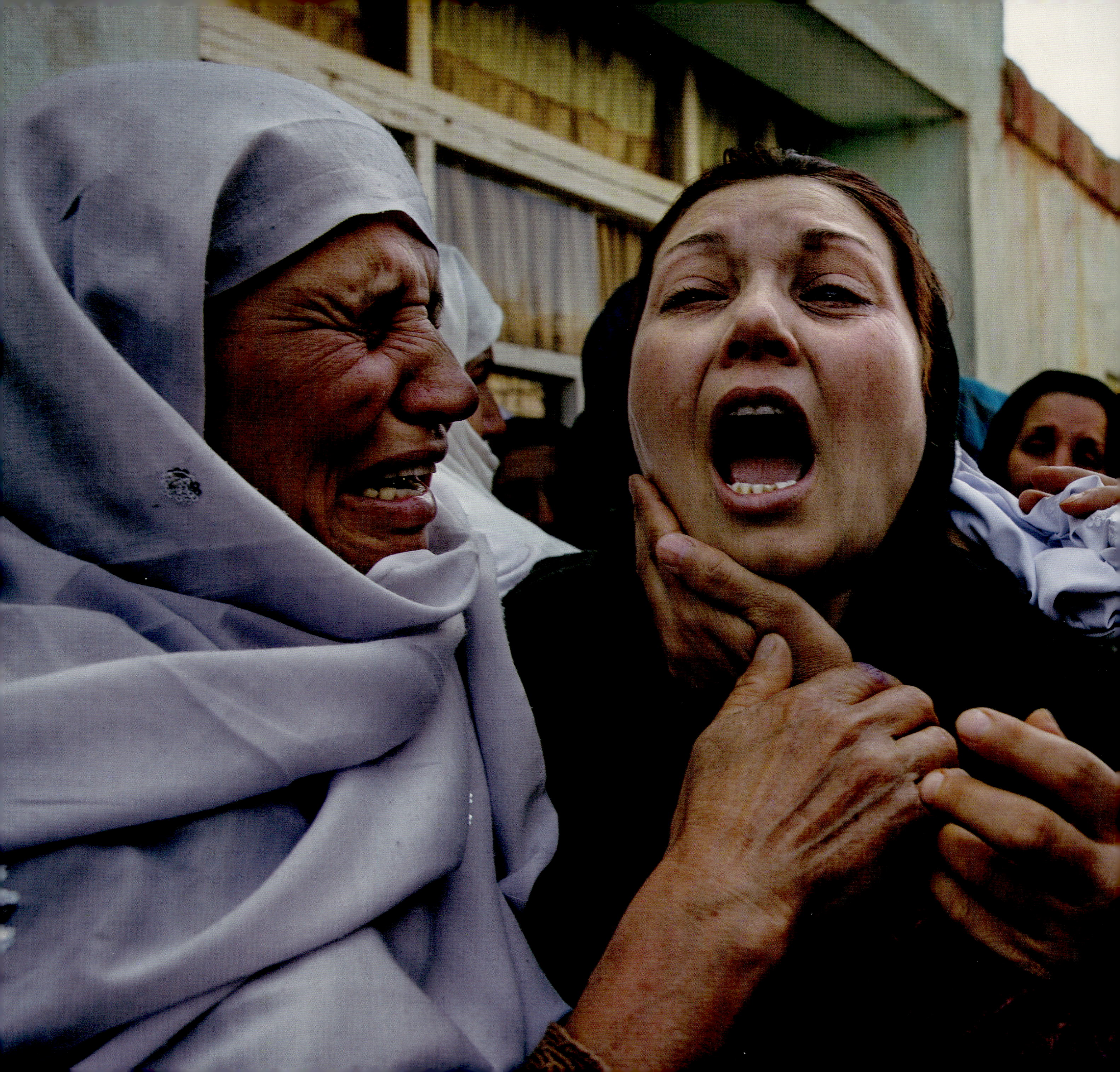

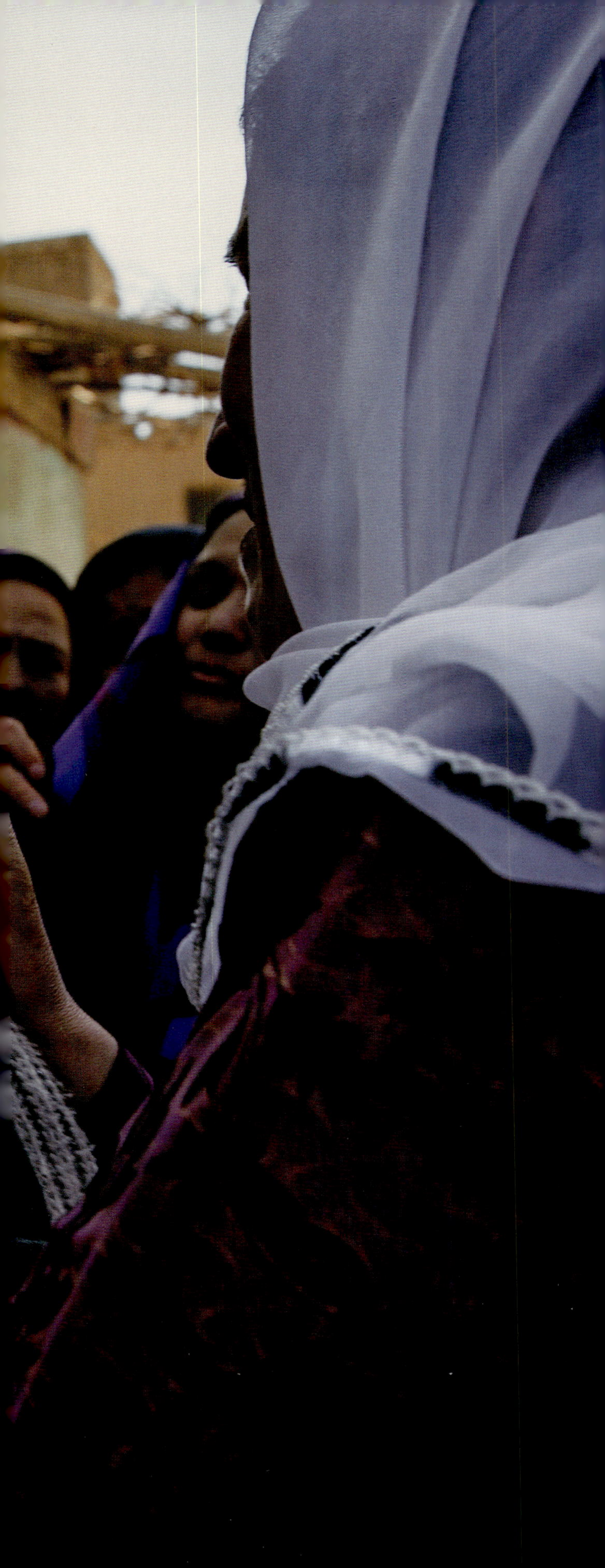

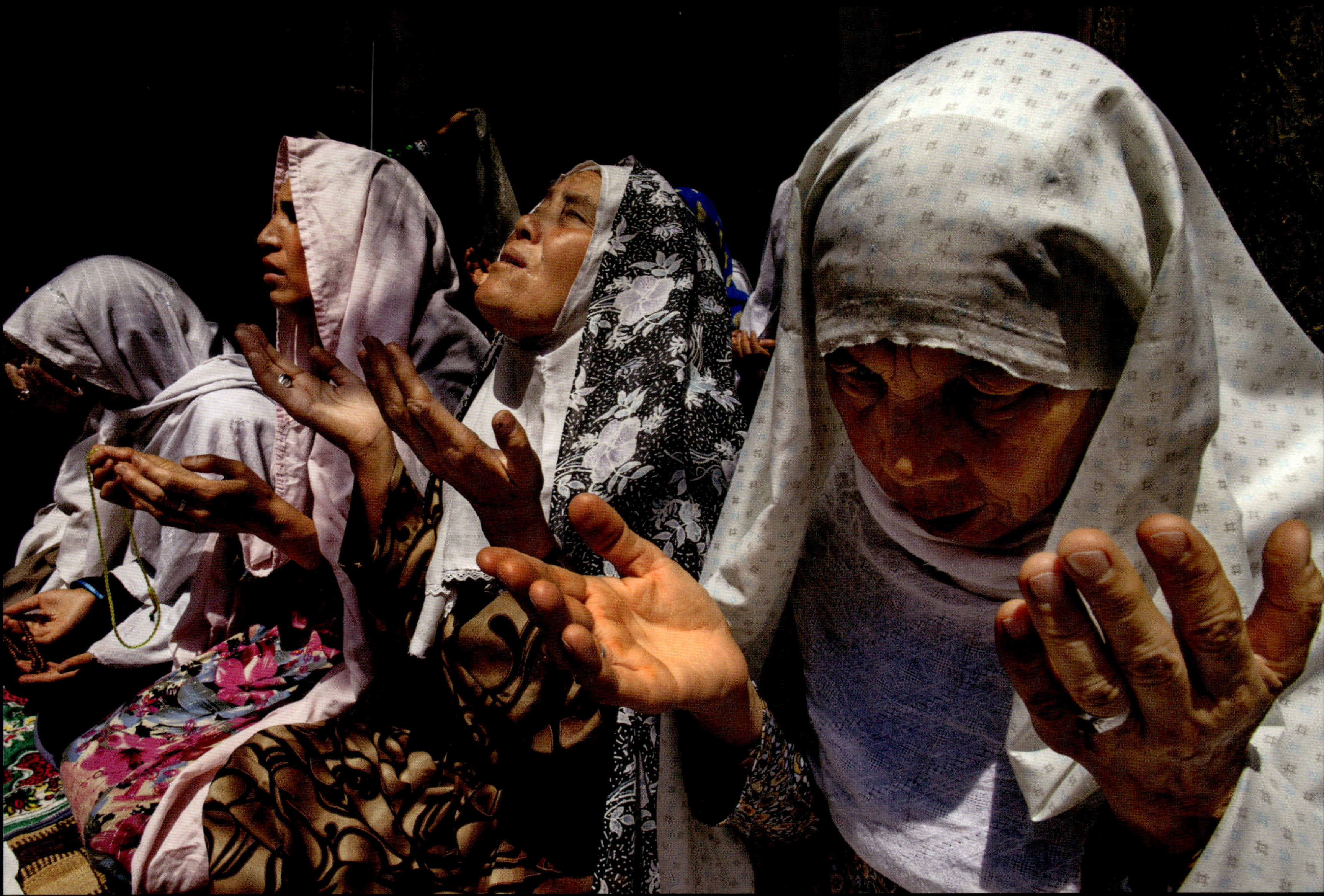

KABUL, JUNE 3, 2011.

Women participate in Friday prayers at the Madinatul-Elm Mosque. Mosques that admit women for prayer segregate them in sections completely separate from the main chambers, where the men say their prayers.

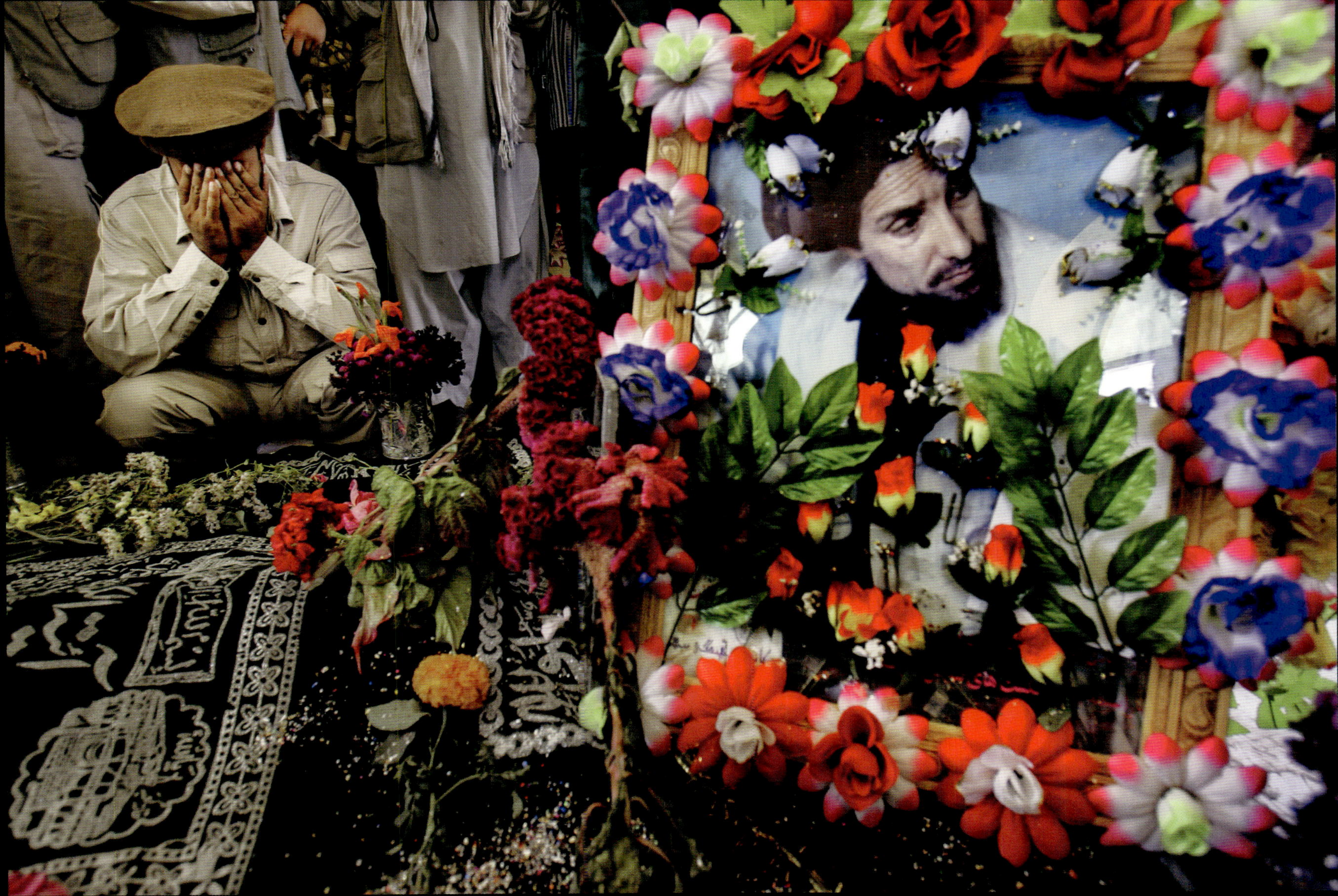

PANJSHIR VALLEY,
SEPTEMBER 10, 2005.

Afghans pay tribute to their "national hero," Ahmad Shah Massoud, at his tomb in the

The Reality

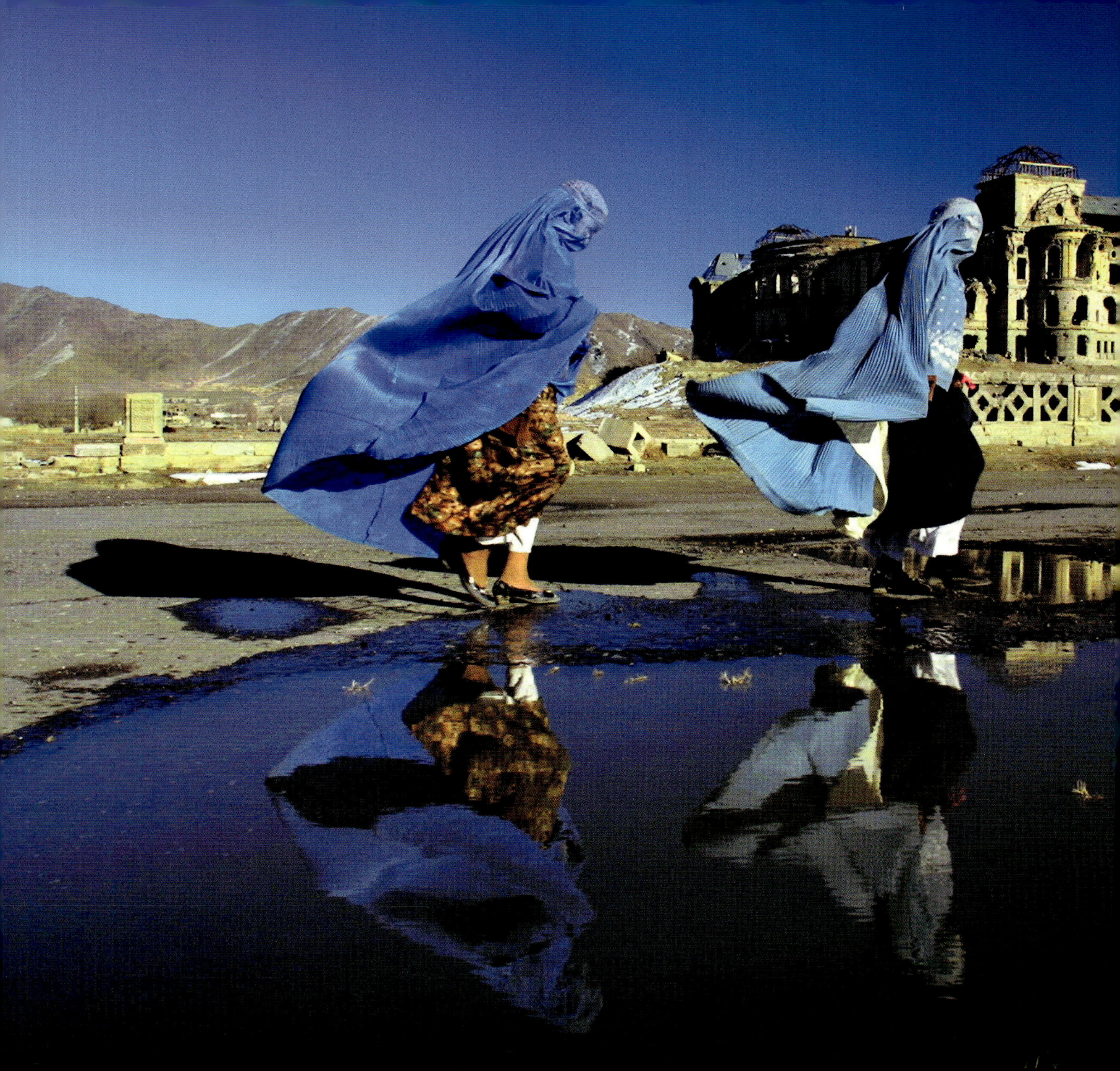

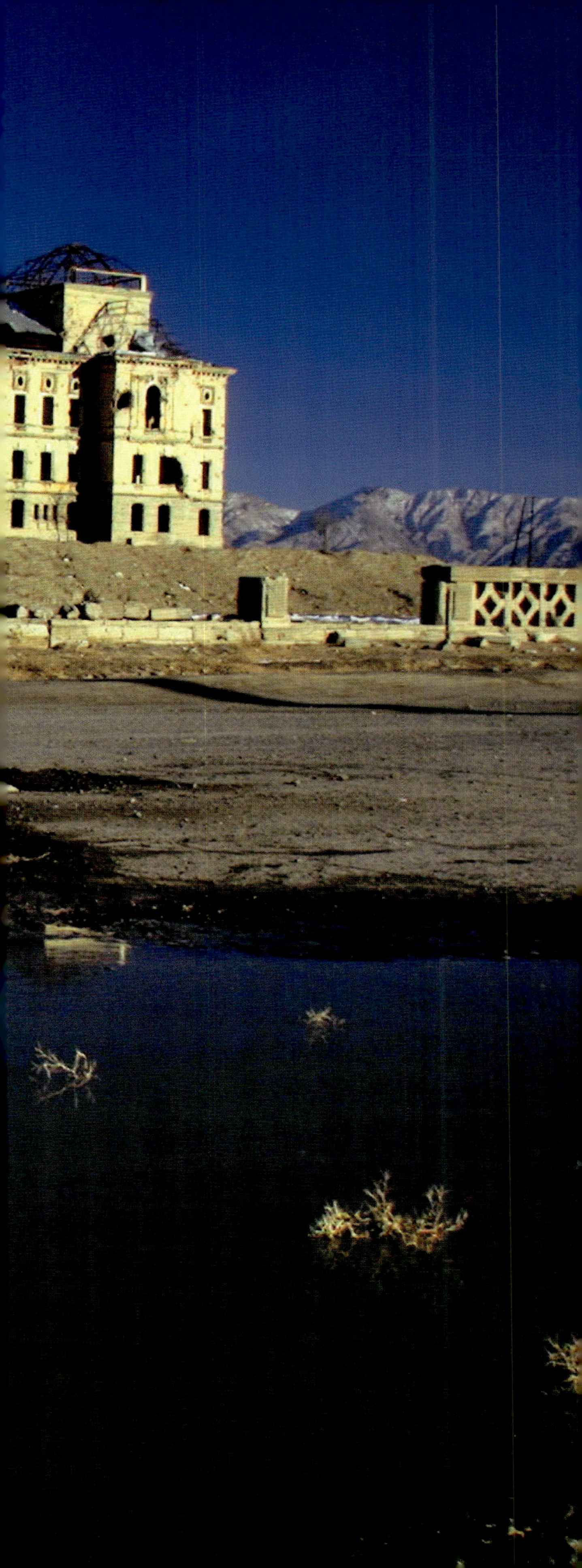

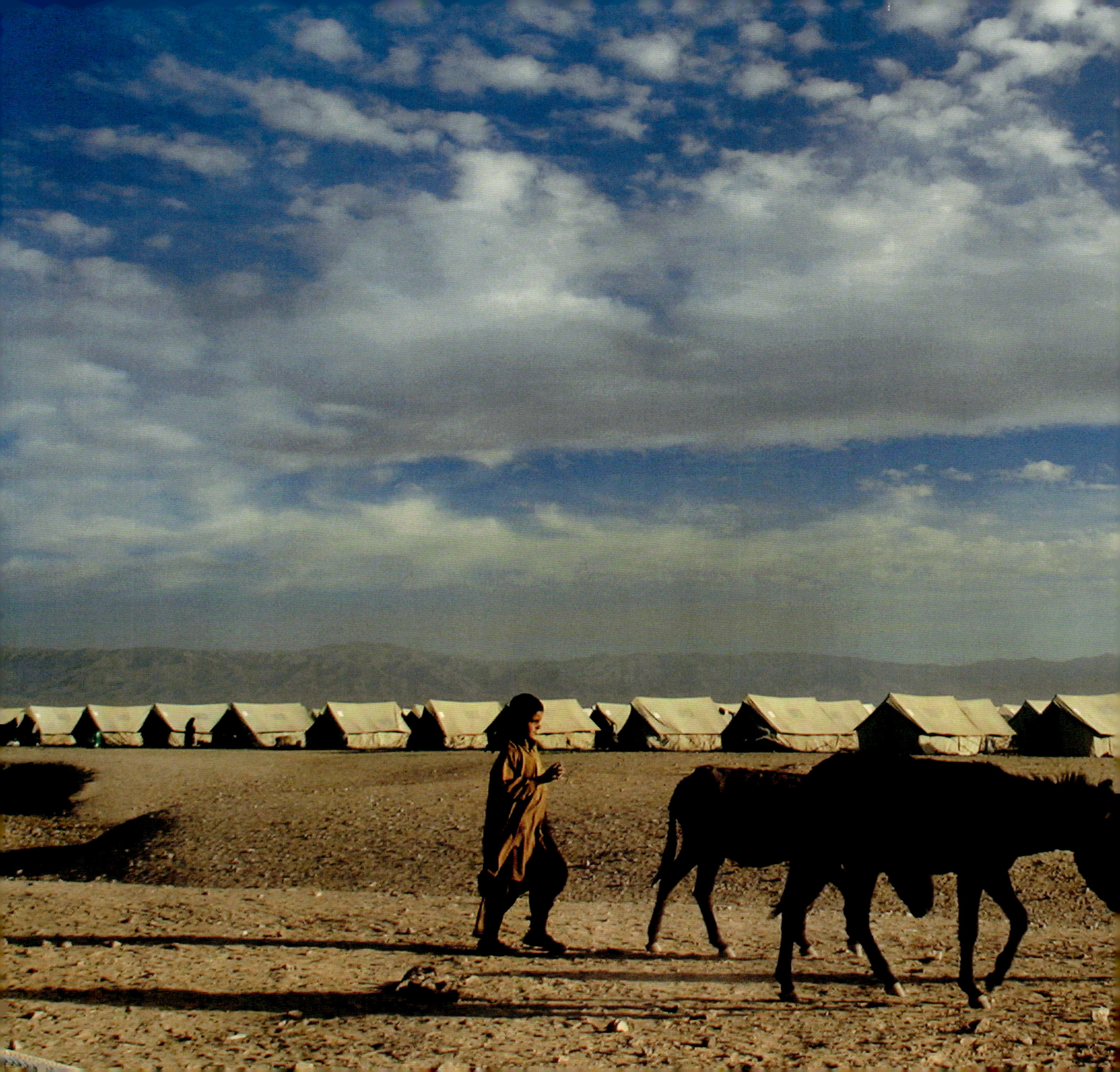

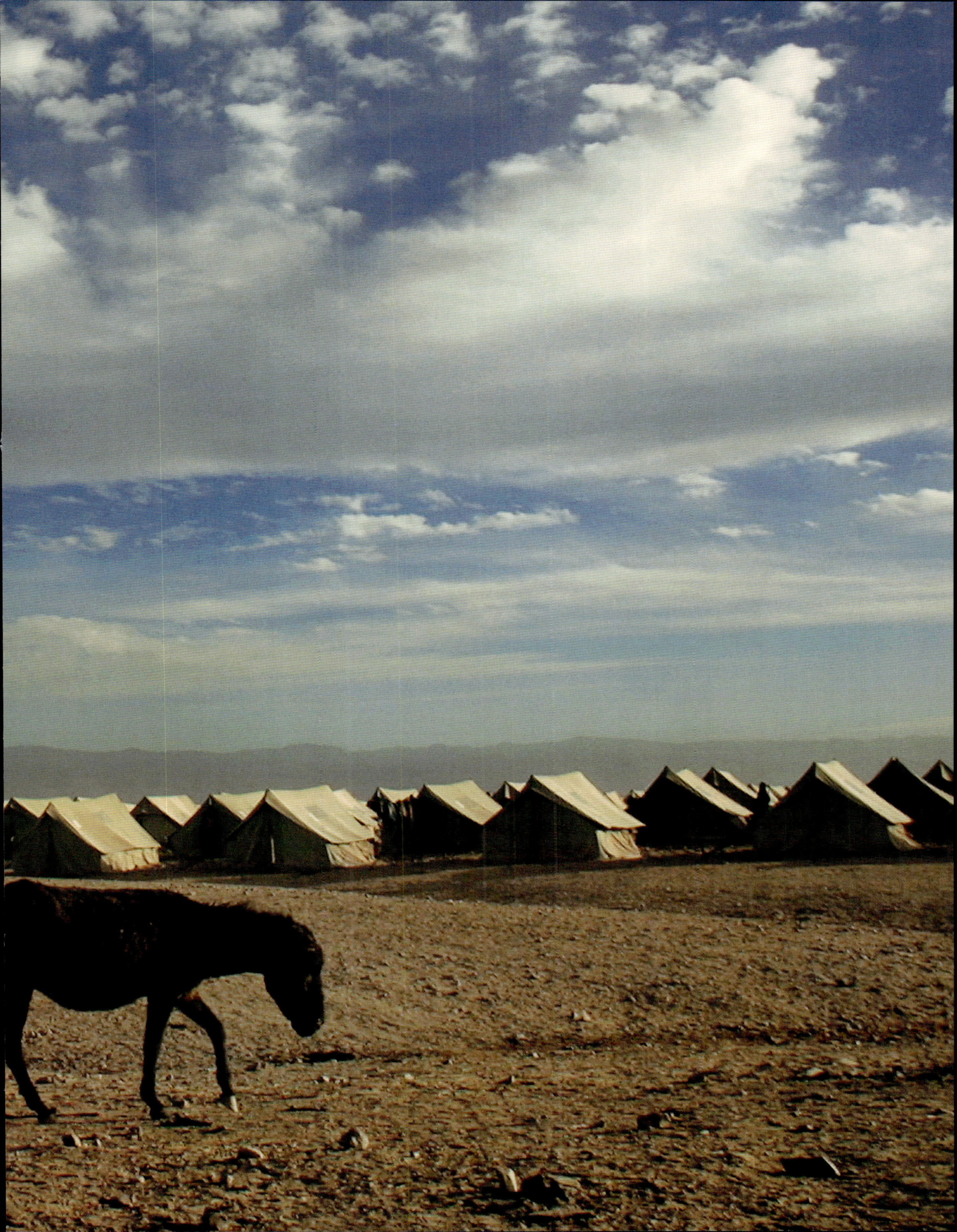

CHAMAN, PAKISTAN, DECEMBER 4, 2001.

A boy walks his donkeys at the Killi Faizo refugee camp, along the Pakistan-Afghanistan border. Tens of thousands crossed the border into Pakistan in an attempt to flee the bombing that began with the US-led invasion.

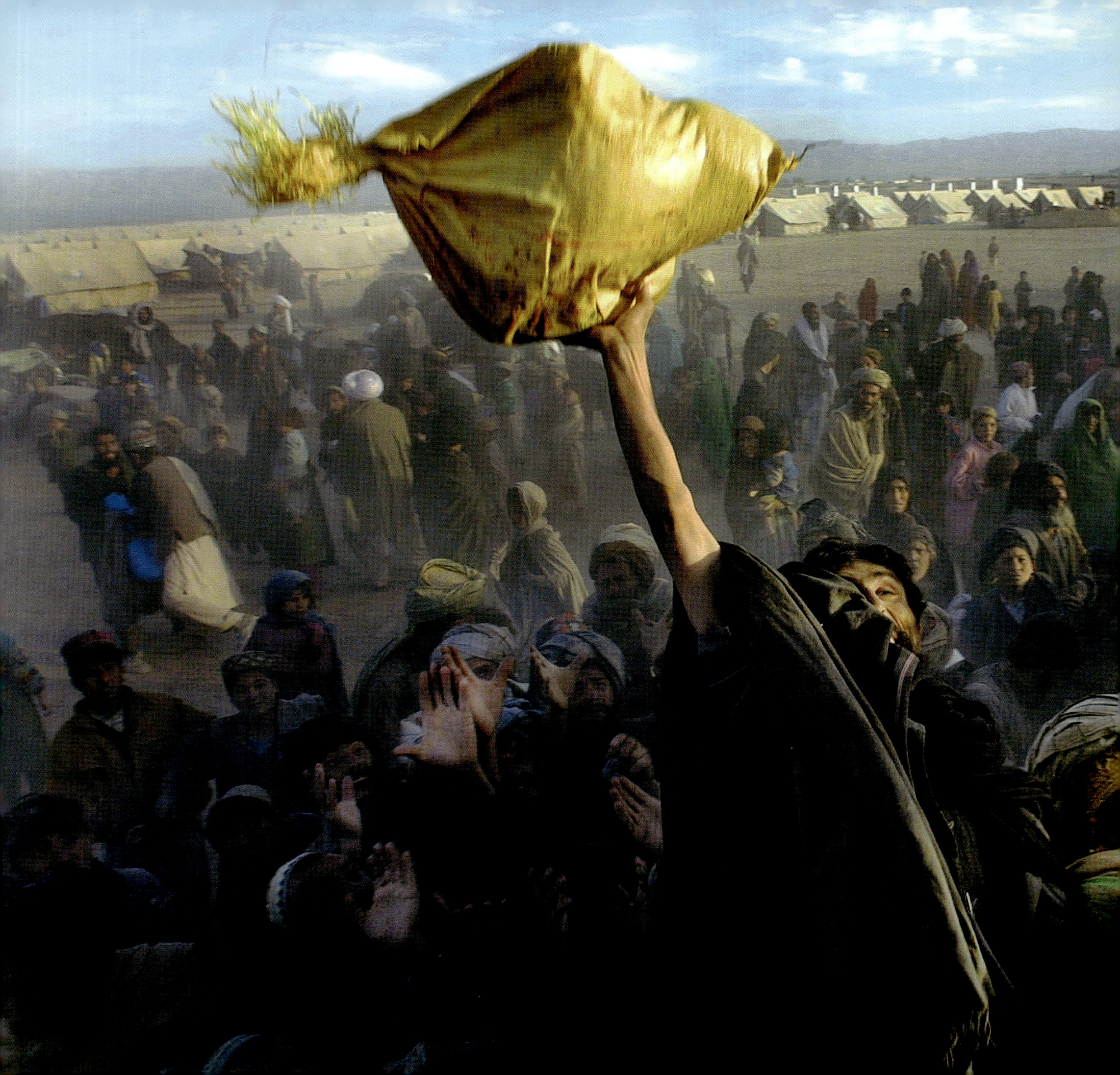

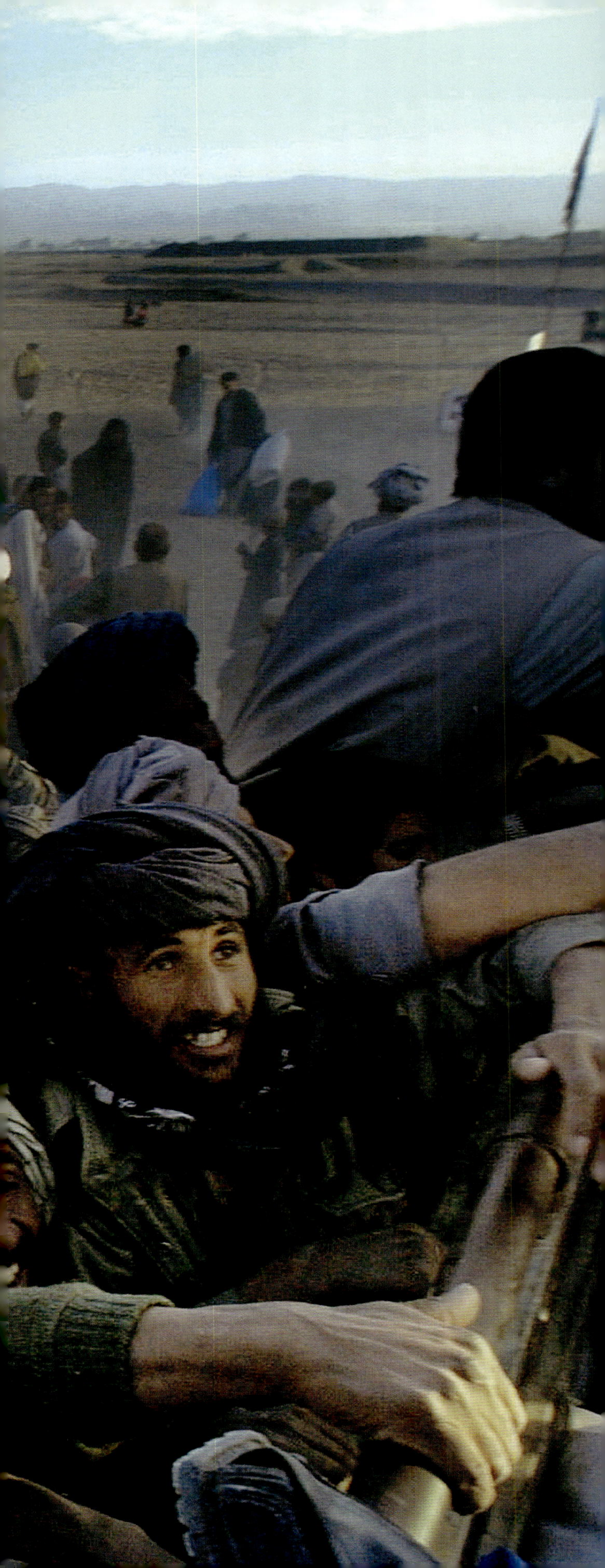

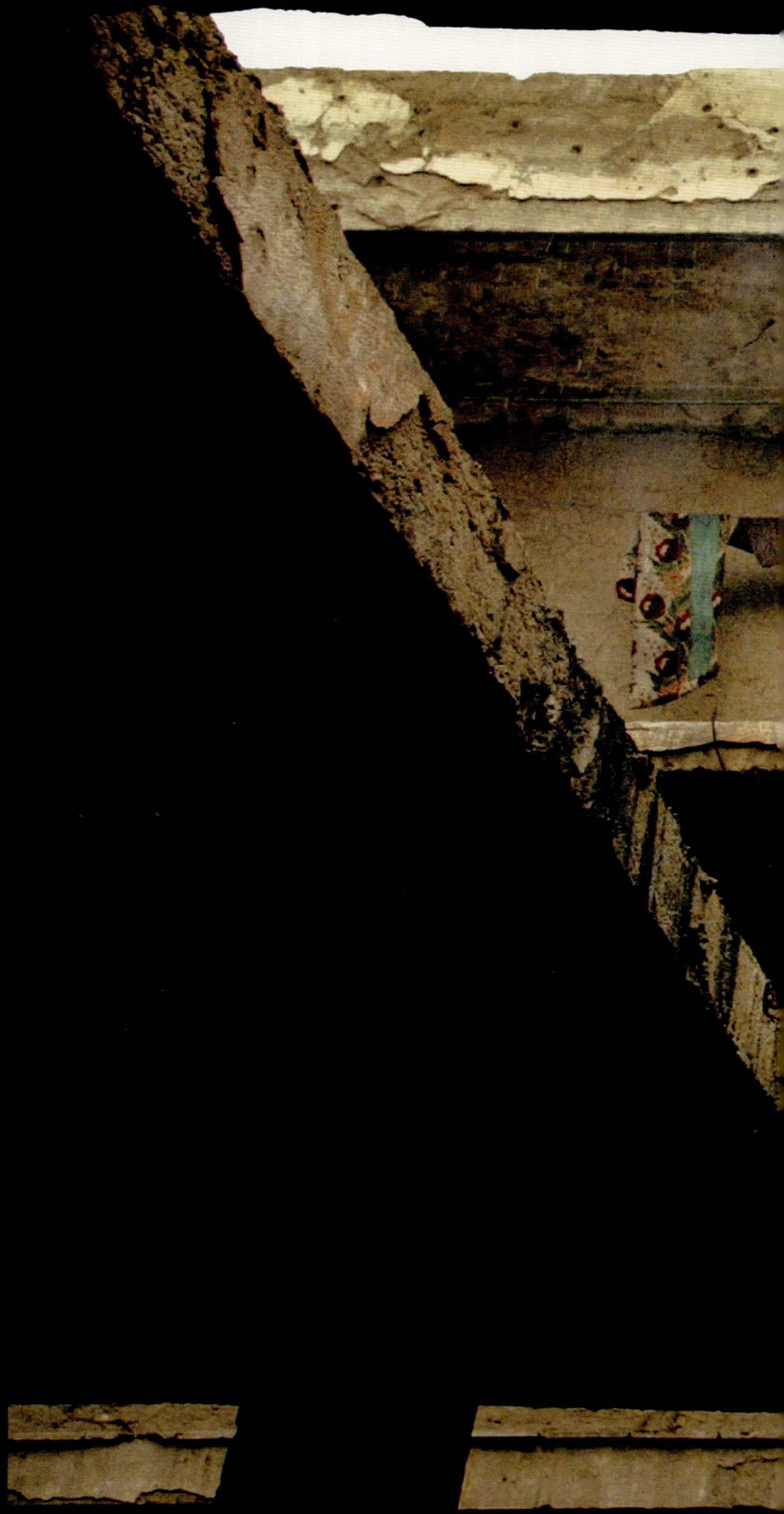

KABUL, JANUARY 29, 2003.

Afghans try to keep warm outside a broken-down and vacant housing complex. The internally displaced families came from Pakistani refugee camps eight months earlier with no money or jobs.

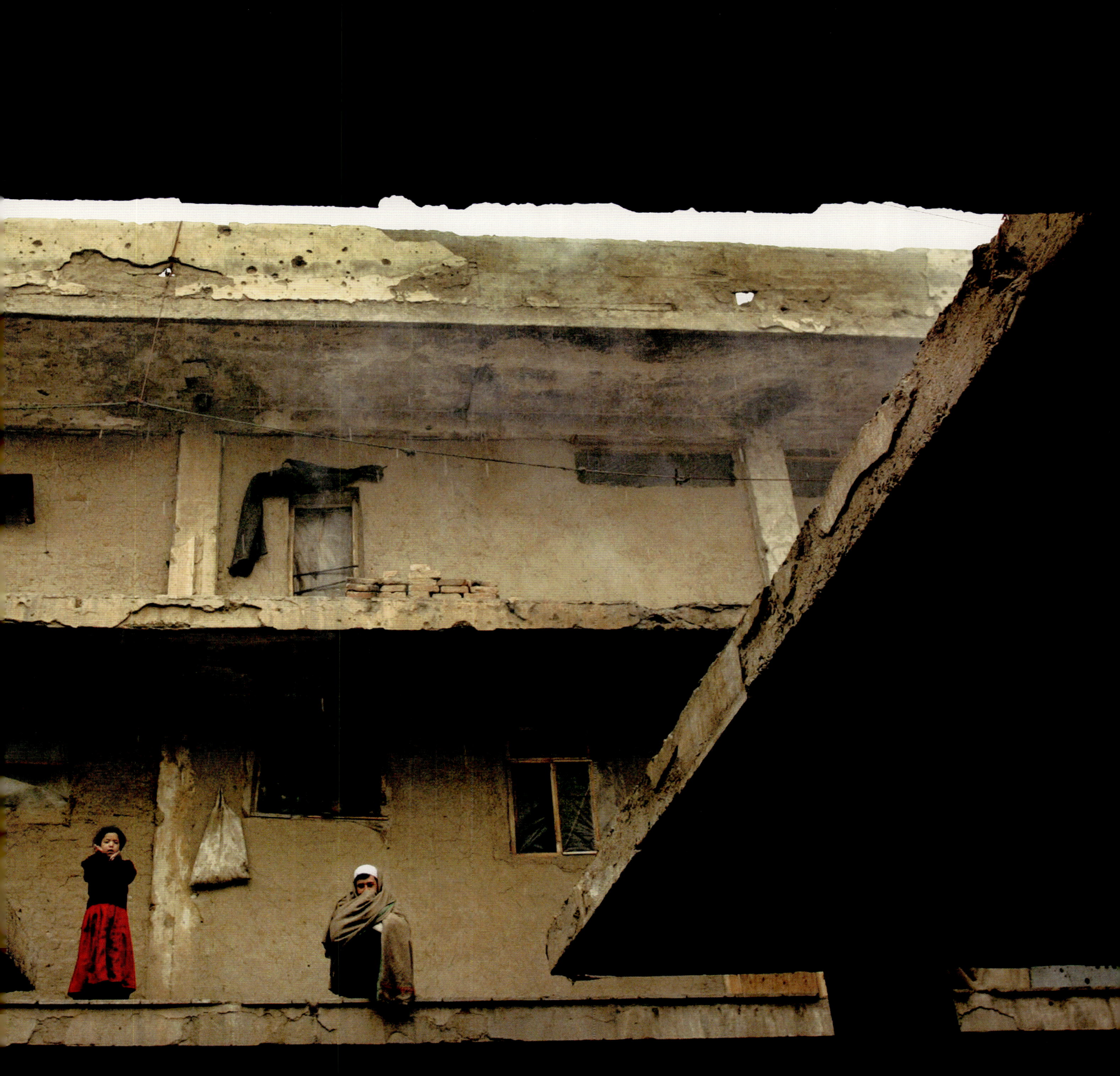

BAMIYAN, SEPTEMBER 2, 2009.

Sima holds her one-year-old baby, Farzana, outside their cave dwelling. Many such families, who belong to a culturally distinct and often persecuted group called the Hazara, are too poor to live anywhere else. The government insists that they are damaging the area around Bamiyan's Buddha statues, which constitute a rare archaeological site.

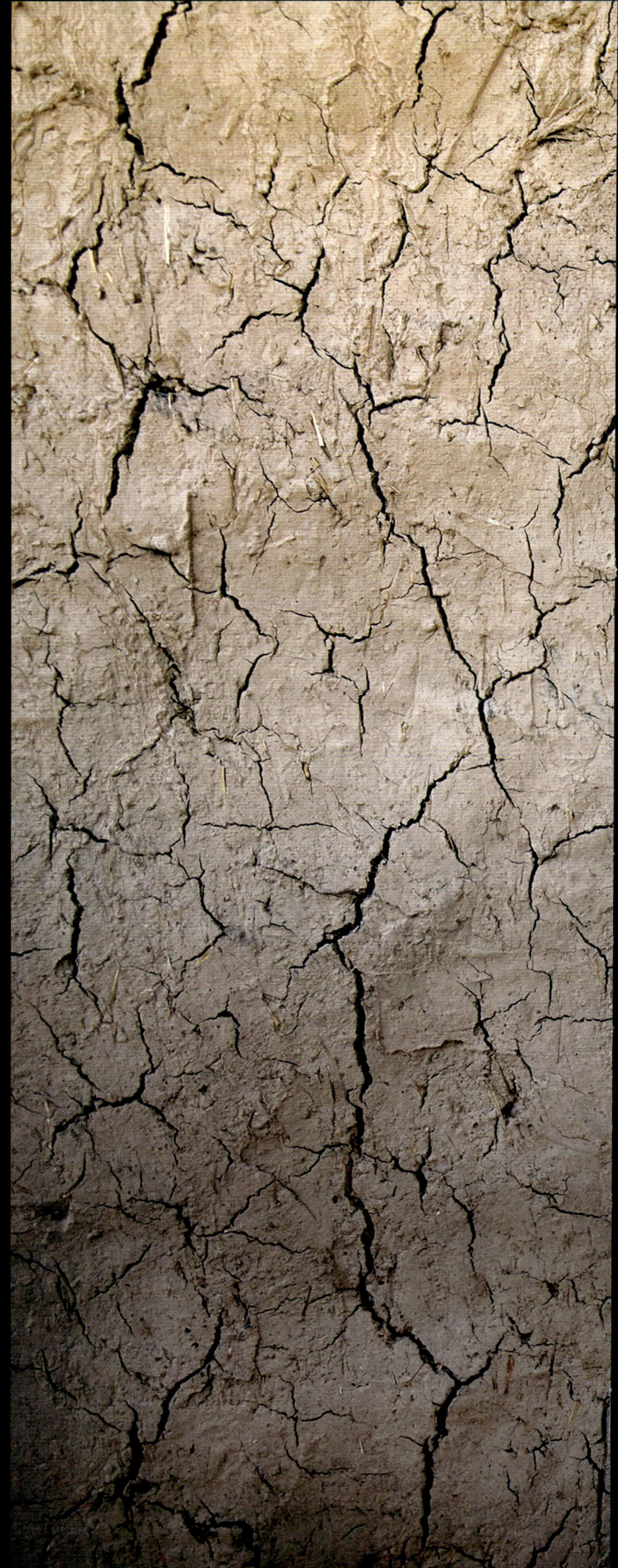

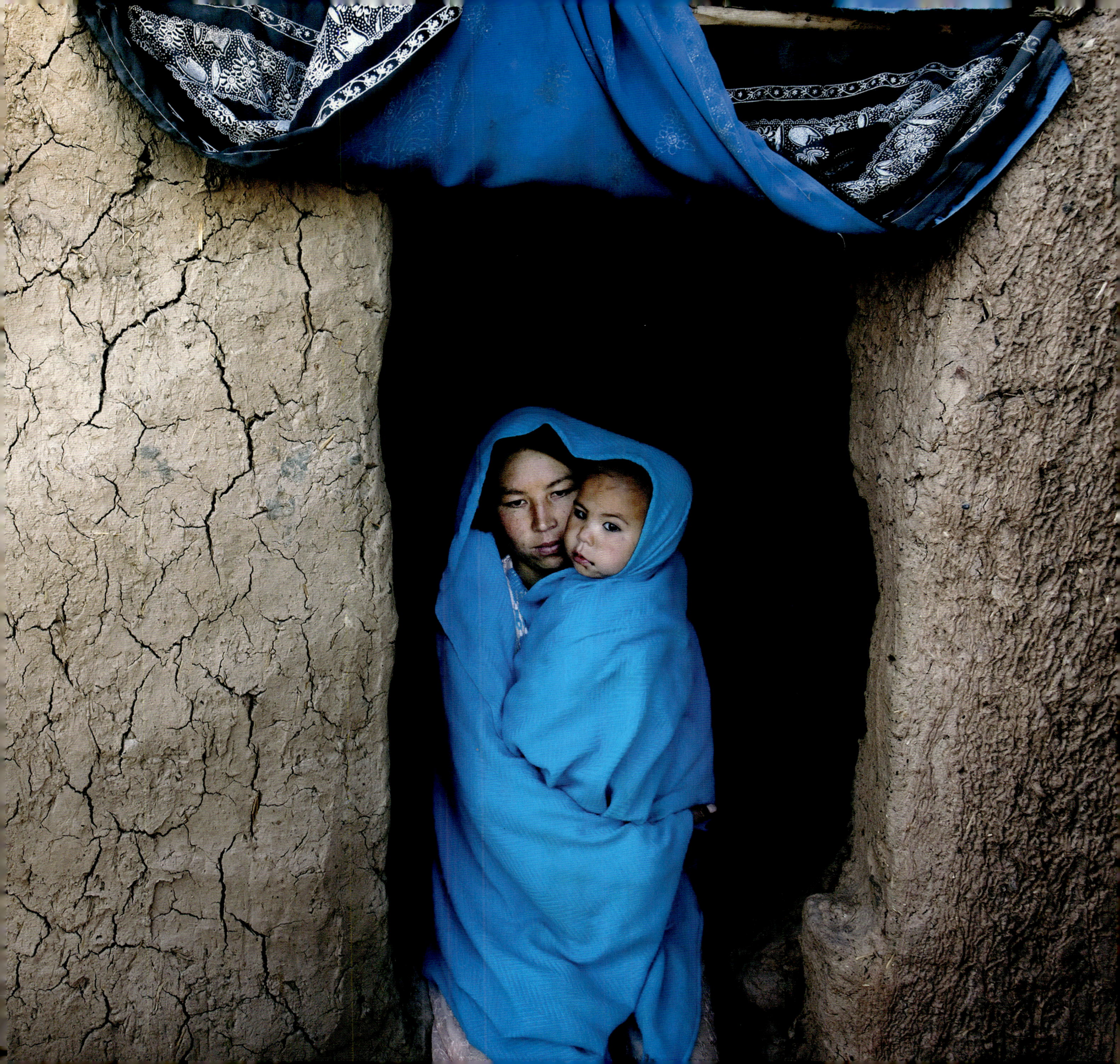

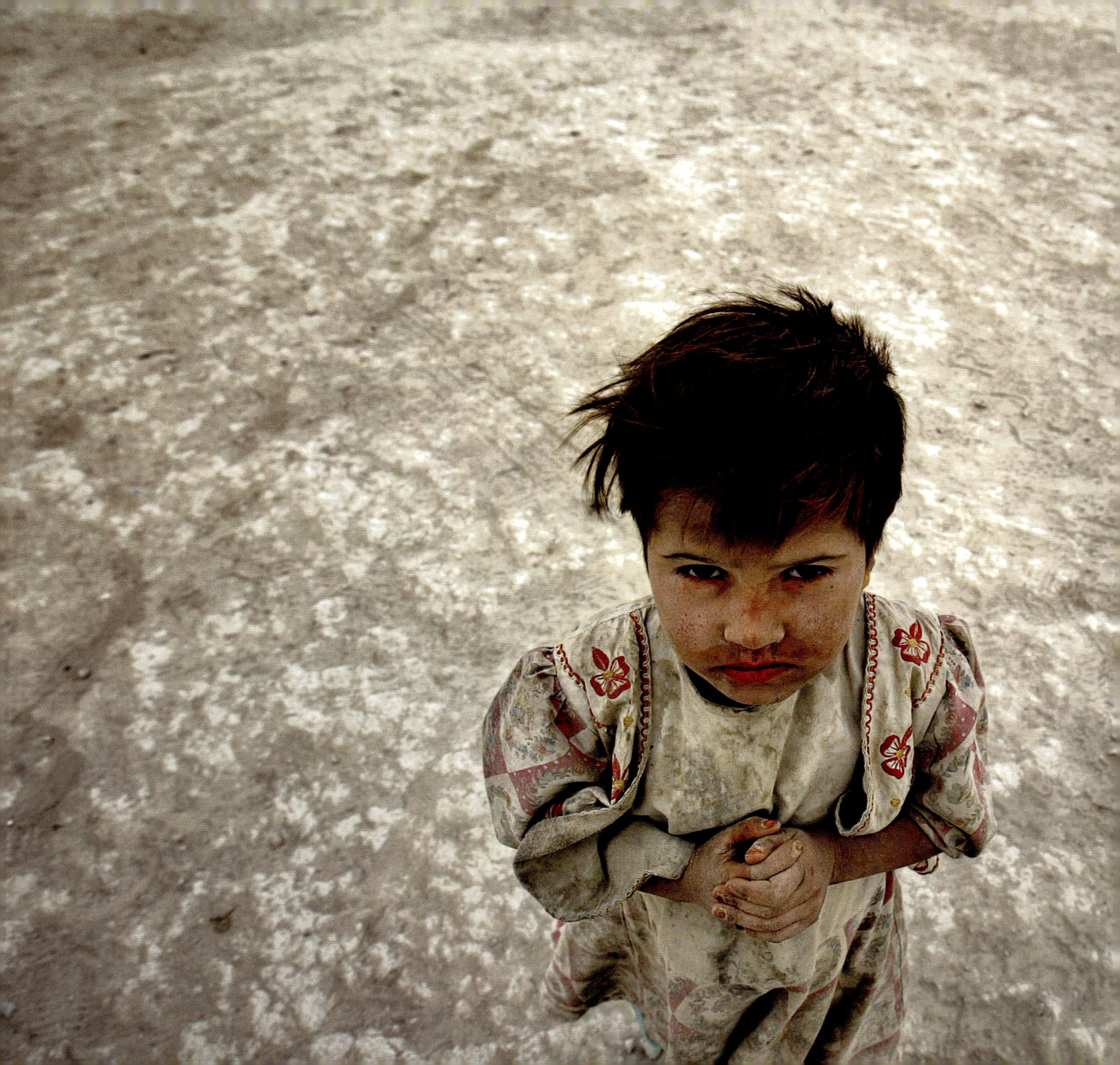

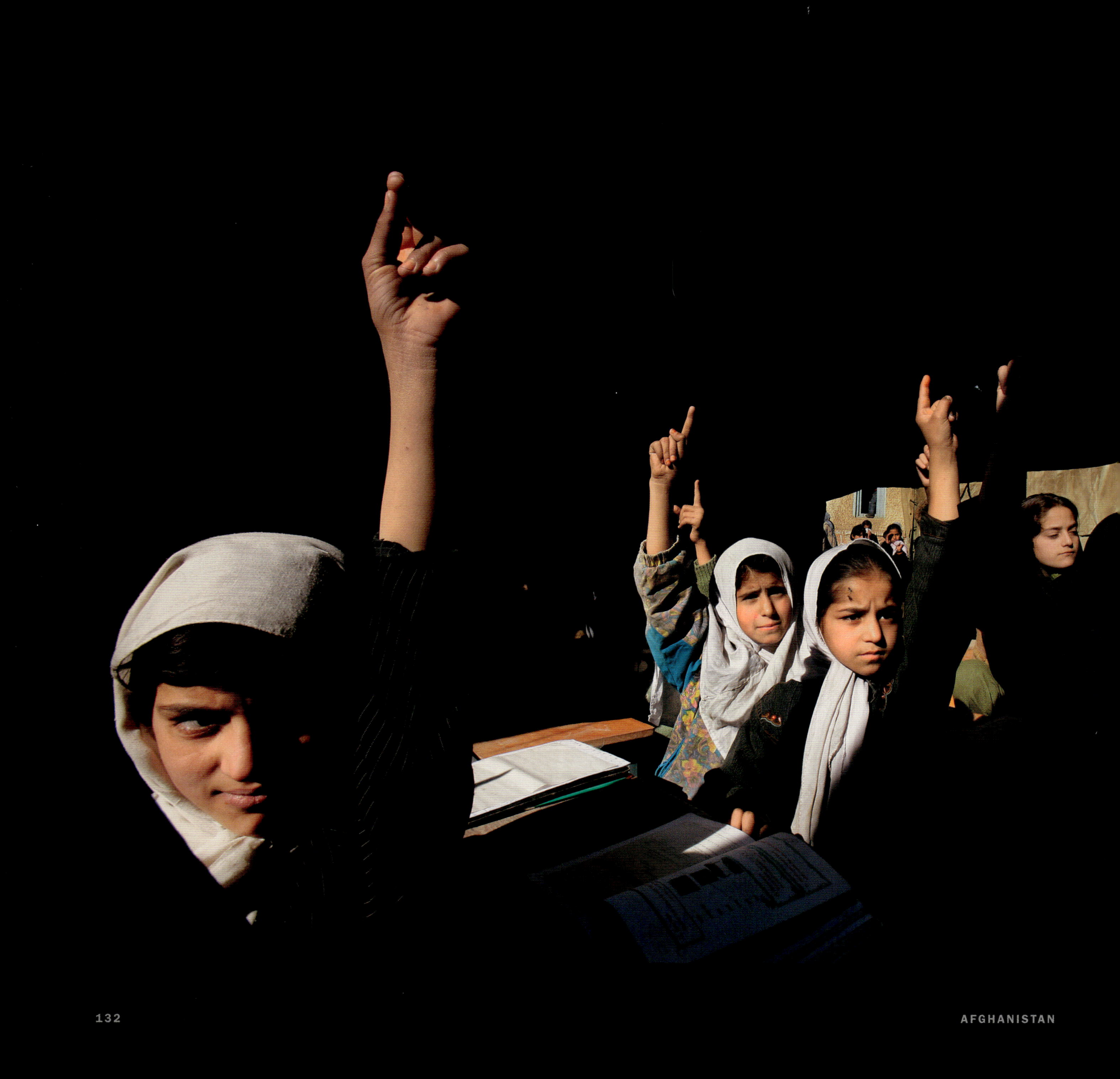

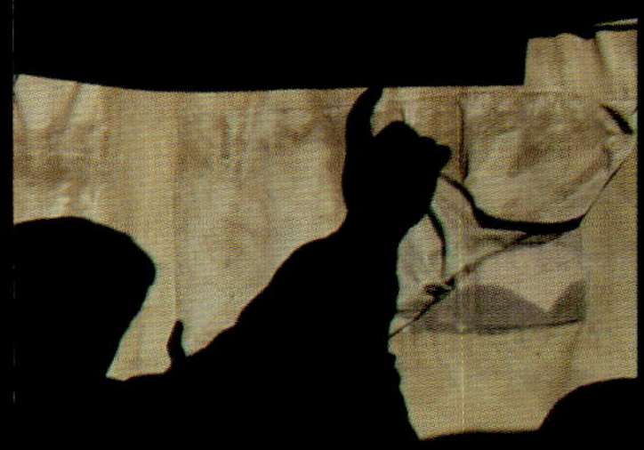

KABUL, NOVEMBER 22, 2006.

LEFT: Girls raise their hands during an English class at Bibi Mahroo High School. The overcrowded school is housed in tents supplied by UNICEF.

KABUL, OCTOBER 31, 2002.

RIGHT: A girl reads during a Persian class at the Khana-e-Noor school for Afghan refugees. Many children had no opportunities for formal education during the Taliban regime, and so this school, which was funded by a Japanese nongovernmental agency, provided such students their first chance to attend classes.

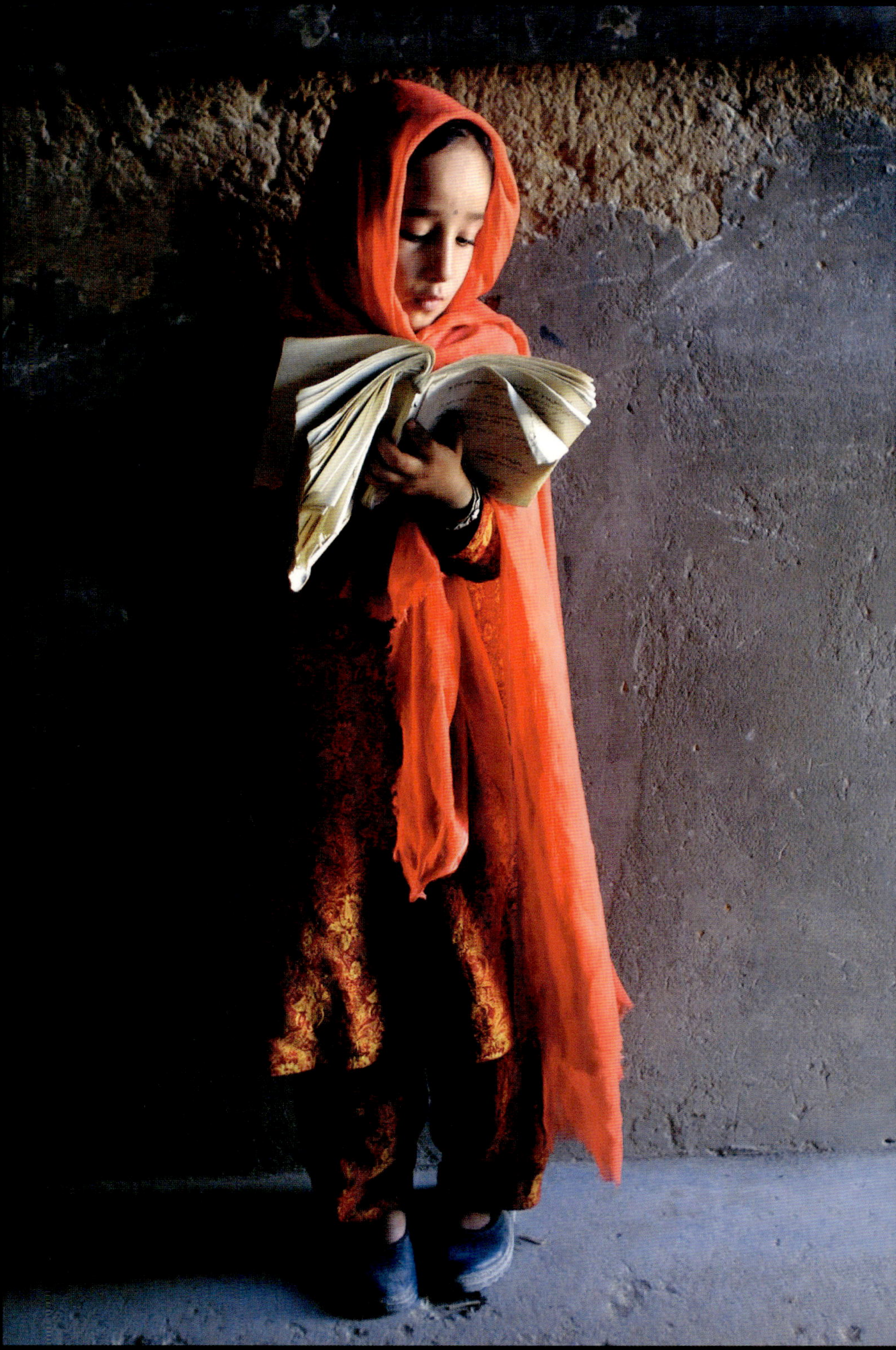

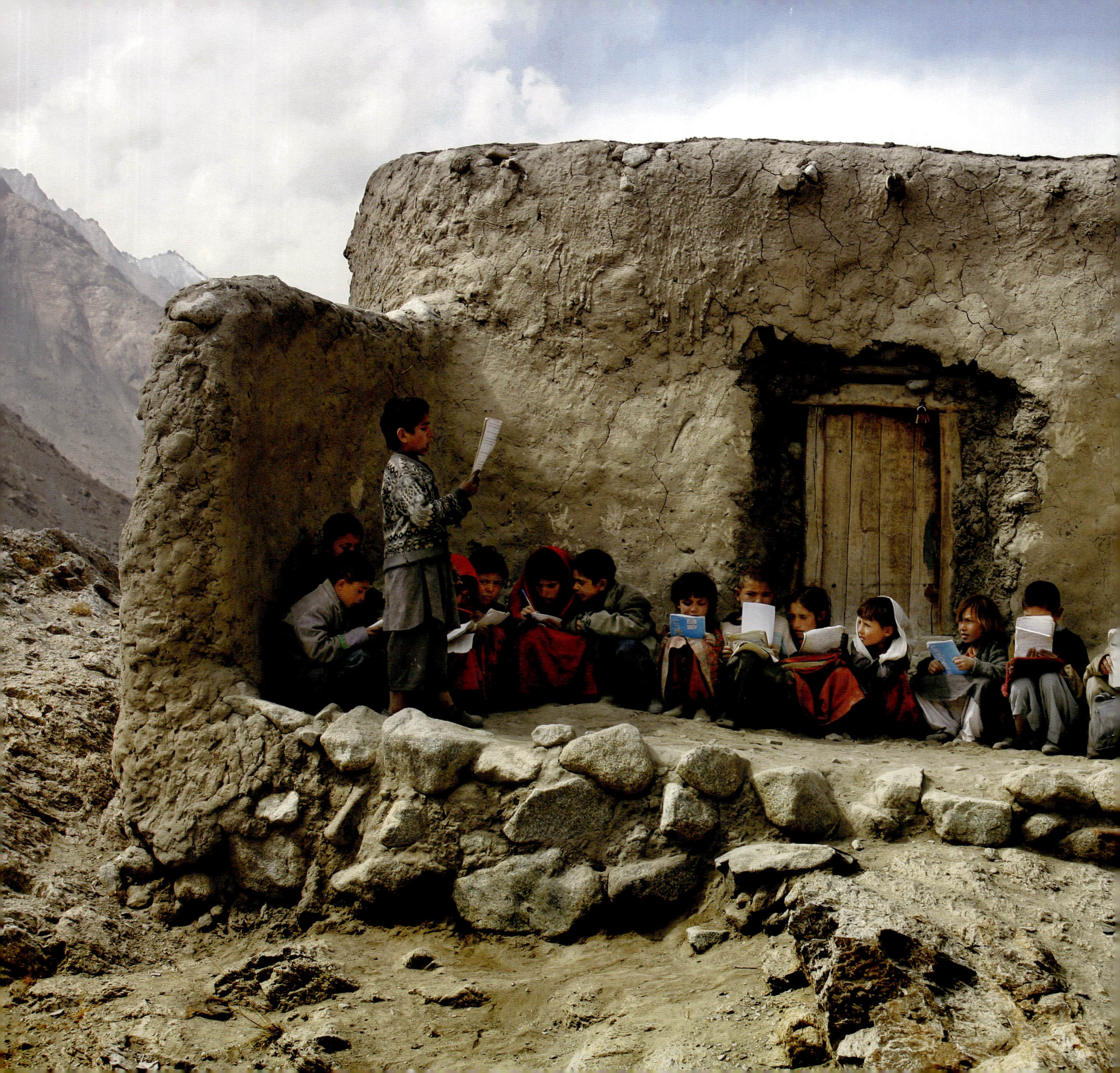

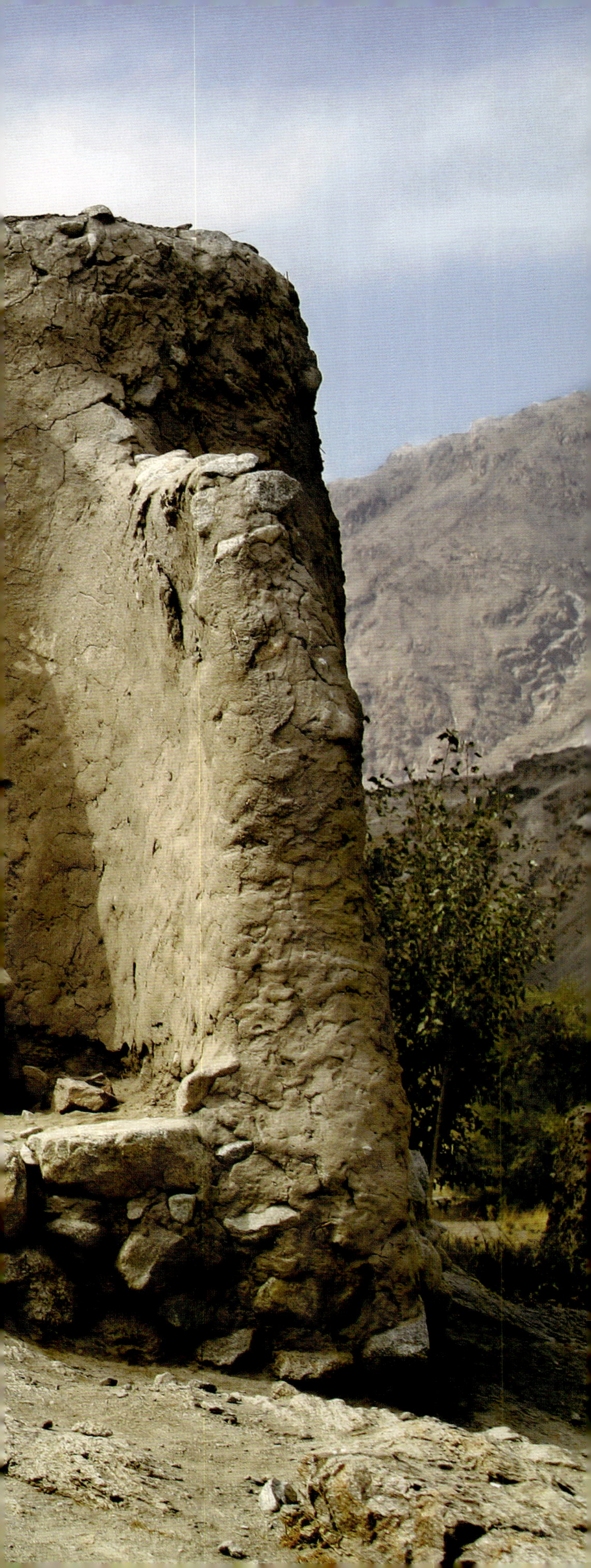

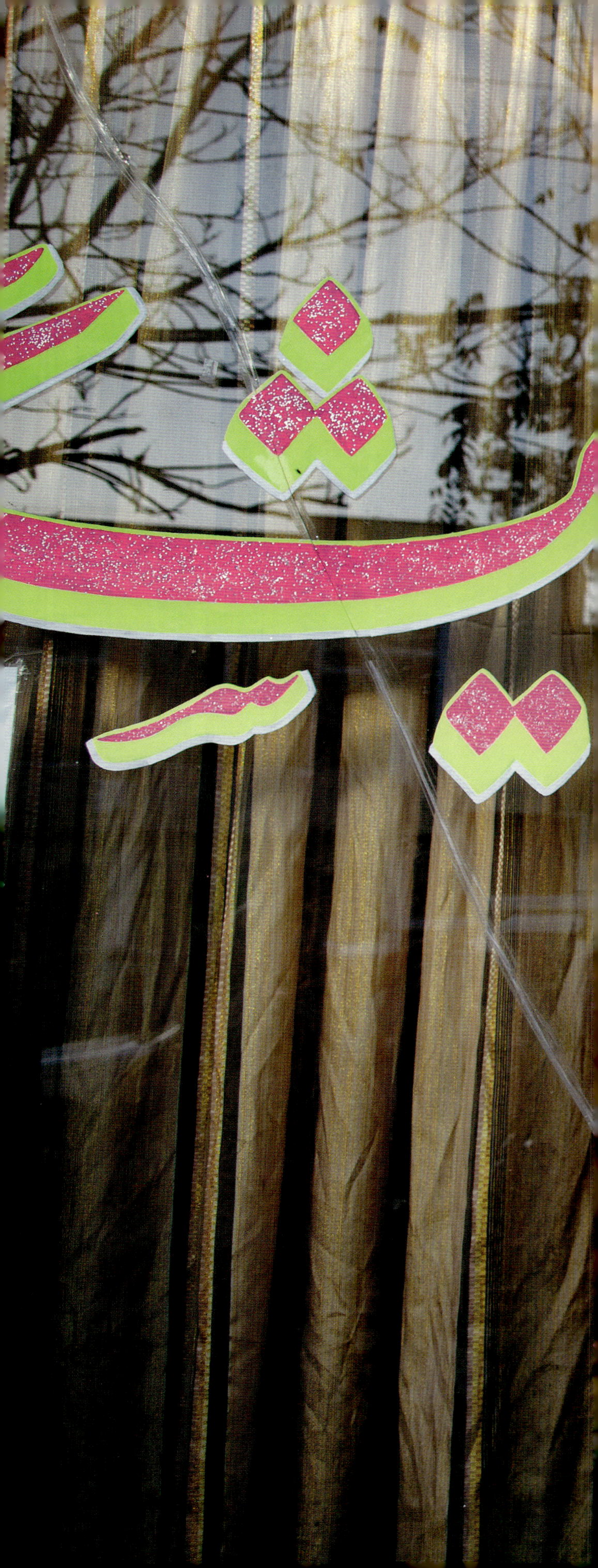

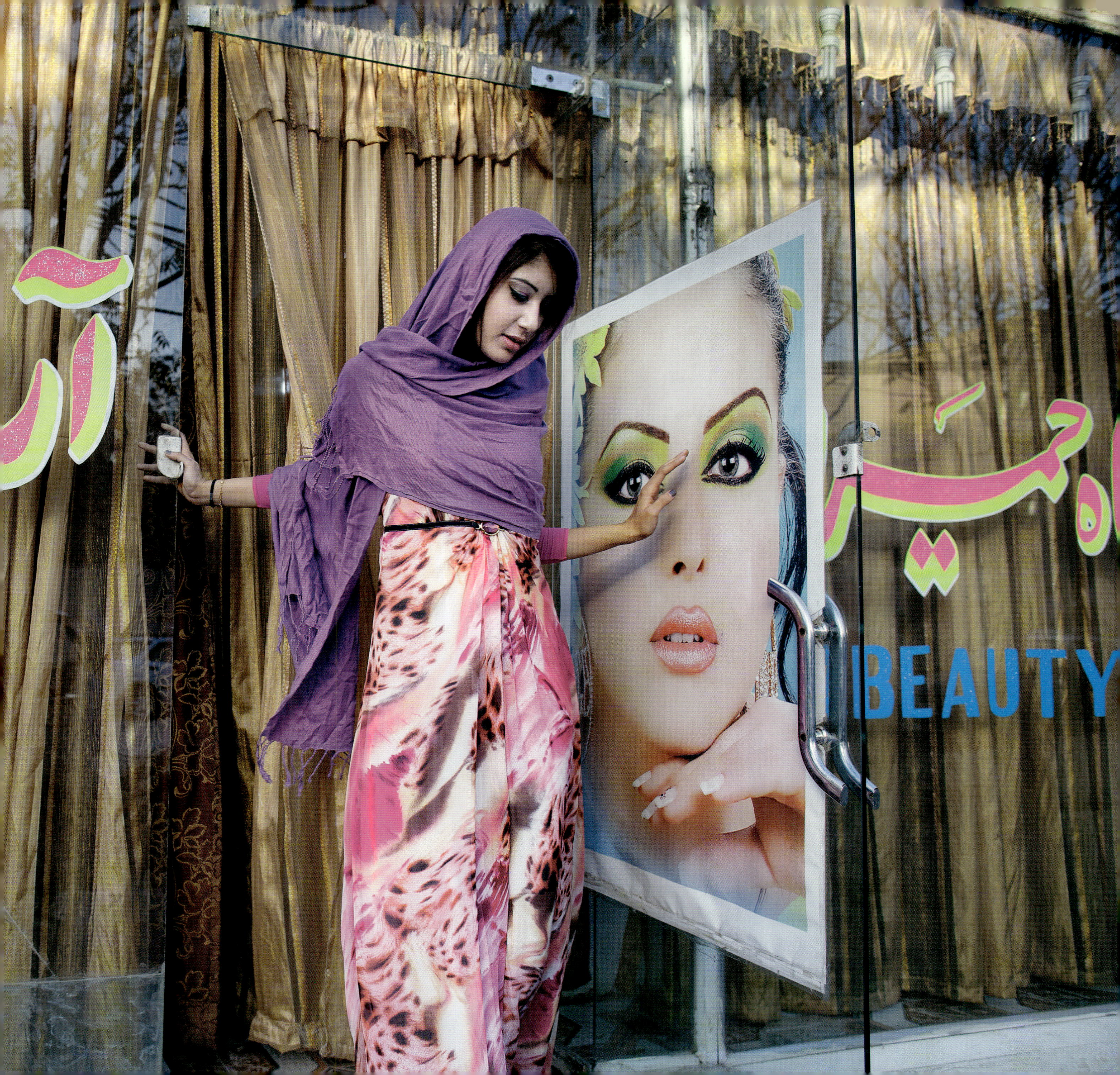
BEAUTY

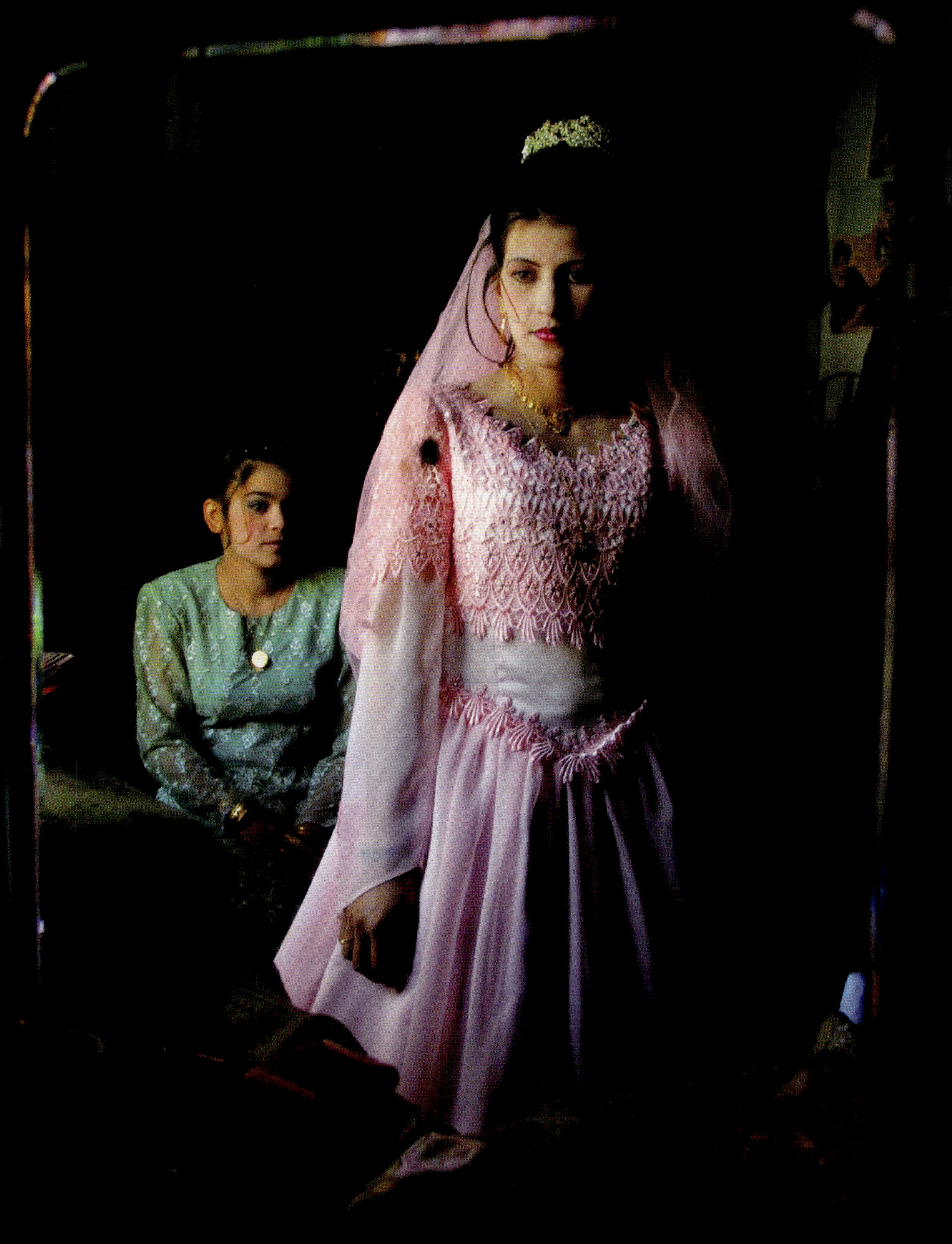

KABUL, JANUARY 4, 2001.

LEFT: Najila Ahmadi, a bride-to-be, gets her wedding dress ready at the local beauty parlor, where her family helps get her dressed for a big engagement party.

KABUL, JULY 31, 2007.

RIGHT: Sitting in a Lincoln limousine outside a bridal salon, nineteen-year-old Qais Habibi patiently waits for his fiancée to finish getting ready for their wedding. Sham, the Lincoln's owner, rents his limo, which is almost always in use during the busy wedding season, at $150 for ten hours, a rate he believes to be the lowest in the world.

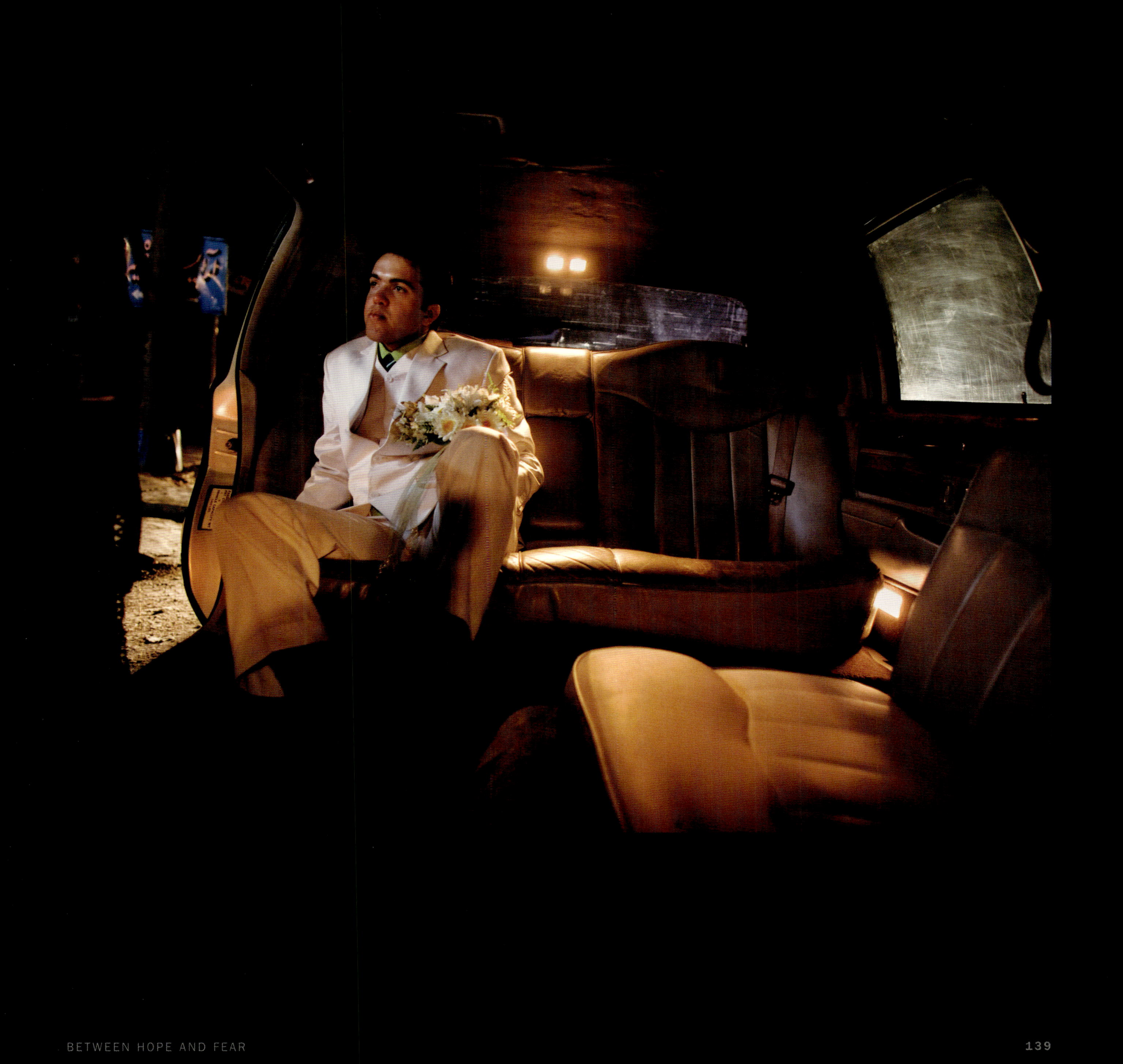

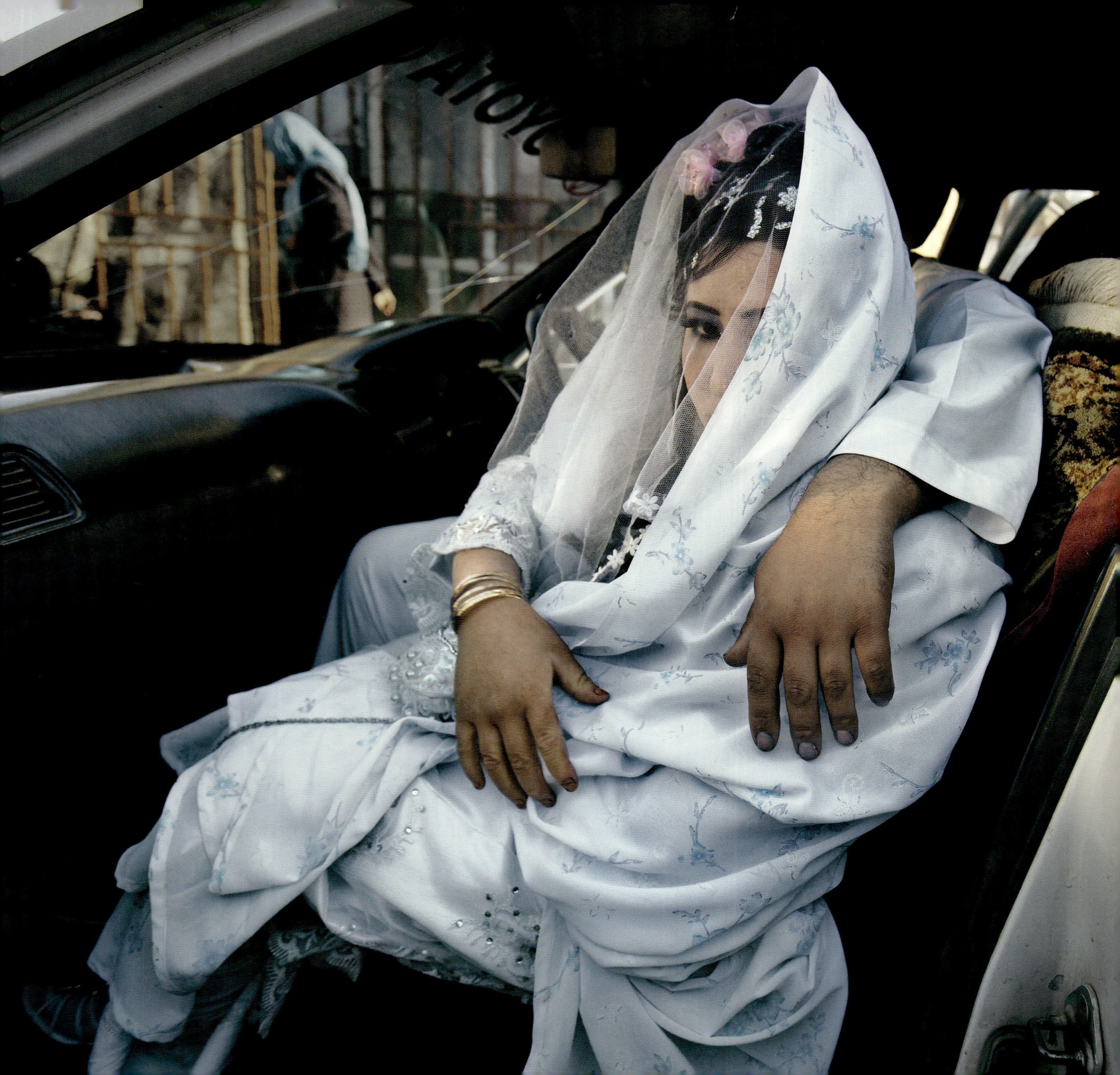

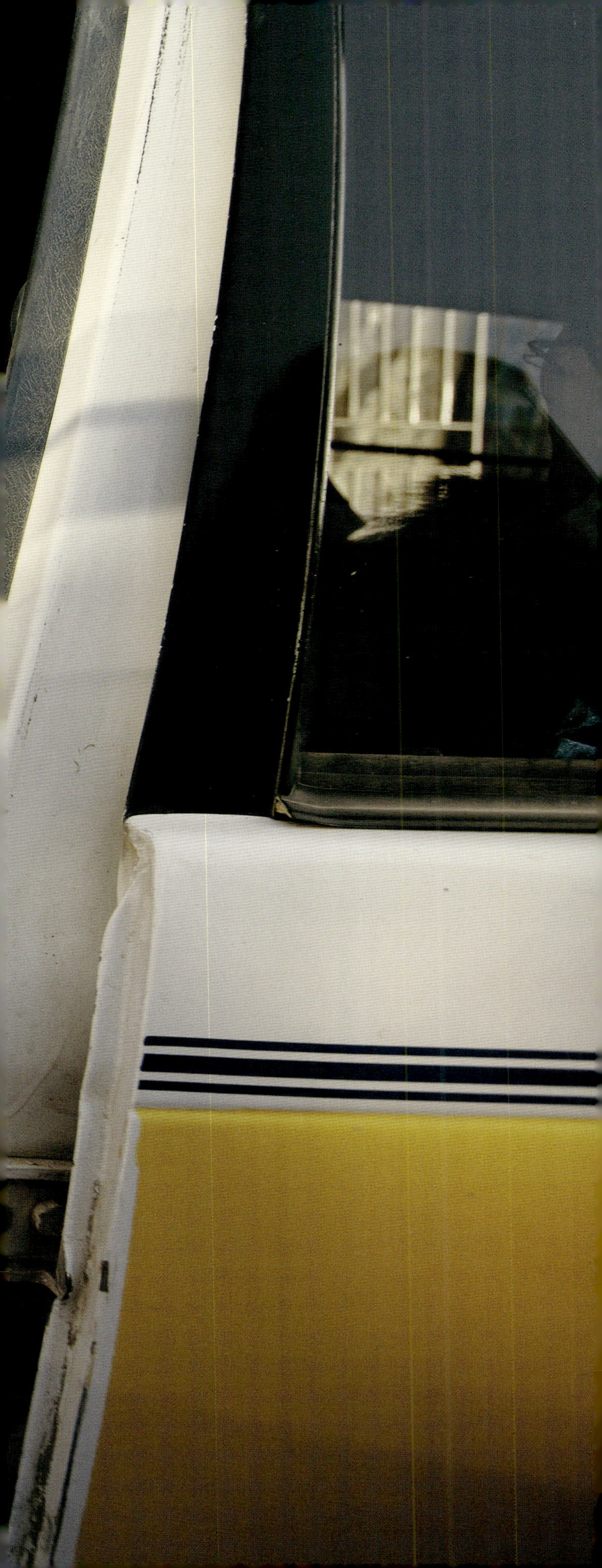

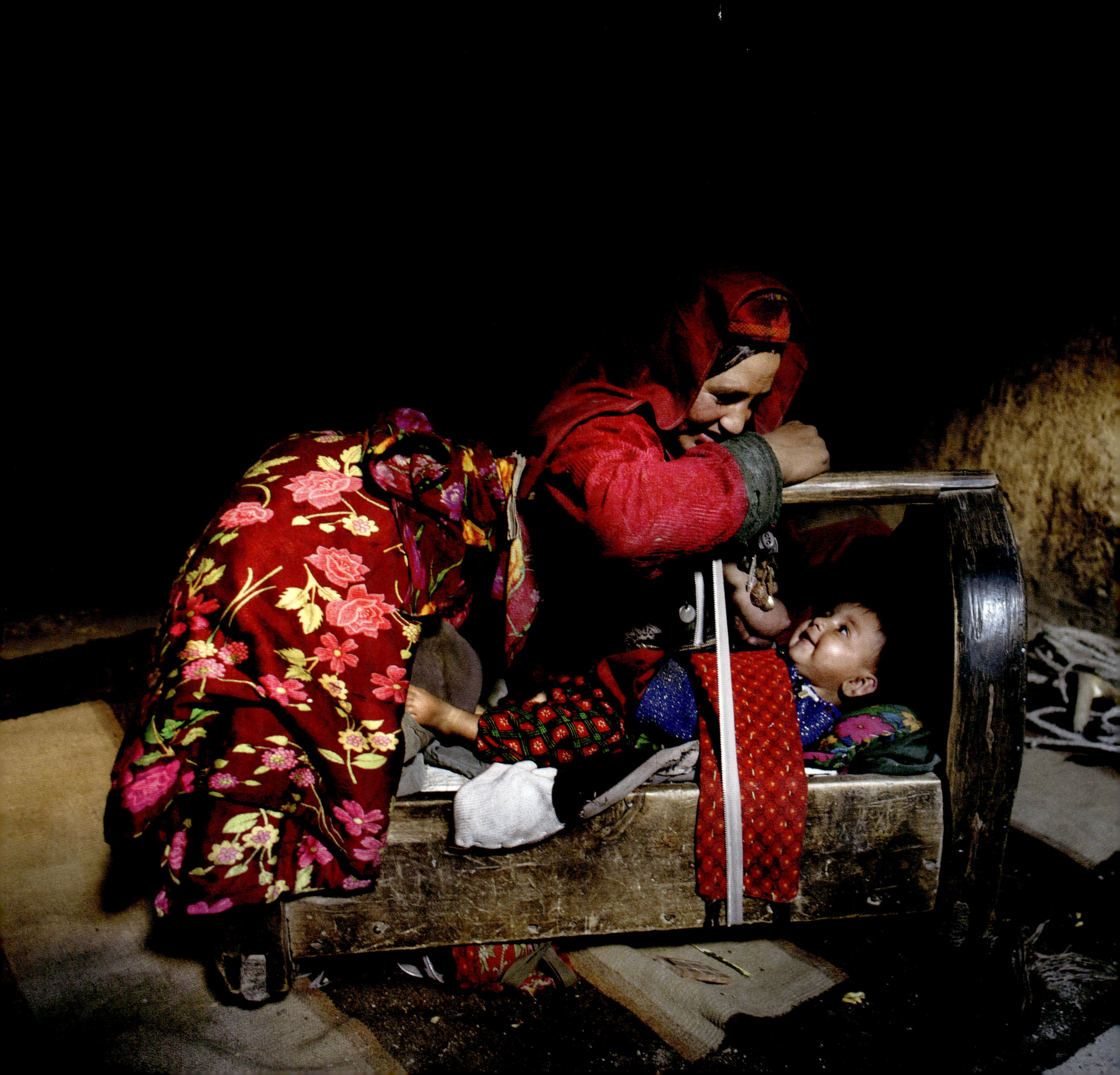

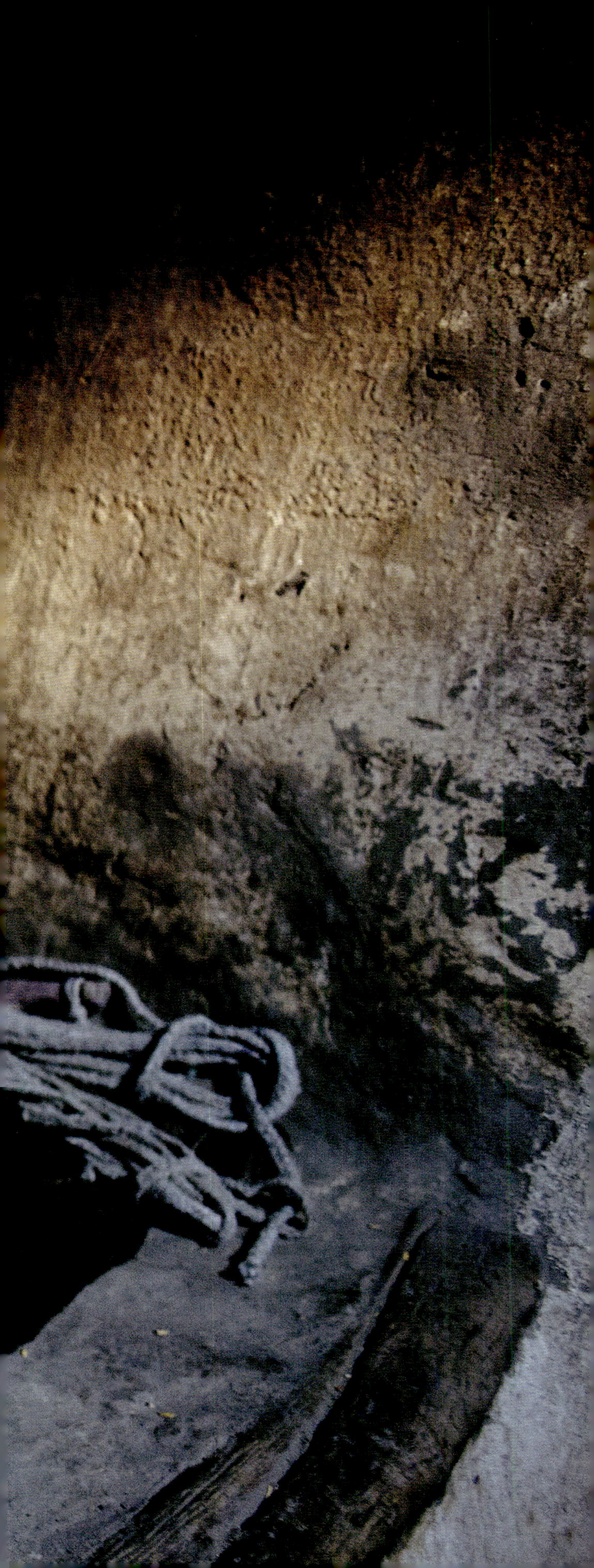

, APRIL 24, 2011.

watches her mother read
the Qur'an after Friday
rs at a local mosque.

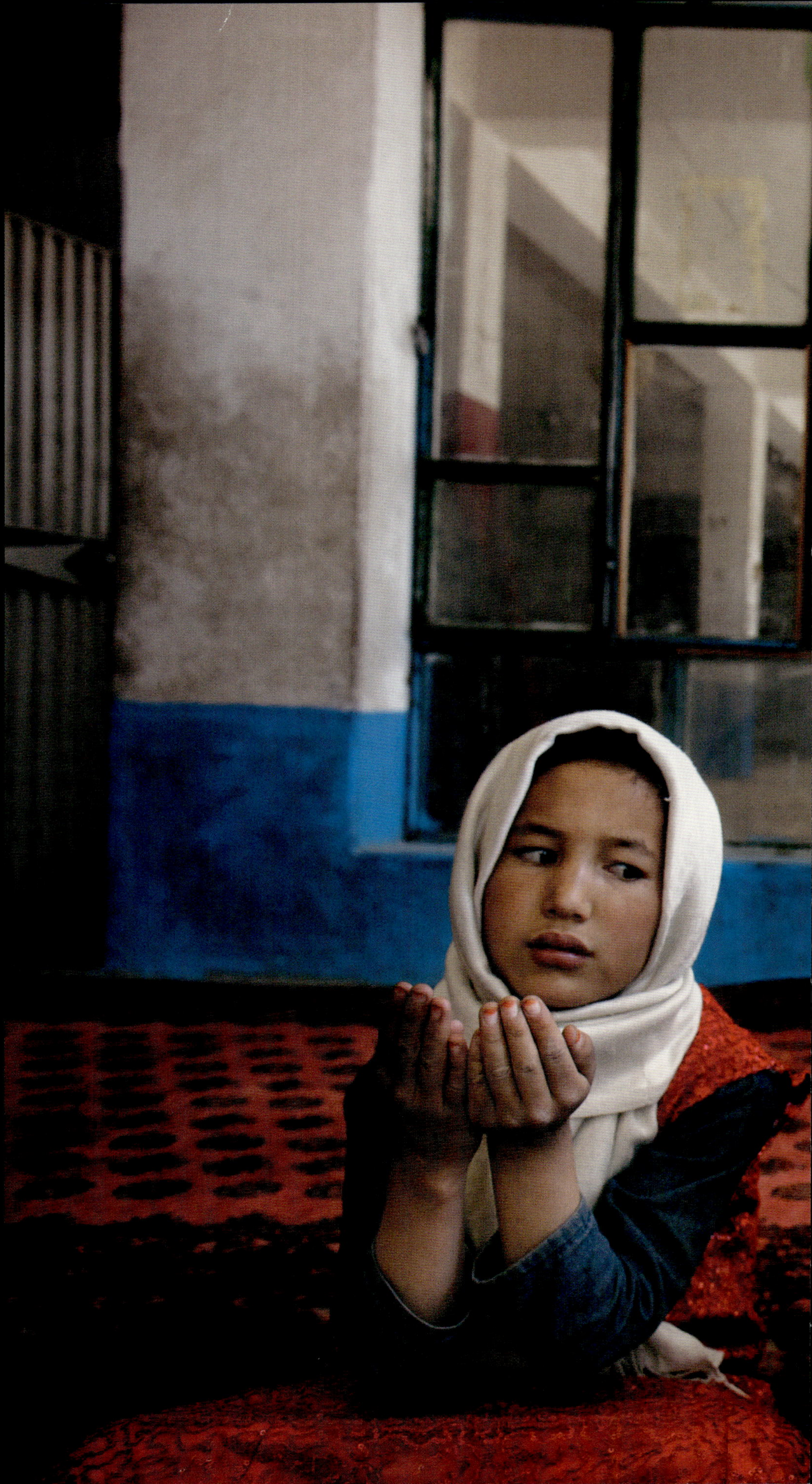

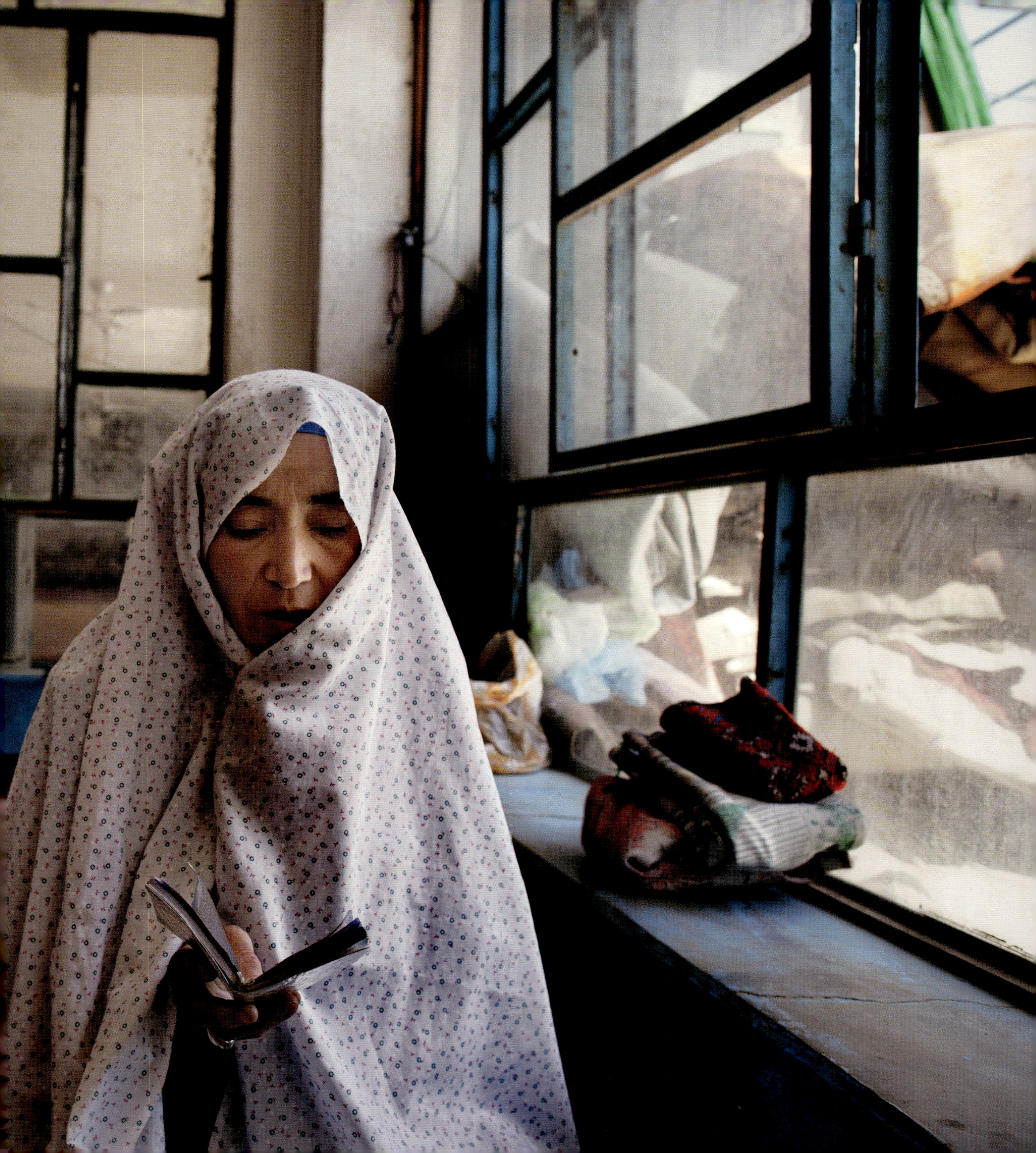

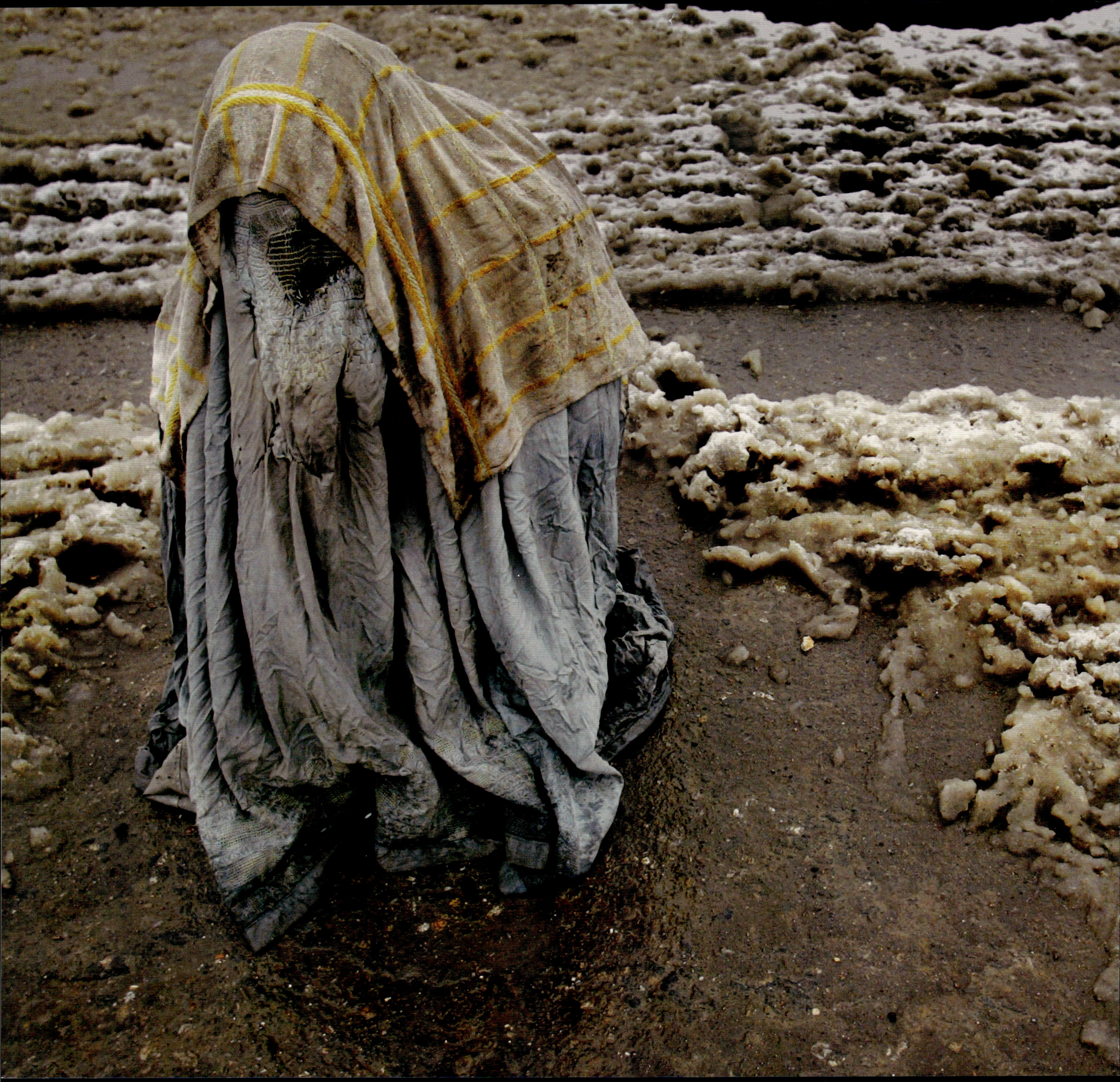

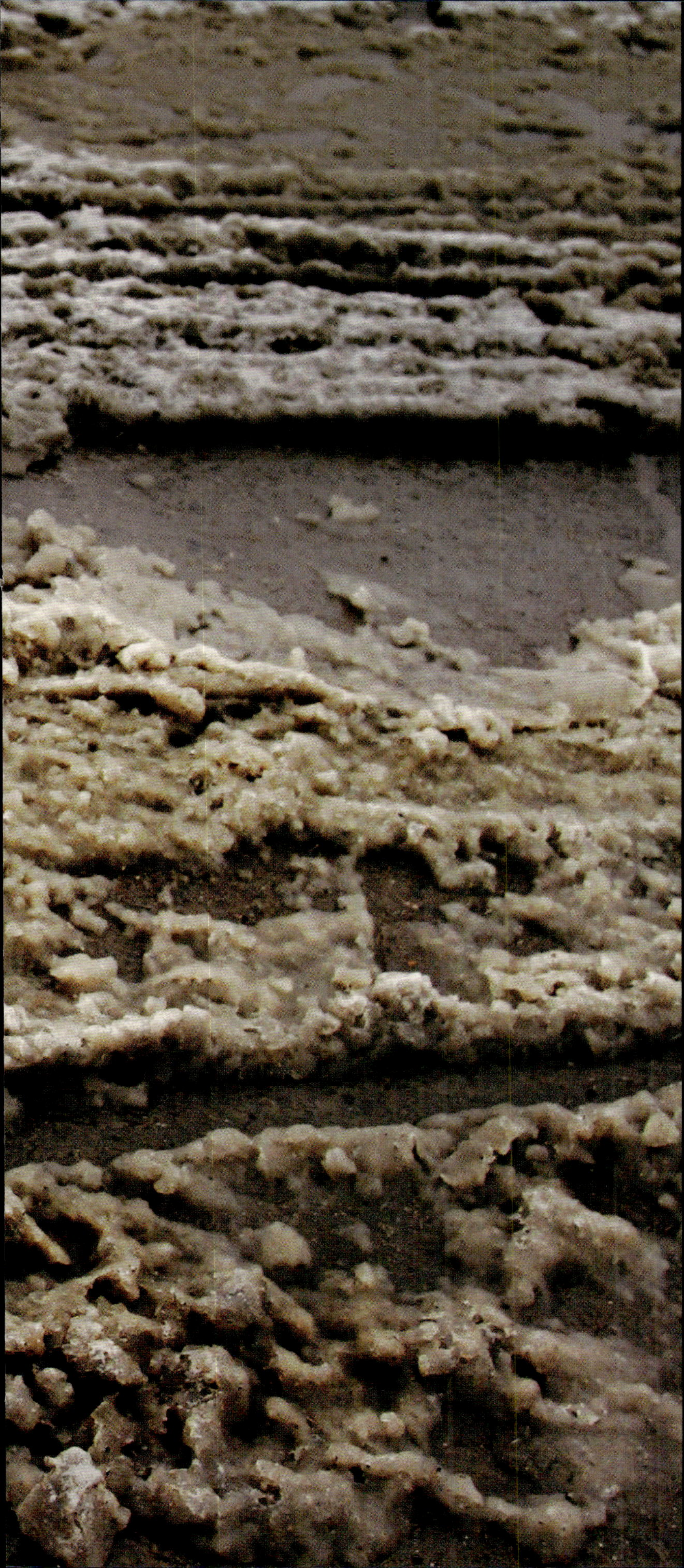

KABUL, FEBRUARY 16, 2003.

A woman covered in a wet, dirty burqa sits on a street begging for money during a snowfall.

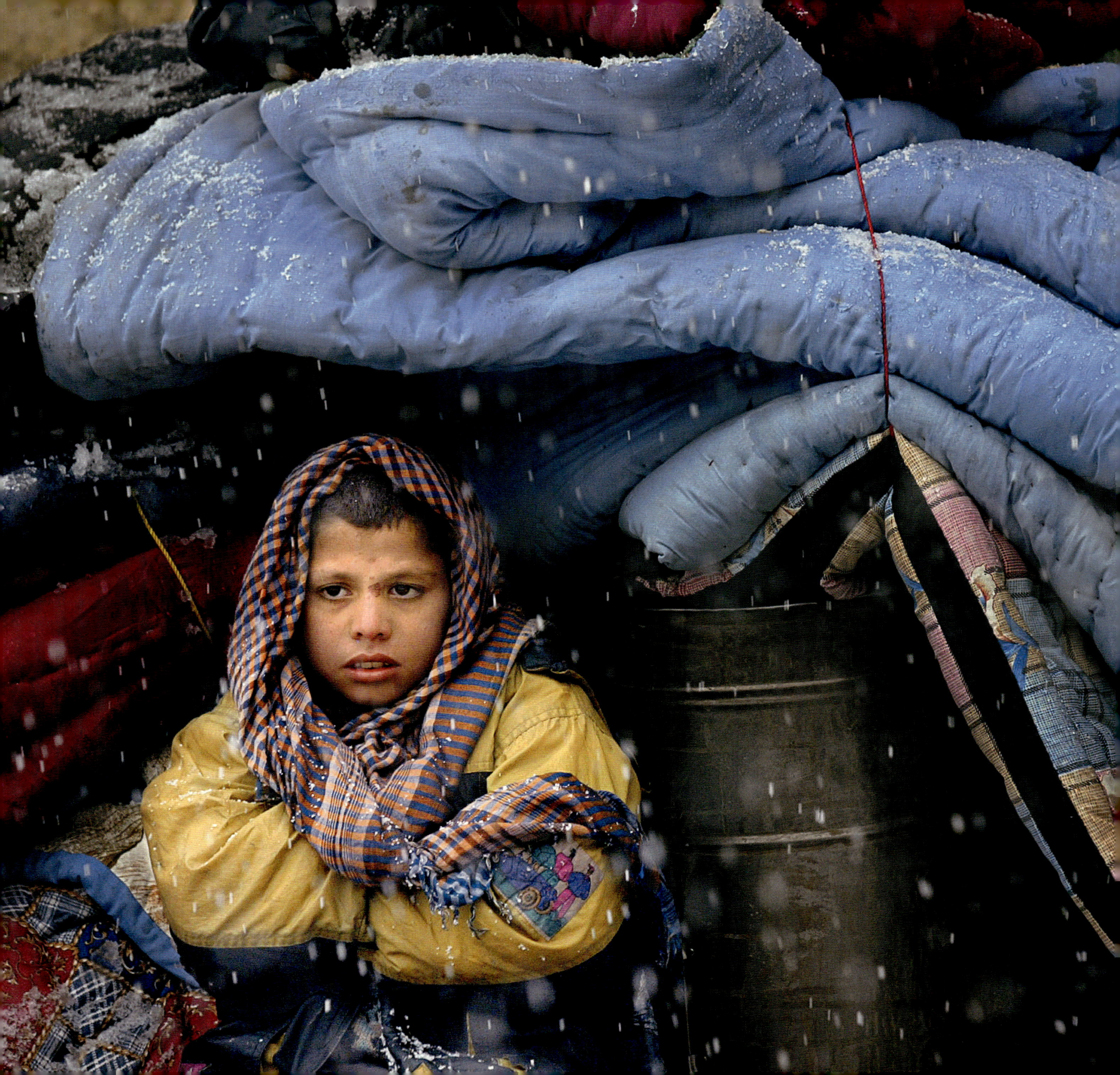

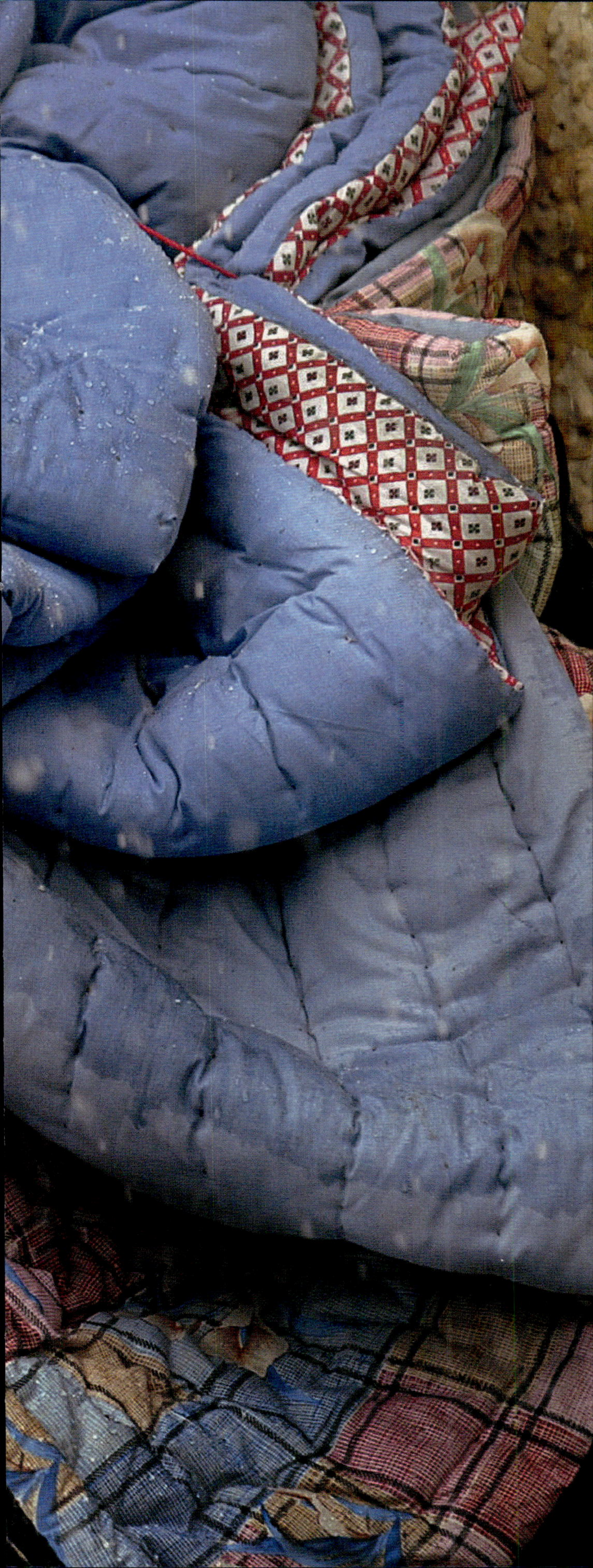

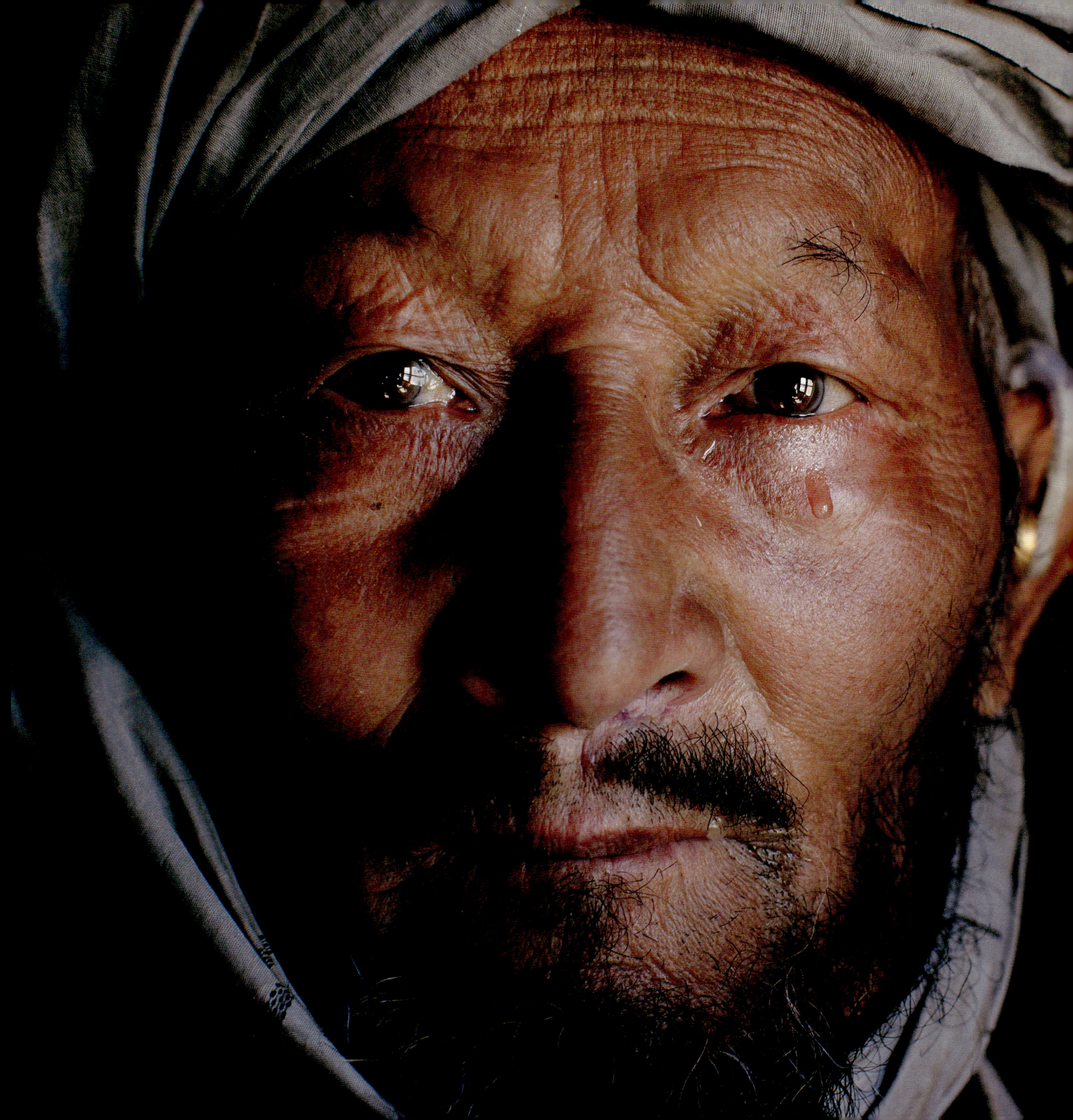

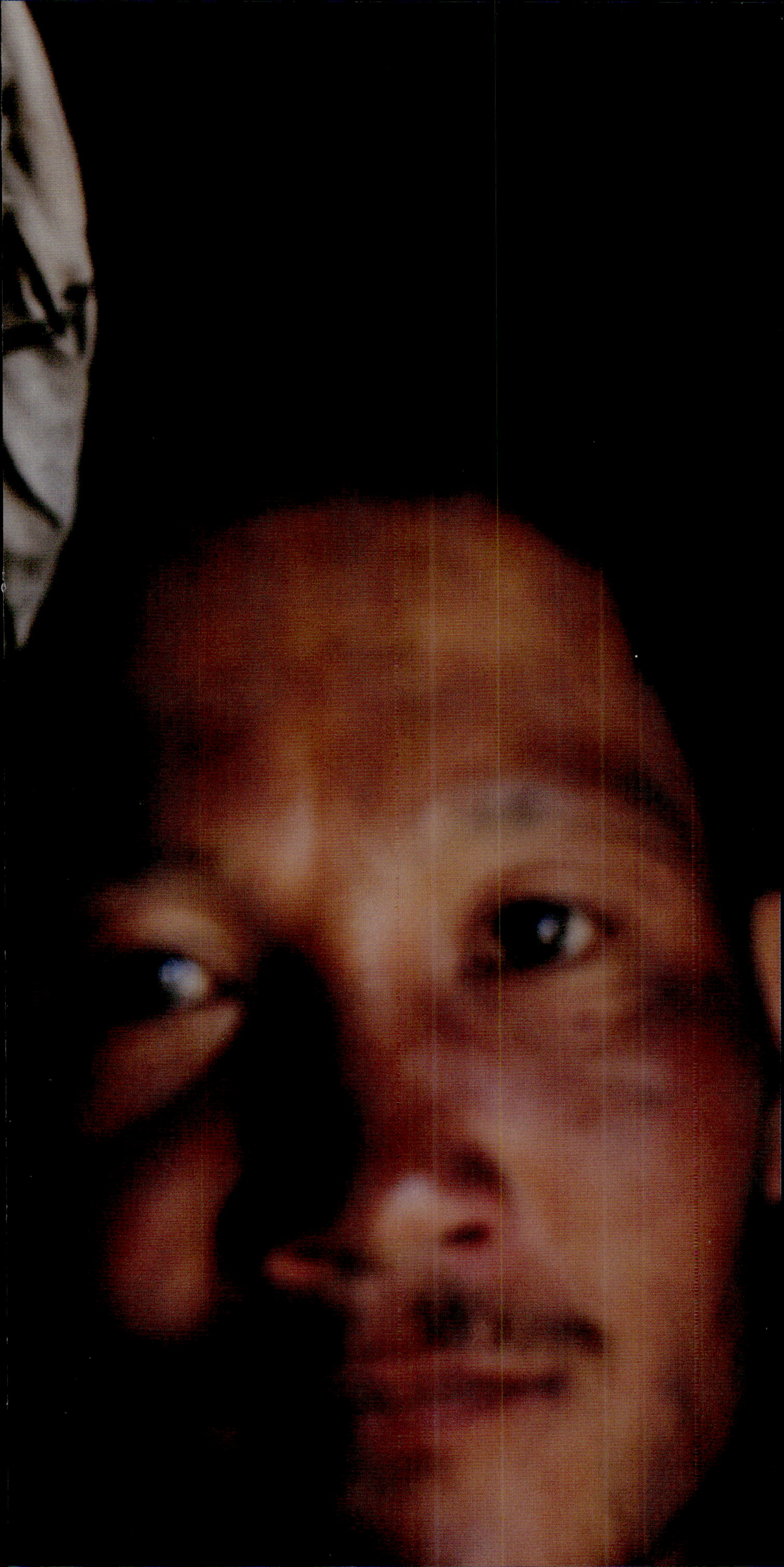

YAKAWLANG, OCTOBER 12, 2010

Seventy-year-old Muhammad Ali stands alongside his son, Yonus, age twenty-five, in a remote village; both are in the early, treatable stages of leprosy. The disease has left Muhammad also suffering from dacryocystitis, an inflammatory condition that causes his eyes to water constantly.

KABUL, AUGUST 27, 2007.

Zaher, fourteen, smokes heroin alongside his heroin-addicted mother, Sabera, and his eleven-year-old sister, Gulparai, in their home. The children began using the drug after watching their widowed mother, an addict for four years.

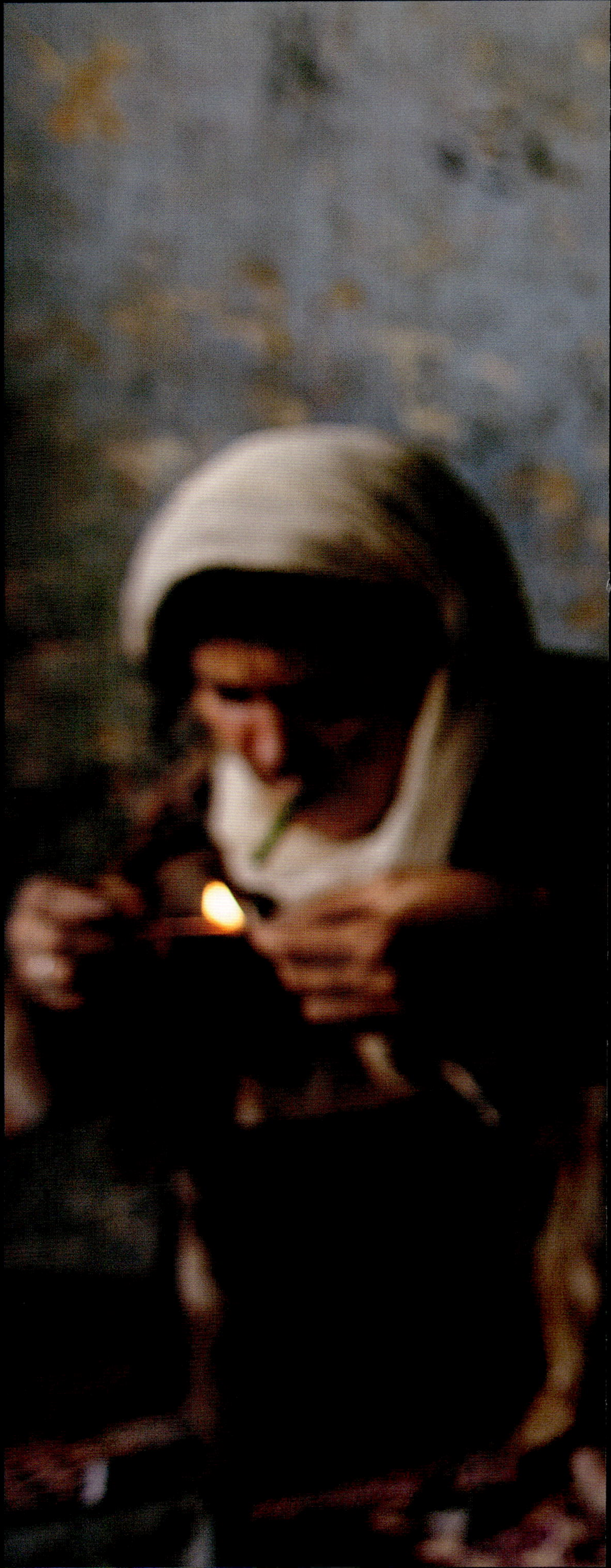

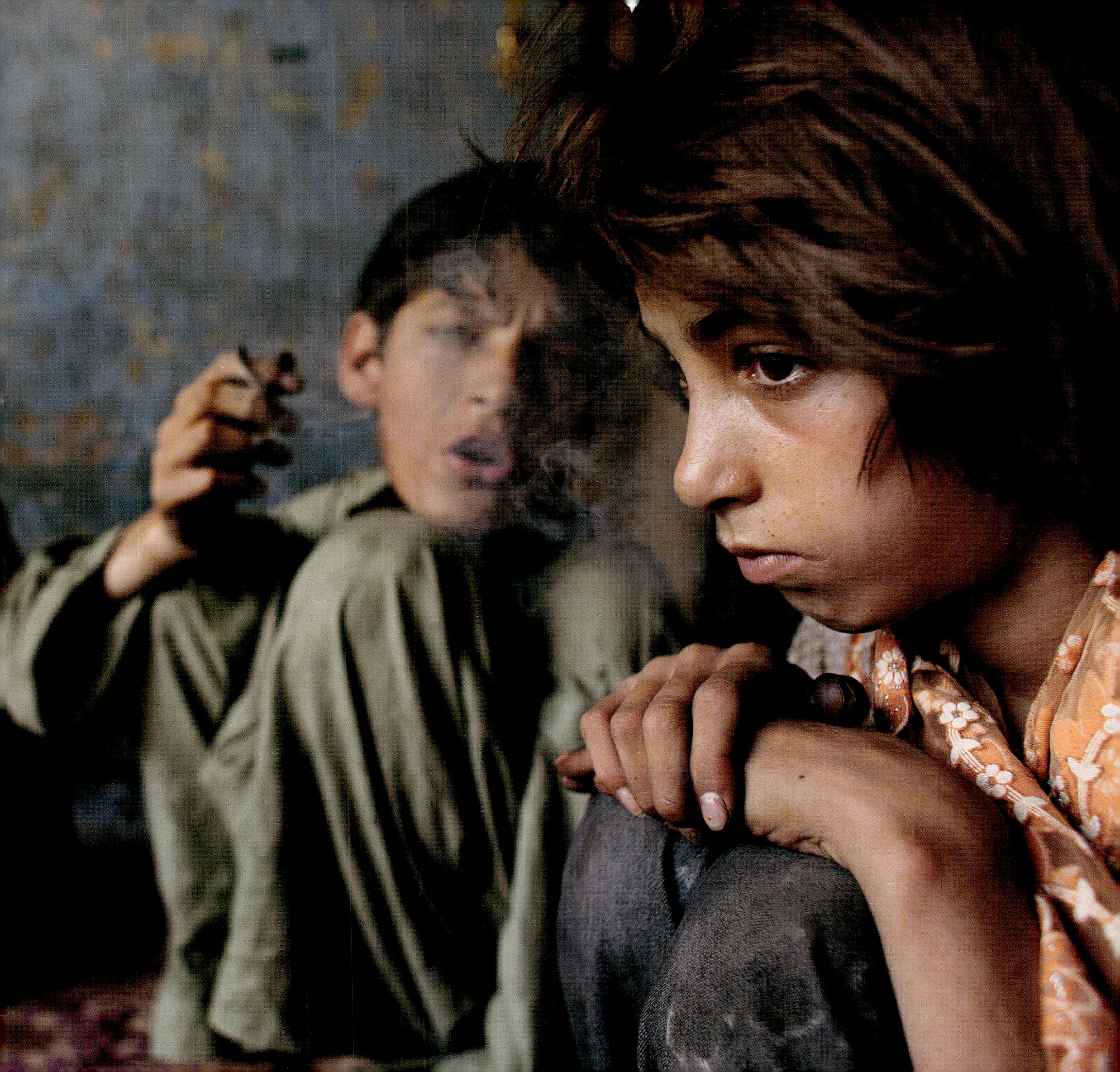

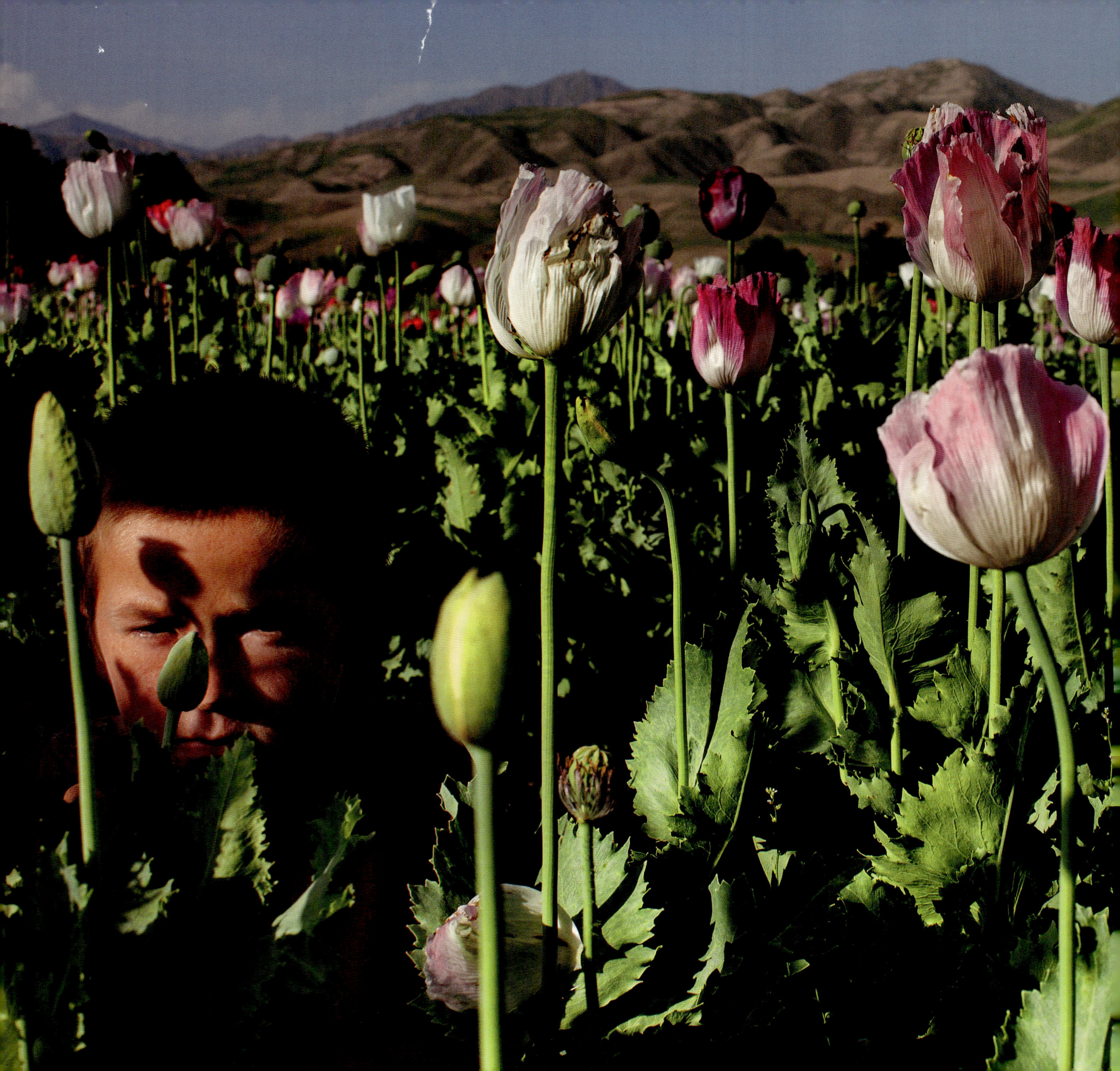

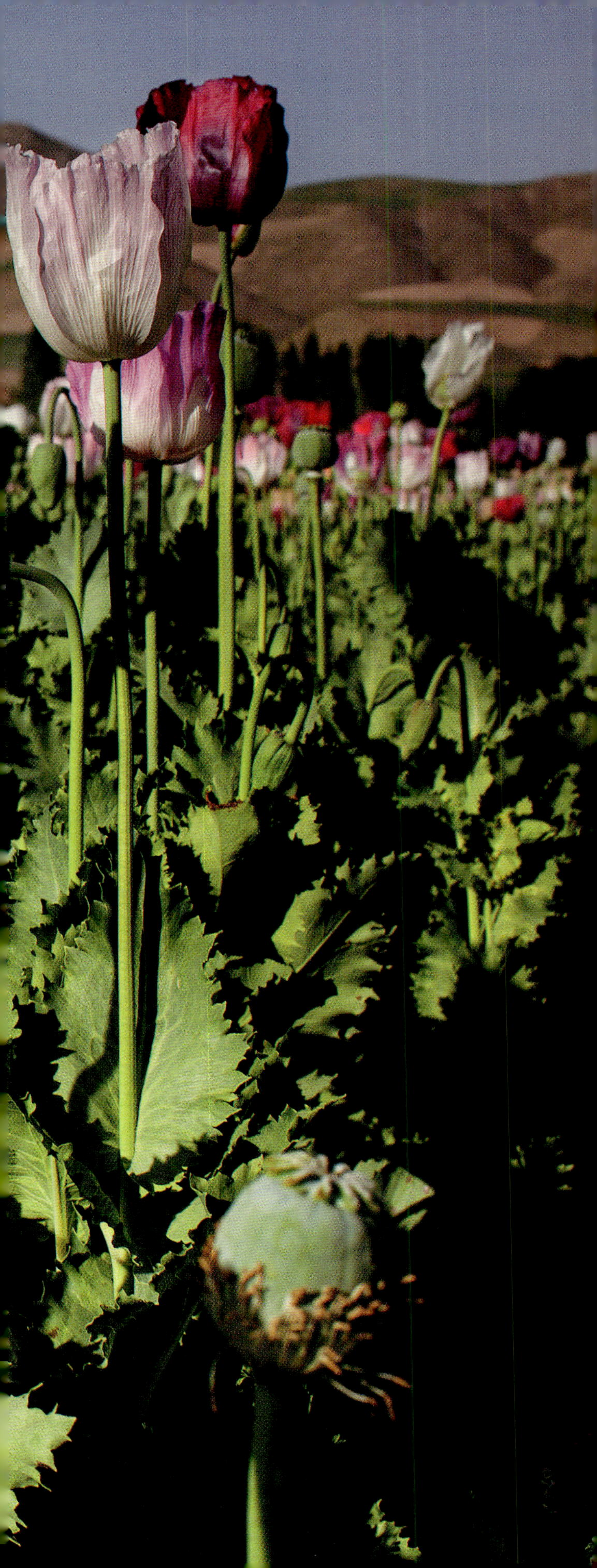

KABUL, MAY 23, 2005.

Naseem, a heroin addict, stares into space after getting high in an old bullet-riddled container popular with addicts in Kabul. Naseem claimed that he has smoked four times a day for the previous twenty years.

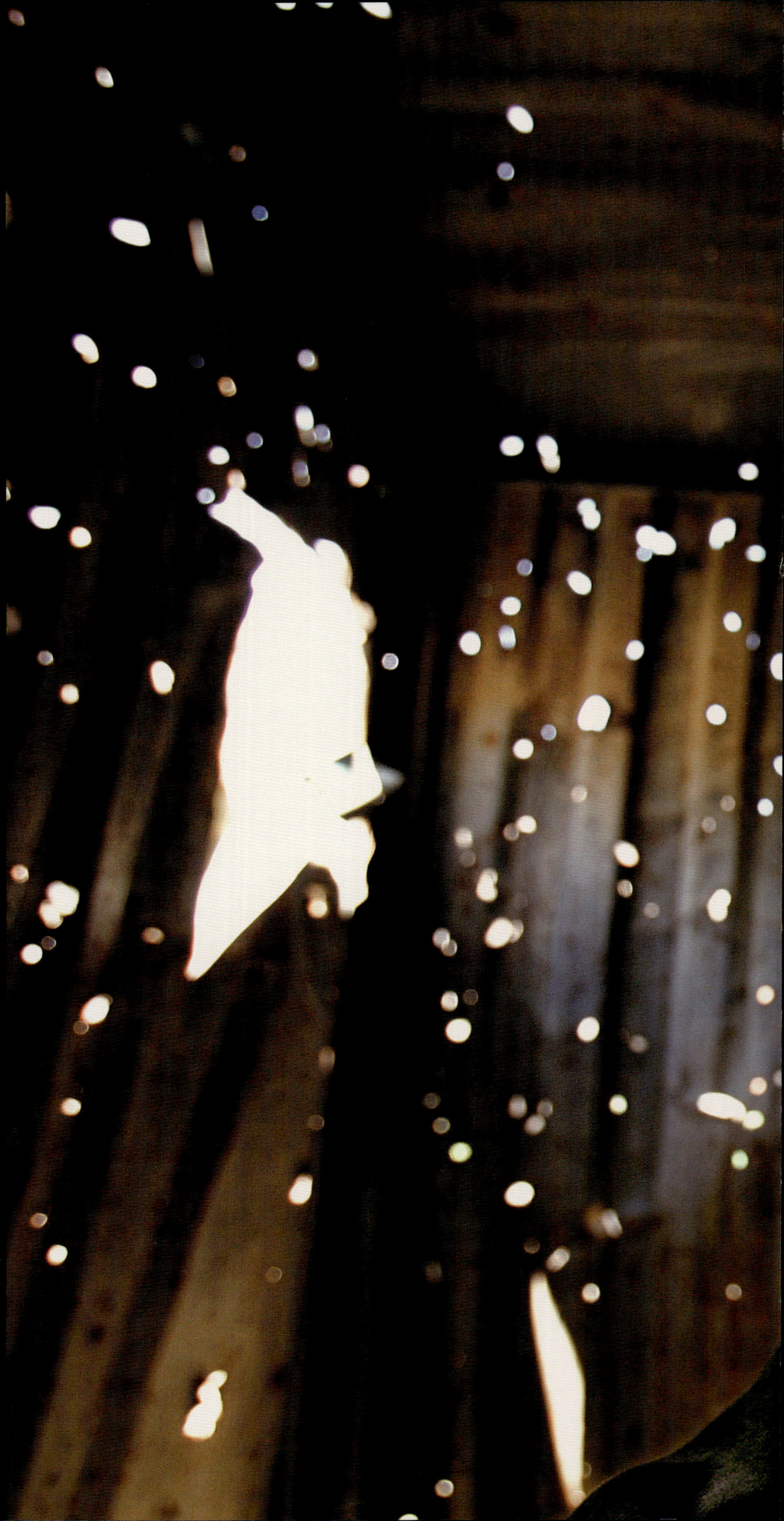

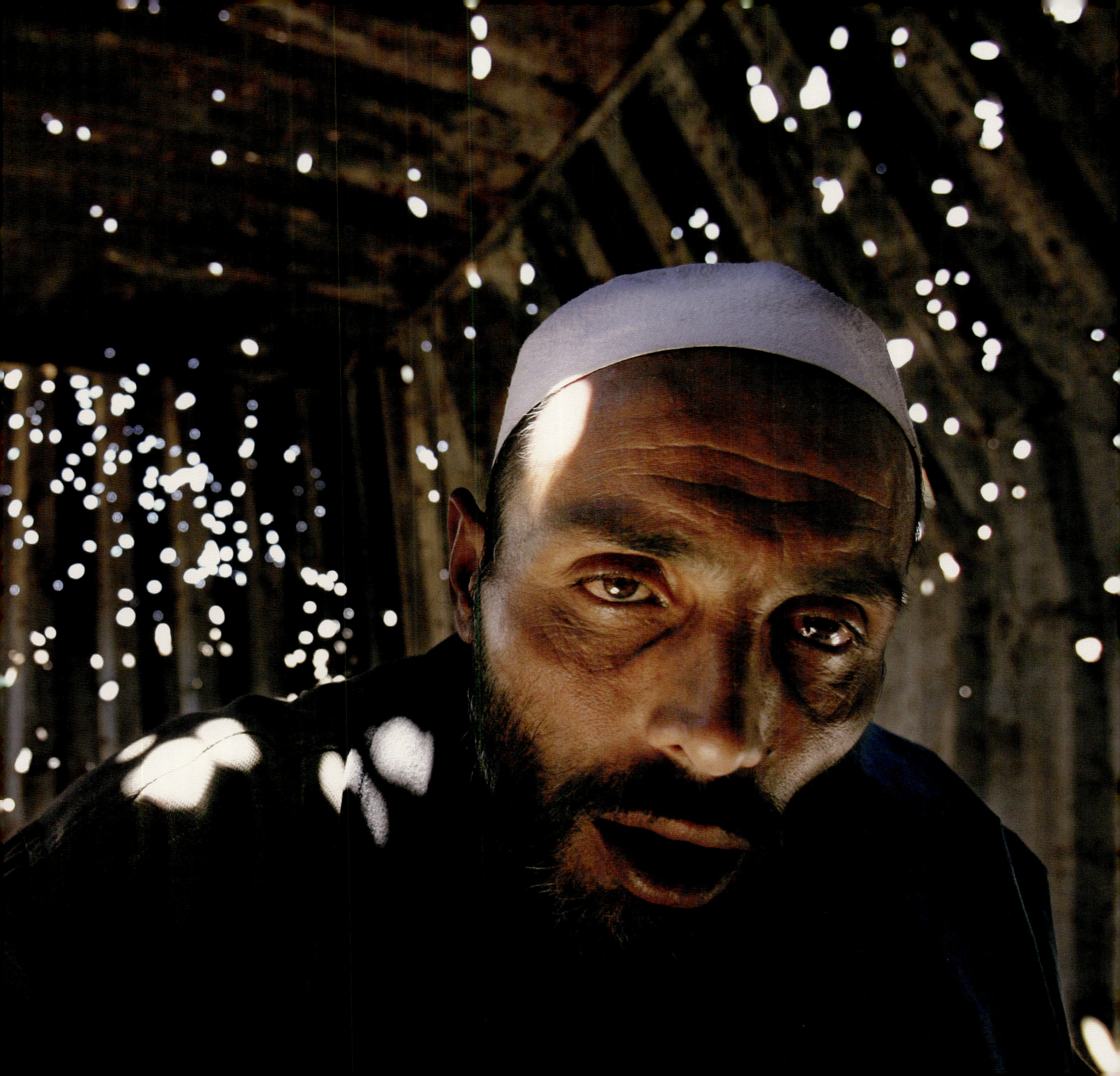

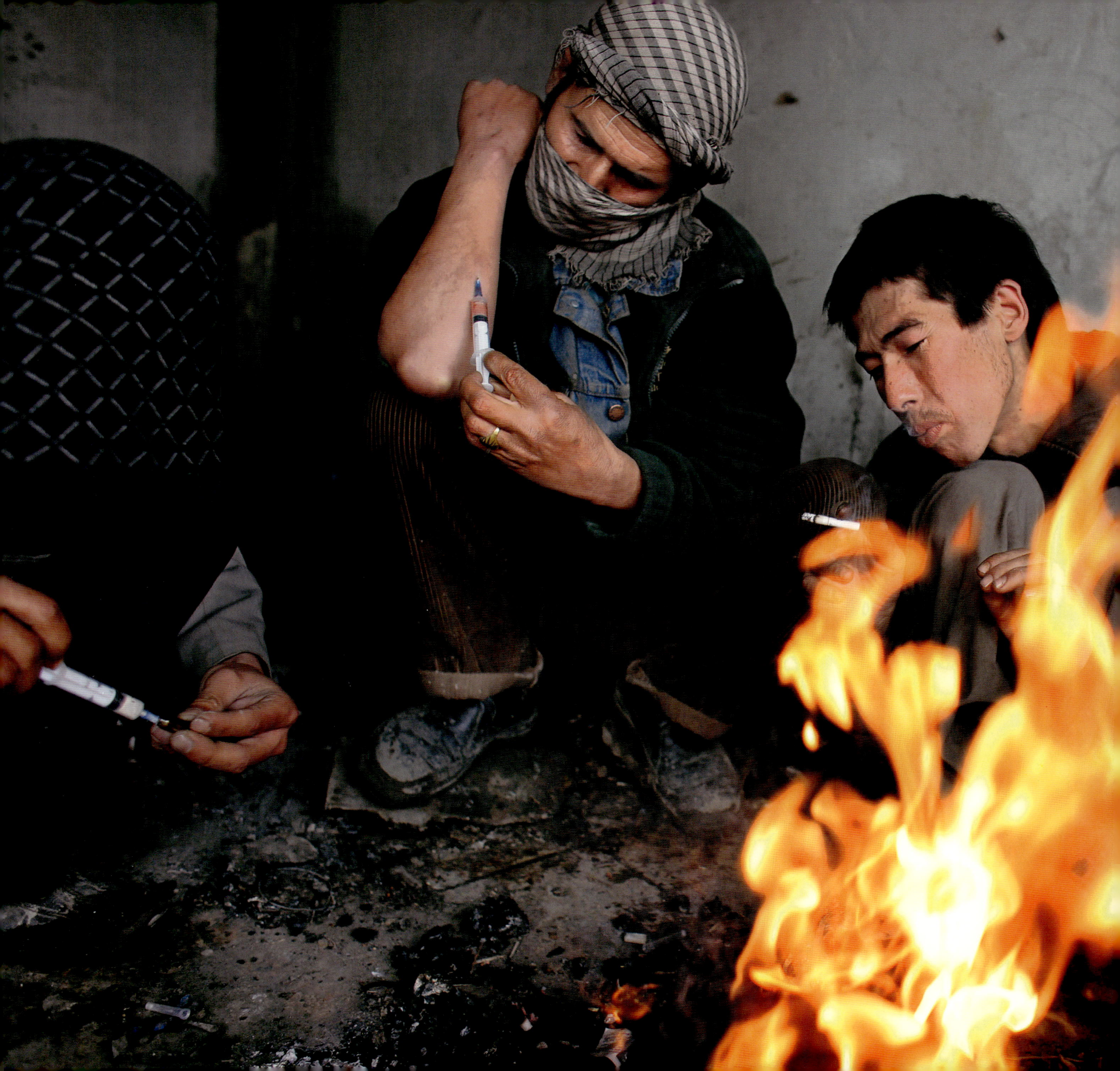

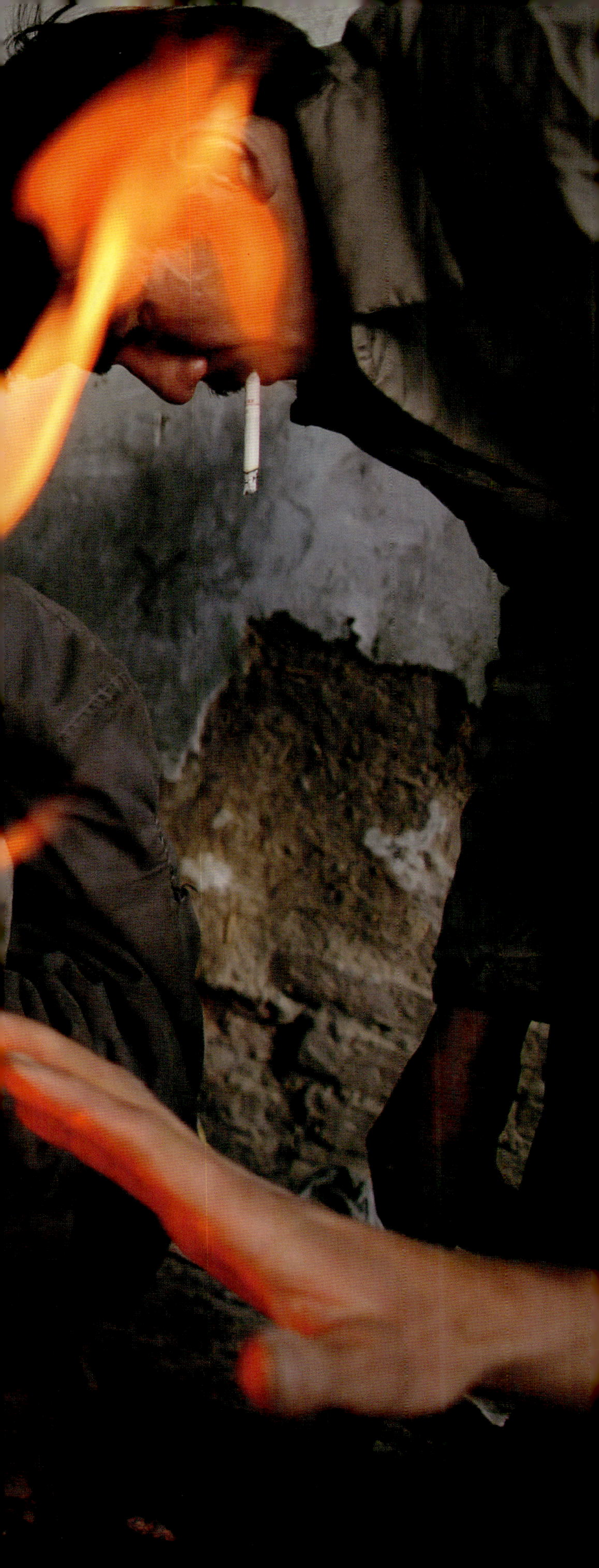

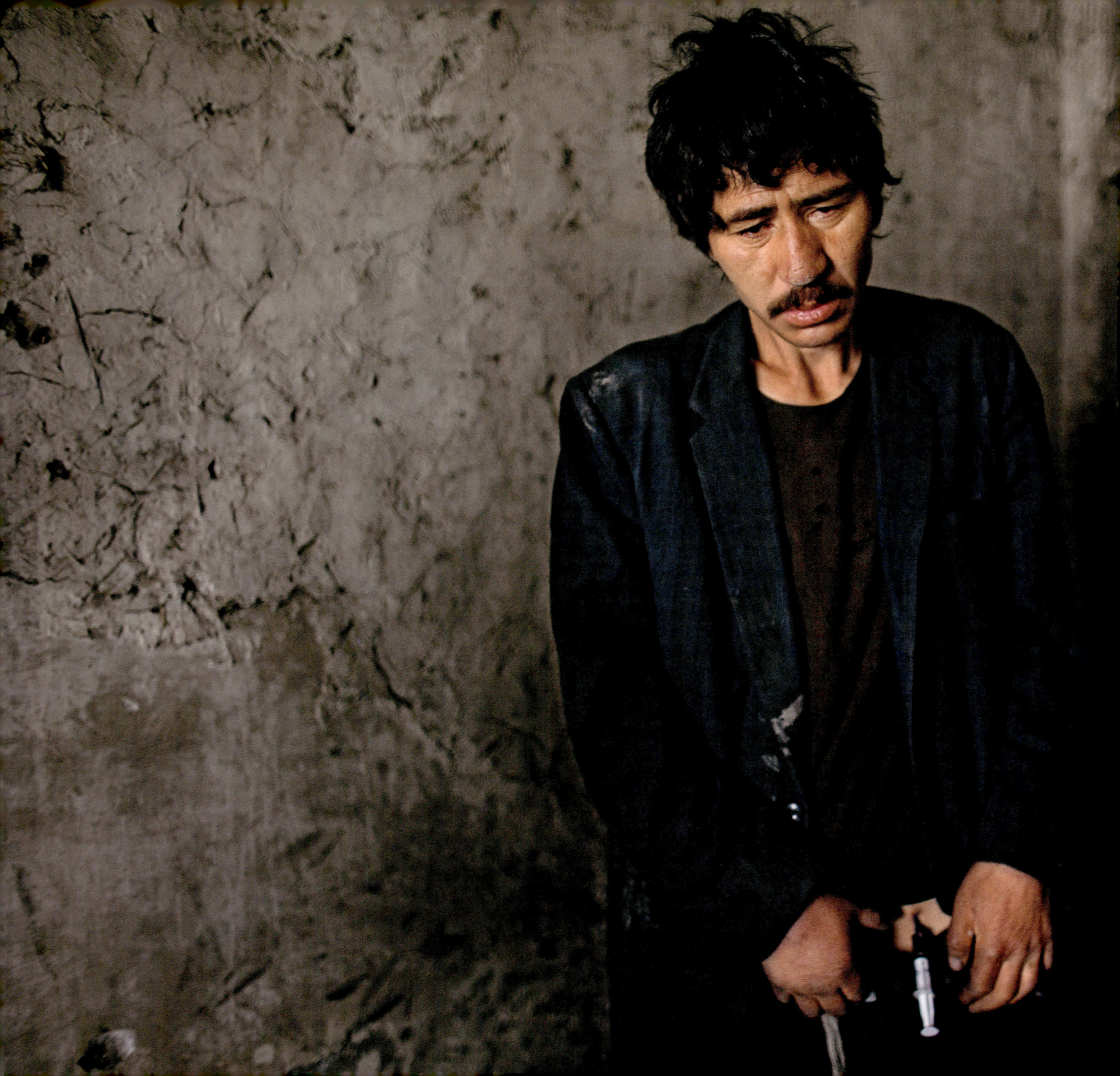

KABUL, FEBRUARY 10, 2009.

A heroin addict injects the drug into his thigh inside the abandoned Russian Cultural Center.

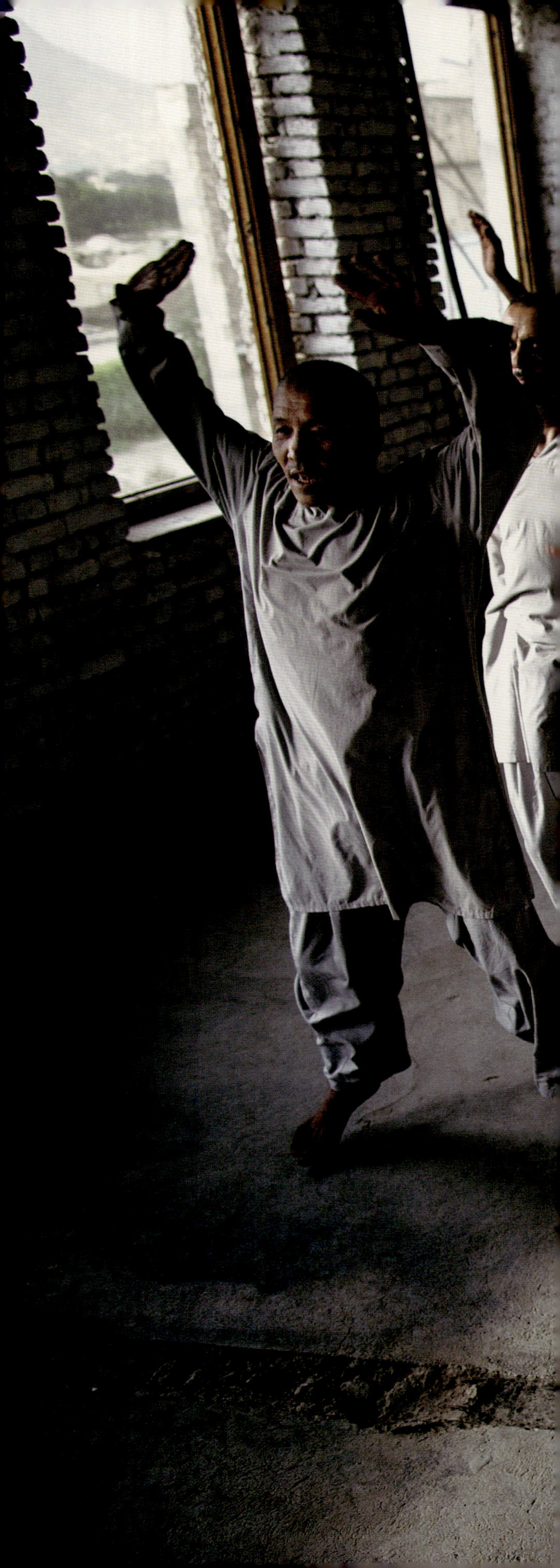

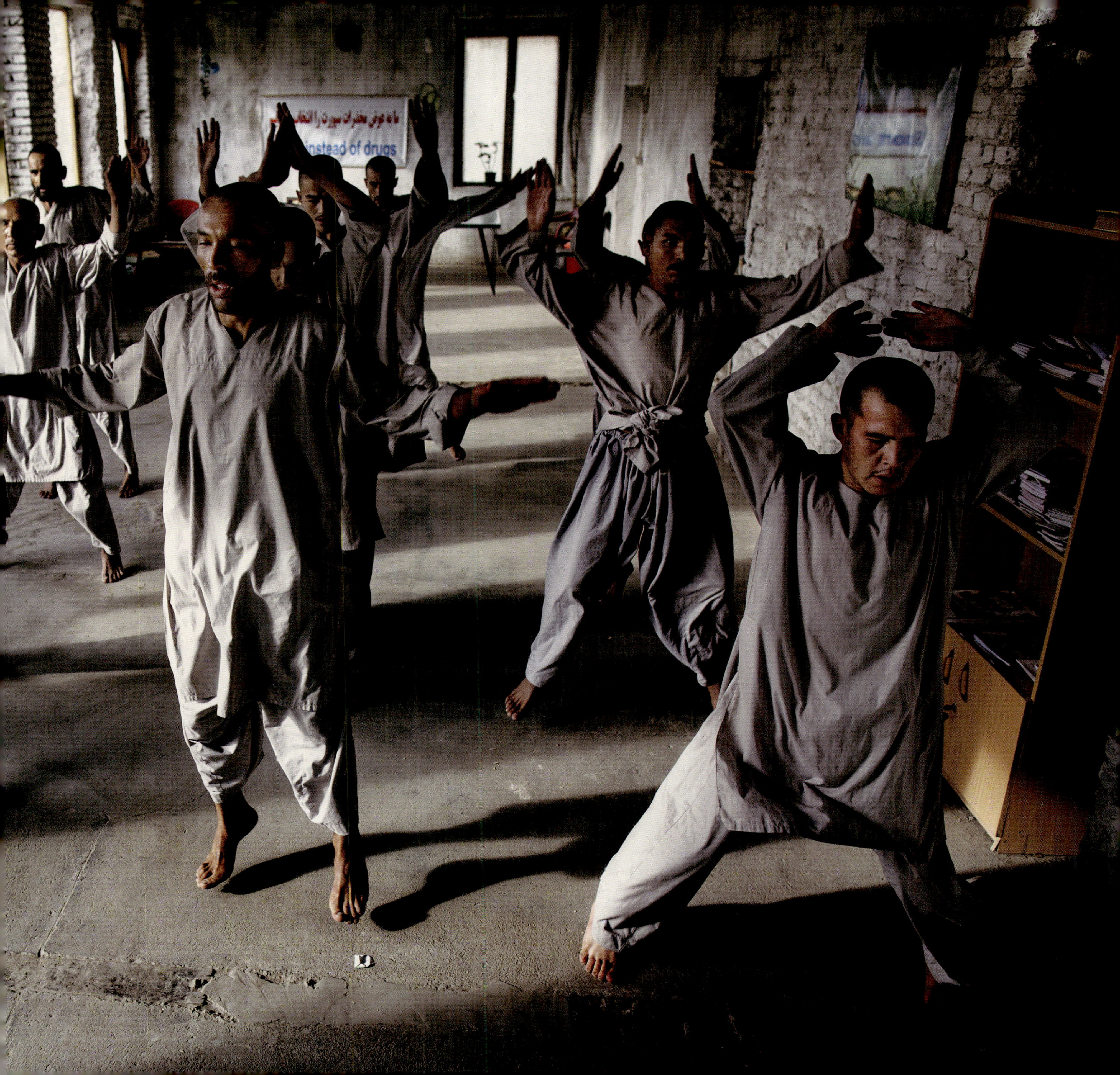
instead of drugs

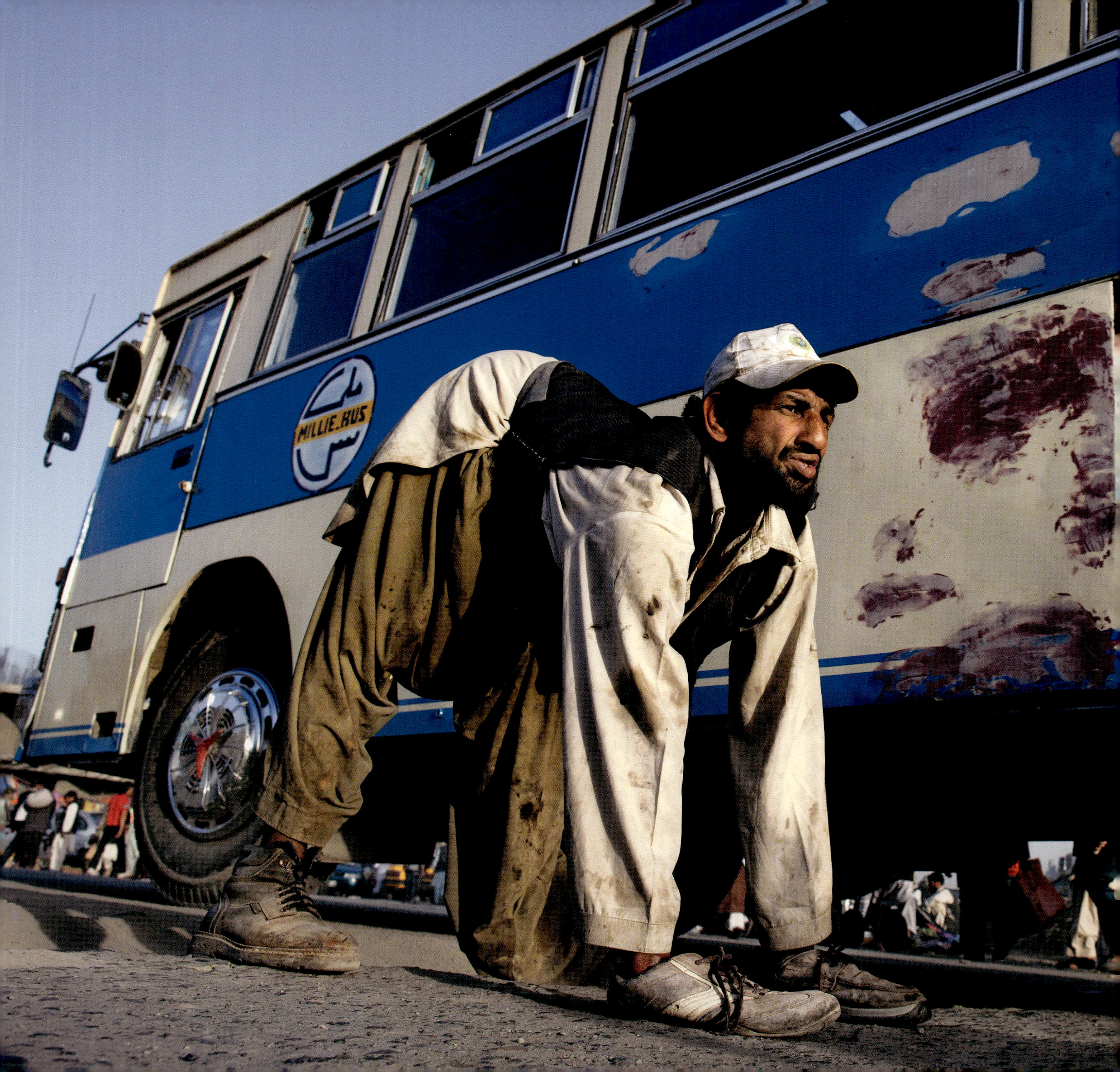
MILLIE BUS

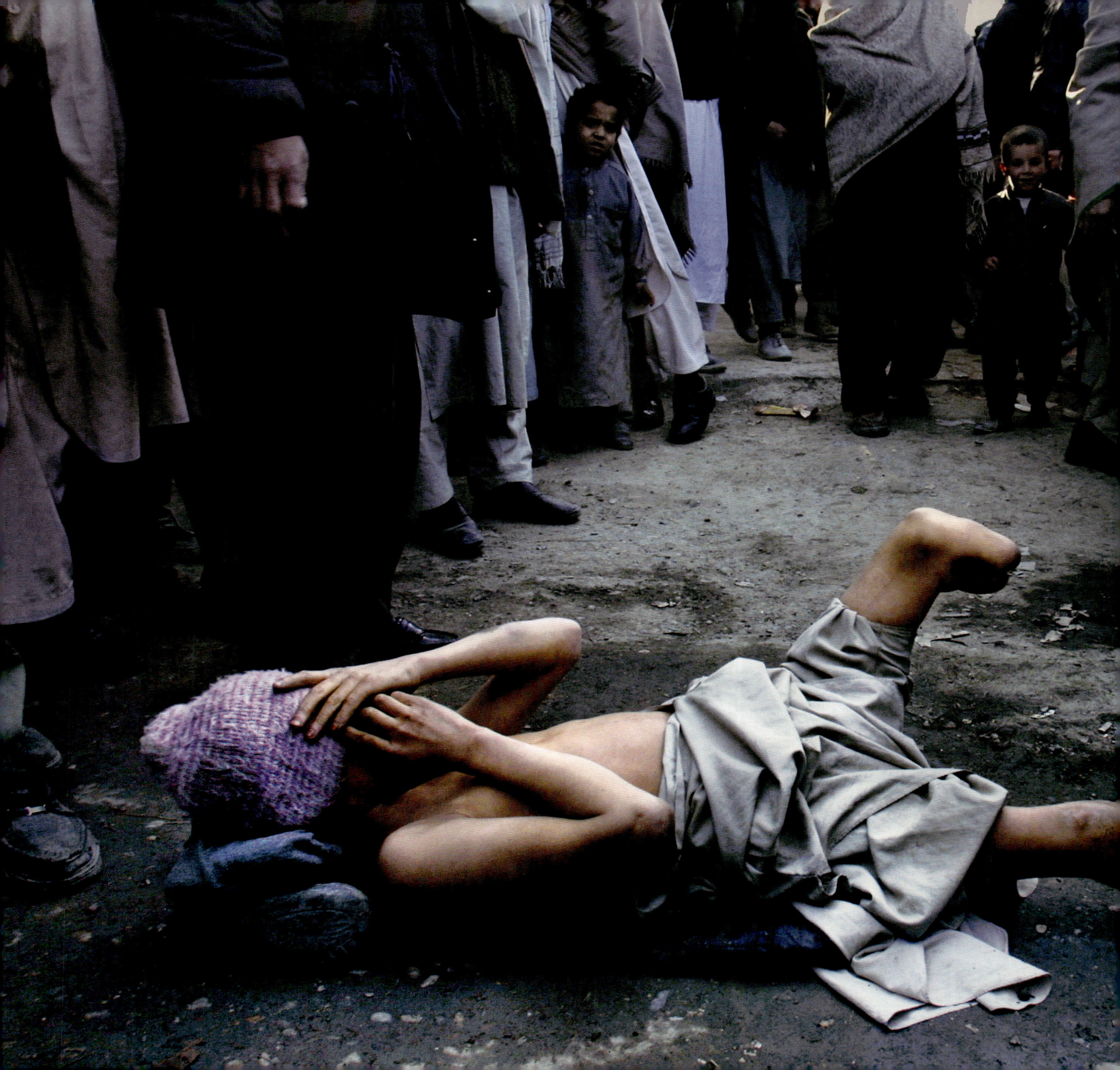

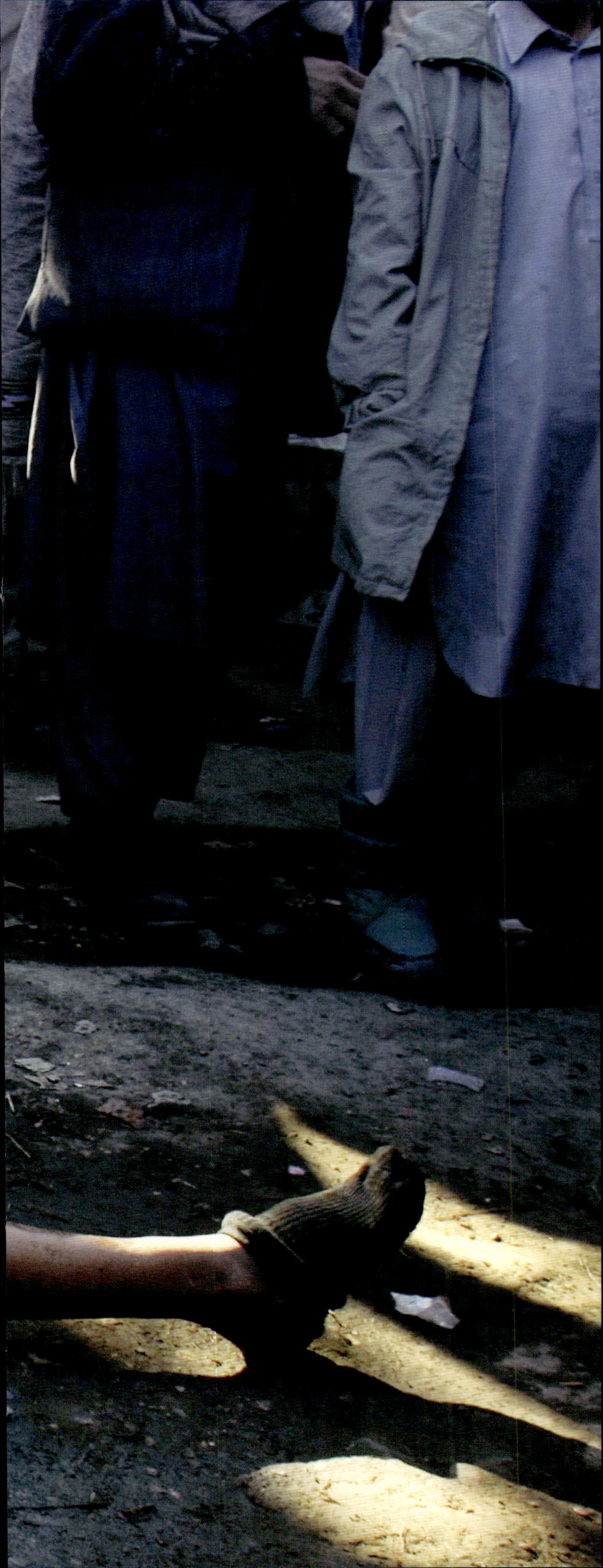

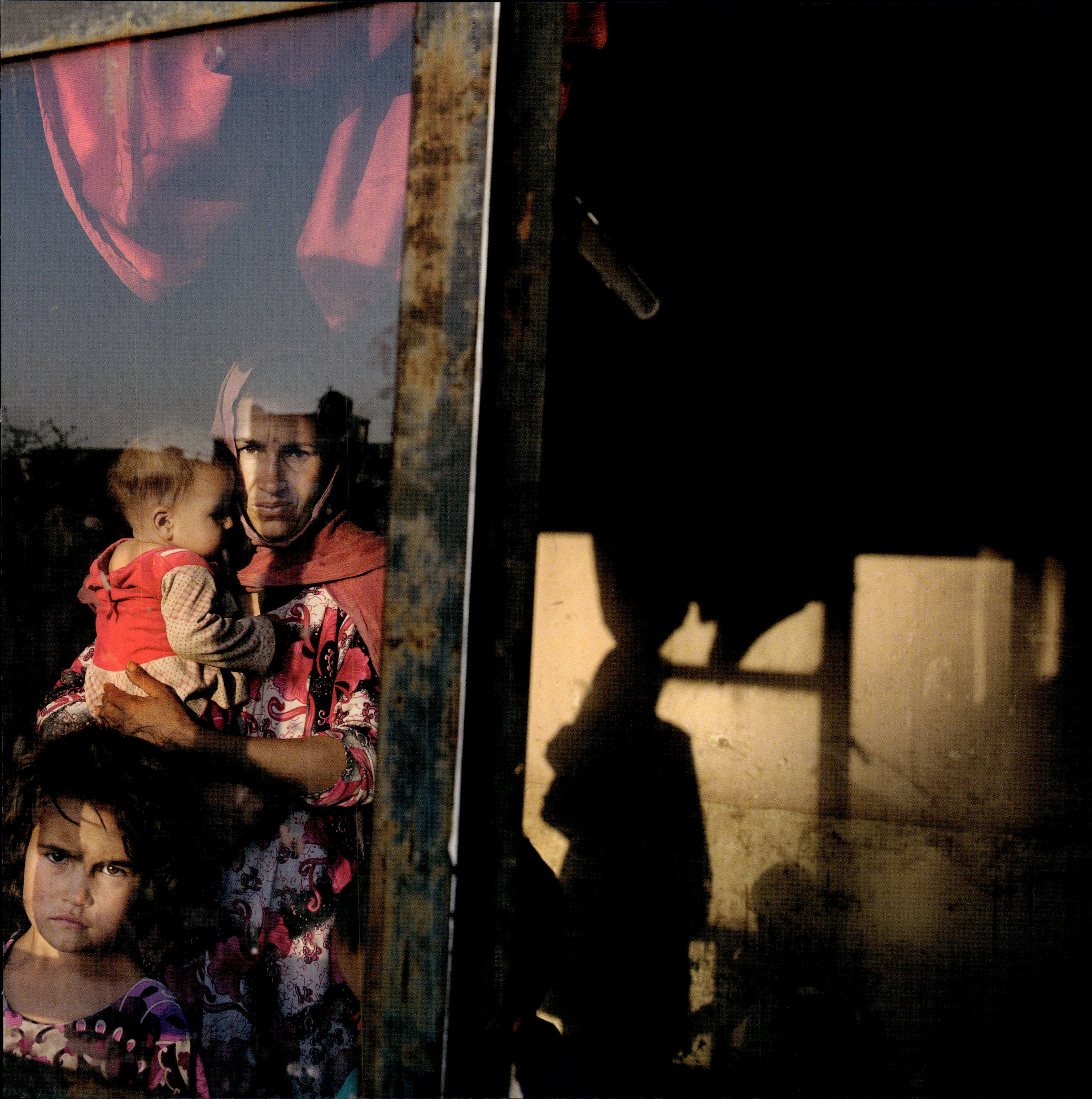

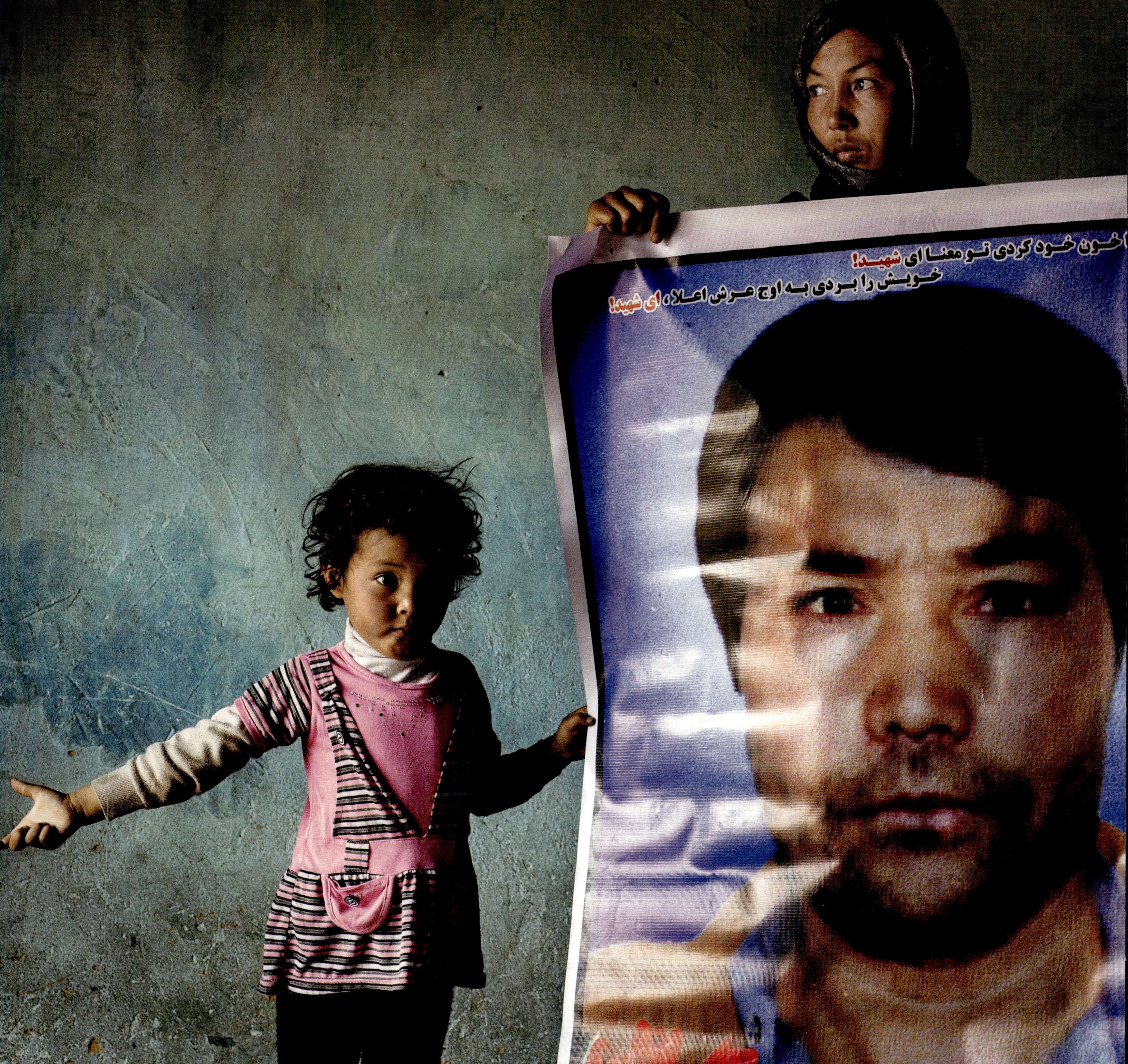
خون خود کردی تو معنا ای شهید!
خویش را بردی به اوج عرش اعلا، ای شهید!

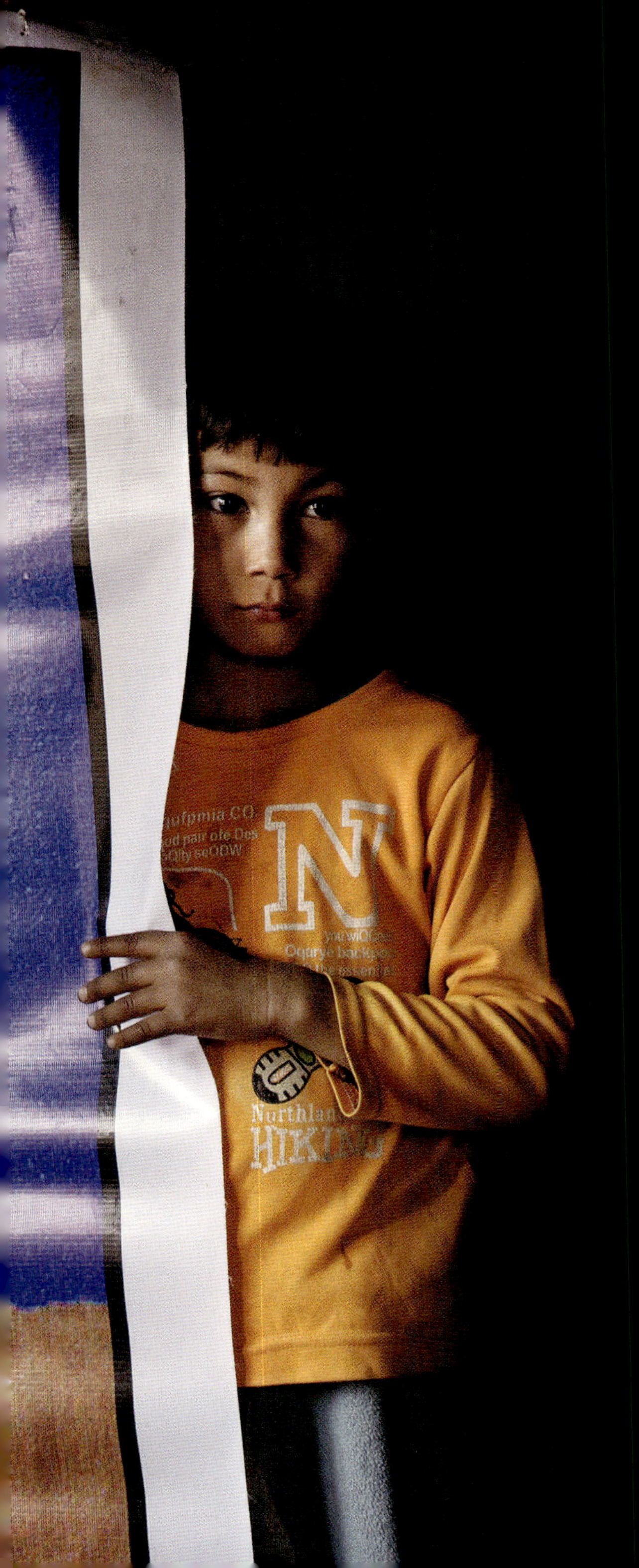

KABUL, MARCH 30, 2015.

Jamila, age thirty-three, stands with her two children, seven-year-old Salad and four-year-old Bahara. Her husband, Muhammad Hussain, who died six months ago, is shown on his martyr poster. He was killed in an attack just eighteen days after joining the national police force in Helmand.

CHAGCHARAN, OCTOBER 21, 2002.

Women in Chagcharan, in the mountainous Ghor Province, carry water from a river; their homes lack any other water supply. Many women in this area cover their heads but traditionally do not wear burqas.

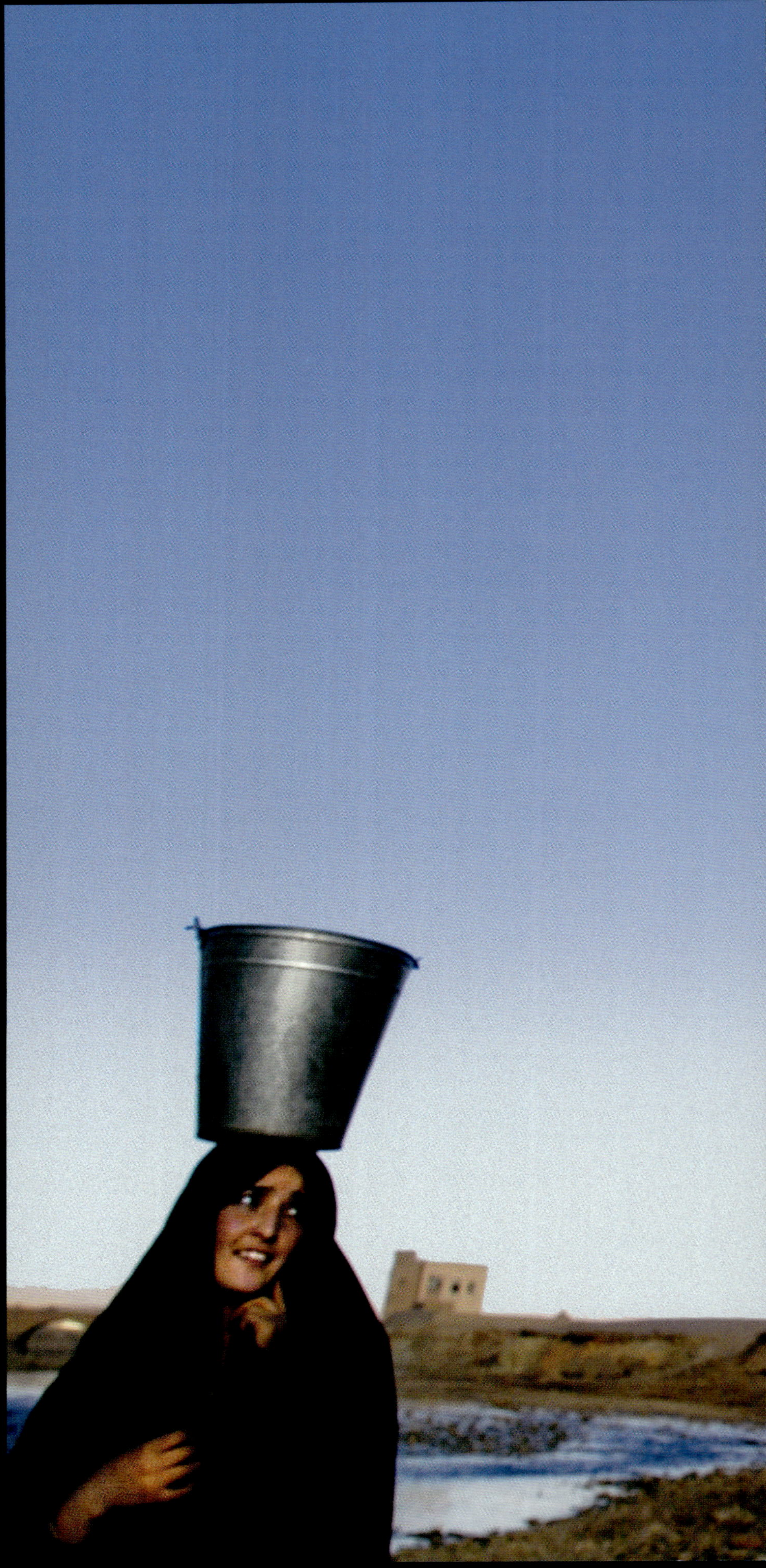

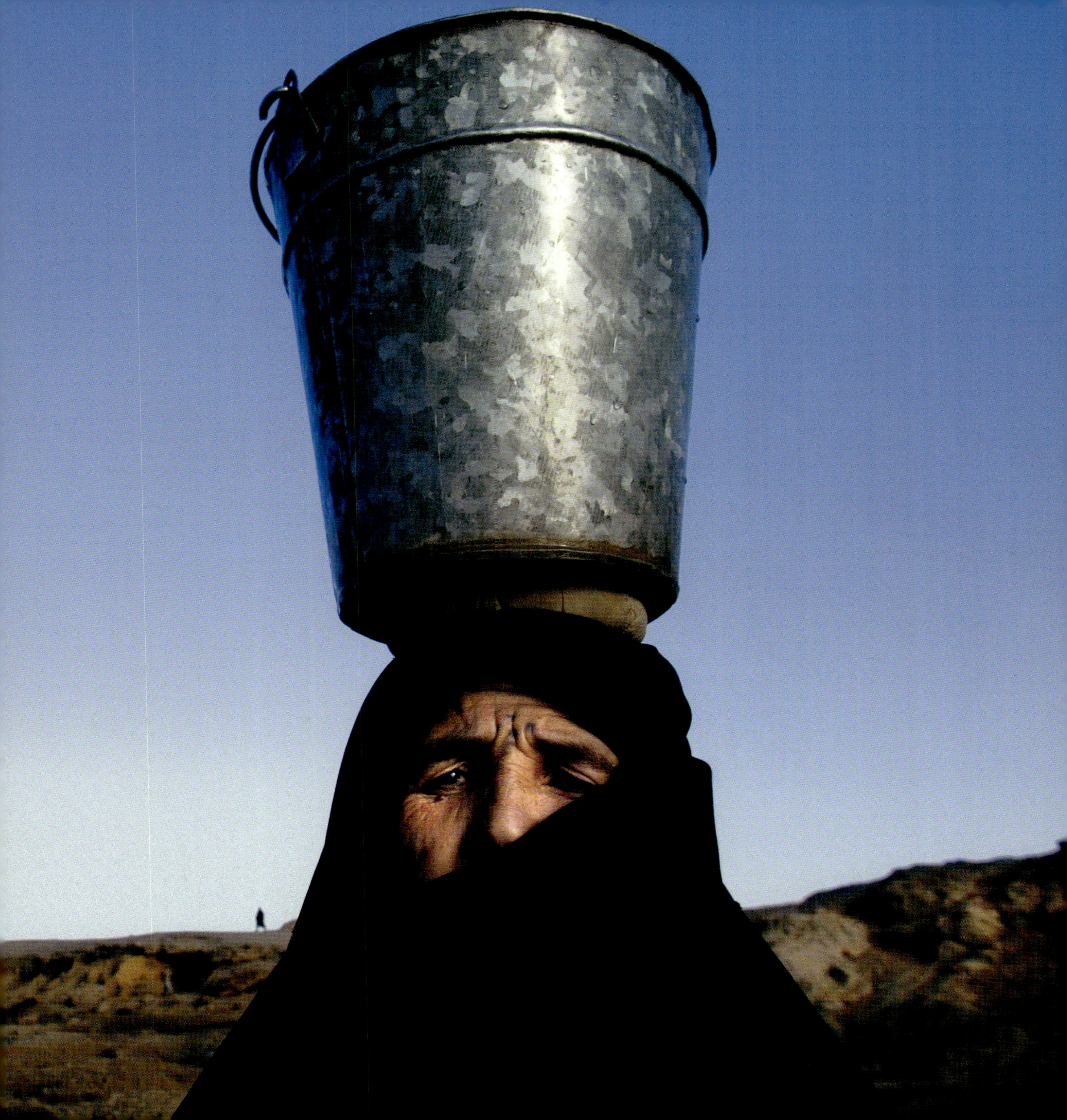

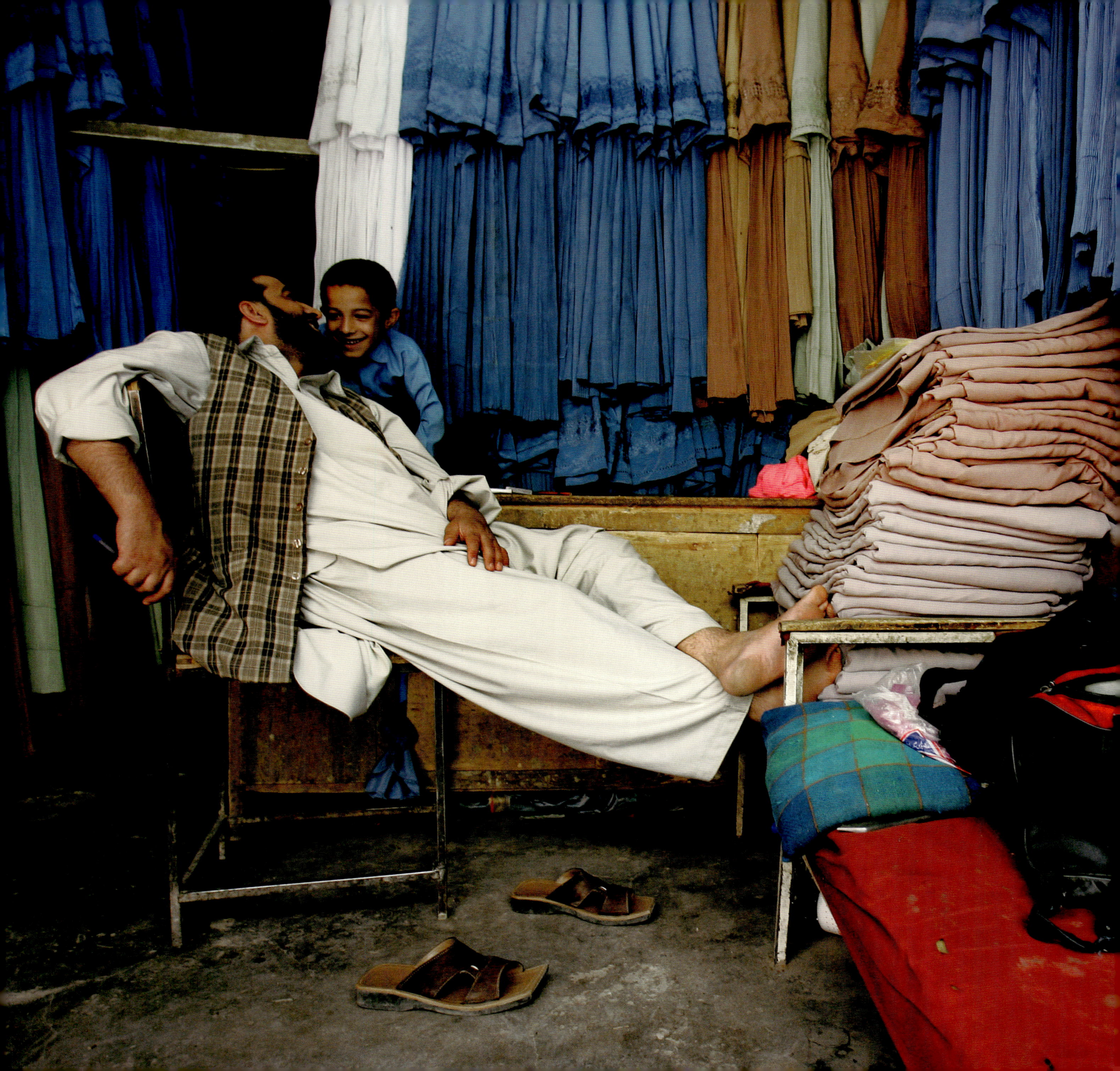

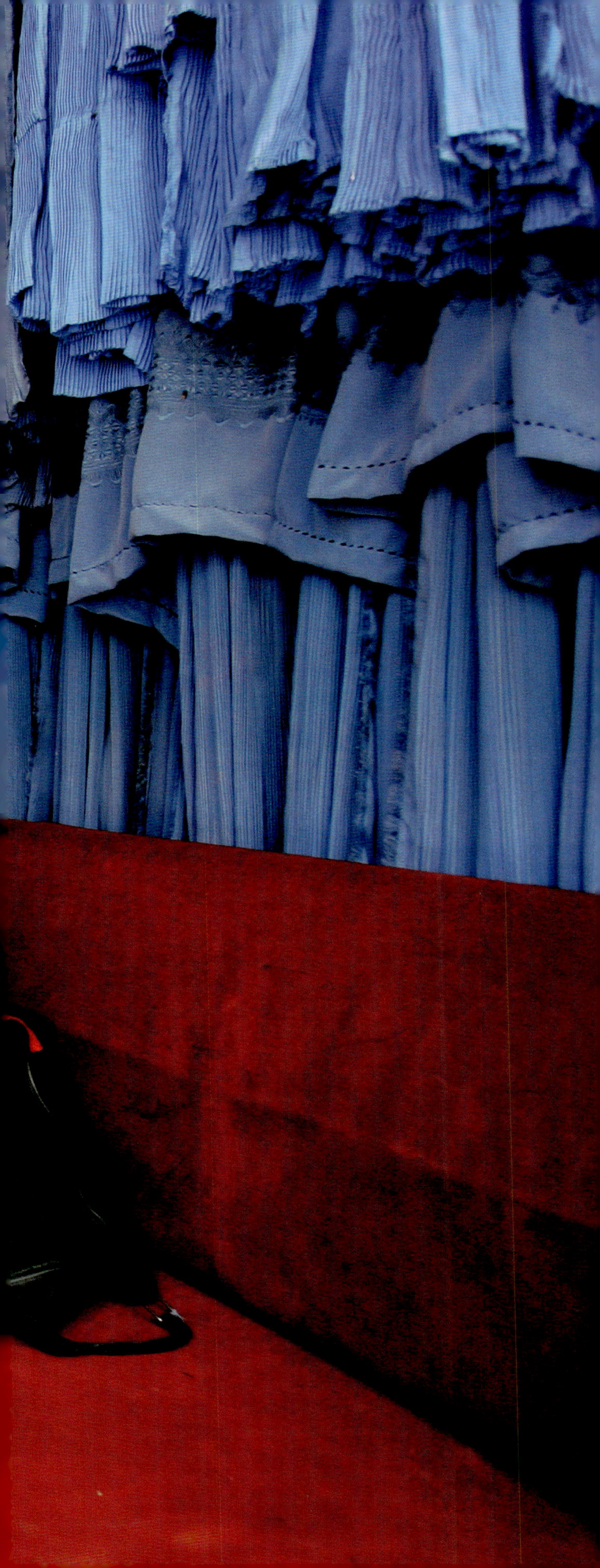

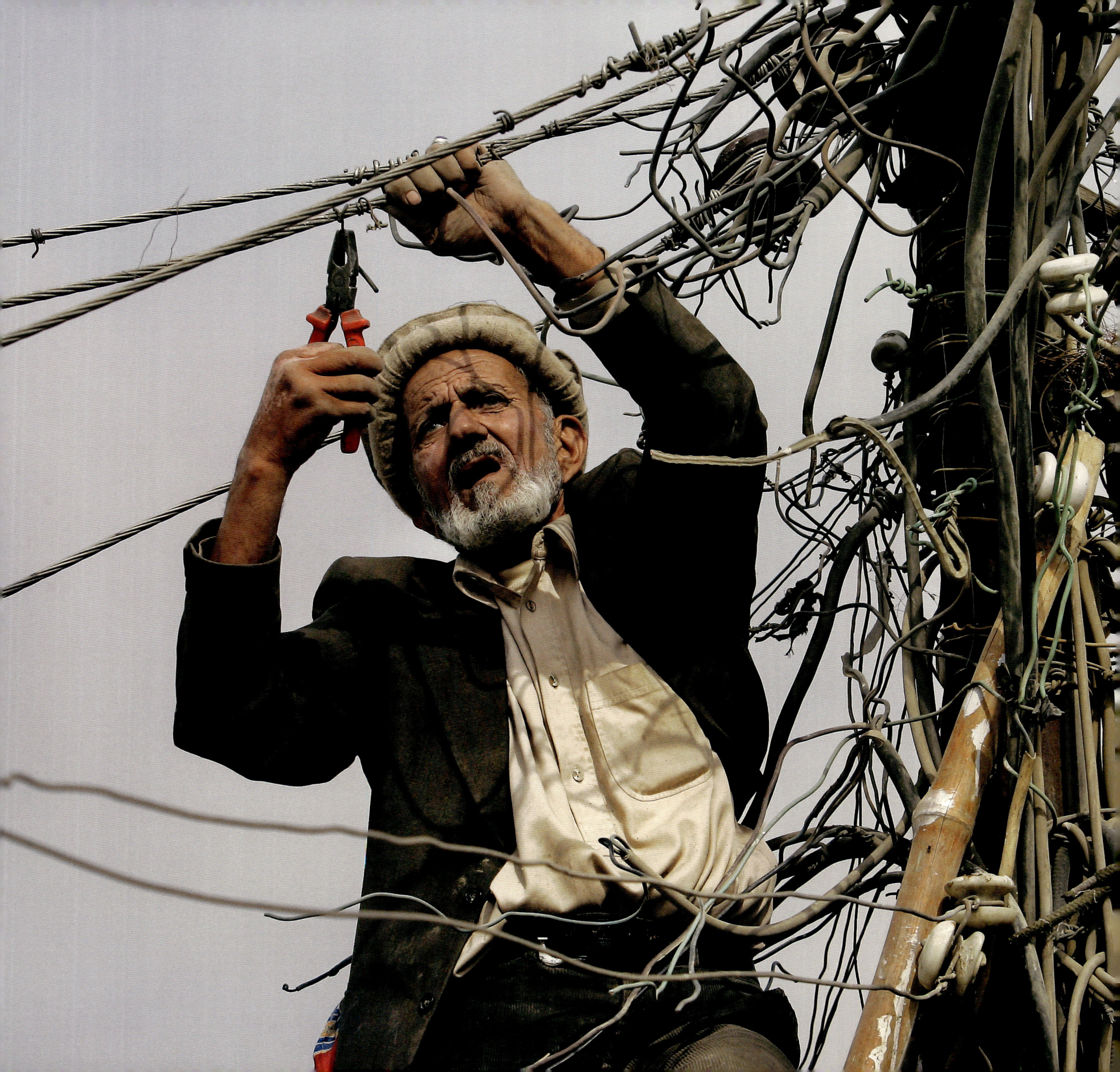

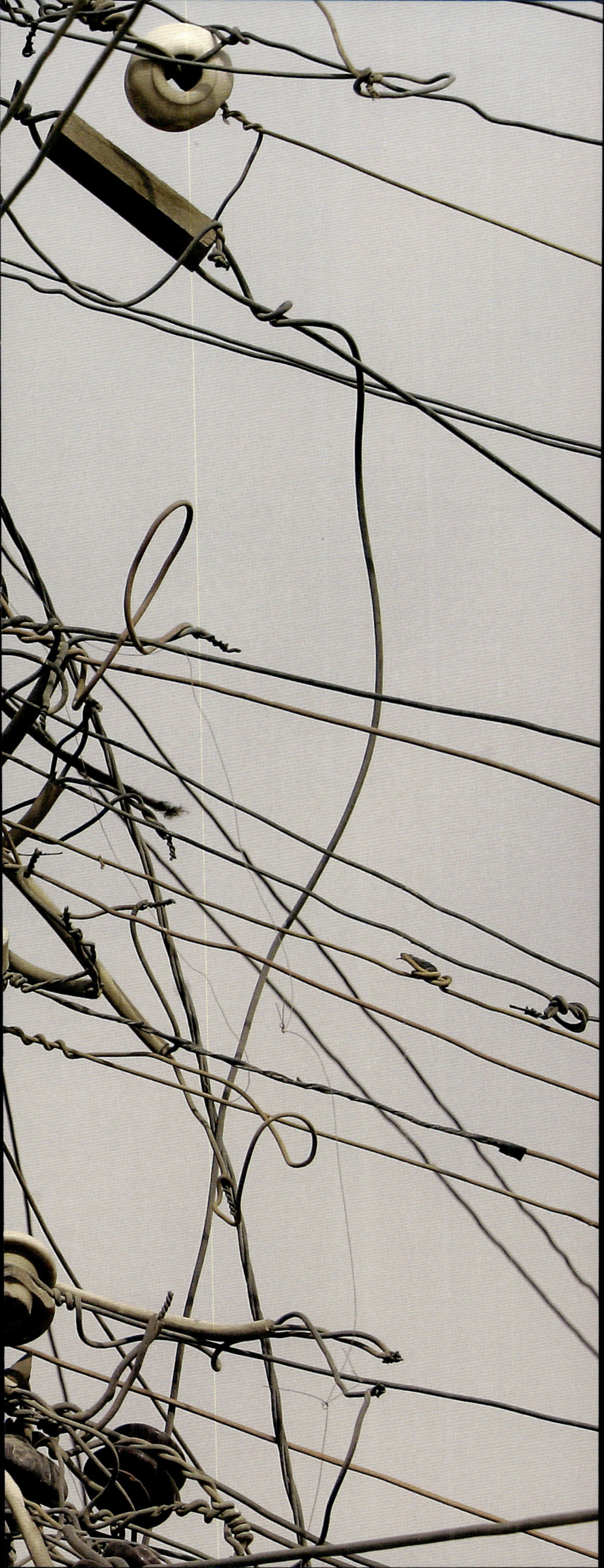

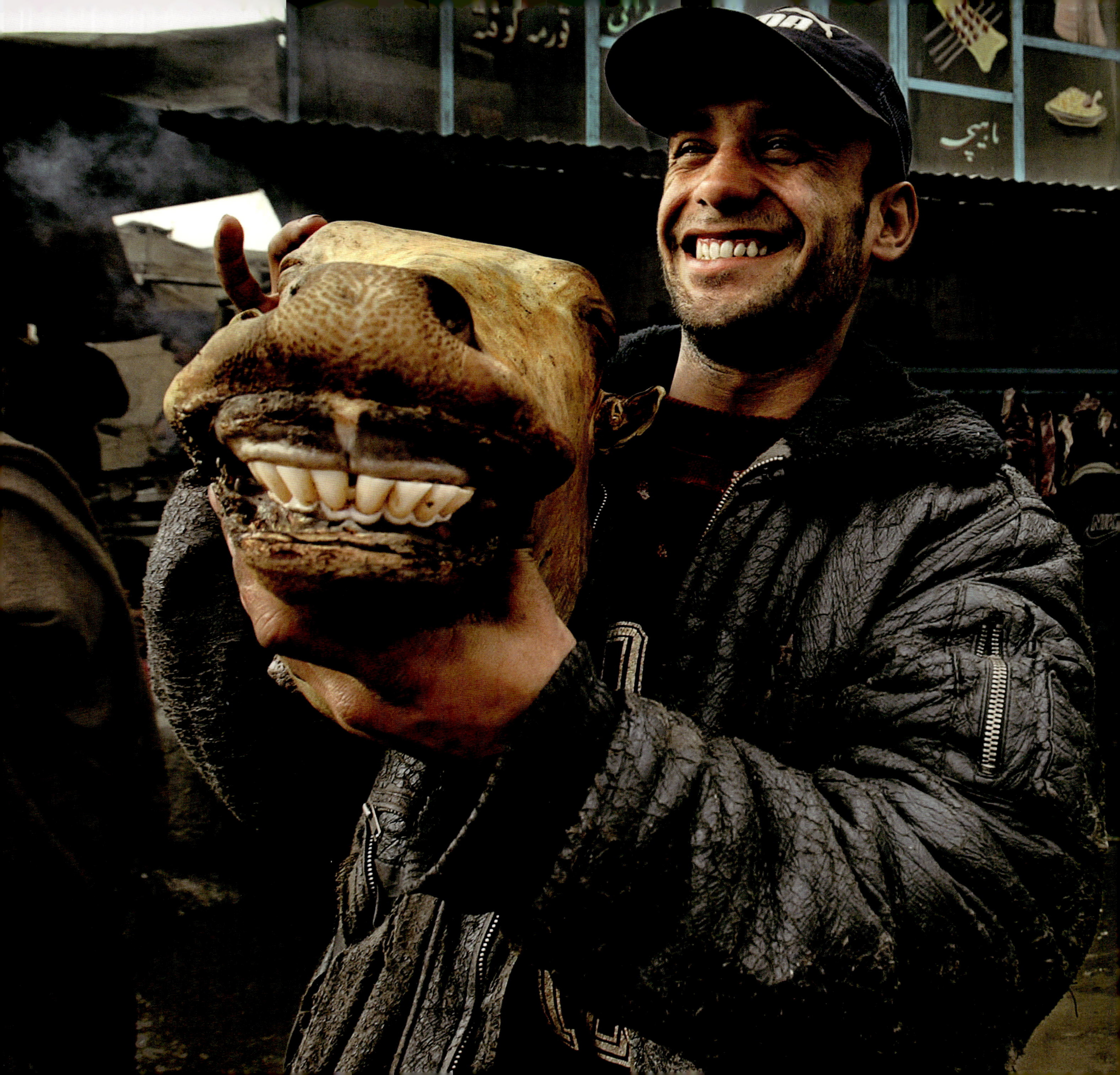

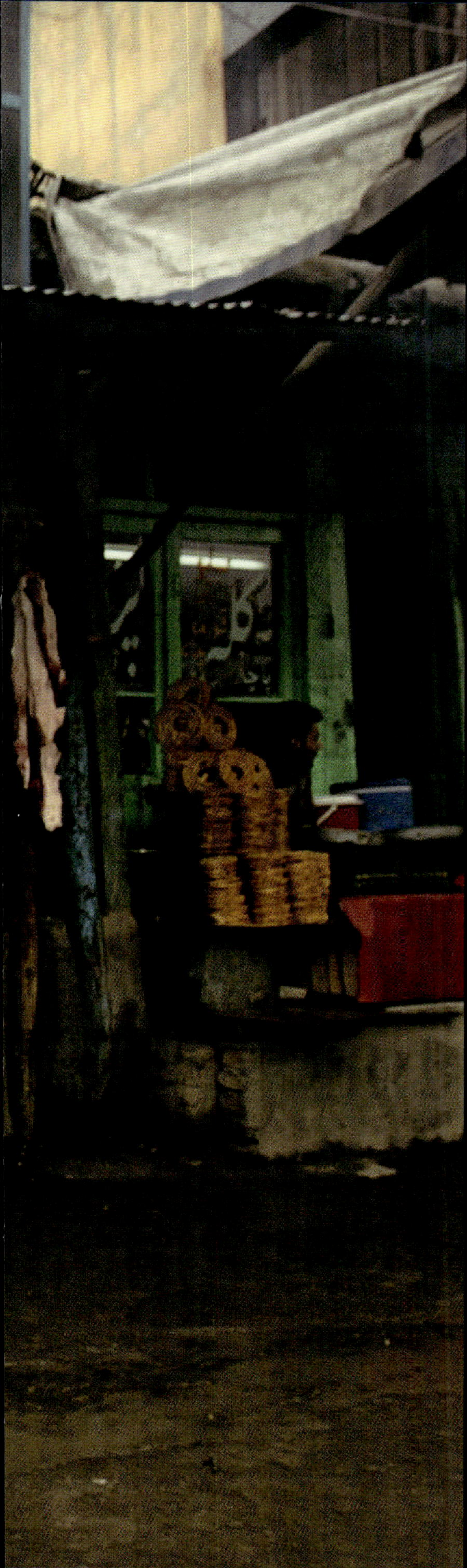

KABUL BAZAAR,
FEBRUARY 23, 2003.

A man proudly shows off a cow's head that he is selling at a bazaar. These animal parts are popular among Afghans because they are cheap and used for soup. They are also thought to be an aphrodisiac.

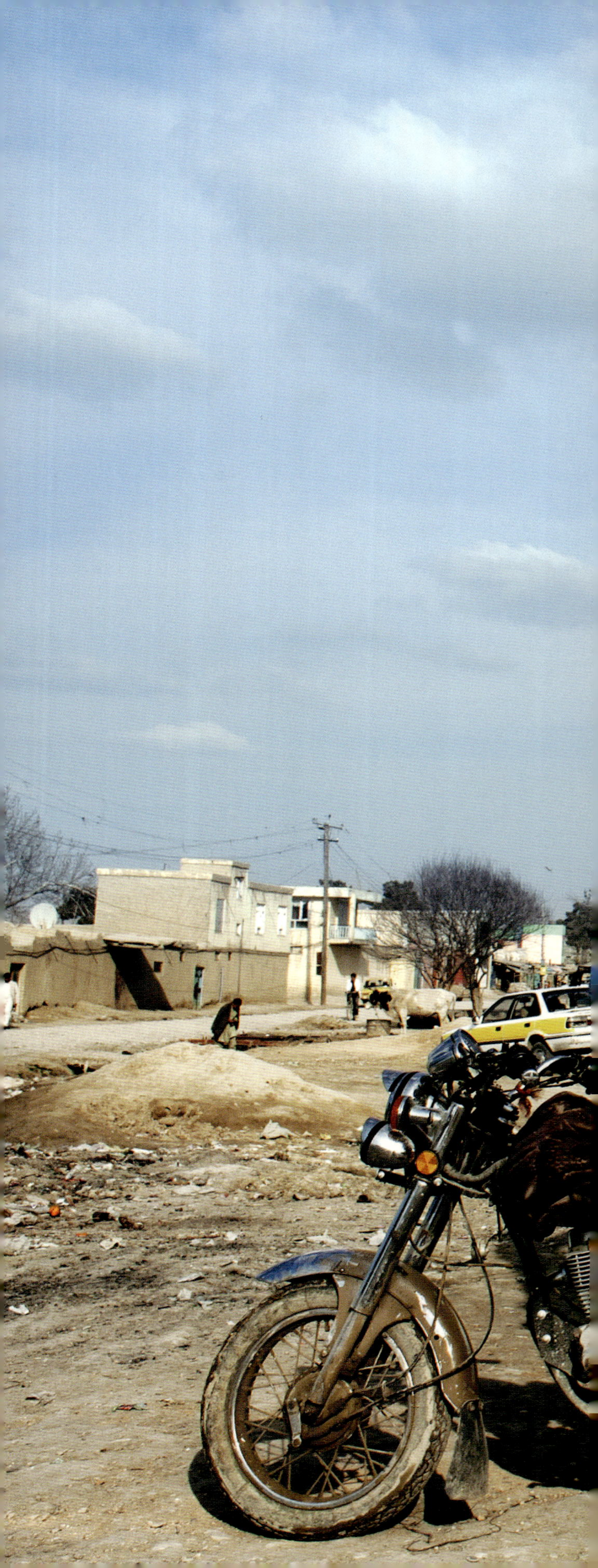

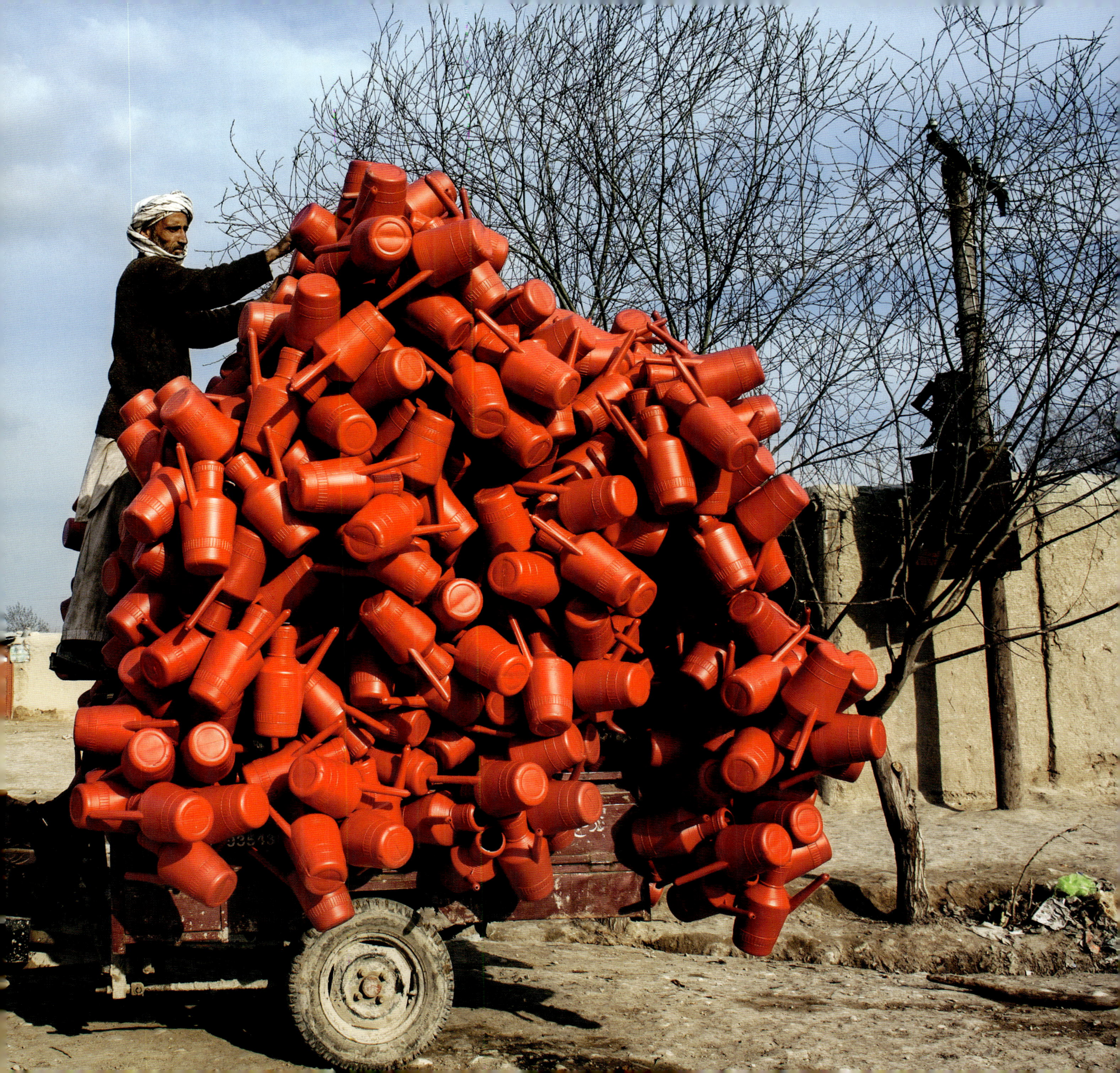

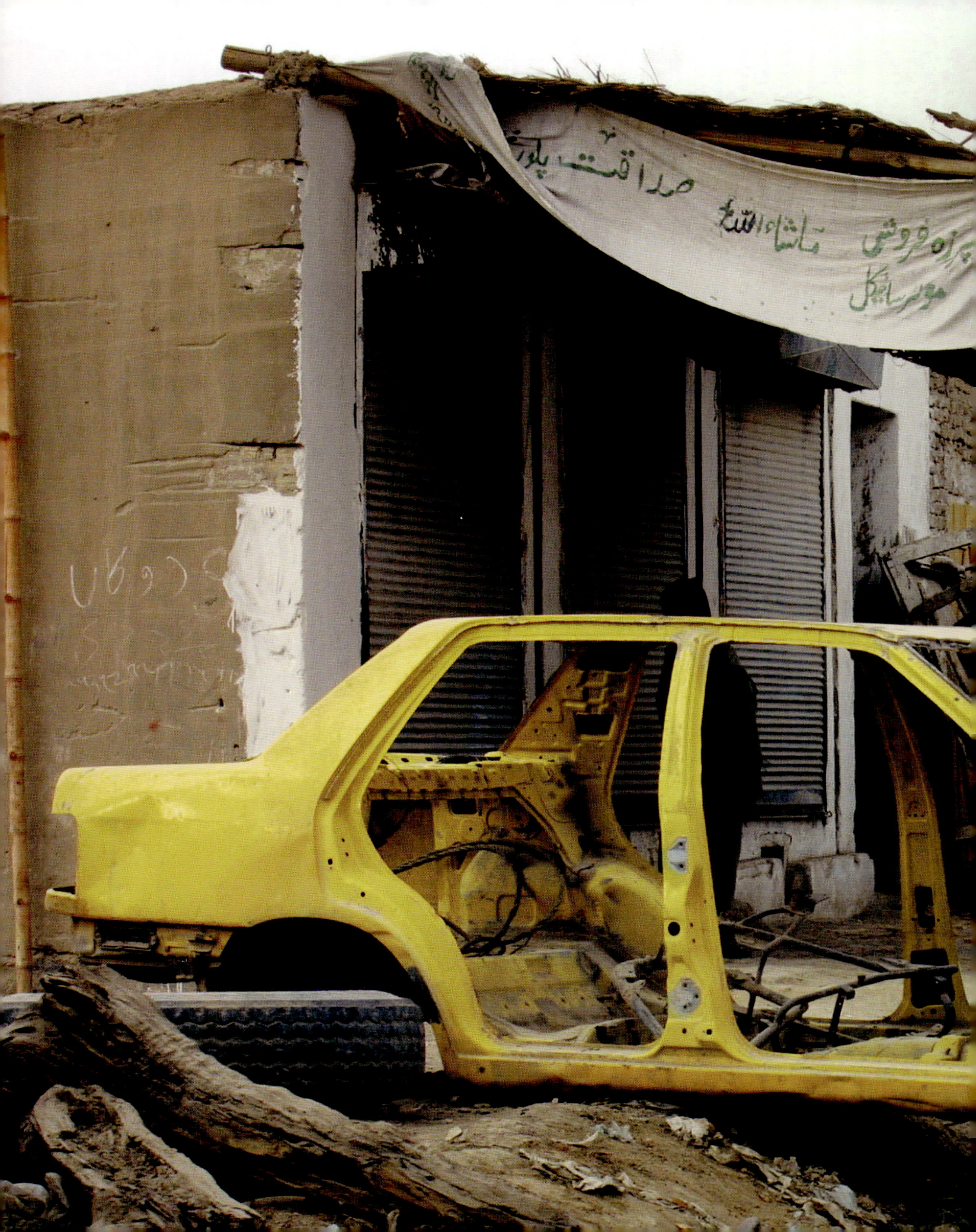
ماشاءاللہ
پرزہ فروش
موٹرسائیکل

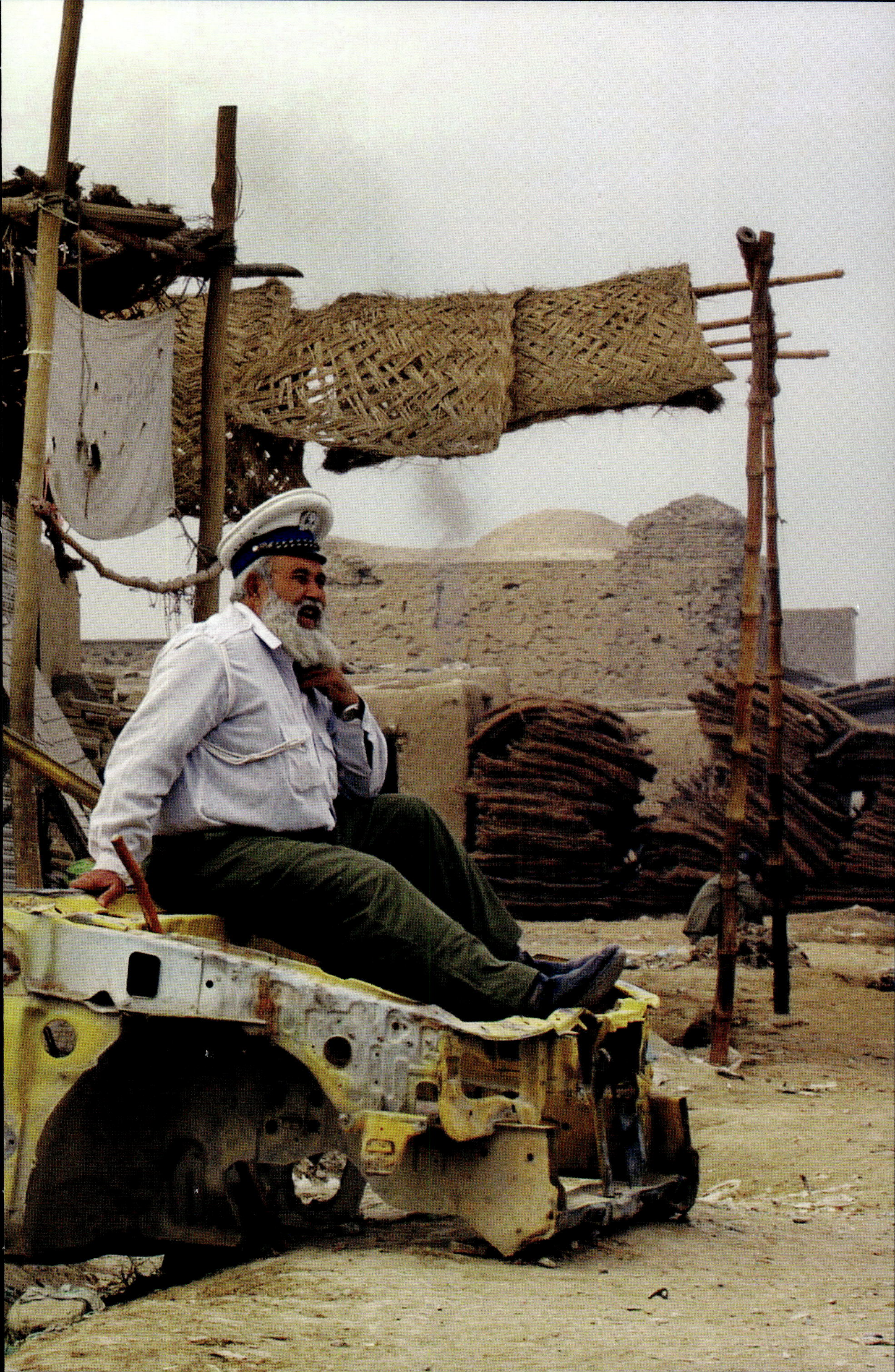

KANDAHAR, DECEMBER 13, 2001.

A policeman takes a break atop an abandoned vehicle.

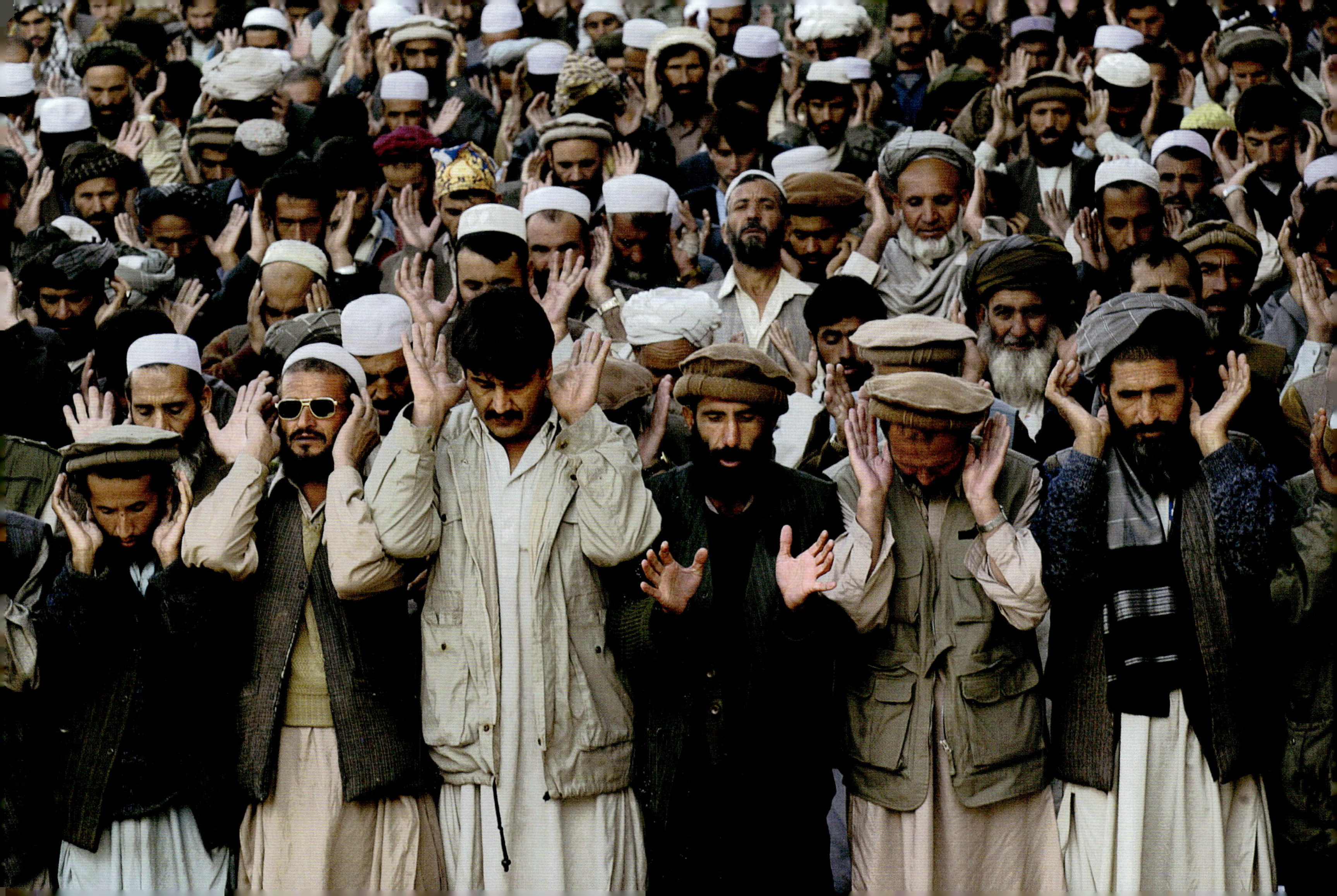

KABUL, NOVEMBER 8, 2002.

LEFT: Men pray at the Blue Mosque on the first Friday of the fasting month of Ramadan.

KABUL, OCTOBER 12, 2007.

RIGHT: A man attends a special prayer at the Eid Gah Mosque on the first day of Eid al-Fitr, a three-day holiday marking the end of Ramadan.

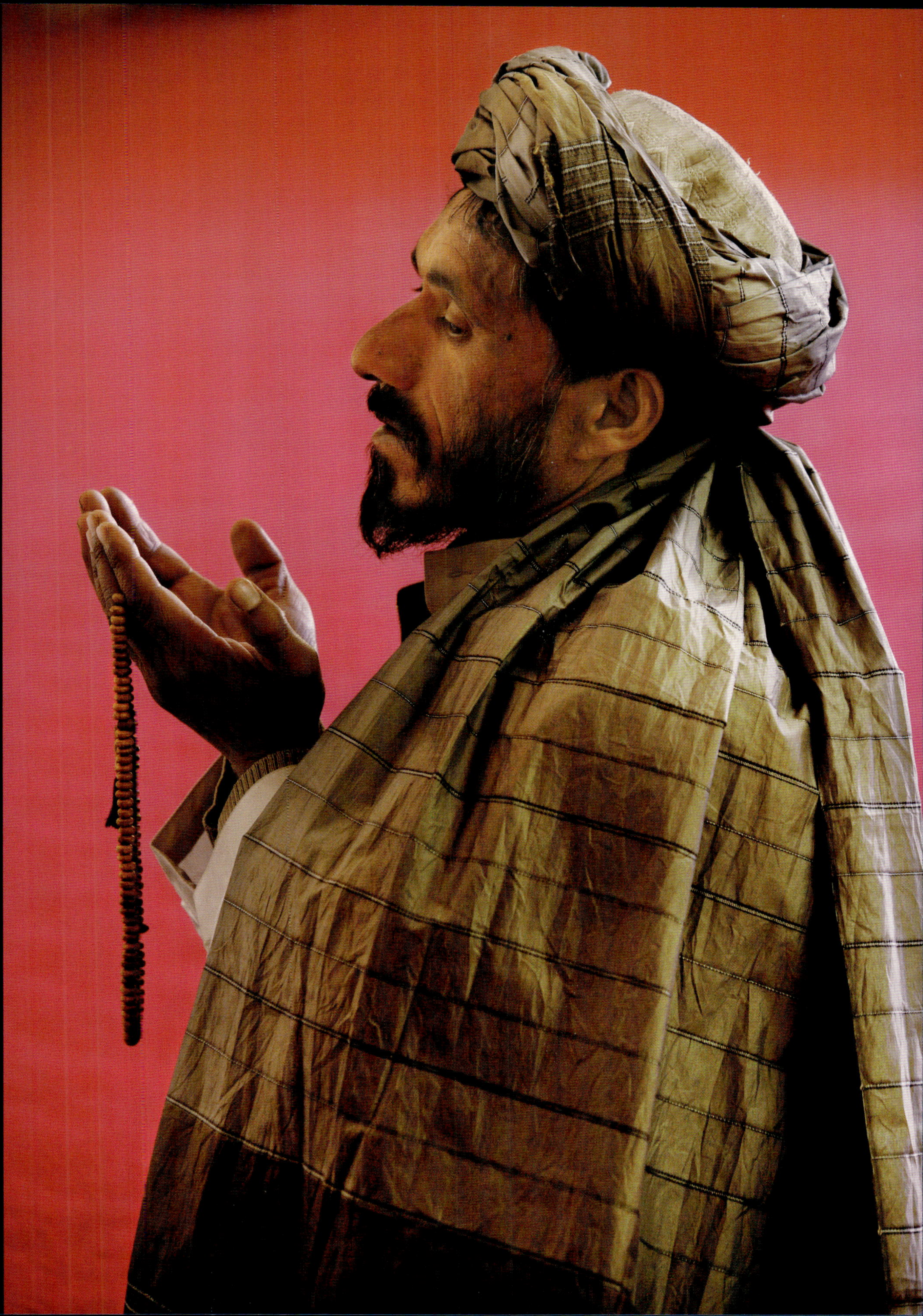

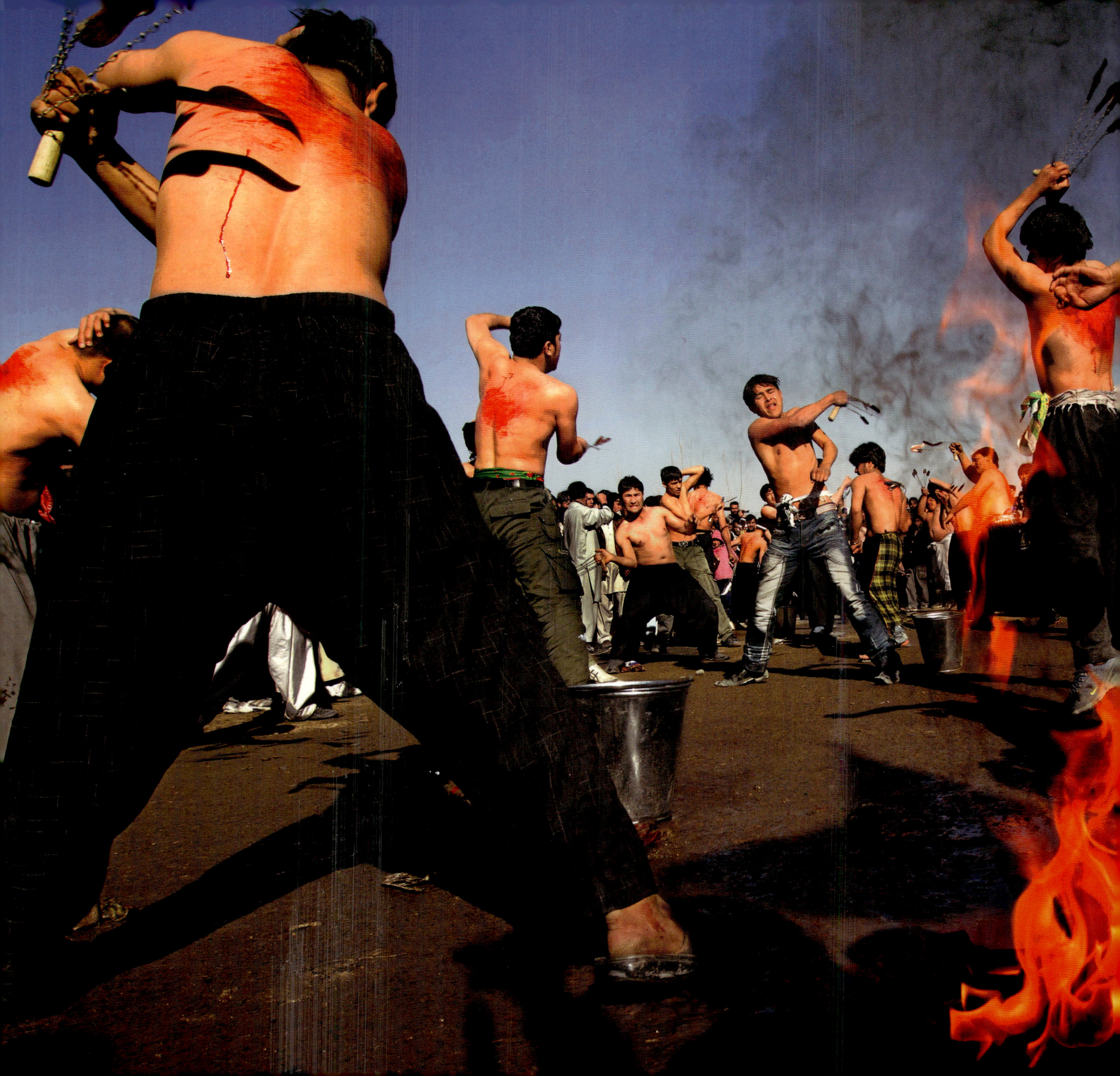

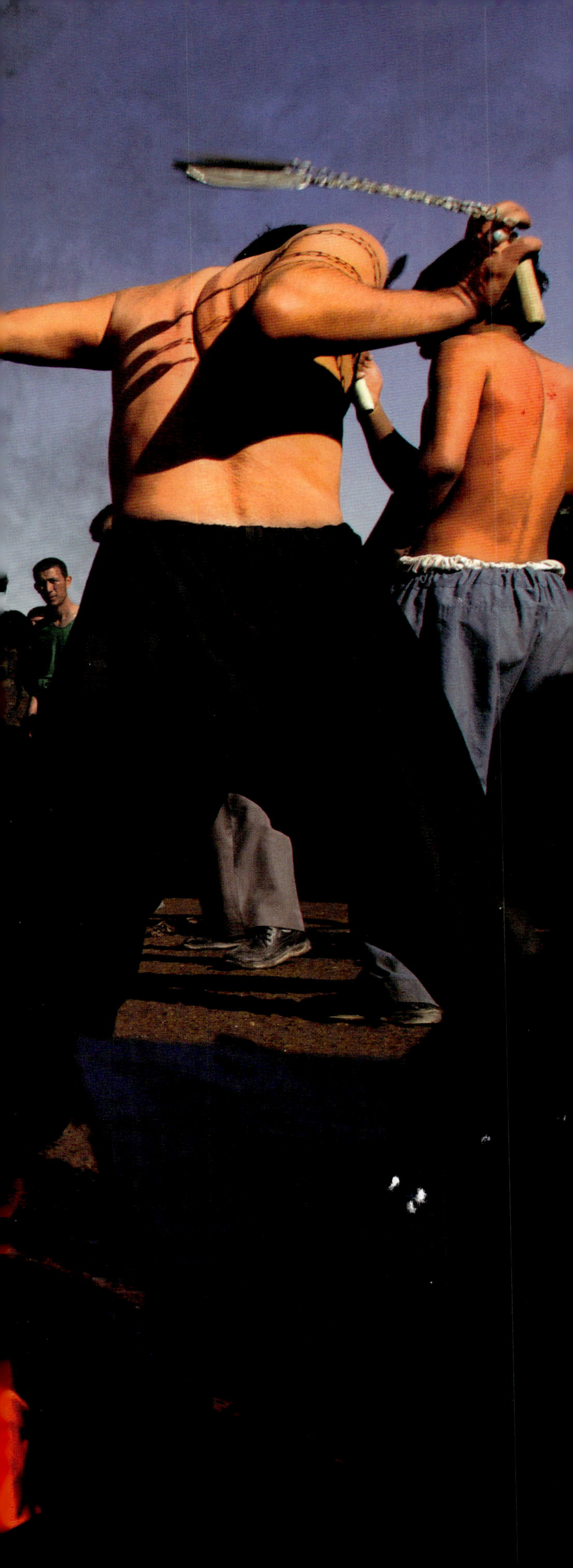

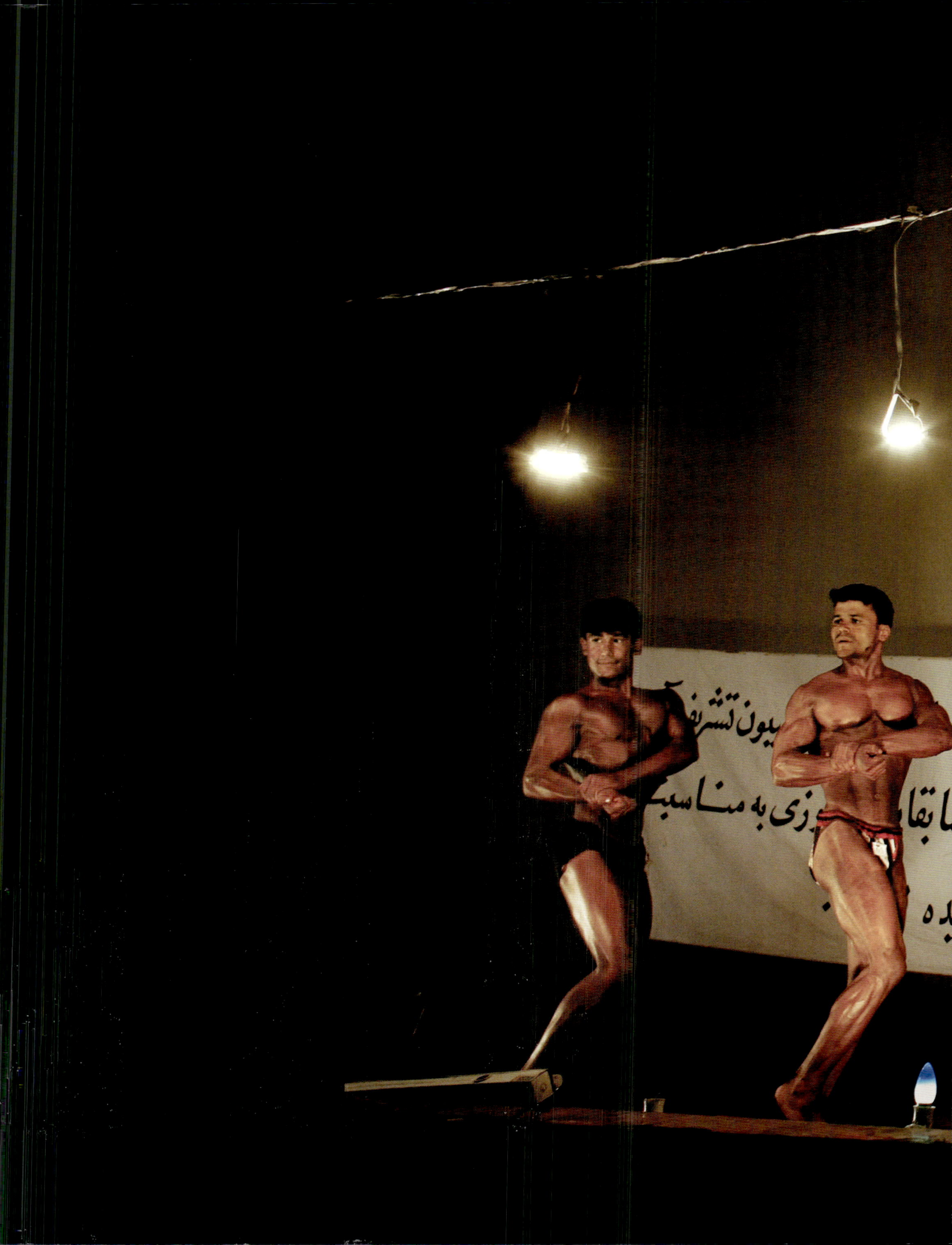

KABUL, AUGUST 6, 2007.

Bodybuilders in the 55–60 kg category square off during a regional bodybuilding competition. Many Afghan men, like others around the world, feel that a macho image of physical strength is important.

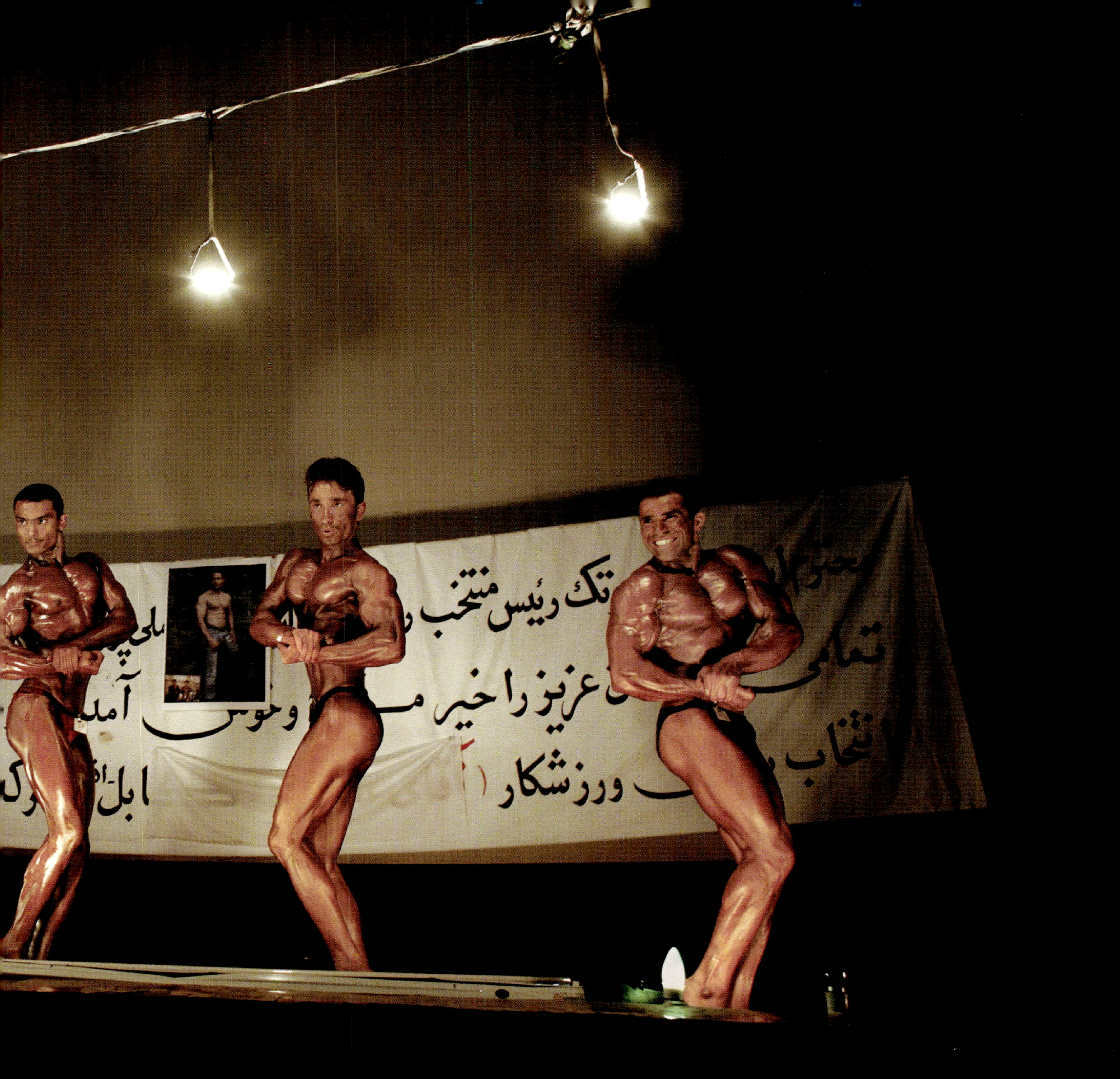

تک رئیس منتخب
عزیز را خیر
ورزشکار

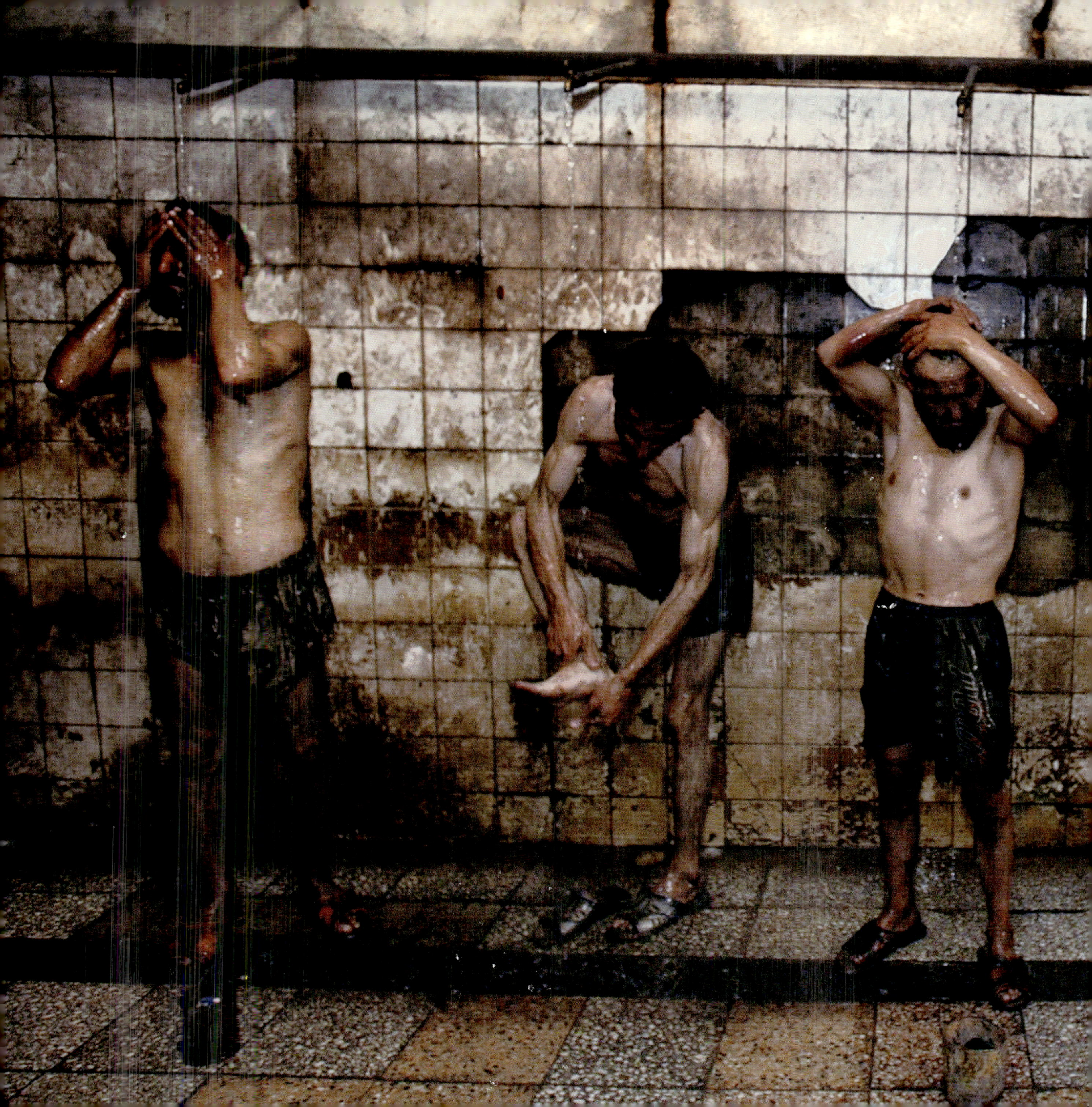

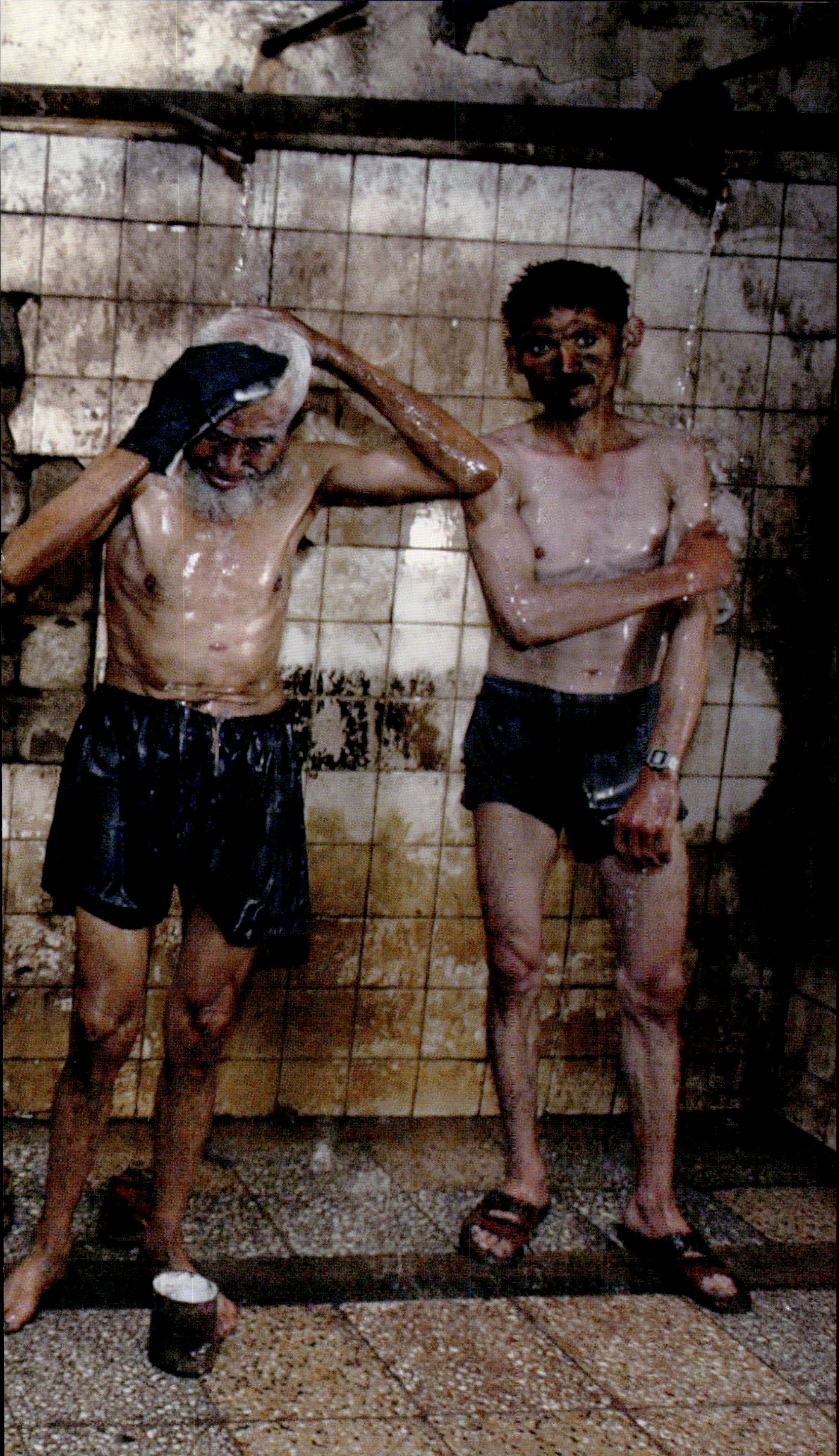

NEAR POL-E-KHOMRI,
OCTOBER 31, 2004.

Miners shower in a bathhouse after working in the Karkar coal mine. The workers make an average of four dollars per day.

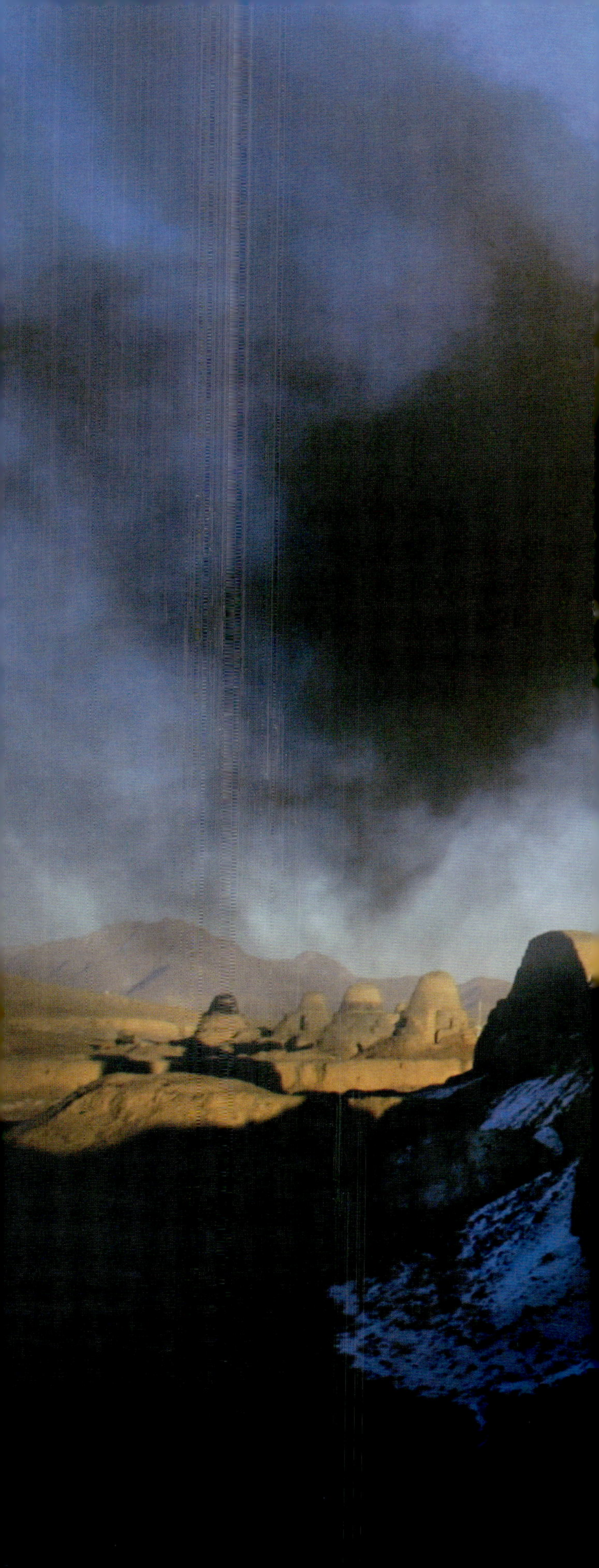

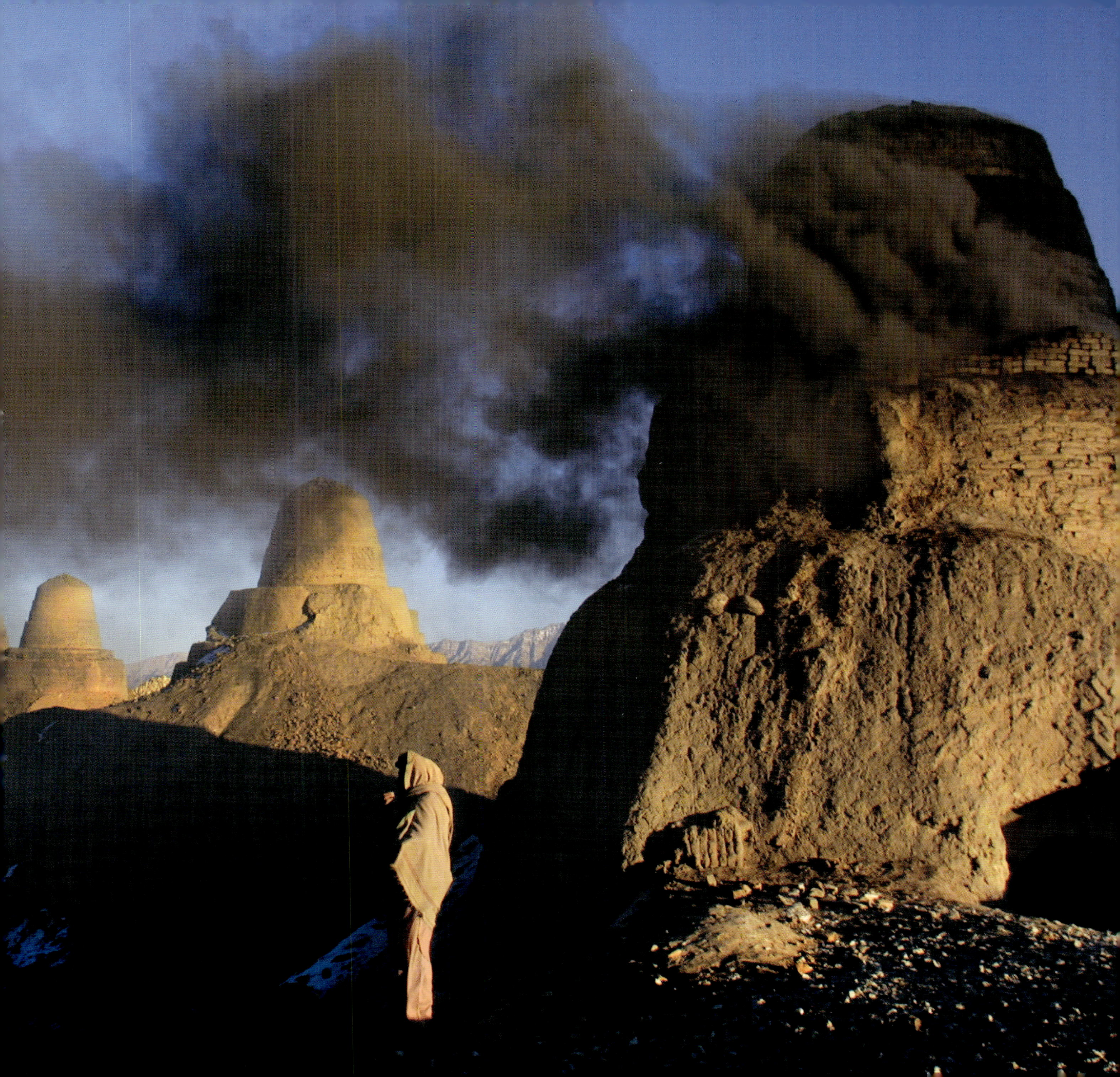

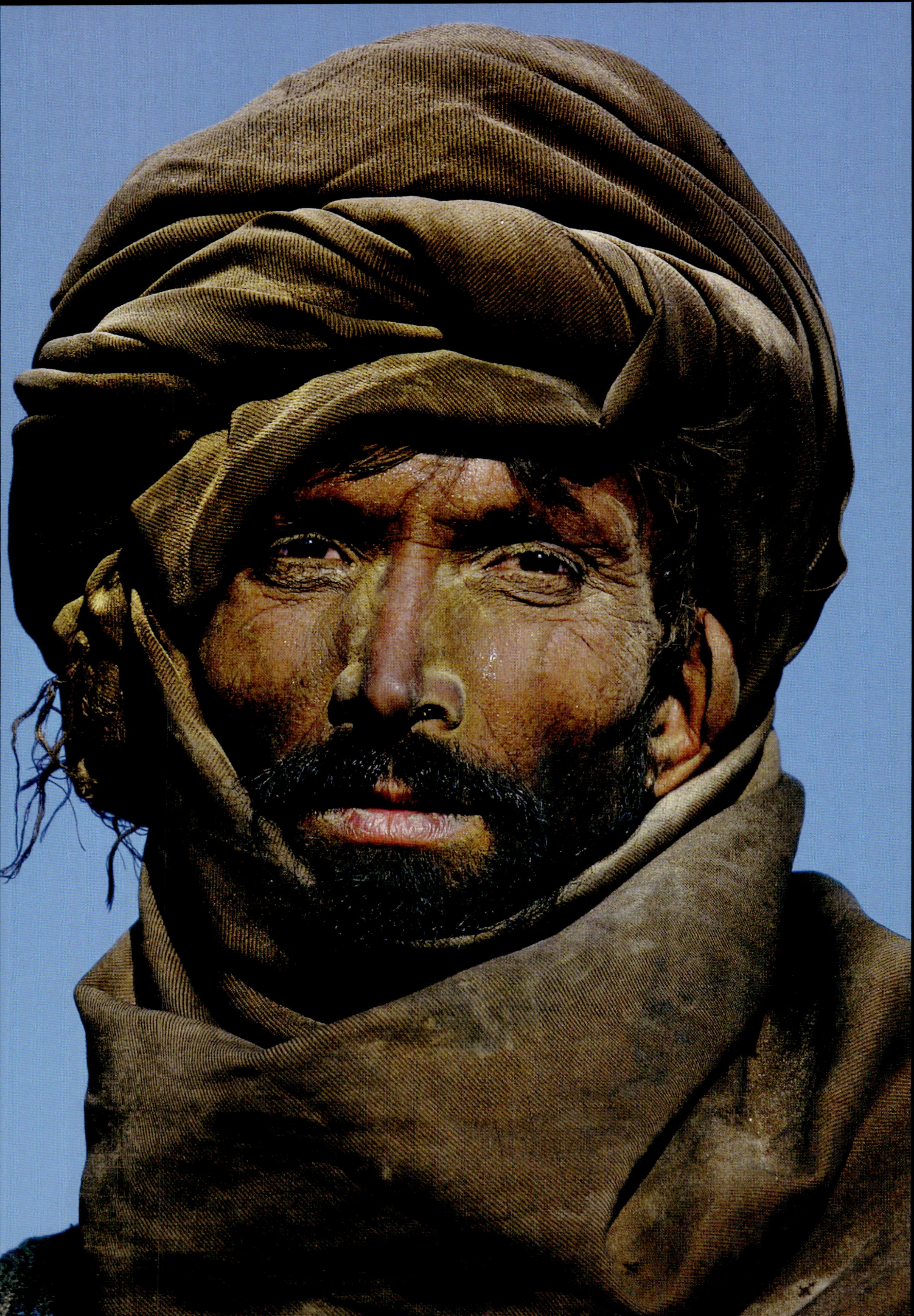

KABUL, FEBRUARY 14, 2002.

LEFT: A worker is covered in dust after a day's labor at a brick factory.

KABUL, NOVEMBER 6, 2009.

RIGHT: A worker stands inside a cloud of smoke as he fires the coal-burning kiln at the Sadat, Ltd., brick factory. The surrounding land is dry and barren, which is perfect for making bricks, thus providing almost year-round work.

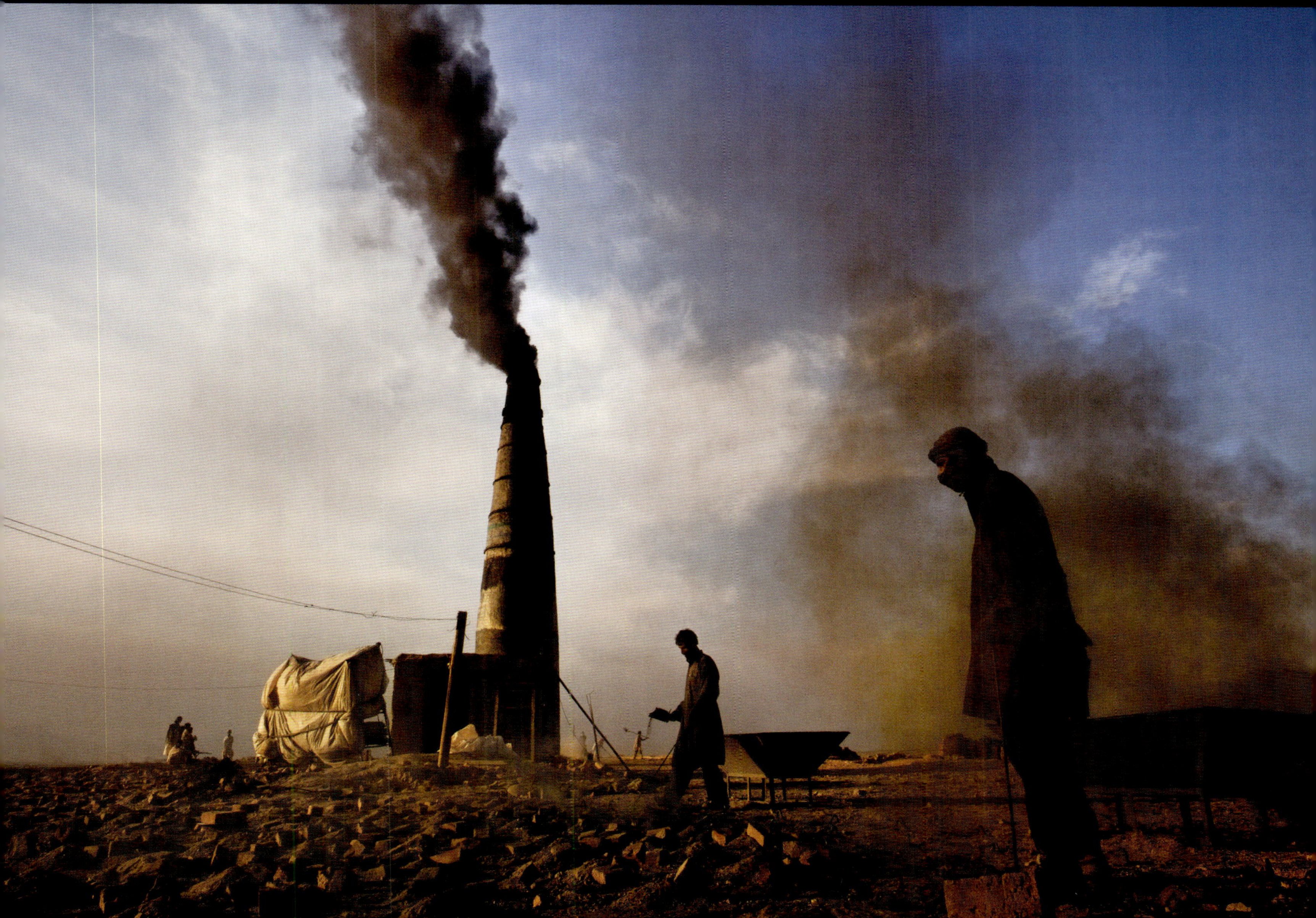

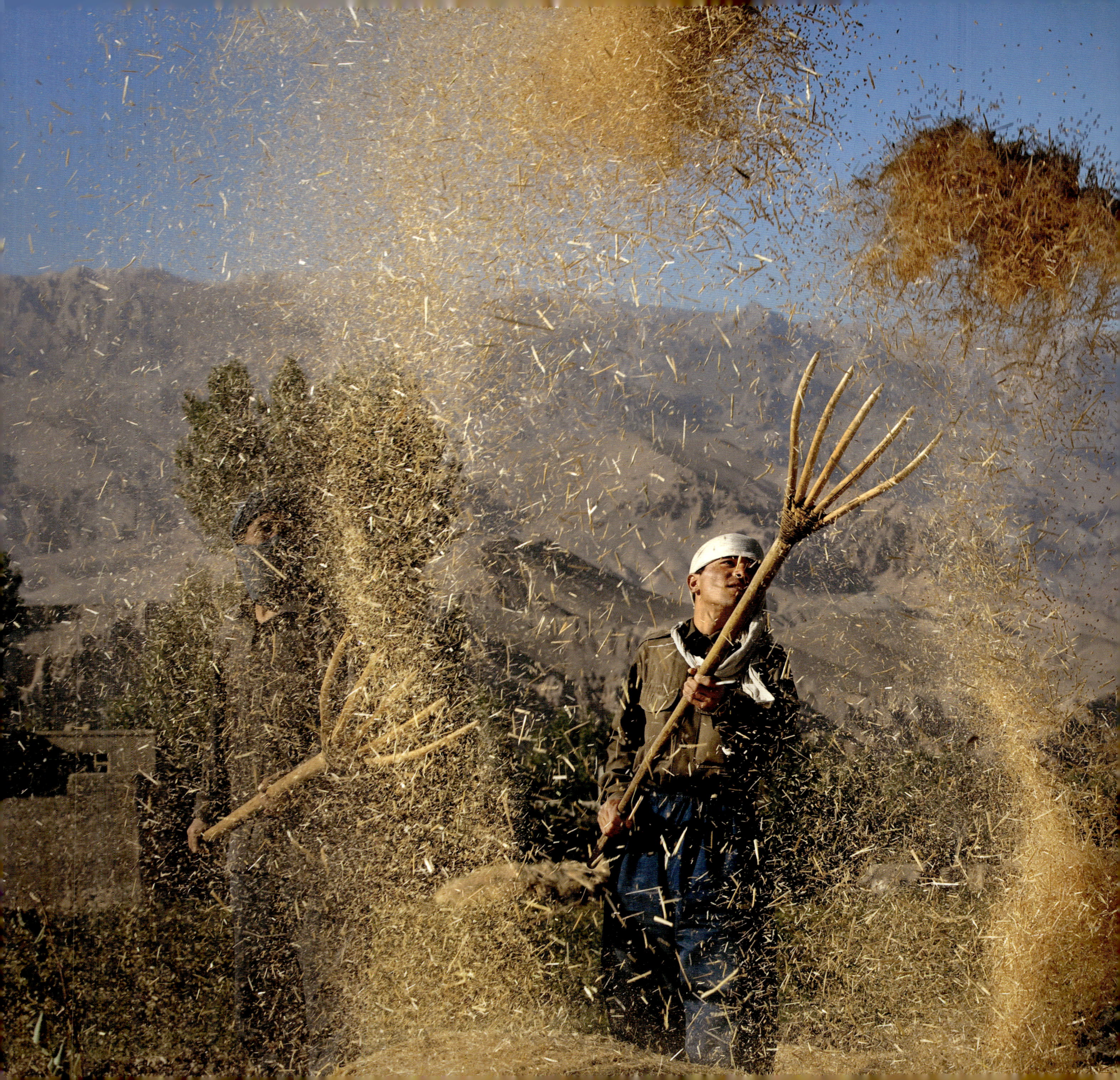

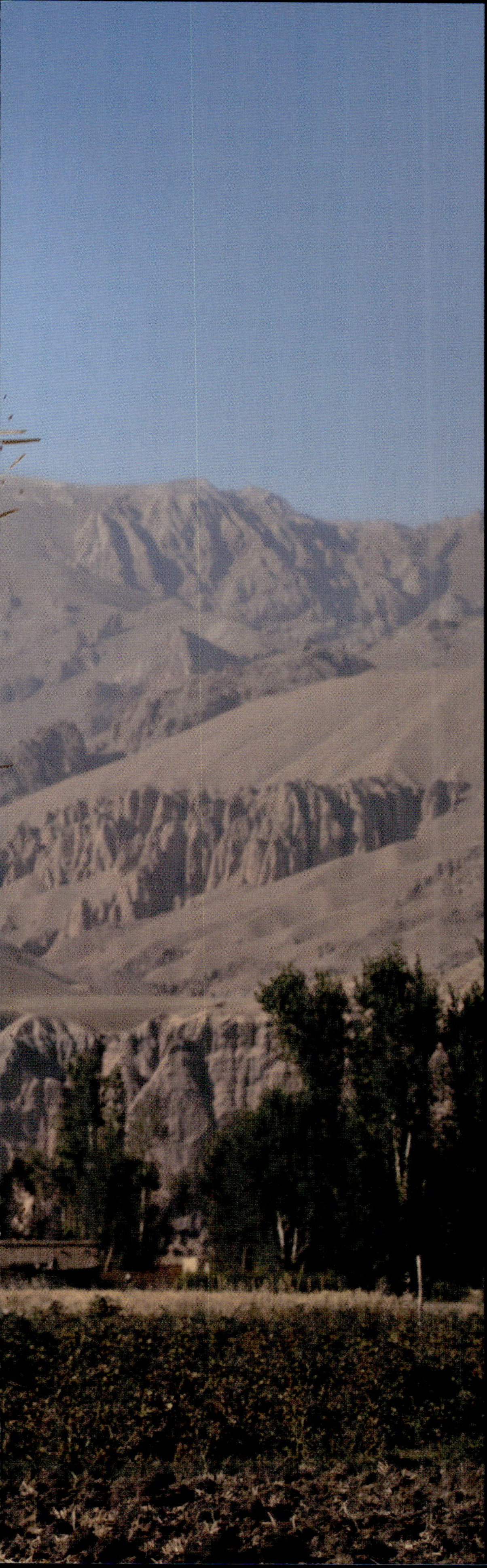

BAMIYAN. SEPTEMBER 7, 2009.

Farmers thresh a healthy crop of wheat as autumn approaches in Bamiyan. Wheat and potatoes are the main crops of this fertile region.

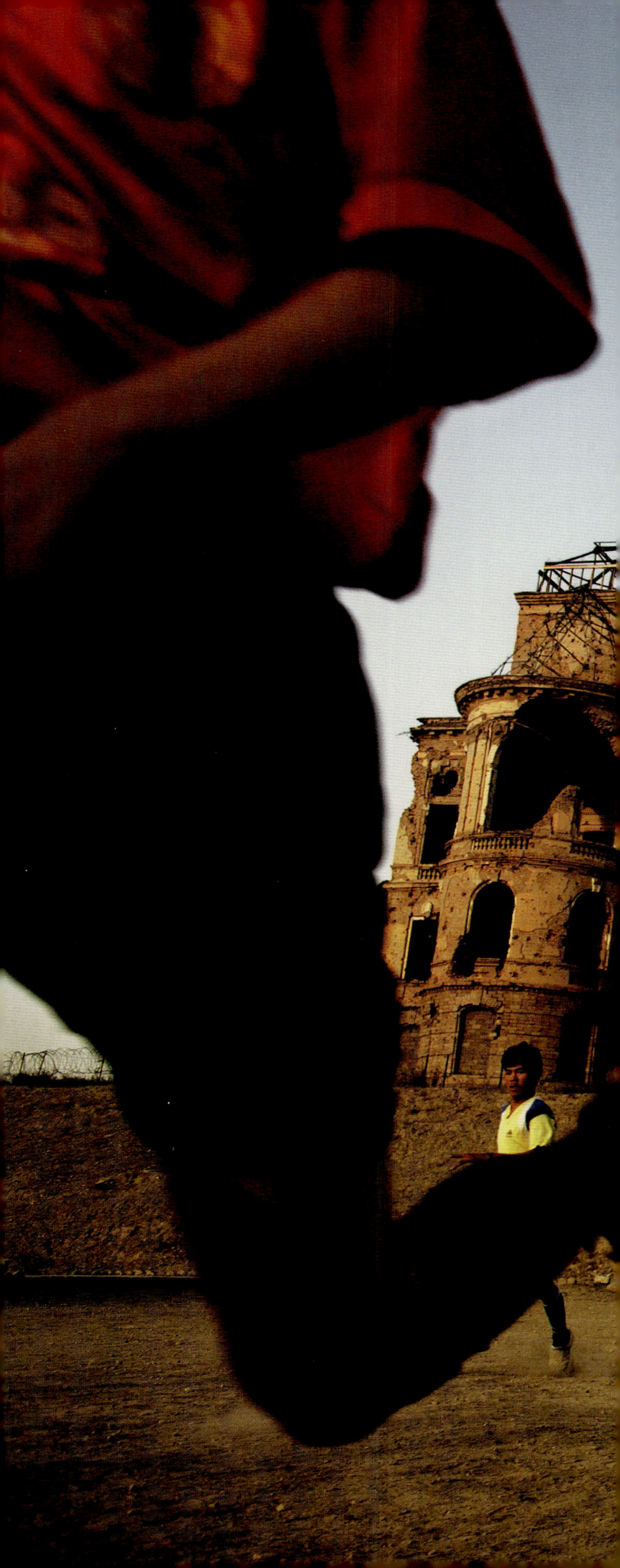

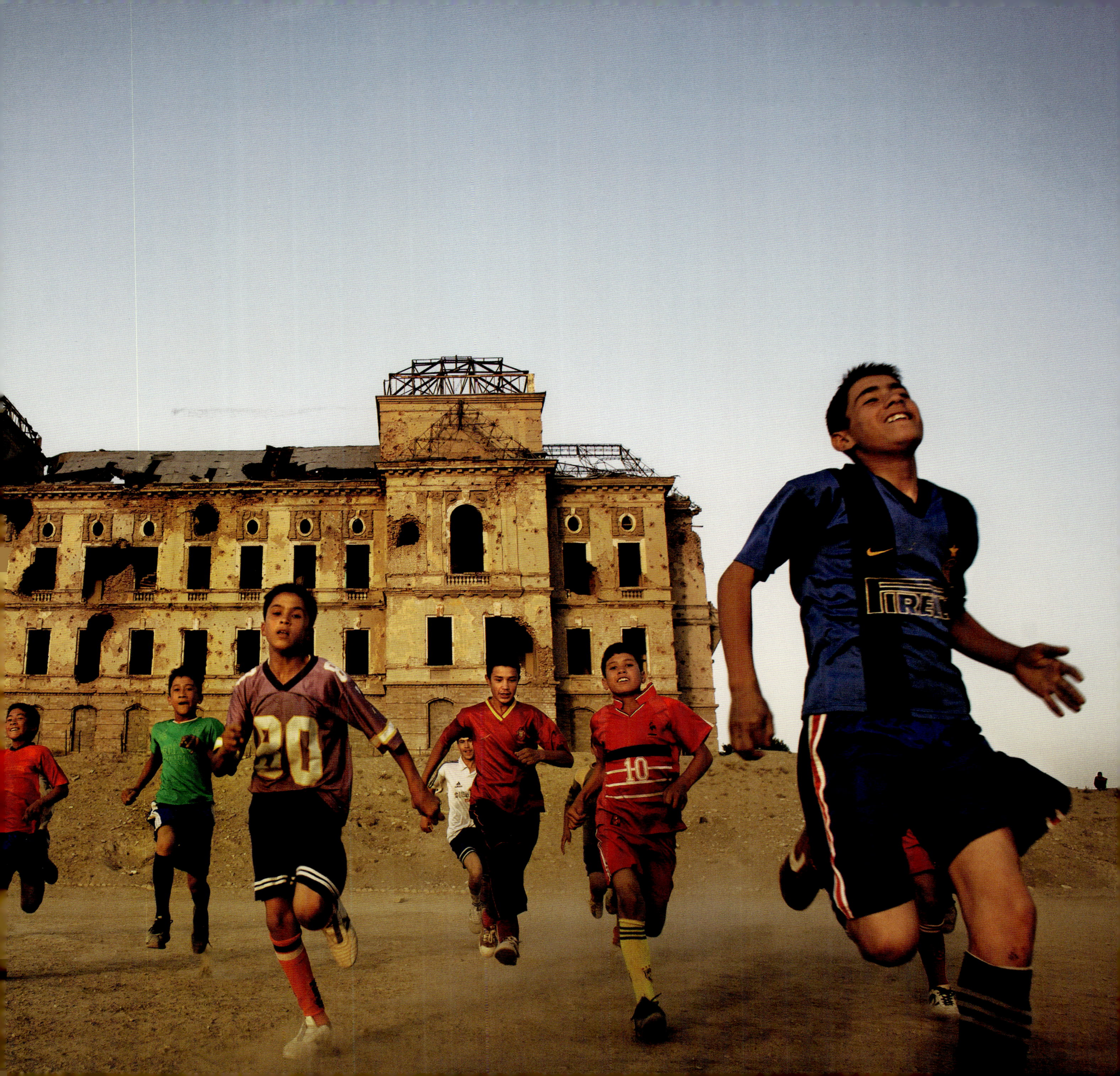
20
10

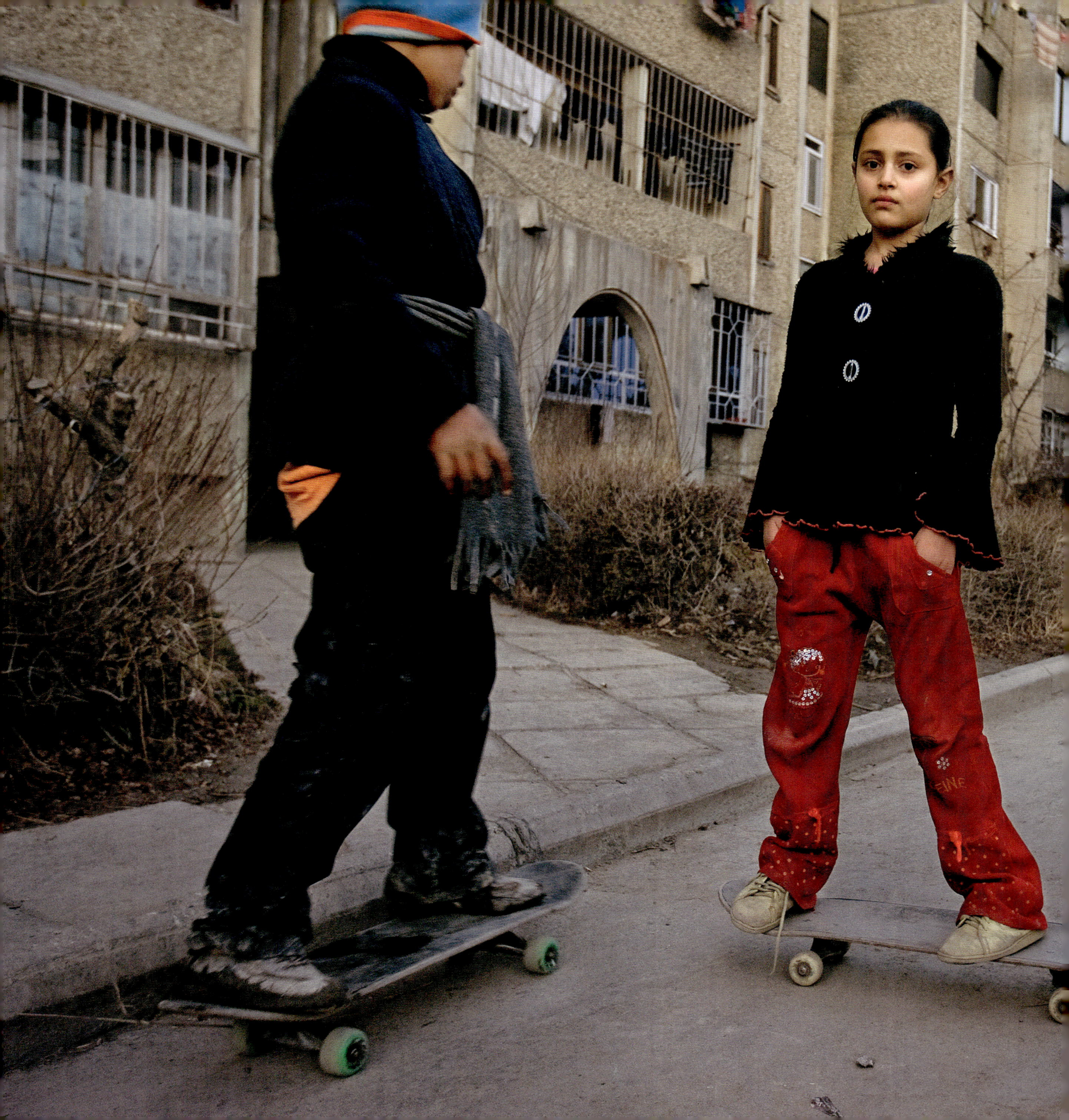

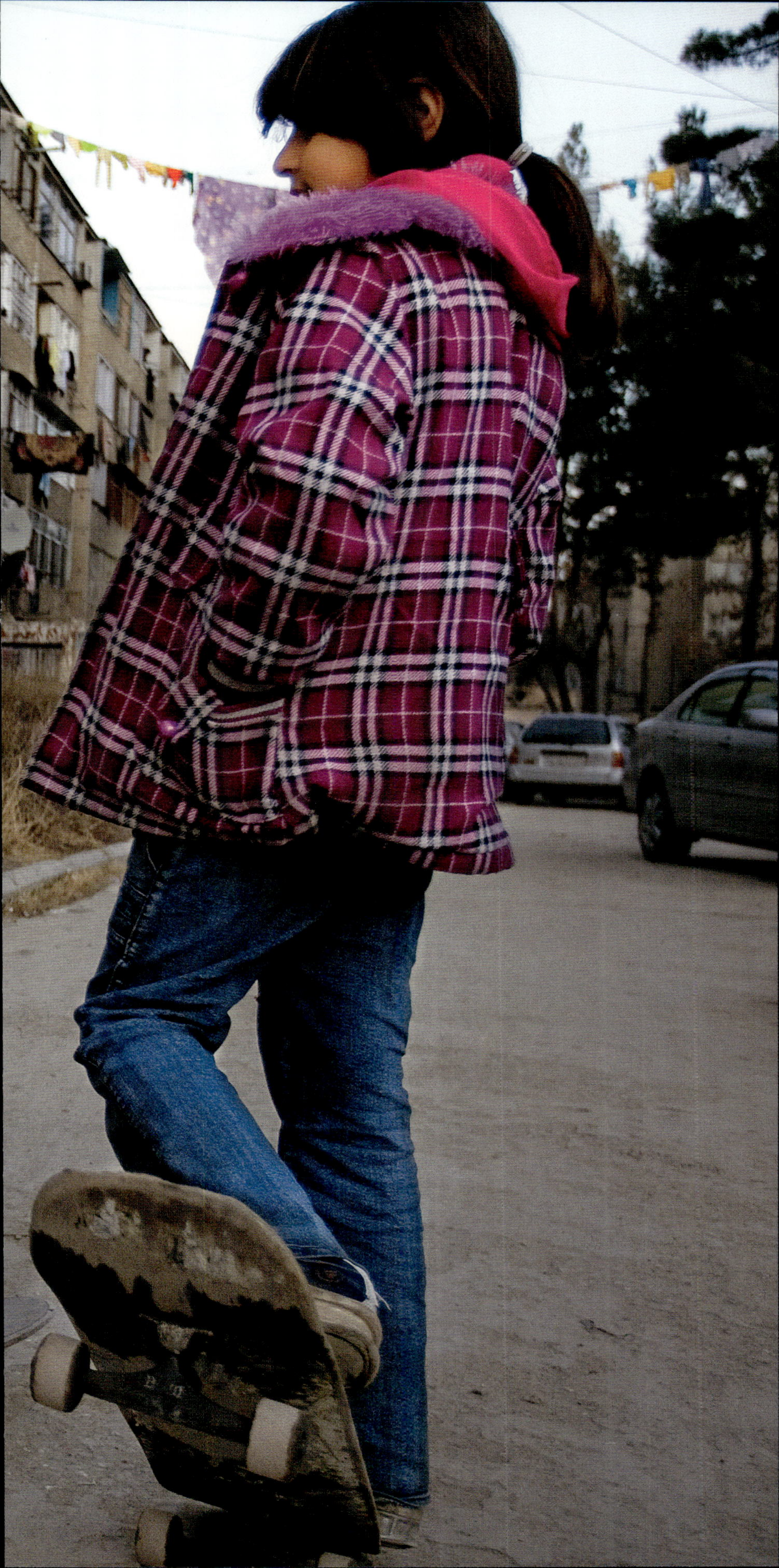

KABUL, JANUARY 31, 2009.

Children skateboard around a middle-class neighborhood. After decades of war, many Afghan youths badly need opportunities for recreation.

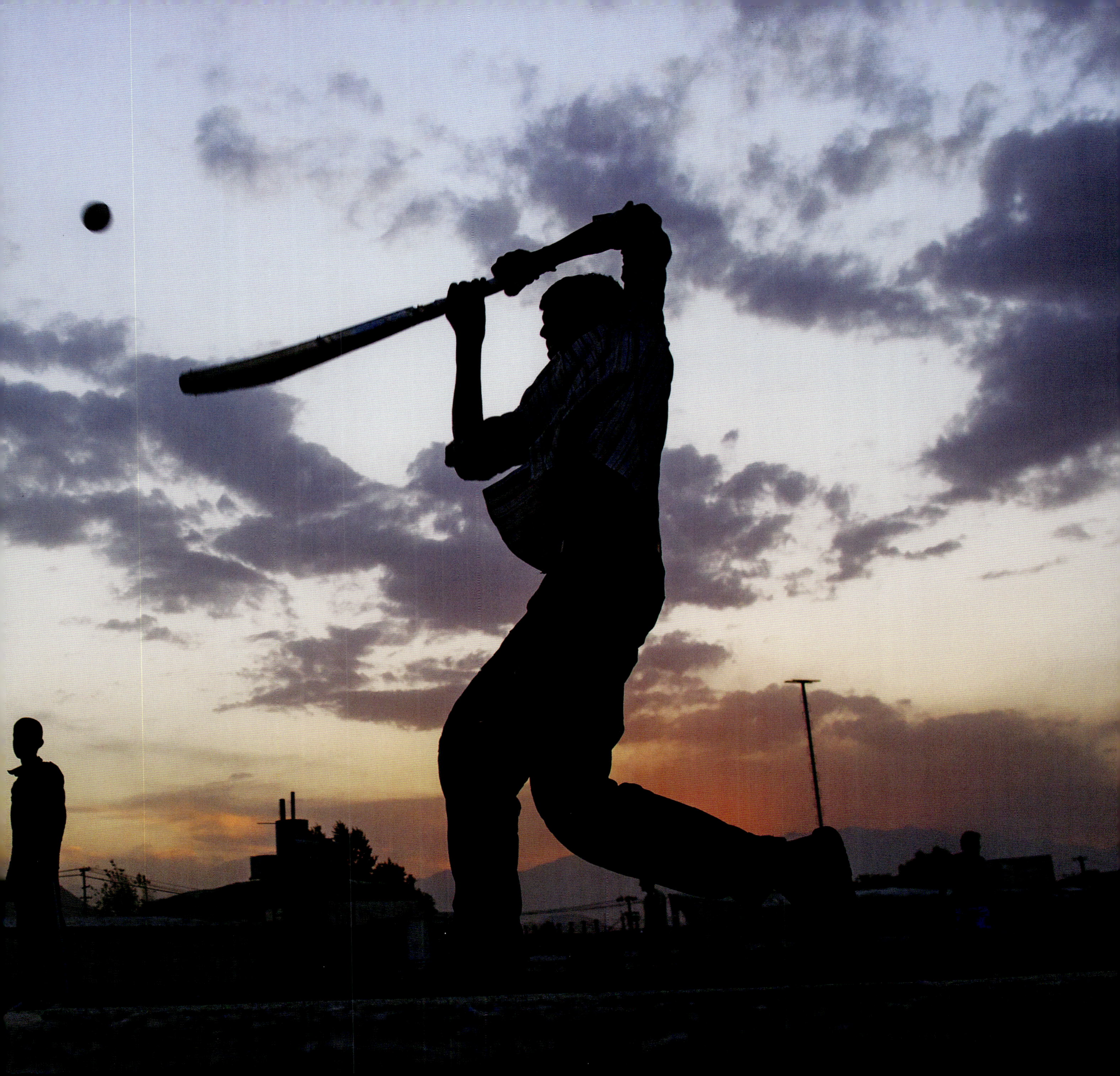

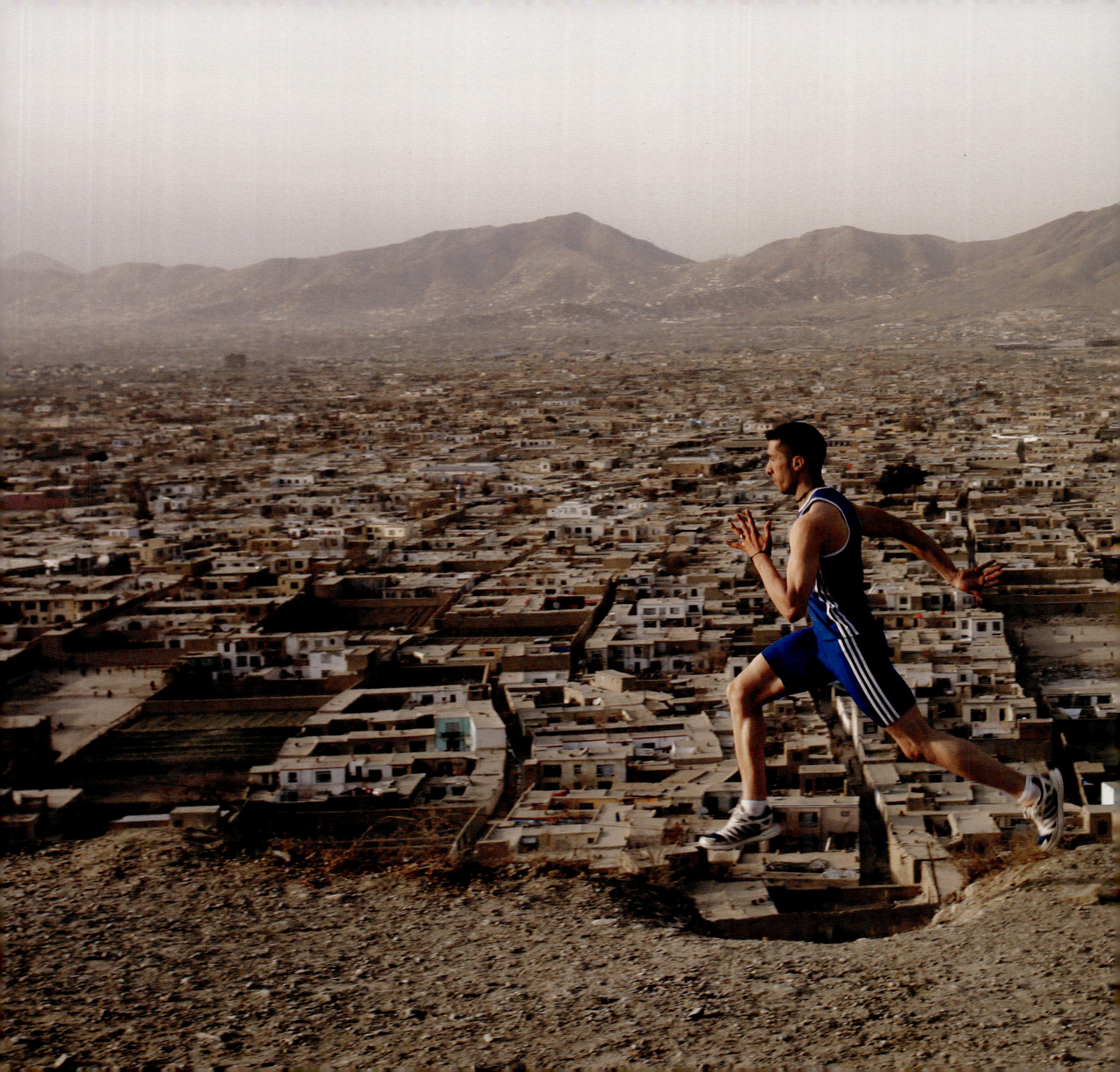

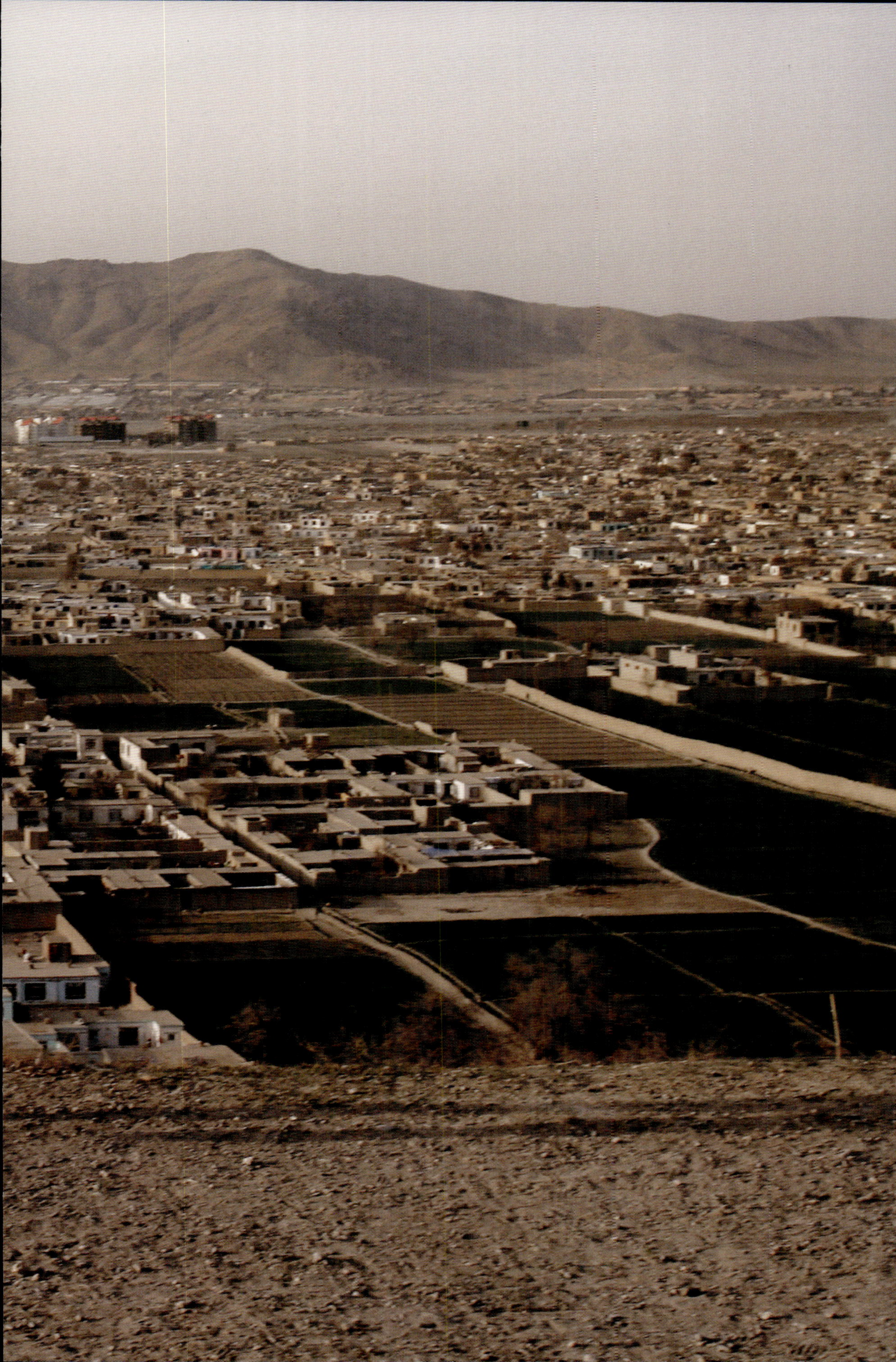

KABUL, MARCH 12, 2008.

Twenty-year-old Massoud Aziz trains along a dirt track on a hill overlooking the capital city. He is the most celebrated runner in Afghanistan, having competed in the 2004 and 2008 Olympics.

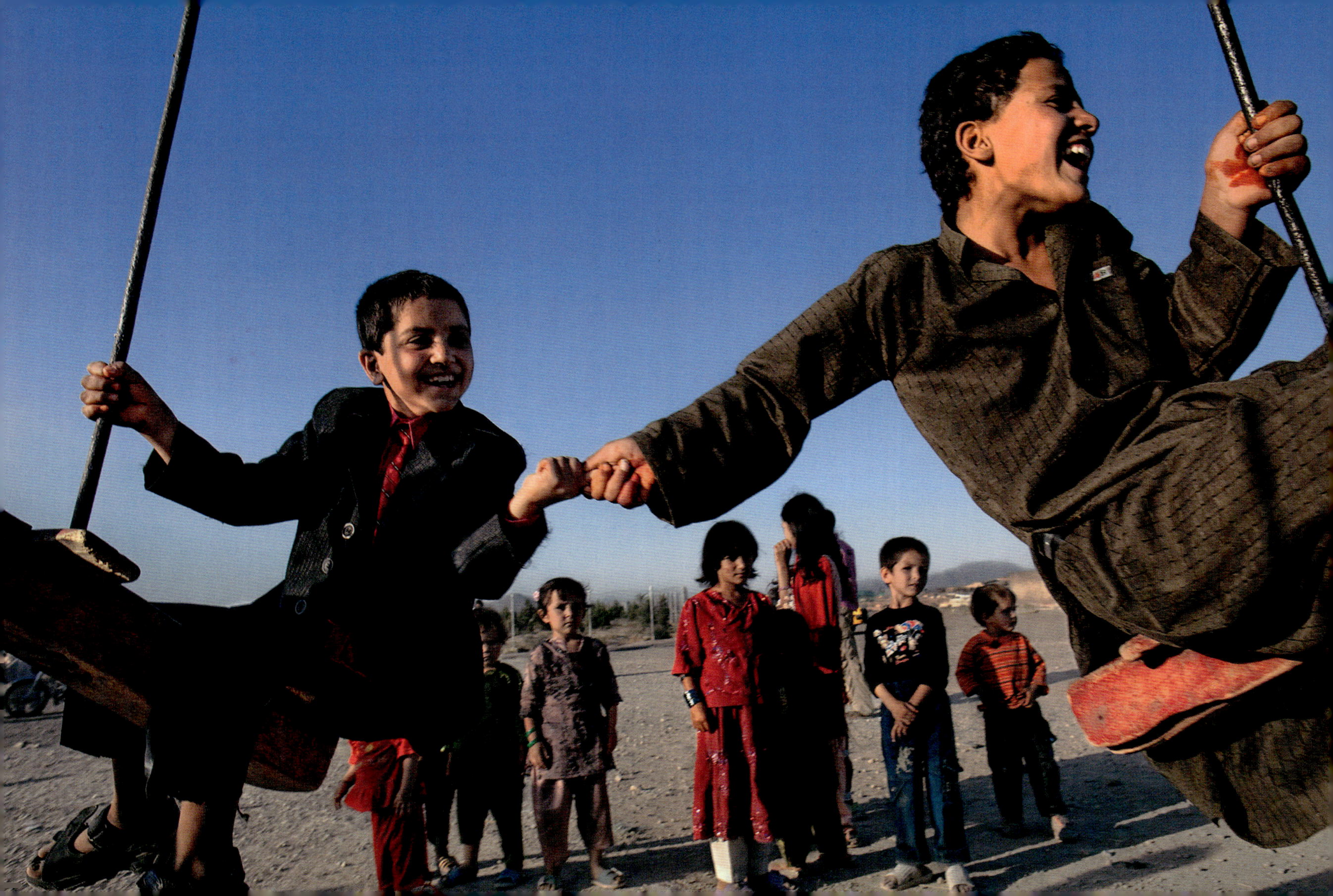

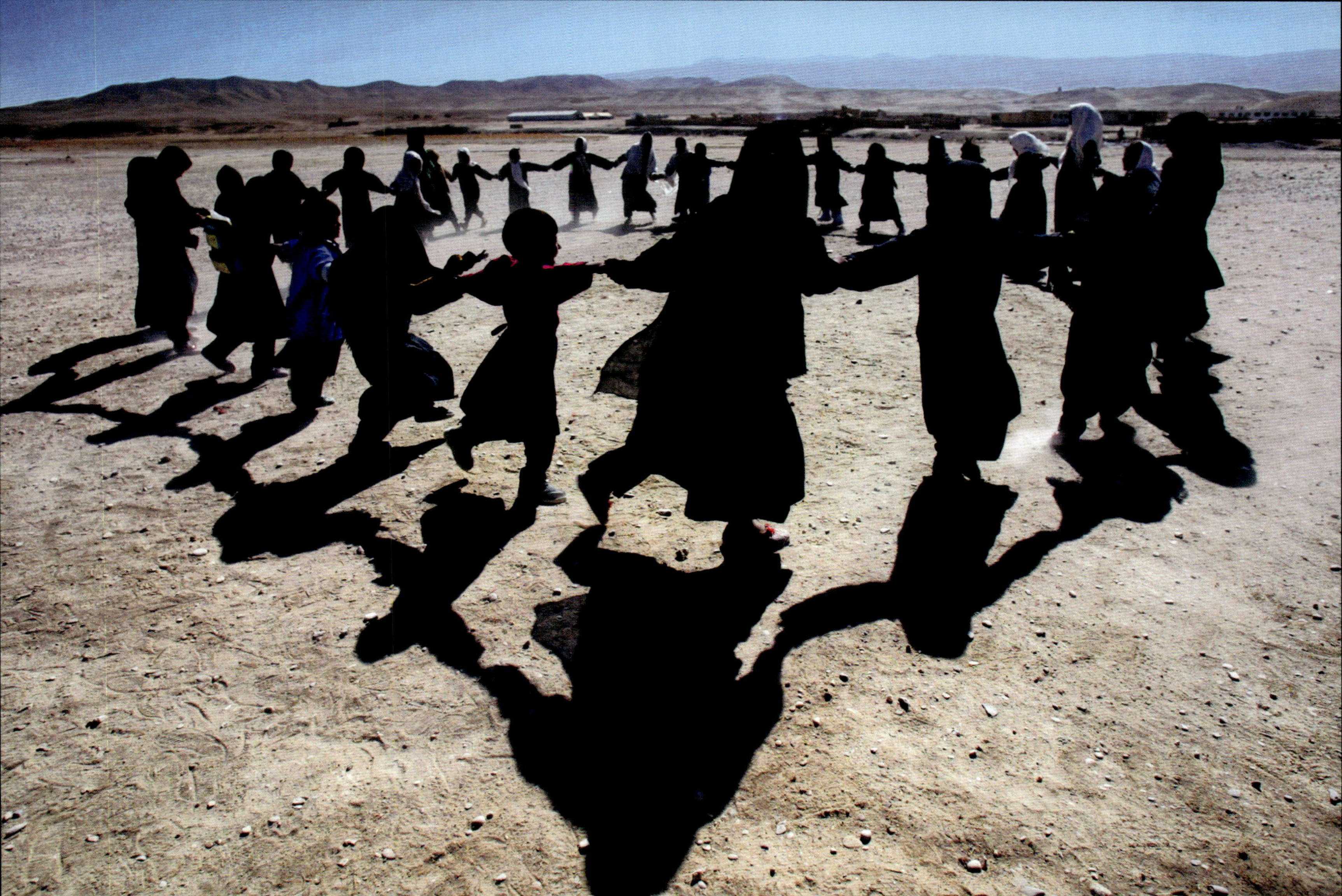

CHAGHCHARAN,
OCTOBER 21, 2002.

Schoolgirls enjoy playing during recess in Chaghcharan, which has a population of

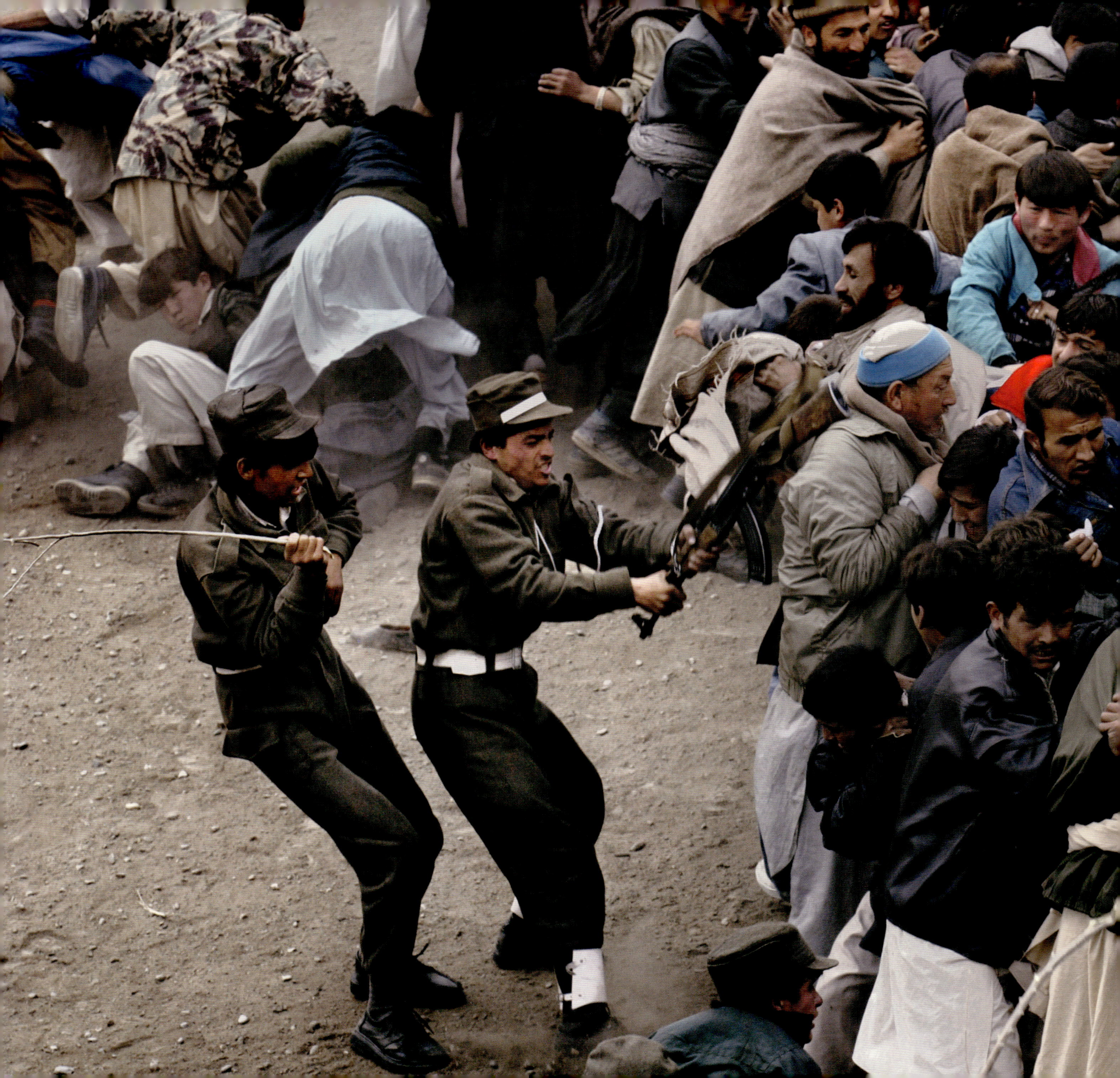

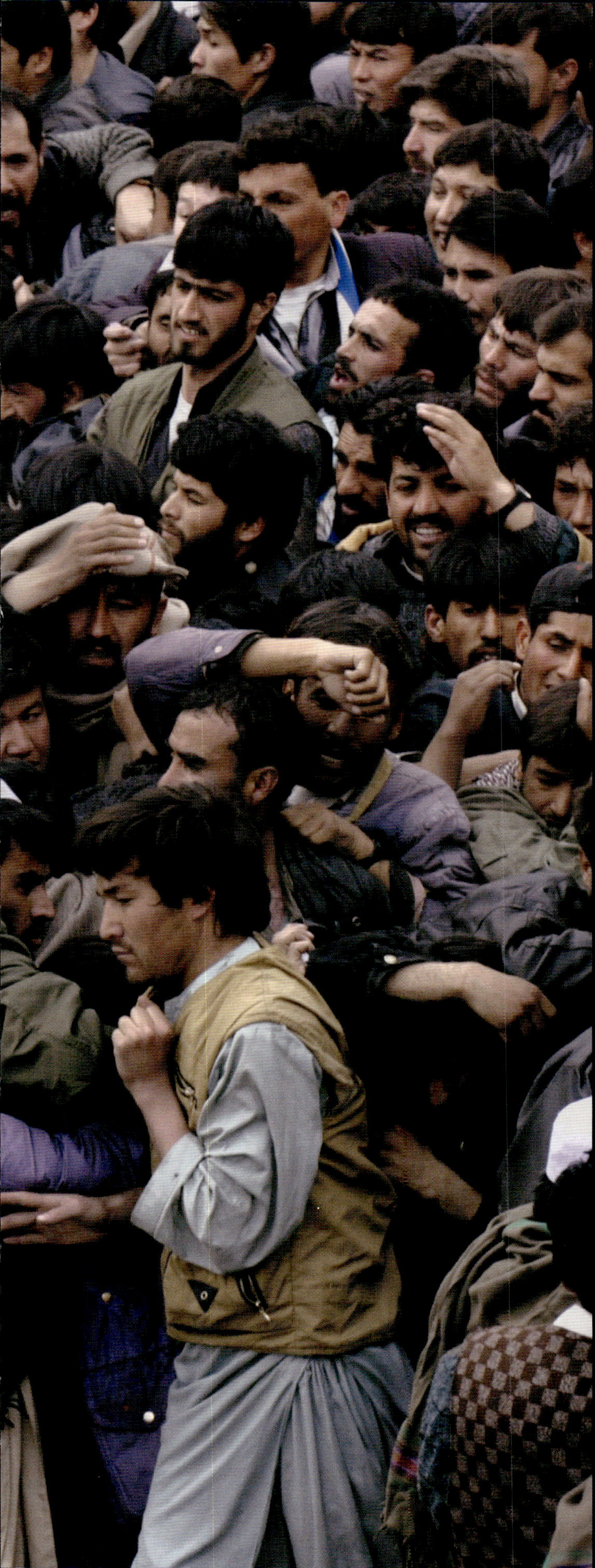

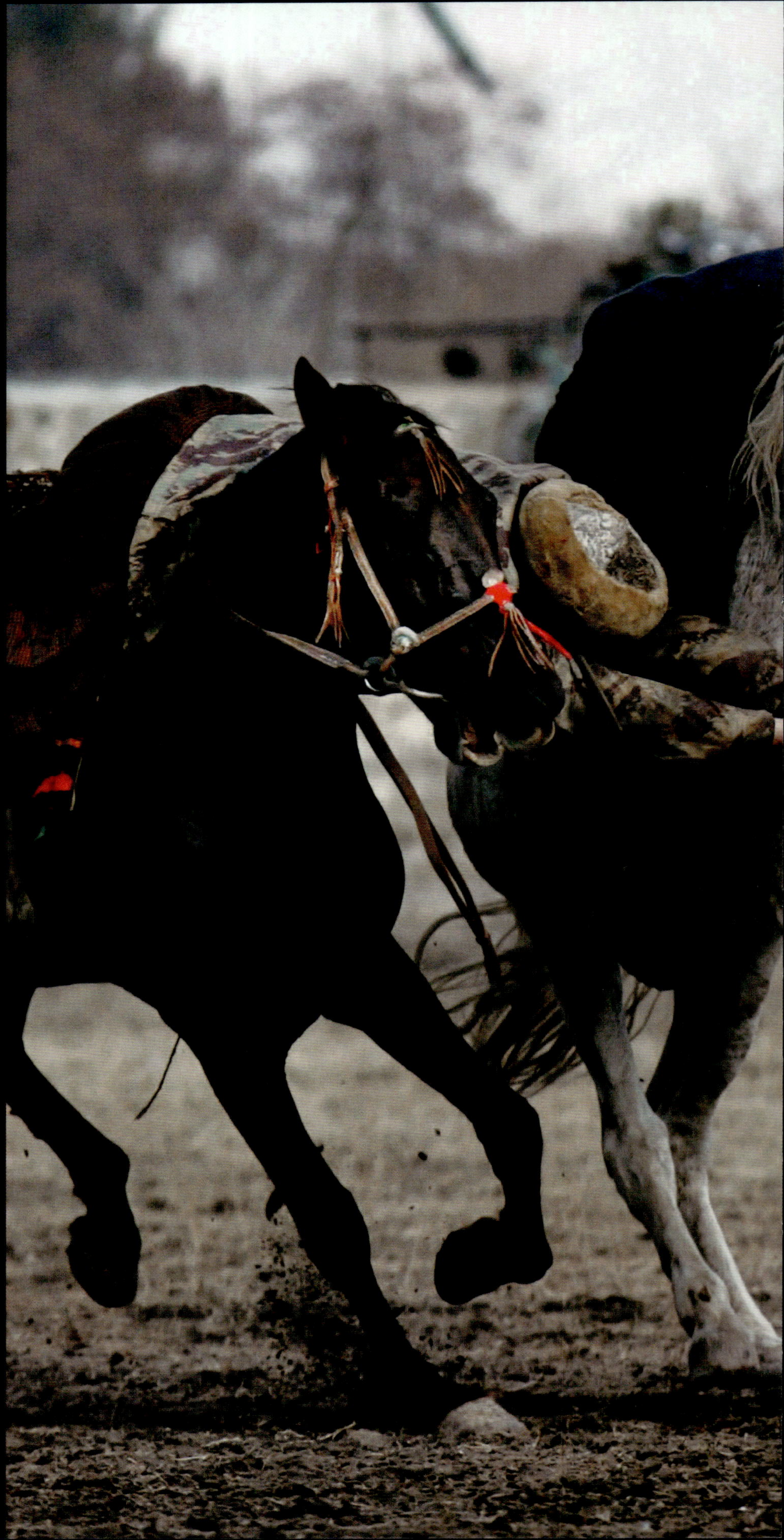

KABUL, FEBRUARY 24, 2002.

Buzkashi players carry a headless calf toward a goal zone. Though banned under the Taliban, buzkashi is considered Afghanistan's national sport.

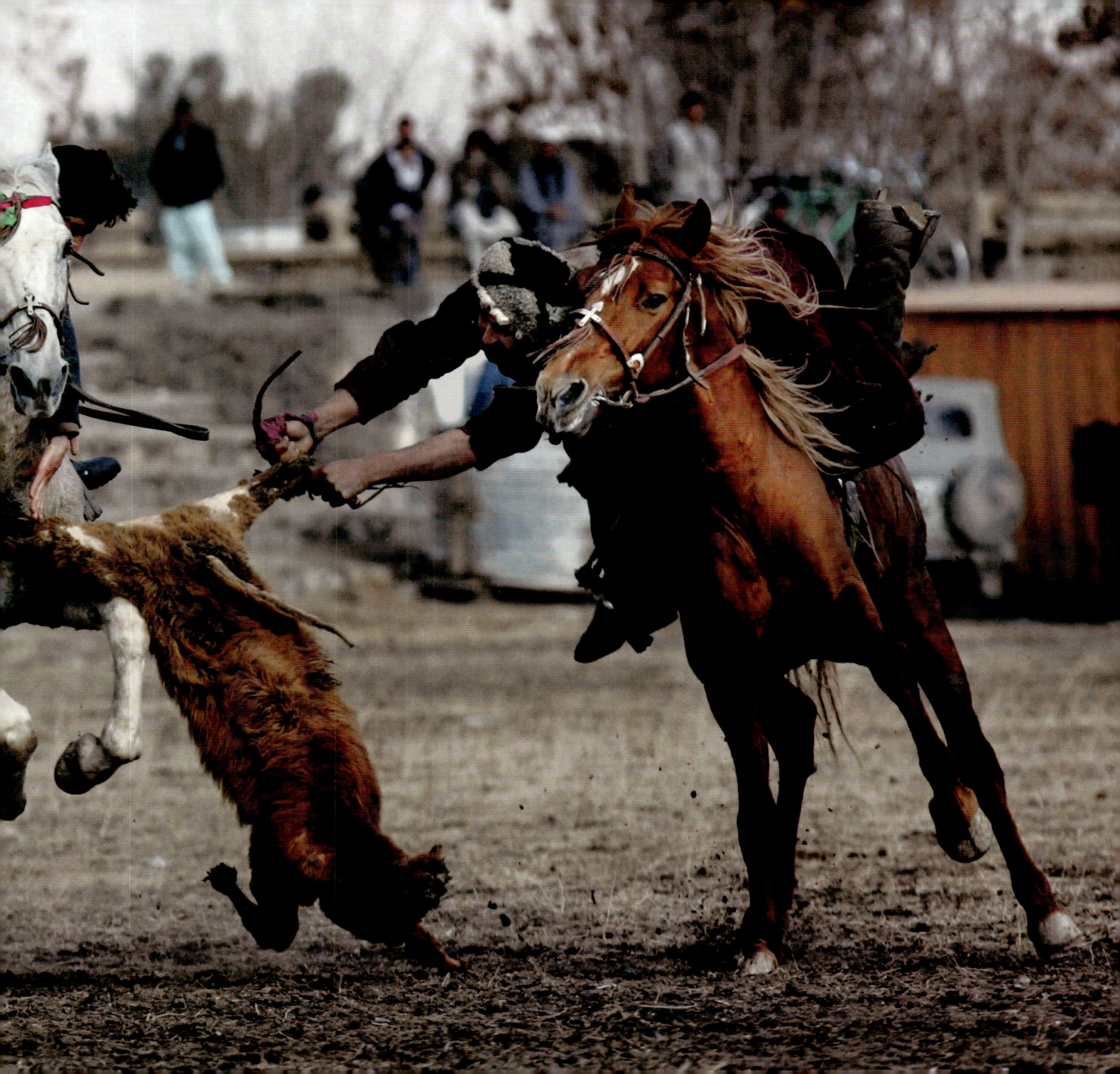

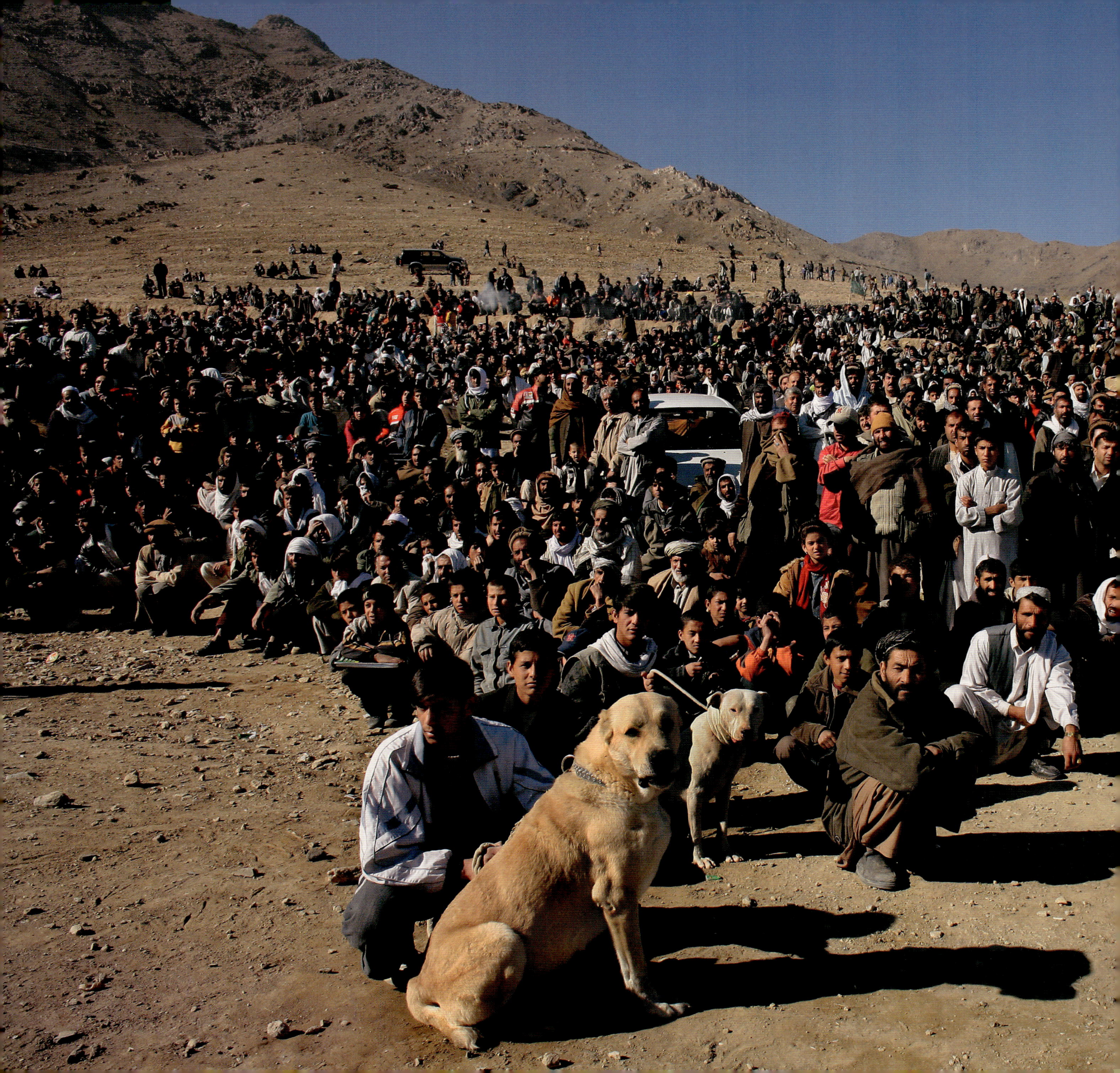

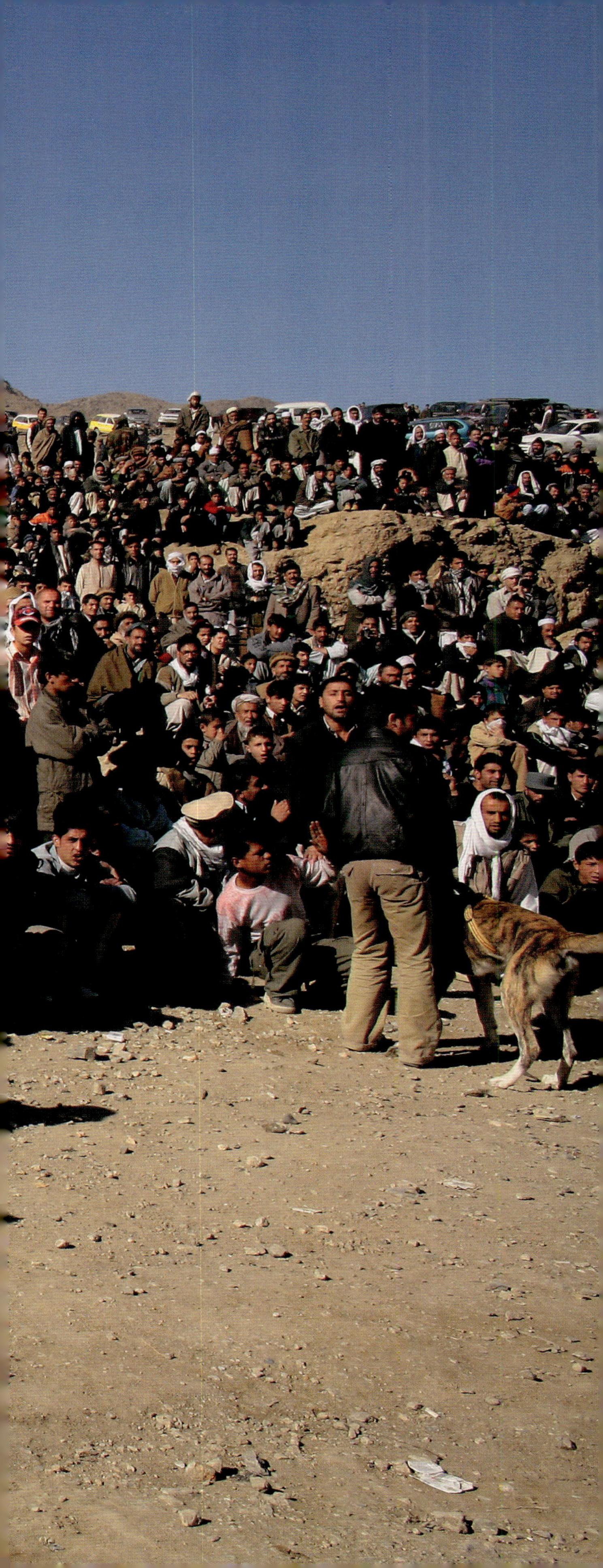

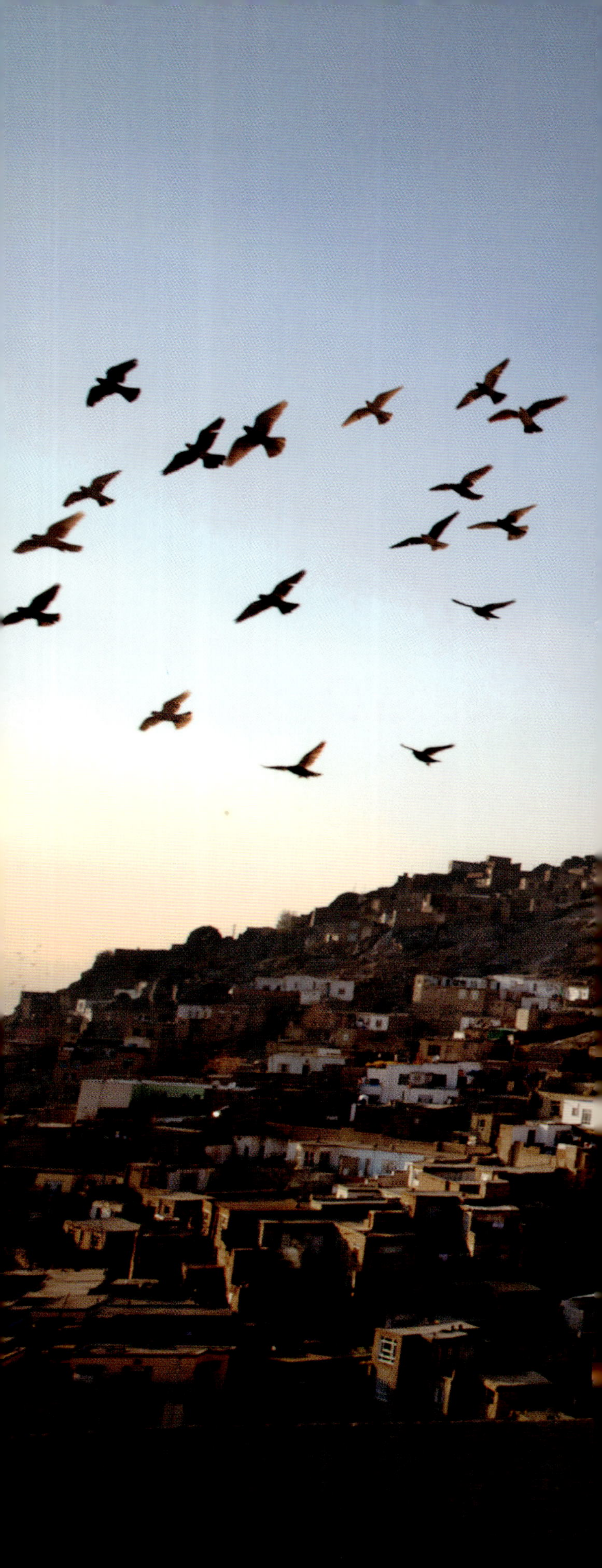

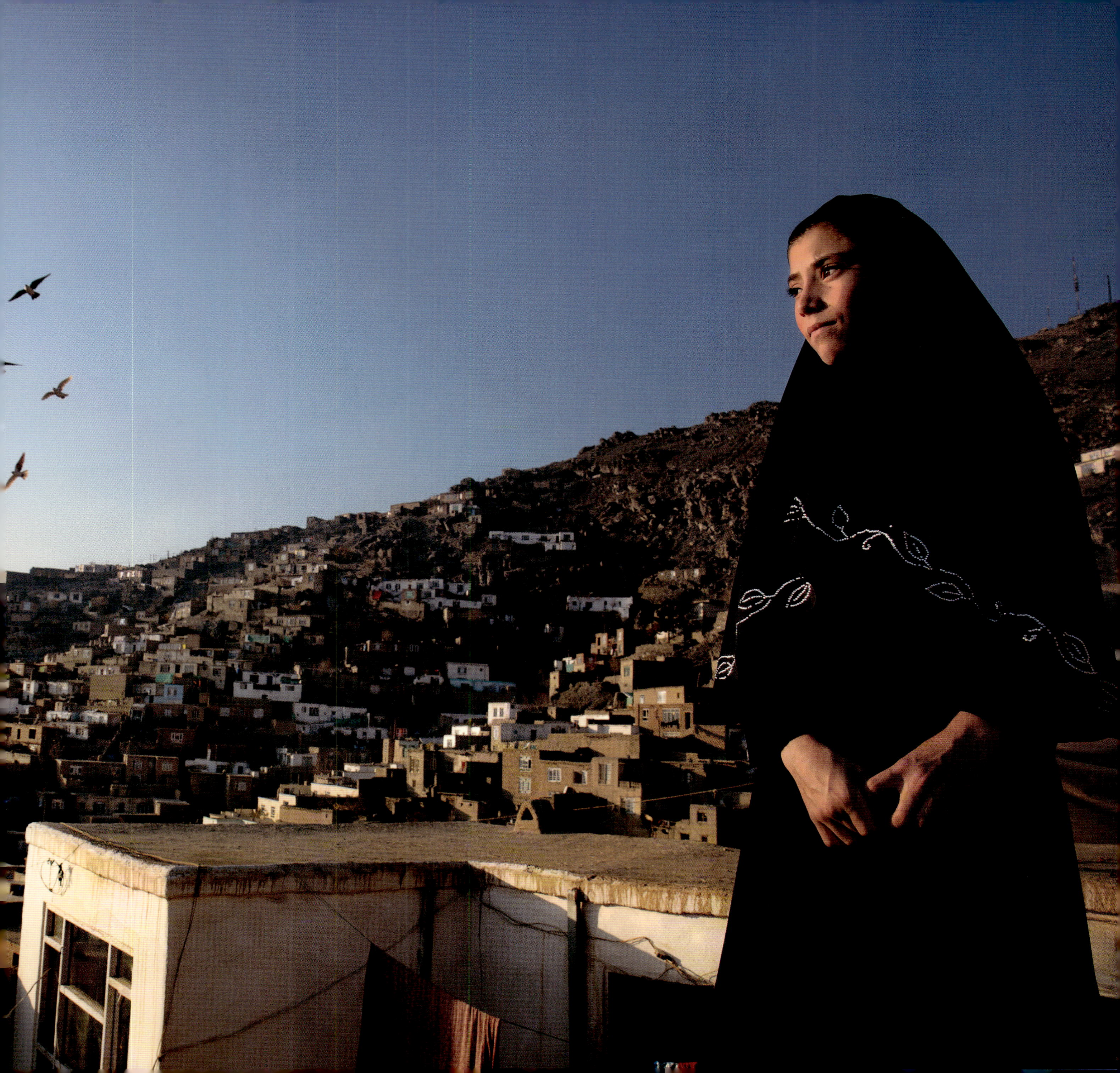

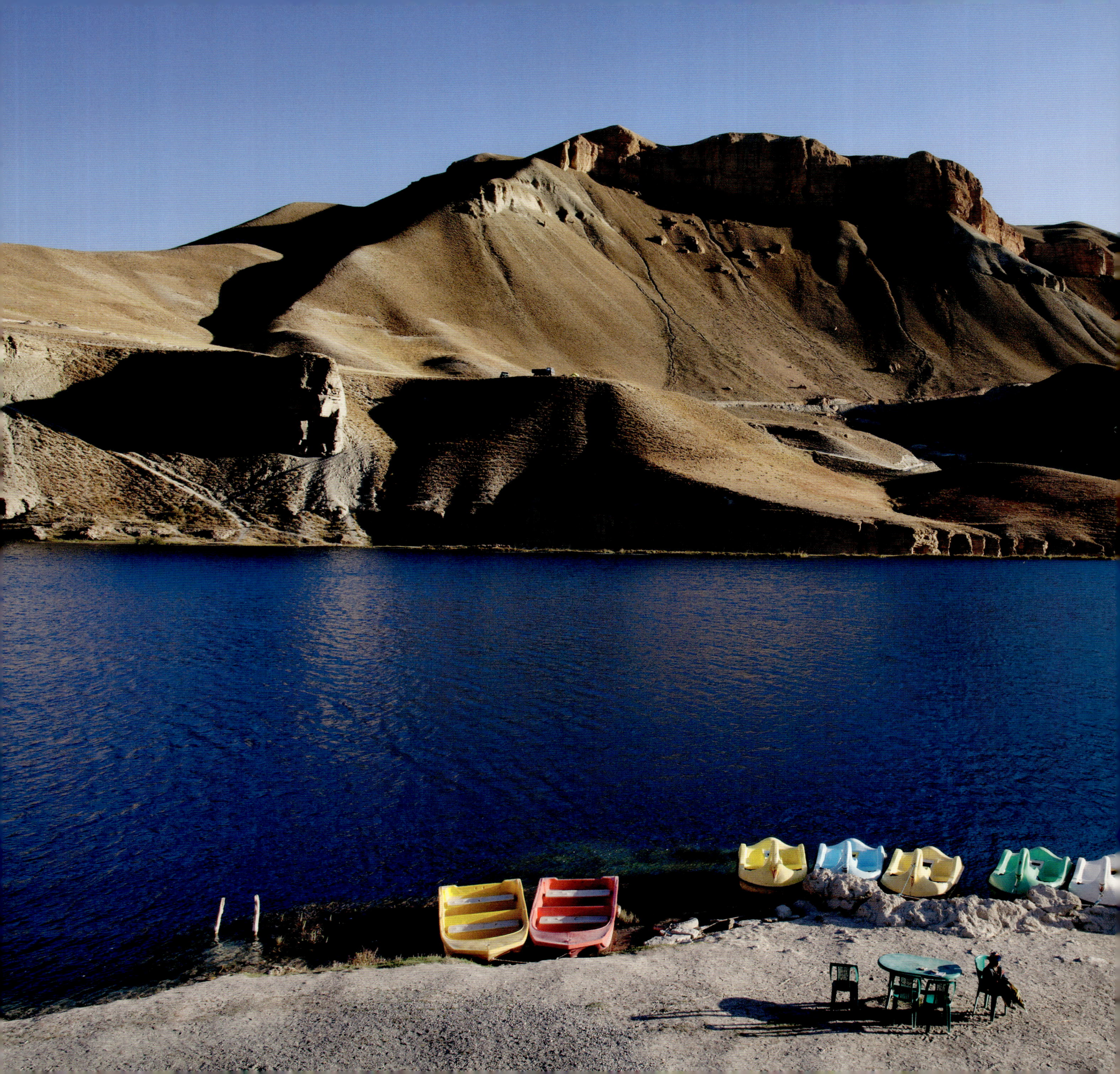

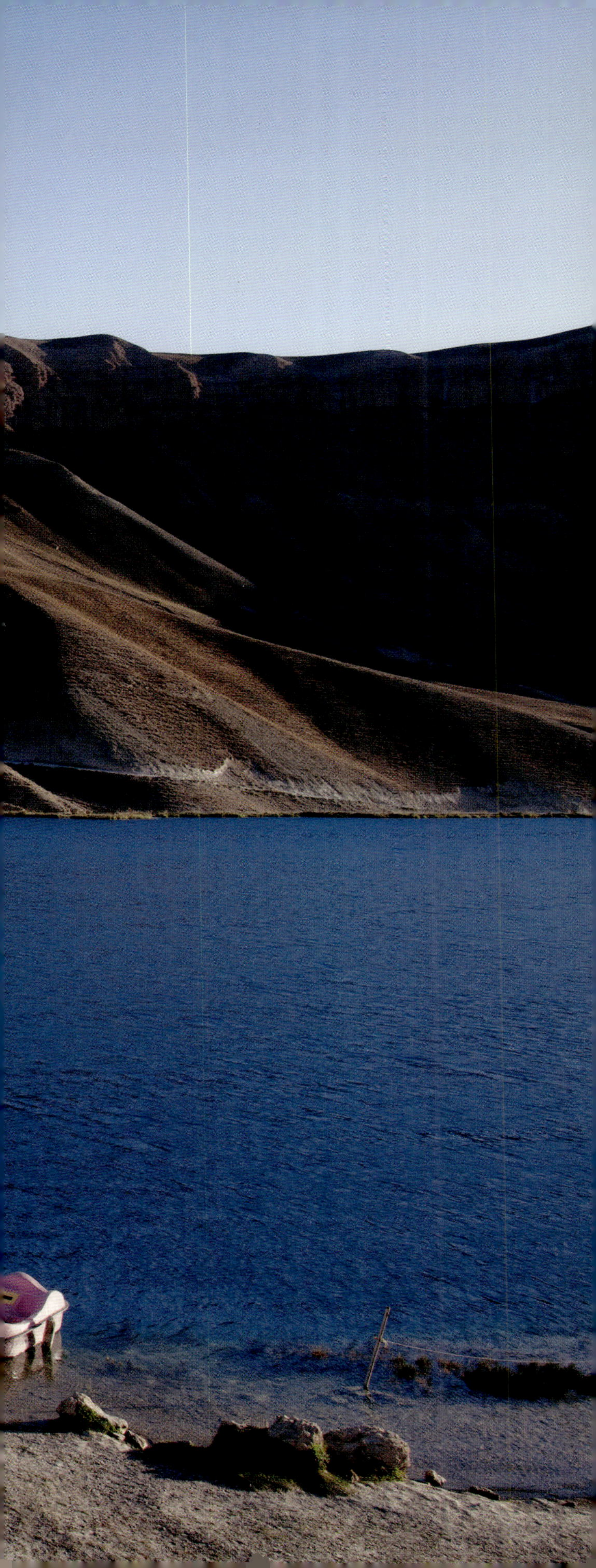

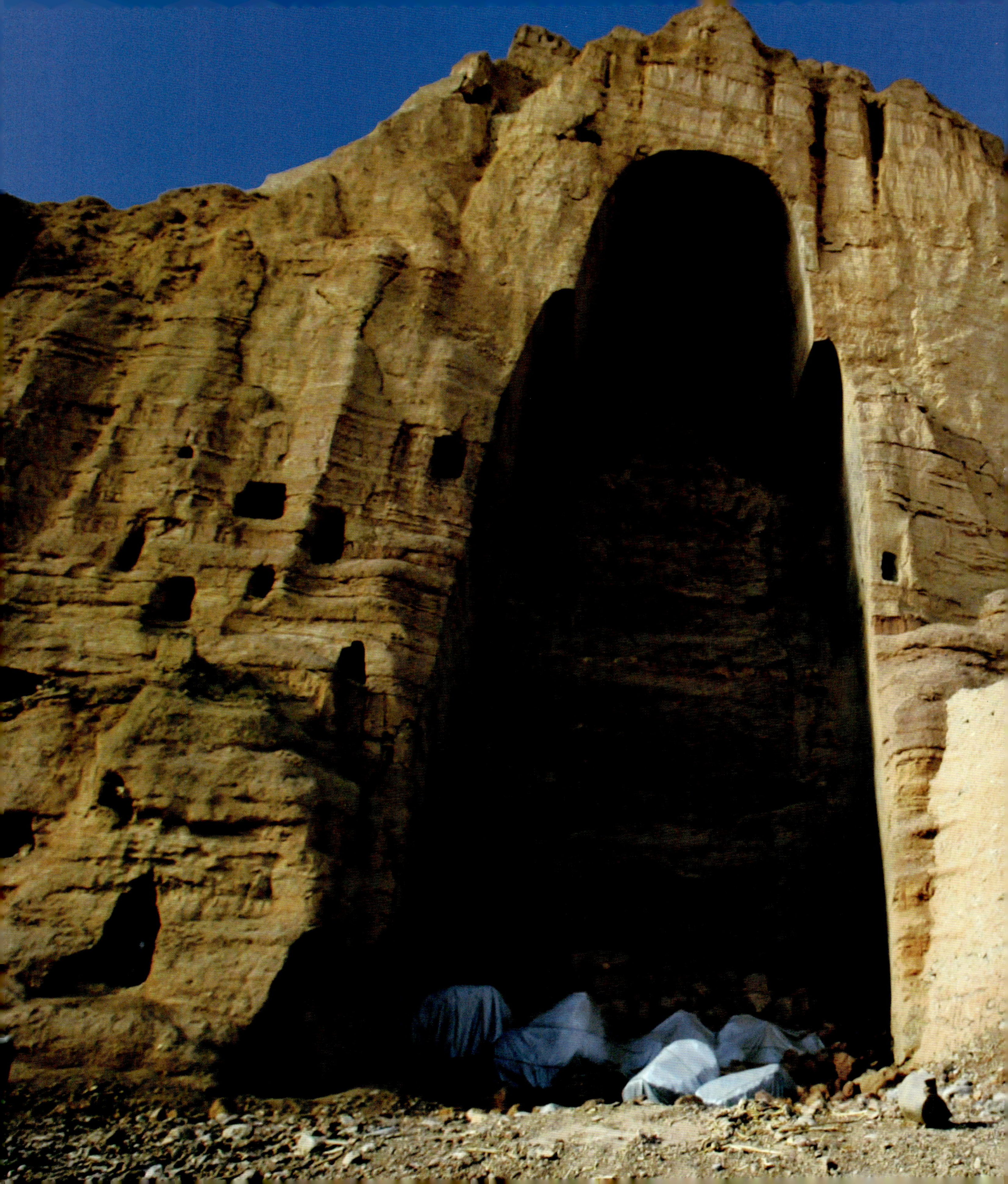

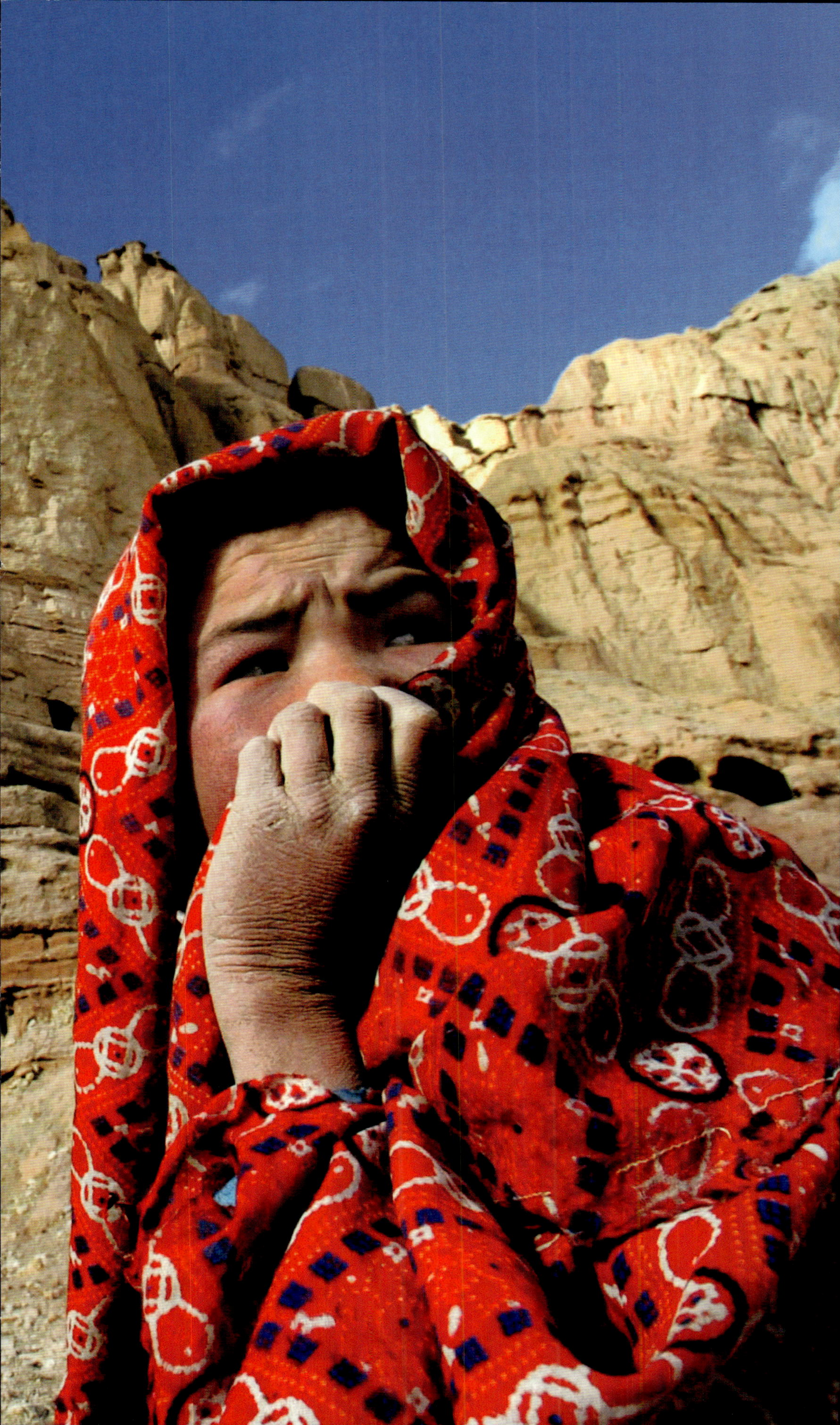

BAMIYAN, FEBRUARY 19,2002.

An Afghan girl who lives in the caves of Bamiyan sits in front of the ruins of a Buddha statue that the Taliban blew up the previous year.

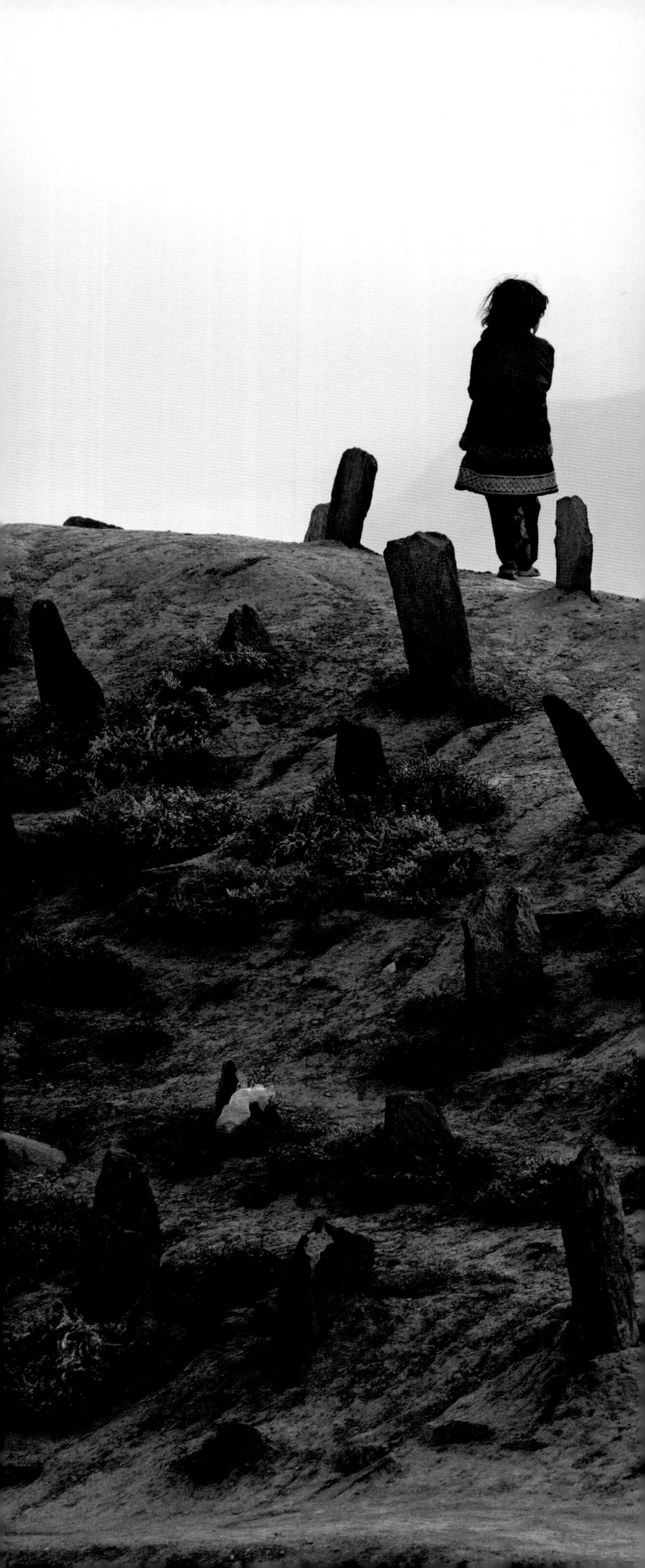

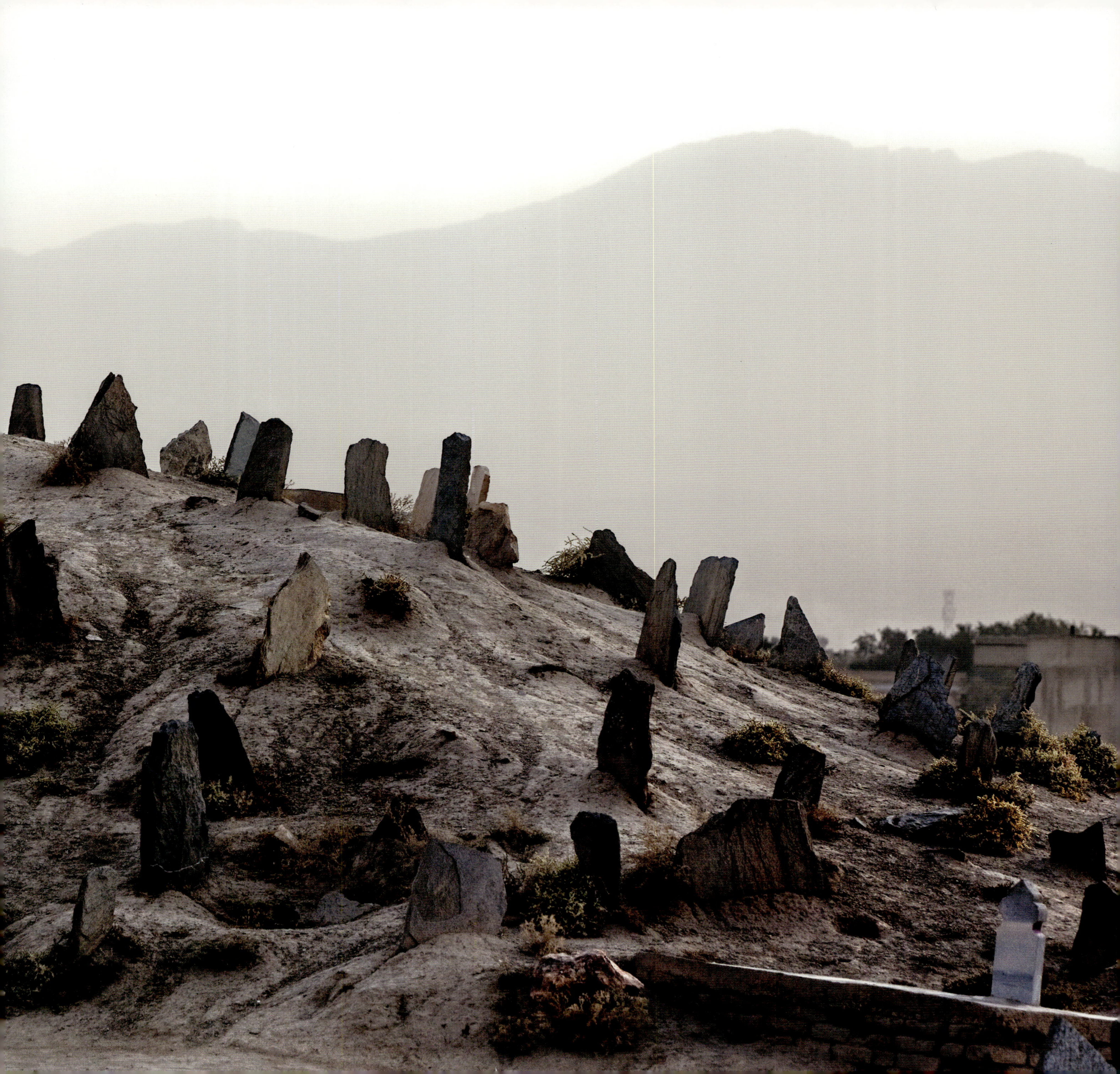

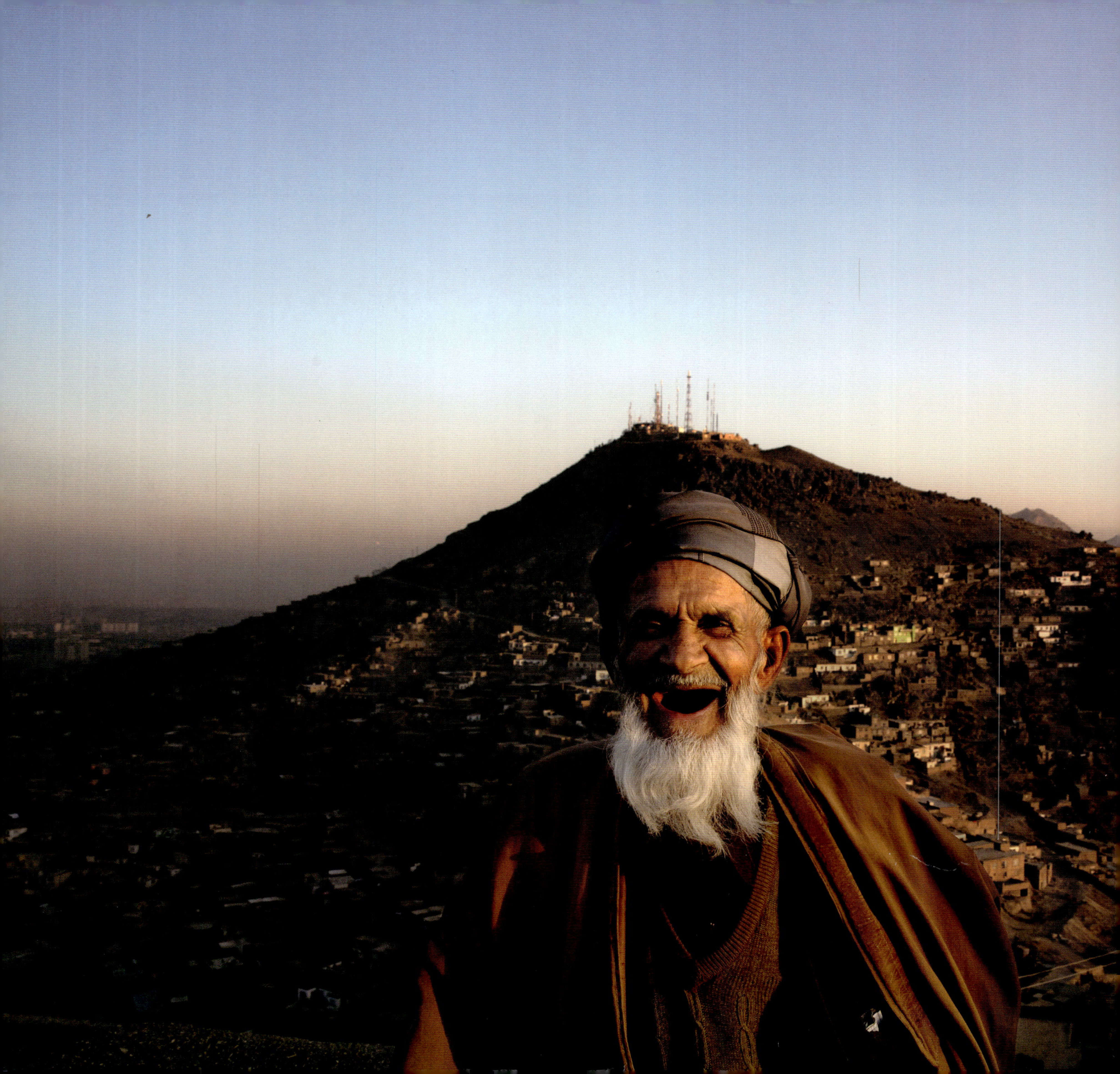

KABUL, MARCH 2015

AFTERWORD

PAULA BRONSTEIN

My Air India flight heads into Kabul, past the snowcapped peaks of the Hindu Kush. I worship these mountains. Indeed, I'm in awe of Afghanistan's rugged landscape; it overwhelms me each time I return, and I always feel as if I am seeing it for the first time. The mountains offer a serenity unknown in the populated areas below, where terrorism, violence, and oppression are the norm. I have been coming to this country since the United States began bombing it, in 2001, shortly after the 9/11 terrorist attacks on US sites. I went there initially on assignment for Getty Images news service and then later from my own desire to catalogue the daily lives of the Afghan people—from the chattering women in the beauty parlors to the boys who kick soccer balls around dusty fields or fly kites in the hills above Kabul. I want to tell these stories in a way that will make the outside world take a second look and see beyond the suicide bombs. I want to show that the Afghans and this war-ravaged country have suffered enough, though their tribulations continue unabated.

Outside the newly renovated Kabul airport, I board a dilapidated bus crowded mostly with Afghans. I see no other Westerners. The international presence seems to have shrunk each time I return. It is spring, and the blooming flowers and trees take me back to New England, where I grew up, a welcome distraction from thoughts about possible Taliban attacks (the road from the airport has always been a target). But my mind wanders only momentarily, and then I am back here in rugged Afghanistan. I check Twitter on my iPhone for any threat alerts—the world now being very different from the one in place when I first arrived; in 2001, we had to use satellite phones.

The technical side may have improved, but working in Afghanistan as a female photojournalist has its unique difficulties, including cultural and religious taboos. For example, prayer is so important to Muslim culture that it seemed vital for me to document people worshiping in this way. In moderate countries it may be easier for me to enter a mosque, but in Afghan culture, at least during my first years there, I could enter only on the women's side, and I had to stand in the back without photographing anyone. I did overcome that obstacle when my male translator finally managed to get me permission to photograph women during their Friday prayer at Kabul's Madinatul-Elm mosque. (In some parts of the country where the Taliban rule, women are rarely seen on the streets and pray only inside the home.)

Of course, being a woman does offer some advantages; unlike men, I can go into the closed-off women's quarters of homes. But ultimately Afghan men hold the power and call the shots, often deciding what women may do, as well as where and when they may do it. On a recent trip for a project on war widows, for example, I often had only one chance to visit and photograph inside a home because one of the male relatives refused to allow me to return.

Even when I felt things were going smoothly, the door might be abruptly slammed in my face. Some people suggested that I could increase my security by wearing a burqa, because then the neighbors wouldn't notice me. But who can say? One young widow I met with the help of a female fixer seemed to be an ideal subject to photograph as we talked casually over tea. But I wasn't allowed back, and even though I had taken no photographs while I was in her home, I heard she was beaten after we left. In the only picture I have of her, she is standing, completely veiled, at her husband's graveside. For Afghan women, violence goes far beyond the casualties and trauma of war.

The deteriorating security situation also creates barriers. Roads that I traveled years ago are hardly safe now. On many occasions, going as far back as 2003, I easily drove to Bamiyan, which remains one of the most beautiful and peaceful parts of the country despite the jarring destruction of the massive Buddhist statues that were carved into a mountainside there some fourteen hundred years ago. In 2009 I photographed an irresistible eight-year-old Hazara girl wearing a pink headscarf and standing in the doorway of a cave where her impoverished family lived. I wonder whether she is married now—most likely she is, for Afghan girls marry in their early teens, many of them forced into it. For me she represents the beauty and the harsh reality of this war-torn country. Today I can take a commercial flight to Bamiyan, but I certainly can't drive there anymore because of the potential threats from bandits or the Taliban. These threats merely keep me from making pictures, but for Afghans, they can mean not making it to a health clinic or hospital until it's too late or not making it there at all.

In this country sadness is a way of life—though sometimes, so too is happiness. I have made some of the most extraordinary photos of my career in Afghanistan, with face after face offering a complex and intriguing gaze and revealing the constant tension between optimism and reality that shapes the lives of so many here. I keep going back, motivated and inspired by those faces, pushing against the difficulties, hoping to find fewer doors slamming shut and more people seeing reasons to smile. Many stories, both warmhearted and harrowing, remain to be told. And they need to be told. Grateful for the access I have been given, I haven't let go of the many photos I wish I could have taken if only I had been granted access.

Every time I return to Afghanistan, I go back knowing I will make photos that show me an existence I could not otherwise have imagined. I took one such photo in 2014, the third time I covered a presidential election there. Several women were waiting to vote in the gender-segregated polling center; "faceless" behind their veils, they cowered when I raised my camera, turning away or hiding behind their burqa-covered arms as if I would otherwise expose them. These women can't be seen, but they are still afraid they will be disclosed. And that, for me, is Afghanistan: an odd closeness between hope and fear. The tiny distance between those two poles emerges everywhere. When I photographed Nowruz, the Afghan New Year—a day Afghanis spend with family, enjoying life—two young boys dressed in their best clothes proudly posed with their toy guns for me. If conflict is all you ever experience, can happiness ever be defined without it?

ACKNOWLEDGMENTS

Special thanks are due to Mike Kamber, who introduced me to Dave Hamrick, the director of the University of Texas Press. I am immensely grateful to everyone at the press for embracing this book project.

To the videographer Bradley Cox, who kindly donated his talents producing the promotional video, and to publishing expert Greg Lowe, who generously offered guidance and advice, I also extend immense gratitude.

I am very grateful to both Kim Barker and Christina Lamb, along with the author Bette Dam, for contributing to this book with their incredible talents.

Much appreciation goes to the sharp and insightful Renee C. Byer and Judy Walgren, who took time from their busy schedules to review this book.

To Massoud Khalili, the lovely Afghan poet and linguist who invited me into his Kabul home for tea and who brilliantly suggested the title for my book, I remain grateful for the privilege of time with you.

More special thanks go to my friends who sat with me during editing sessions in Bangkok: Karen Emmons, Greg Constantine, Jack Kurtz, and Yvan Cohen—thank you all for your aesthetic expertise.

I have been a member of the Getty Images family since 2001, and their unwavering support has enabled me to create this important body of work. I would like to add my best wishes to Jonathan Klein, who has led Getty Images as CEO and founder and has, after twenty years, become its chairman. In addition, I would like to acknowledge the editors of Getty Images News who trusted my ability to work in a conflict zone, sending me to cover Afghanistan in the early days of the war, especially Hugh Pinney, Sandy Ciric, and Pancho Bernasconi. Many thanks go as well to the amazing team at Getty Images Reportage: Patrick DiNola, Patrick Llewellyn,

Aidan Sullivan, Lauren Steele, James Price, Jay Davies, Stewart Stanley, and Emily Krzan. And thanks to those who contributed to the crowdfunding campaign.

Heartfelt thanks to all my friends and colleagues who have given me encouragement and support all these years, helping in a variety of ways to bring this book to life. There are too many of you to mention on this page, and I apologize for not being able to name everyone, but the list includes Palani Mohan, Sarah Stewart, Kate Brooks, Adam Dean, Lynsey Addario, Heidi Levine, Rick Loomis, Paul Kitagaki, Ed Ornelas, Liz Baylen, Dan Haar, Michael Kodas, Stacy Waters, Patrick Whalen, Daniel Berehulak, Robert Nickelsberg, Seth Mydans, Mariko Takayasu, Carolyn Cole, Adrees Latif, Ami Vitale, Mahnaz Rezai, Shannon Galpin, Kathy Gannon, Farzana Wahidy, Mathilde Vu, Ahmad Zia Haidary, Mansoor Bakhtar Qurban, Sophie Barry, Jim Nachtwey, Maggie Steber, Mario Tama, John Moore, Spencer Platt, Chris Hondros, Ron Haviv, Claire Rosen, John Stanmeyer, Mathew Lynn, Andrea Bruce, and Melina Mara.

I feel privileged to have worked over the past year on some great stories for the *Wall Street Journal* with the foreign correspondents Margherita Stancati and Nathan Hodge; many of the photos for those assignments are included in this book. Thanks especially to the WSJ International picture editor Patrick Whalen and the entire photo desk team.

This book would not be here without the 206 Kickstarter backers who gave generously and patiently waited for it to be published. I will be indebted to them forever. Though I would like to mention each of them, space prevents me from doing so, but I have to single out Margie Katz for digging deep into her pockets as the loving sister she has always been.

Finally, special thanks to Mark Bloom and Samai at Bloom Pro Lab in Bangkok for their hard work on retouching and printing my photographs.

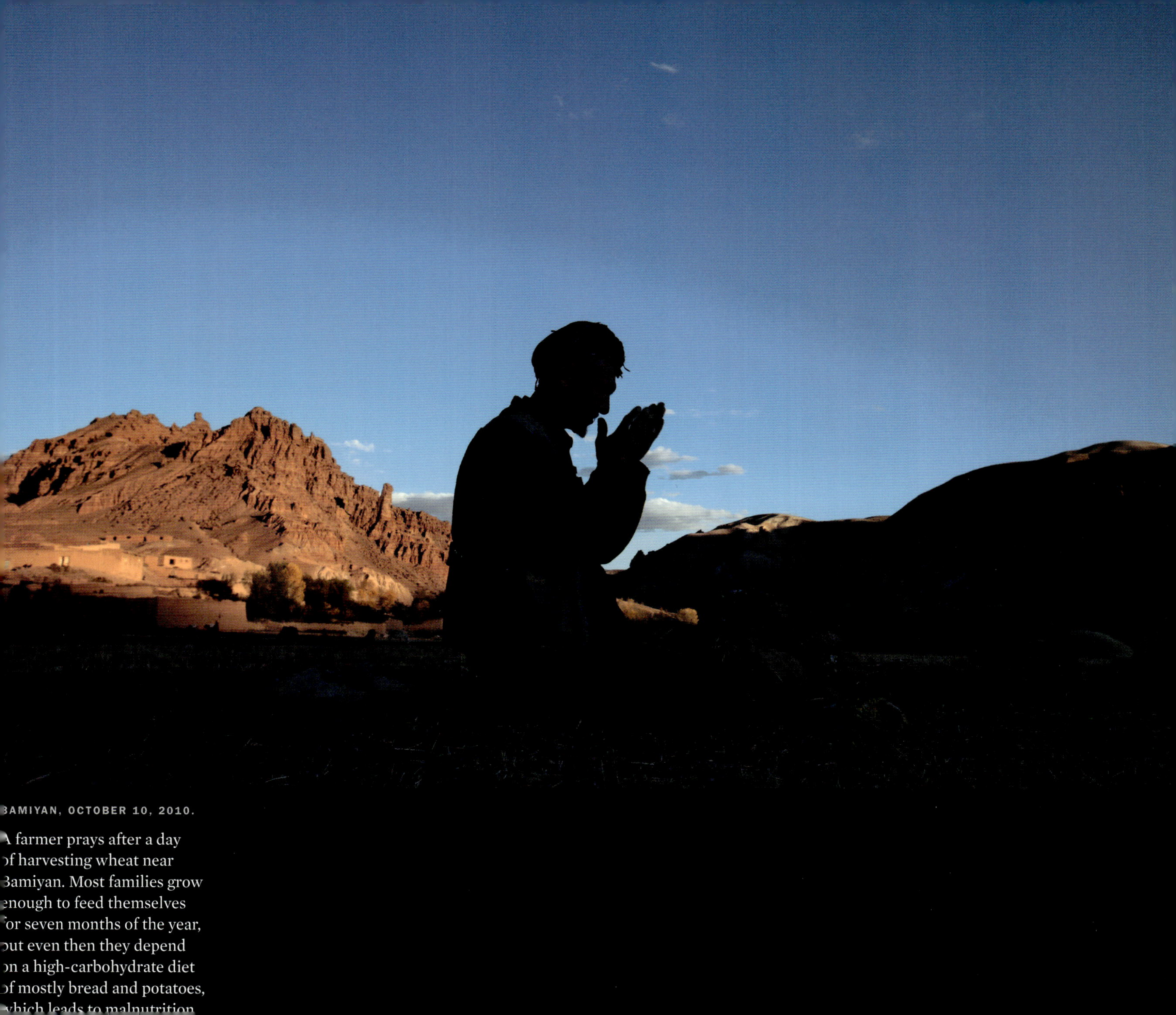

ɜAMIYAN, OCTOBER 10, 2010.

\ farmer prays after a day
ɔf harvesting wheat near
Bamiyan. Most families grow
enough to feed themselves
for seven months of the year,
ɔut even then they depend
ɔn a high-carbohydrate diet
ɔf mostly bread and potatoes,
which leads to malnutrition

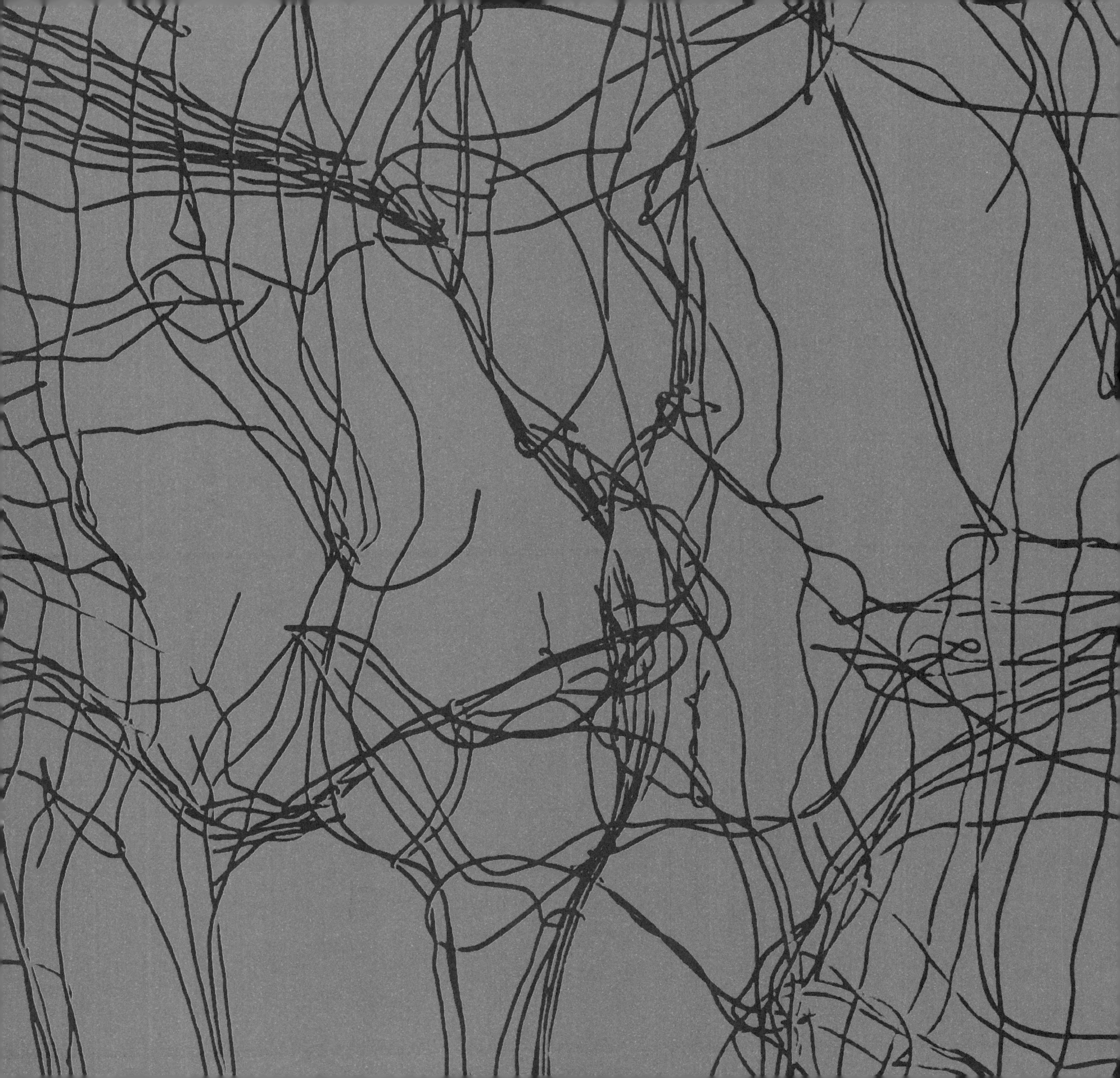